Gender and Education in Ontario:
An Historical Reader

Edited by
Ruby Heap and
Alison Prentice

Canadian Scholars' Press   Toronto 1991

Gender and Education in Ontario: An Historical Reader

First published in 1991 by
Canadian Scholars' Press Inc.
339 Bloor Street West, Suite 220
Toronto, M5S 1W7
Canada

Canadian Cataloguing in Publication Data

Main entry under title:

Gender and Education

ISBN 0-921627-78-5

1. Women — Education — Ontario — History. I. Heap, Ruby
II. Prentice, Alison, 1934-

LC1768.05G46   1991   376.9713   C91-094012-6

Table of Contents

Part One: The Emergence of Gender as a Focus

Part Two: The Different Worlds of Turn of the Century Teachers

Part Three: Vocationalism and Its Meaning for Girls' Schooling

Gender and Education in Ontario: An Historical Reader

Credits

We wish to acknowledge permission to reprint the following essays and their sources:

Ian E. Davey, "Trends in Female School Attendance in Mid-Nineteenth Century Ontario" *Histoire sociale/Social History* 8, 16 (November 1975): 238-254.

Alison Prentice, "From Household to School House: The Emergence of the Teacher as Servant of the State" *Material History Bulletin/Bulletin d'histoire de la culture matérielle* 20 (Fall 1984): 19-29.

John R. Abbott, "Accomplishing 'a Man's Task': Rural Women Teachers, Male Culture and the School Inspectorate in Turn of the Century Ontario" *Ontario History* 78, 4 (December 1986): 314-330.

Susan Gelman, "The 'Feminization' of the High School: Women Secondary School Teachers in Toronto: 1871-1930" *Historical Studies in Education/Revue d'histoire de l'éducation* 2, 1 (Spring 1990): 119-148.

Marta Danylewycz, "Domestic Science Education in Ontario, 1900-1940" J. Donald Wilson, ed., *A Not Imperfect Past: Education and Society in Canadian History* (Vancouver: UBC Centre for the Study of Curriculum and Instruction, 1984): 20-58, 94-109, 115-119.

Nancy S. Jackson and Jane S. Gaskell, "White Collar Vocationalism: The Rise of Commercial Education in Ontario and British Columbia, 1870-1920" *Curriculum Inquiry* 17,2 (Summer 1987): 177-201.

Lynne Marks, "Kale Meydelach or Shulamith Girls: Cultural Change and Continuity Among Jewish Parents and Daughters–a Case Study of Toronto's Harbord Collegiate in the 1920s" *Canadian Women Studies/les cahiers de la femme* 7, 3 (Fall 1986): 85-89.

Jo LaPierre, "The Academic Life of Canadian Coeds, 1880-1900" *Historical Studies in Education/Revue d'histoire de l'éducation* 2,2 (Fall 1990): 225-245.

Nicole Neatby, "Preparing for the Working World: Women and Queen's During the 1920s" *Historical Studies in Education/Revue d'histoire de l'éducation* 1, 1 (Spring 1989): 53-72.

Introduction: Gender and Education in Ontario's Past

This book explores various aspects of the relationship between gender, education and social change in Ontario. At the same time, it is intended to provide students and teachers with a sampling of the fruits of over fifteen years of scholarship in the history of women and education in this central Canadian province.

The essays in the volume reflect the rapid growth not only of women's history, but of educational history during the past two decades. More importantly, they illustrate a growing interaction between the two fields, as feminist historiography has increasingly challenged the study of the educational past.[1] Certainly, women's movements have been concerned with women's access to learning and this issue has therefore always figured in the history of women and education. But feminist historians now look at broader questions. Perhaps their major contribution has been to focus our attention on the relations between women and men in educational history. This has meant comparing the access to schooling of women with that of men in the past, as well as analysing gender relations within educational institutions over time. It has also meant examining the relations between educational practices and the gendered social structures that have surrounded them and been the context for educational debate, practice and change. New feminist interpretations are also leading to new questions about the relations of power in the world of learning. Who has defined what we perceive to be knowledge? Who has controlled the production and dissemination of knowledge and how have these controls been put into place?

At the same time, students of educational history have been raising questions about the multiple meanings of education, and especially of state-controlled and mass-produced educational forms, as these have developed over the past century and a half.[2] If we speak of formal schooling—and we must always be careful to distinguish between education broadly considered and the experiences that take place in institutional settings that we call schools, colleges or universities—what has such schooling meant for women in general, or for particular groups of women? Have most women sought schooling for themselves, or have they merely endured it? What impact has the institutionalization of education, particularly its institutionalization under state auspices, had on women, individually and collectively?

All of these questions have informed the development of new work on the history of women and education. Earlier histories tended to dwell on the admission of women to the various institutions devoted to learning, especially the "higher" learning that led to professional occupations and possible economic independence for individual women. Taken for granted in such accounts was that access was invariably a positive step and constituted an obvious improvement in the status of women.[3] While not neglecting this topic or denying altogether the truth of this interpretation, newer work has begun to raise questions about women's access to schooling and to explore women's actual experience in various educational settings over time. And its aim has been not only to understand the ways in which educational ideologies and forms have dictated and modified the patterns of women's lives, but also to explore the roles that women themselves played in various educational arenas and educational processes, not to mention in the creation and management of educational institutions, in the past.

Early feminist reproduction theory stressed the ways in which sexist practices in schools have reproduced and continue to reproduce gender inequalities and women's subordination or oppression in society. More specifically, it examined the ways in which schools have prepared girls to accept their roles as low-paid or unpaid domestic workers in capitalist economic systems.[4] Like reproduction theory in general, however, this approach has been criticized as reductionist and mechanistic. What it failed to consider was individual consciousness and also the possibility of resistance and change. Women have not been simply acted upon; they have also been active agents capable of contesting and modifying educational thought and practice. Most recent feminist work in the history of women and education is thus enlightened by an approach which sees women as capable of resisting their subordination or oppression and making choices of their own. One of its main goals has been to focus on women's subjective experience and the reality of their individual lives and social relationships in various educational settings.[5]

Finally, feminists working in the history of women and education are increasingly concerned to explore the diversity of women's educational experiences in the past. The interaction between gender and education is not confined simply to the school and the classroom. It occurs in various contexts: the family, the community, and the workplace as well as social, cultural and political settings. Education is thus an ongoing process which evolves not only in a variety of environments, but which also crosses the life cycle of women. Furthermore, the diversity and complexity of women's educational experience can be revealed only if the categories of class, ethnicity and race are added to those of sex or gender. Black women, for example, insist on the "double oppression" to which they have been subjected, as women and as members of the black community.[6] Similar arguments are put forward by native women and women whose experiences as members of cultures arising out of their immigrant, ethnic, and/or religious backgrounds or affiliations have separated them from the historical mainstream.

Introduction: Gender and Education in Ontario's Past

The essays contained in this book only begin to address this complexity. They contain no definitive answers regarding either the overall character of change in education for women in Ontario or the causes of change in Ontario women's educational experience. They nevertheless document and begin to explore the reasons for some important shifts, as informal and domestic modes of education gradually gave way, in the course of the nineteenth century, to increasingly formalized and state-controlled structures for the schooling of girls and women, and as Ontario witnessed the diversification and increasingly hierarchical nature of these structures in more recent times.

****

Part 1 of this book illustrates the body of work which, in the 1970s and early 1980s, focussed on gender and began to formulate new questions about the place of women in Ontario education. It is proper to mention here, although we do not include an example, the pioneering work of Marion V. Royce in this respect. Three papers that she published, and a later unpublished sketch that focussed on early Upper Canada,[7] revealed significant themes in the educational history of Ontario women during the nineteenth century: the demand, first of all, for schooling for girls and the importance and diversity of the institutions that were created for them. These ranged from small domestic schools which both married and unmarried women ran in their homes to the first of the larger academies admitting young "ladies." Most of the latter developed under church sponsorship and were for girls only but, in several important cases, they were co-educational. When it came to the realm of state-aided institutions, Royce dealt with the common schools for both sexes, but focussed more of her attention on the admission of women to the boys' grammar schools. It was her research that initially revealed the significant debates that developed in the 1860s over co-education in these Upper Canadian institutions, with their mixed goals but aspirations to provide "superior" education. Recent work has reinterpreted some of Royce's findings, offering a more thorough and critical perspective on the schooling of girls in various religious, private and public settings in Upper Canada, and the latter should therefore be read along with the former.[8] At the same time, the work of Marion Royce constituted an important challenge. She was the first to address the following fundamental questions: Who was responsible for the schooling of girls in nineteenth-century Ontario? Why did girls' education become so controversial? And what kind of schooling did girls receive?

Gender and Education in Ontario: An Historical Reader

The first article in Part 1 addresses some of these issues by focussing on the schooling experience of girls in a specific geographical setting, the city of Hamilton. In it, Ian Davey explores the relations between school enrolment, the family and social structure, asking two basic questions: Who went to school and what schools did they attend? The application of quantitative techniques to a rich variety of sources such as the manuscript census permitted Davey to trace over time the changing religious affiliation, class, gender, age and ethnicity of the children attending school. The school attendance of girls, Davey's study demonstrates, was complex and differed from that of boys. His article also shows how the class composition of the clientele for Hamilton's leading privately financed ladies' academies changed when state-aided schooling for adolescent girls became established in that city.

The second article, by Alison Prentice, traces the emergence of the Ontario elementary public schoolteacher as an individual who was most likely to be young, female and single. This study relies on quantitive work that the author did in the late 1970s and early 1980s with Marta Danylewycz and Beth Light, focussing on the social characteristics of teachers in selected localities in mid-nineteenth-century Ontario and Quebec. But it also adds a new dimension in its attention to the conditions and technologies of the classroom, as these evolved in the latter part of the century, and to the ways in which these affected teachers' work in the schools.[9]

Part II highlights the growing body of new research on the history of teachers in Ontario. Taking us to the turn of the century and beyond, the first two articles explore further the dimensions of women teachers' work. John Abbott takes up a theme only alluded to in the Prentice study, namely the complex relations that developed between women teachers and the male inspectorate in rural Ontario. Susan Gelman opens new ground by exploring the gendered character of high school teaching in Toronto and by establishing, with the help of quantitative records, the specific locations of women teachers' work in the high schools, as they became increasingly involved in the delivery of secondary education in the city. These essays explore the power that stereotypes of what was appropriate work for women—and for men—had for both sexes. They also reveal women teachers' resistance in the face of stereotypes that went against the grain or, in some cases, to explicit pressures exerted by individual male authority figures. Early resistance among urban elementary schoolteachers took institutional shape with the formation of the Toronto Women Teachers' Association examined by Harry Smaller. Responding to infrequent promotions, low pay and other injustices they perceived in the conditions of their employment, career-oriented women began to organize their sister teachers in the mid-1880s. Smaller's essay places the

Introduction: Gender and Education in Ontario's Past

WTA in the wider context of teacher organizing and of gender relations at the time and analyses the associations early successes and failures.

All three essays invite us to reflect on the impact of the feminist movement on turn-of-the-century teachers' consciousness of their situation as women. Was the temptation or the power to challenge authority informed by feminist discourse? Can class consciousness also be detected in women teachers' voices? How did class and gender interact to determine the nature and goals of their individual and collective actions? These articles confirm the importance of considering both of these categories in educational history.

Most of the women teachers whose lives and work are the objects of study in this volume were women who were employed in the paid labour force. But women also worked in the household, performing unpaid, private, domestic and family labour. The reality of "women's work" must thus refer to both their paid and unpaid labour. The articles in Part III shed light on the relations between family, education and work by examining the role of schooling in the training of women for work in the home and in the public labour force. At the turn of the century, such a role was conferred on the public schools by educators, government officials, businessmen and social reformers who claimed that, in the wake of increasing industrialization and urbanization, the mid-nineteenth-century curriculum was no longer relevant to the roles that most women would play in modern society. This led to an orchestrated campaign to promote "vocational" education in the public school system. The result was a significant revision of the curriculum based on the introduction of supposedly more practical subjects and courses designed to better prepare students for their future occupations.

As the essays in Part III demonstrate, vocationalism had a major impact on the definition and provision of women's education in the late nineteenth and early twentieth centuries, although the extent of its ultimate impact on society is a complicated question. Certainly, one immediate result was the establishment of various gender specific vocational courses and institutions deemed appropriate for women's attributed roles, as in the case of domestic science. The study by Marta Danylewycz shows how, between 1900 and 1940, domestic science became an integral part of Ontario's educational system, courses being provided at the elementary and secondary levels, as well as in universities. The popularity of the domestic science movement reflects the wide range of support it received from social reformers and educational and political leaders. Middle and upper class women, in particular, had specific motives for promoting the training of girls for their "natural vocation," motives which varied according to the latter's class origins. Although domestic science education was based on the acceptance of separate spheres for men and women, as well as of a domestic service role for many working class and immigrant women, it also favoured the creation of new public roles and career opportunities for some women, particularly as teachers and professors in the field.

The training of women for their roles as mothers, housewives, and domestic servants did not occur only in the classroom. Kari Delhi's examination of the activities of the Toronto Home and School Council between 1916 and 1930 illustrates the way in which its female members focussed on the education of mothers. However, while middle-class women were introduced to the ever-changing scientific child rearing methods promulgated by (largely male) professionals and were encouraged to see themselves as "expert" mothers, working-class and immigrant women were provided with lessons that were less consonant with their circumstances in the world—and particularly the relationship of themselves and their children to the schools. In their efforts to create harmony between schools and families, the women of the Home and School Council were involved in the construction of labels for children and families whose lives or attitudes did not fit well with school practice; the words "defective," "deviant" and "feeble-minded" came into the vocabulary as a result of the psychological testing that the Council helped to promote, along with the streaming that steered "problem" children into low paying jobs. The relationship between gender and class in the educational experience of women, as well as the active involvement of some women in constructing oppressive definitions of motherhood, emerge clearly in this study.

Definitions of appropriate roles for women are also the focus of the third essay in this section, on the rapid development of commercial education in the high schools at the turn of the century. According to Nancy S. Jackson and Jane S. Gaskell, few developments in secondary curriculum have had a greater influence on the education of women. The expansion of commercial education paralleled the revolution in office work and the resulting flow of women into the clerical labour force. Commercial schooling thus increasingly came to mean female schooling and, as the demand for female clerical workers increased, the public high schools gradually superseded the private business schools in the training of girls for "pink collar" jobs. This form of vocational education, conclude the authors, significantly contributed to the segregation and subordination of women in the schools as well as in the paid labour force.

If commercial education became easily identified with female education, the case of technical education was more problematic. What did technical education mean for women? Should women receive training to prepare them for industrial work? At the turn of the century, Ontario women already had a history as industrial workers. In the following decades, female occupations

Introduction: Gender and Education in Ontario's Past

increasingly diversified in the manufacturing sector, while the expanding service sector opened new job opportunities for women. Did employers and educators deem it necessary to provide vocational education for present and future women workers? Ruby Heap sheds light on these questions in her study of the Toronto Technical High School between 1890 and 1930. This school established from the start a distinct curriculum for women which, in the beginning, largely focussed on domestic science. With increasing state intervention in vocational education and the development of new job opportunities for women, the content of this curriculum was expanded and diversified. One important fact remained, however: technical schooling trained women differently from men because it prepared them for "women's work," that is not only for the narrow spectrum of low-skilled jobs available to women, but also for the unpaid work they performed in the home. The type of training provided by the Toronto Technical High School thus reflected prevailing attitudes concerning the nature of female labour as well as the institutional linkages between the school system and the labour market for working-class women.

In Part IV, we turn to a consideration of the feminist impulse in education: in this case, the quest for advanced learning for women. The yearning to be part of the academy is not reducible to a single dimension, however, as the articles in this section suggest. In environments as varied as a Roman Catholic convent school, a Methodist academy, a predominantly Jewish Toronto collegiate institute, and three very different English Canadian universities, young women were bound to have diverse experiences. And yet certain themes permeate most of the essays in this section. One is the pursuit of advanced learning in a protected, and often religious or ethnically separate, setting. A second is the quest, on the part at least of some, of learning for its own sake as well as for the status that advanced studies could confer. At the same time, however, women students consistently valued the practical dimensions of their education. Increasingly, they would expect to seek at least a period of employment in the public labour force after they left the halls of higher learning. The latter, as must be evident from the above discussion, included private academies and public secondary schools, as well as colleges and universities in the eyes of nineteenth- and even many early twentieth-century seekers of knowledge and advanced training. It was only gradually that our present rather fixed notion of three levels of education, with only the third qualifying as "higher education," emerged in western educational systems.[10]

Johanna Selles-Roney and Elizabeth Smyth investigate these themes in their studies of the early years at London's Alma College and Toronto's St. Joseph's Academy, while Lynne Marks explores them in her article on Toronto's Harbord Collegiate in the 1920s. In each of these institutional settings, young women were in some ways encouraged to challenge the conventions of their day. The very presence of Jewish girls at Harbord in the period following the First World War was a challenge to the Eastern European Jewish tradition that scholarship was an exclusively male prerogative. The articles on St. Joseph's and Alma also suggest the liberating possibilities inherent in both the theory and the practice of higher learning for women. At the same time, denominational women's academies, and even Harbord Collegiate in the 1920s, were to some extent closed worlds. The female cultures that these institutions fostered also involved constraints.

Jo LaPierre's investigation of women's experience at Queen's, the University of Toronto, and McGill in the late nineteenth century dwells on the extent to which these constraints could be internalized. Perhaps because the co-educational university was perceived to be an especially dangerous environment for women, and even the label "college woman" seemed a threat to one's feminine identity, the early women students in English-Canadian universities were inclined to melt into the woodwork, rather than burst forth as liberated women. Their public radicalism confined itself to their invasion of these bastions of male privilege and power in the first place; once there, the women's revolution was a quiet one. Like all of the essays in this section, LaPierre's study is innovative in its stitching together of fragmentary evidence on women's experience in the academy from diverse and elusive records.

Both Lynne Marks and Nicole Neatby had the advantage of living participants to interview in their reconstructions of women's educational experiences in the 1920s, in Neatby's case at Queen's University. As we move into more recent times, oral history techniques allow historians of women and schooling to probe new questions and to re-evaluate the impact of feminism on women's educational concerns. Neatby's study demonstrates that, far from retreating after the winning of the franchise in federal and almost all provincial elections, 1920s women were often in pursuit of some potentially liberating goals. Still constrained in many respects by the ideology of domesticity, many Queen's women were nevertheless committed to an educational experience that might ultimately result in their ability to be financially independent. Neatby emphasizes the radical implications of this aim.

****

The present collection, which covers selected themes and ends with the interwar years, reflects only partly the state of Ontario historiography on gender and education. There exist studies of women's education in Ontario that take

Introduction: Gender and Education in Ontario's Past

us past the 1920s and 1930s and that explore themes not dealt with here. Indeed, both the contents and gaps in this volume are suggestive both of the rich veins that have been explored and of those that remain to be explored or that deserve further study.

One area in which research is urgently needed, is the education—and miseducation—of First Nations women or of other special groups of Ontario women. Analysis of women's education in particular racial or ethnic or class settings is only in its infancy and is clearly deserving of much more attention.[11] We also need to study further the ways in which the organization of schools and the structuring of the curriculum in Ontario have promoted gender differentiation.[12] In addition, the specialized training of Ontario women for such female professions as elementary school teaching, nursing and librarianship, and for the "higher professions" of medicine and law, is an area that has been overlooked by historians until recently.[13] On the other hand, while the presence and work of female teachers in elementary schools have been of great interest to historians, we are only beginning to delve into the history of gender and secondary school, college, or university teaching in Ontario.[14] Finally, there is a need to explore further in an historical perspective the various links between educational institutions and the gender-segregated paid and unpaid labour markets.

Several essays in this collection have taken us beyond the borders of Ontario to include material on Quebec or British Columbia, or historiographical discussion of countries other than Canada. We would argue that such comparative and cross-institutional approaches deserve encouragement. Several essays have also explored, either directly or indirectly, the ways in which religious concerns and the education of women have intersected in the past. Certainly the impact of denominational and cultural pluralism on girls' and young women's schooling is a subject worthy of further investigation in the Ontario context.[15] Finally, although our collection has focussed almost exclusively on education in "school" settings, it is clear that educational history must not be confined to such studies. On the contrary, explorations of women's work in the Young Women's Christian Association and the Canadian Girls in Training, among many other organizations, have demonstrated the importance of the informal, extra- or non-institutional mode in women's education, in Ontario as elsewhere.[16]

Some of the questions touched on in these essays are developed further in broader studies or have been addressed from a different perspective by Ontario historians.[17] On the other hand, we believe that these articles stand on their own as an introduction to the richness and diversity of the work that the last fifteen years have produced in the history of gender and education in Ontario.

Gender and Education in Ontario: An Historical Reader

We hope that they will not only introduce the field but encourage further work on a subject that richly deserves our analysis and deeper understanding.

Introduction: Gender and Education in Ontario's Past

Notes

1. For a discussion of feminism and educational history in the Canadian context, see Alison Prentice, "Towards a Feminist History of Women and Education," in David Jones, ed., *Approaches to Educational History* (University of Manitoba, Monographs in Education, 1981); Ruth Pierson and Alison Prentice, "Feminism and the Writing and Teaching of History," in Angela R. Miles and Geraldine Finn, eds., *Feminism: From Pressure to Politics* (Montreal: Black Rose Books, 1989); and Ruth Pierson, "Historical Moments in the Development of a Feminist Perspective on Education," *Resources for Feminist Research/Documentation sur la recherche féministe* 13, 1 (March 1984).

2. See Alison Prentice, *The School Promoters: Education and Social Class in Mid-Nineteenth Century Upper Canada* (Toronto: McClelland & Stewart, 1977). More recent studies include Susan E. Houston and Alison Prentice, *Schooling and Scholars in Nineteenth-Century Ontario* (Toronto: University of Toronto Press, 1988); Bruce Curtis, *Building the Educational State: Canada West. 1836-1871* (London: The Falmer Press, 1988); and R.D. Gidney and W.J.P. Millar, *Inventing Secondary Education: The Rise of the High School in Nineteenth-Century Ontario* (Montreal: Queen's-McGill University Press, 1990). Until now, only Quebec historians have produced volumes focussing exclusively on the elementary and secondary schooling of Canadian women in the past. See, Nadia Fahmy-Eid and Micheline Dumont, eds., *Maîtresses de maison, maîtresses d'école: Femmes, famille et éducation dans l'histoire de Québec* (Montréal: Boréal Express, 1983) and *Les couventines: L'éducation des filles au Québec dans les congrégations religieuses enseignantes, 1840-1960 (Montréal: Boréal, 1986). For recent studies on the education of women in Britain, see Felicity Hunt, ed., *Lessons for Life: The Schooling of Girls and Women 1850-1950* (Oxford: Basil Blackwell, 1987); Carol Dyhouse, *Girls Growing Up in Late Victorian and Edwardian England* (London: Routledge & Kegan Paul, 1981); and Sara Delamont, *Knowledgeable Women: Structuralism and the Reproduction of Elites* (London: Routledge, 1989). Recent American studies include Barbara Solomon, *In the Company of Educated Women: A History of Women and Higher Education in America* (New Haven: Yale University Press, 1985) and David Tyack and Elizabeth Hansot, *Learning Together: A History of Co-education in American Public Schools* (New Haven: Yale University Press, 1990).

3. See, for example, Thomas Woody, *A History of Women's Education in the United States* 2 vols. (New York: The Science Press, 1929); Charles E. Phillips, *The Development of Education in Canada* (Toronto: W.J. Gage, 1957) especially chapter 20, "Women and Girls"; Phyllis Stock, *Better Than Rubies: A History of Women's Education* (New York: Longman, 1978). For an early American critique of this approach, see Jill Conway, "Perspectives on the History of Women's Education in the United States," *History of Education Quarterly* 14, 1 (Spring 1974).

4. The work of Ann Marie Wolpe, Rosemary Deem and Madeleine MacDonald (later Arnot) best exemplifies feminist reproduction theory. See, for example, Wolpe, "Education and the Sexual Division of Labour" in Anne Marie Wolpe and Annette Kuhn, eds., *Feminism and Materialism* (Boston and London: Routledge and Kegan Paul, 1978); Deem, *Women and Schooling* (London and Boston: Routledge and Kegan Paul, 1978) and Deem, ed., *Schooling for Women's Work* (Boston and London: Routledge and Kegan Paul, 1980); MacDonald, "Socio-cultural Reproduction and Women's Education," in Deem, ed., *Schooling for Women's Work.*

5. For a discussion of feminist "resistance and cultural production" theory, see Kathleen Weiler, *Women Teaching for Change: Gender, Class & Power* (New York: Bergin & Garvey, 1988).

6. In the United States, studies dealing in whole or in part with the history and status of black women in education are beginning to accumulate. They include Jacqueline Jones, *Soldiers of Light and Love: Northern Teachers and Georgia Blacks, 1865-1873* (Chapel Hill: University of North Carolina Press, 1980); Linda M. Perkins, "The Black Female American Missionary Association Teacher in the South, 1861-1870," in Jeffrey J. Crow and Flora J. Hatley, eds., *Black Americans in North Carolina and the South* (Chapel Hill: University of North Carolina Press, 1984) and "The History of Blacks in Teaching: Growth and Decline within a Profession," in Donald Warren, ed., *American Teachers: Histories of a Profession at Work* (New York: Macmillan, 1989); and Dorothy Sterling, ed. *We Are Your Sisters: Black Women in the Nineteenth Century* (New York: W.W. Norton, 1984). Similar studies are beginning in Canada as well. See Afua Cooper, "The Search for Mary Bibb, Black Woman Teacher in Canada West during the Mid-Nineteenth Century," *Ontario History* 83, 1 (March 1991) as well as her essay on Mary Bibb in *We're Rooted Here and They Can't Pull Us Down: Essays in African Canadian Women's History* (Toronto: University of Toronto Press, forthcoming).

7. Marion V. Royce, "Arguments over the Education of girls: Their Admission to Grammar Schools in this Province," *Ontario History* 47 (March 1975): 1-13; "Education for Girls in Quaker Schools in Ontario," *Atlantis* 3, 1 (Fall 1977): 181-92; "Methodism and the Education of Women in Nineteenth Century Ontario," *Atlantis* 3, 2 pt 1 (Spring 1978): 131-43; "Notes on Schooling for Girls in Upper Canada from the Pre-Conquest Period until the Mid-Nineteenth Century," Canadian Women's History Series, No. 10, Department of History & Philosophy, Ontario Institute for Studies in Education, 1978.

8. See especially Houston and Prentice, *Schooling and Scholars in Nineteenth-Century Ontario* and Gidney and Millar, *Inventing Secondary Education: The Rise of the High School in Nineteenth-Century Ontario.*

9. The subject of the work that teachers did was further explored in an essay not yet published when "From Household to Schoolhouse" appeared. See Marta Danylewycz and Alison Prentice, "Teachers' Work: Changing Patterns and Perceptions in the Emerging School Systems of Nineteenth- and Early Twentieth-Century Central Canada," *Labour/le travail* 17 (Spring 1986), reprinted in Alison Prentice and Marjorie R. Theobald, eds., *Women Who Taught: Perspectives on the History of Women and Teaching* (Toronto: University of Toronto Press, 1991). For the more detailed explorations of who taught school, see Marta Danylewycz, Beth Light and Alison Prentice, "The Evolution of the Sexual Division of Labour in Teaching: A Nineteenth Century Ontario and Quebec Case Study," *Histoire sociale/Social History* 16, 2 (May 1983) and Marta Danylewycz and Alison Prentice, "Teachers, Gender and Bureaucratizing School Systems in Nineteenth Century Montreal and Toronto," *History of Education Quarterly* 24, 1 (Spring 1984).

10. For an analysis of the processes involved in this development in Ontario, as well as the important role played by the question of women's education in it, see Gidney and Millar, *Inventing Secondary Education.*

11. Paul Bennett, "'Little Worlds': The Forging of Identities in Ontario's Protestant Denominational Schools and Special Institutions" (University of Toronto: Ed.D Thesis, 1991) contains chapters on native residential schools, black separate schools, Mennonite schools, single-sex upper class private schools and industrial schools for boys and girls, as well as extensive discussion of gender and class relations in these educational settings. See also the essays by Afua Cooper, cited in endnote 6. Cooper's M.A. thesis, soon to be completed at the Ontario Institute for Studies in Education, will deal with black teachers in mid-nineteenth-century Upper Canada.

12. See for example, Bruce Curtis, "'Illicit' Sexuality and Public Education in Ontario, 1840-1907," *Historical Studies in Education/Revue d'histoire de l'éducation*, 1, 1 (Spring 1989), and Helen Lenskyj, "Training for 'True Womanhood': Physical Education for Girls in Ontario Schools, 1890-1920," *ibid.*, 2, 2 (Fall 1990). On teachers, see Judith Arbus, "Grateful to be Working: Women Teachers During the Great Depression," Alison Prentice, "Multiple Realities: The History of Women Teachers in Canada," and Cecilia Reynolds, "Too Limiting a Liberation: Discourse and Actuality in the Case of Married Women Teachers," in Frieda Forman, *et al.,* eds., *Feminism and Education: A Canadian Perspective* (Toronto: Centre for Women's Studies in Education, Ontario Institute for Studies in Education, 1990); also Cecilia Reynolds, "Hegemony and Hierarchy: Becoming a Teacher in Toronto, 1930-1980," *Historical Studies in Education/Revue d'histoire de l'éducation* 2, 1 (Spring 1990).

13. Existing studies include Alison Prentice, "'Friendly Atoms in Chemistry': Women and Men at Normal School in Mid-Nineteenth-Century Toronto," in David Keane & Colin Read, eds., *Old Ontario: Essays in Honour of J.M.S. Careless* (Toronto: Dundurn Press, 1990); Lykke De La Cour and Rose Sheinin, "The Ontario Medical College for Women, 1883-1906: Lessons from Gender-Separatism in Medical Education," *Canadian Woman Studies/Les cahiers de la femme.* 7, 3 (Fall, 1986), and E.W. Stieb, Gail C. Coulas and Joyce A. Ferguson, "Women in Ontario Pharmacy, 1867-1927," in *Pharmacy in History*, 28, 3 (1986), American Institute of Pharmacy. The last two articles have been reprinted in Marianne Gosztonyi Ainley, ed., *Despite the Odds. Essays on Canadian Women and Science* (Montreal: Vehicule Press, 1990).

14. For college and university teaching, see Alison Prentice, "Scholarly Passion: Two Persons Who Caught It," *Historical Studies in Education/Revue d'histoire de l'éducation*, 1, 1 (Spring 1989): 7-27, reprinted in Prentice and Theobald, eds., *Women Who Taught*.

15. These themes have already been the subject of much research in Quebec. See Fahmy-Eid and Dumont, eds., *Maîtresses de maison, maîtresses d'école,* and *Les couventines*; Anne Drummond, "Gender, Profession, and Principals: The Teachers of Quebec Protestant Academies, 1875-1900, *Historical Studies in Education/Revue d'histoire de l'éducation* 2, 1 (Spring 1990). Readers should also watch for a collection of essays edited by Elizabeth Muir and Marilyn Whitely on women and the Christian Church in Canada, a number of which will deal with educational themes.

16. See especially Terry Crowley, "The Origin of Continuing Education for Women: The Ontario Women's Institutes," *Canadian Woman Studies/les cahiers de la femme* 7, 3 (Fall 1986): 78-81; Diana Pedersen, " 'Keeping Our Good Girls Good': The YWCA and the 'Girl Problem,' 1870-1930," *Canadian Woman Studies/les cahiers de la femme* 7, 4 (Winter 1986):20-24, and " 'The Call to Service': The YWCA and the Canadian College Woman, 1886-1920," in Axelrod and Reid, eds. *Youth, University and Canadian Society;* Margaret Prang, " 'The Girl God Would Have Me Be': The Canadian Girls in Training, 1915-39," *Canadian Historical Review* 66, 2 (1985): 154-84.

17. Comprehensive studies include Curtis, *Building the Educational State;* Houston and Prentice, *Schooling and Scholars;* and Gidney and Millar, *Inventing Secondary Education.* On domestic science education, see Diana Pedersen, " 'The Scientific Training of Mothers': The Campaign for Domestic Science in Ontario Schools, 1890-1913," in Richard Jarell and Arnold E. Roos, ed., *Critical Issues in the History of Canadian Science, Technology and Medicine* (Thornhill: HSTC Publications, 1983) and Terry Crowley, "Madonnas before Magdalenes: Adelaide Hoodless and the Making of the Canadian Gibson Girl," *Canadian Historical Review*, 67, 4 (1986). On women university students during the Second World War, see Nancy Kiefer and Ruth Pierson, "The War Efforts and Women Students at the University of Toronto, 1939-1945," in Paul Axelrod and John Reid, eds., *Youth, University and Canadian Society: Essays in the Social History of Higher Education* (Montreal: Queen's University Press, 1989).

Gender and Education in Ontario: An Historical Reader

Contributors

John Abbott teaches history at Algoma University College in Sault Ste. Marie. He has published articles on the transmission of educational policy to Northern Ontario and is currently completing a book on this subject.

Marta Danylewycz taught history at Atkinson College, York University, at the time of her untimely death in 1985. The author and co-author of articles dealing with women and education, she is also known for her monograph on religious women in Quebec.

Ian E. Davey studied in Ontario before taking up teaching and administrative posts at the University of Adelaide in Australia, where he continues his research and writing on the history of class, gender and schooling.

Kari Dehli teaches at the Ontario Institute for Studies in Education. Her thesis explored how middle-class women organized gender and class relations in the Home and School Association in early twentieth-century Toronto, and she is currently completing a project on skills training in Ontario and Norway.

Jane S. Gaskell has published widely on the sociology of gender and education, with a special emphasis on vocational education for women. She is a professor and department chair in the Faculty of Education at the University of British Columbia.

Susan Gelman is a doctoral student at the Ontario Institute for Studies in Education. Her research and writing focus on the history of work, community and education in turn of the century Ontario, and currently on the history of teachers in secondary schools.

Ruby Heap teaches history at the University of Ottawa. She has published articles on the history of education and the history of women in Quebec and is currently researching the development of vocational education for women in Quebec and Ontario.

Nancy S. Jackson does work on the social organization of knowledge, with a special focus on work and education, skills training, and gender issues. She teaches in the Faculty of Education at McGill.

Jo LaPierre is completing a Ph.D. thesis on nineteenth-century women university students for the Ontario Institute for Studies in Education. She teaches at Vanier College and is currently on loan to the Research Branch of the Royal Commission on New Reproductive Technologies in Ottawa.

Lynne Marks has written on women in both secondary school and university settings. She is currently completing a doctoral thesis for York University, focussing on class and gender dimensions of involvement in religion and leisure in three late nineteenth century Ontario towns.

Contributors

Nicole Neatby is completing a doctoral thesis at the Université de Montreal on the history of the student movement at that institution during the 1950s. Her research interests also include the history of secondary and higher education for Roman Catholic women in Ontario.

Alison Prentice teaches history at the Ontario Institute for Studies in Education. Her writing has explored class and gender issues in nineteenth- and early twentieth-century Ontario schooling and she is currently involved in research on the work of women in Ontario universities.

Johanna Selles-Roney has published articles on women's religious and educational experience in the early twentieth century. Her doctoral thesis, for the Ontario Institute for Studies in Education, will examine Methodist schooling for young women in Ontario between 1830 and 1925.

Harry Smaller works in community and educational development in Toronto alternative school settings and has also taught at the Ontario Institute for Studies in Education. His Ph.D. thesis and published articles deal with teacher education and teacher unionism in Ontario.

Elizabeth Smyth has taught in secondary schools and published on the history of religion in Ontario, as well as on topics in contemporary special education and gender and education. She is currently a member of the Northwestern Centre and the Curriculum Department of the Ontario Institute for Studies in Education.

Part One:

The Emergence of Gender as a Focus

Trends in Female School Attendance in Mid-Nineteenth-Century Ontario

Ian E. Davey

Introduction[1]

One of the most extraordinary gaps in the writing of social history in general and educational history in particular is the lack of studies of school attendance patterns.[2] Our understanding of the profound changes in childhood experience resulting from the expansion of schooling in the nineteenth century remains minimal because we have little information on who actually attended school, the number of years devoted to schooling and the regularity of attendance. The aim of this paper is to suggest ways of remedying this situation. It focusses on changes in female school attendance patterns in Ontario during the 1850s and 1860s—the years when Egerton Ryerson's free school program brought an increasing number of children into the schools. The paper surveys overall attendance patterns in the province, quantitatively analyses the social structure of female students in one community, Hamilton, and examines the changing function of the private academy for girls in the period.

The Changing Pattern of Female School Attendance, 1847-71: An Overview

From 1846 each local superintendent of schools in the province was required to submit an annual report listing the number of children of school-age in his area, the number of pupils, male and female, enrolled in the schools and the average attendance of these pupils at school. From this information it is possible to construct a composite picture of the extent of and changes in female school attendance in Ontario. There is, however, one major limitation regarding the figures. The reports list the number of males and females enrolled in the various common schools in each year, not the number regularly attending. In consequence, they exaggerate the actual number of pupils found in the schools in any one month or on any one day. Yearly enrolments included all of those who entered the school regardless of their length of stay in the school and in the area. As it is becoming increasingly clear that geographic mobility in the period was immense, a considerable number of children must have moved from one area to another and from one school to another during each year, thus

1

inflating the actual number of pupils.[3] Nevertheless, there is no reason to believe that the overall enrolment pattern is seriously distorted or that the yearly male-female ratio among pupils is inaccurate.

The most obvious feature of female enrolment in the province's common schools during the period of the free school campaign from the late forties to 1871 was the steady increase in enrolment from 55,254 in 1847 to 211,260 in 1871 (see Table 1). This increase reflected not only the rise in population in Ontario but also the increasing proportion of girls attending the schools. Moreover, the increase in common school enrolment accounted for most of the increase in girls' attendance as the enrolment at the private schools and academies, both male and female, only increased from 6,753 in 1850 to 8,562 in 1870. Thus, Ryerson's school reform program had the effect of bringing large numbers of girls into contact with the schools for the first time. Although, throughout the period, there were always more boys enrolled than girls, the disparity between the sexes steadily diminished. Whereas in 1850 only 43.6% of those enrolled in the common schools were girls, by 1871 the proportion had steadily increased to 47.3%. If, as Ryerson claimed, there were more girls attending private schools than boys, the proportional gap between the sexes must have been even narrower.[4]

The most spectacular advances in female attendance occurred in the province's cities. In 1848, for example, only 26.2% of school-age (five to sixteen) children in Toronto, Kingston and Hamilton attended the common schools and of these only 35.8% were girls. By 1871 over 85% of the school-age children of the province's cities were enrolled in the public schools and 49% of them were girls. In the rural areas, where the majority of the population lived, the influx of girls to the common schools was less spectacular. Although, by 1871, a similar proportion of school-age children were enrolled in the public schools, the proportion of girls was only 47%. In both rural and urban areas, the period of most rapid increase in female enrolment was the commercial boom years of the early fifties. However, the female enrolment figures were far more volatile in the urban areas than in the rural sections where the increase, both numerically and proportionately, was more of a steady upward trend.

Trends in Female School Attendance

Table 1—NUMBER OF FEMALES ATTENDING COMMON SCHOOLS 1847-71

YEAR	ONTARIO		COUNTIES		CITIES*	
	Number	% of Students	Number	% of Students	Number	% of Students
1847	55254	44.3	—	—	1268	40.2
1848	57714	44.1	—	—	1086	35.8
1849	61929	44.7	—	—	1619	44.5
1850	66173	43.6	61197	44.0	1601	34.9
1851	75815	44.5	68679	44.8	2322	43.7
1852	80323	44.7	71790	44.8	2782	45.1
1853	87344	44.9	77578	44.9	3028	44.3
1854	91283	44.7	80022	45.3	3691	43.3
1855	102186	44.8	90652	45.3	4899	41.0
1856	113725	45.3	98864	45.3	6616	45.8
1857	122608	45.0	104437	44.9	8688	47.5
1858	133050	45.3	111828	45.2	9059	47.4
1859	135904	45.1	114231	45.1	8687	45.6
1860	143708	45.5	119869	45.5	9106	46.0
1861	151483	45.9	127196	46.0	9343	47.3
1862	158292	46.1	132280	45.9	9839	48.3
1863	167818	46.5	139079	46.3	10792	49.1
1864	173671	46.7	143920	46.6	10711	48.3
1865	179332	46.7	148576	46.7	10815	46.8
1866	182306	46.6	150619	46.6	10700	46.9
1867	188642	47.0	154789	46.8	11238	49.1
1868	198092	47.2	161690	47.0	12007	48.8
1869	202745	46.9	164955	46.7	12649	48.7
1870	209137	47.3	169198	47.0	13081	48.6
1871	211260	47.3	168708	47.0	13913	49.0

* Toronto, Kingston and Hamilton until 1855 when Ottawa and London added.
Source: *Annual Report of the Normal, Model, Grammar and Common Schools*, 1847-1871.

Gender And Education In Ontario: An Historical Reader

In the cities, the rapid increase in enrolment in the fifties was brought to a halt by the onset of the Depression. Although the numbers of both male and females enrolled were affected, reflecting the net loss of population from some of the urban areas, the proportional disparity between the sexes widened indicating that in times of hardship parents were more likely to dispense with their daughters' education. The comment of the local superintendent for Beverly Township in Wentworth County is instructive on this point. After noting that almost four boys to every three girls attended the schools in the township, he continued that "one must infer from this fact that the opinion seems yet to prevail that girls need less Common School education than boys. The natural disparity between the sexes does not justify the above disproportion."[5]

If the trend throughout the period was towards increased enrolment in the common schools, the picture of educational progress in Ontario was muddied by the low average attendance of those enrolled. The proportion of those on the rolls who attended for 100 days or less (out of a possible 260) hovered around 55% from 1856 through 1871. Unfortunately, the reports only give a sex breakdown on average attendance in the early years although the comments of the local superintendents throughout the period suggest that the patterns evident in those years remained constant to 1871. The most important feature of the summer and winter attendance patterns was the seasonal variation in the rural areas (see Table 2). In each of the years between 1850 and 1854, more boys than girls attended in both summer and winter but in the season of greater attendance, winter, the discrepancy between the sexes was approximately twice that of the summer. That is, many more boys and fewer girls attended in winter. In the cities it seems that the seasonal pattern was reversed for, apart from 1854, attendance was notably higher in summer than winter. As in the rural areas, however, in winter the proportion of boys was higher than in summer although they remained in the majority in both seasons.

The factors affecting school attendance in mid-nineteenth-century Ontario were many and varied. Commercial depressions resulting in high unemployment in the urban areas and increased transience affected school attendance. Similarly, in rural areas, bad crops and prices meant fewer children were sent to school: "as soon as farmers are blessed with better harvest and more remunerative markets, the children will be more regular in their attendance, they will be sent longer to school, and far more attention will be given to furnishing the school houses."[6] The pronounced seasonal pattern of attendance in the farming areas was similar to that noted by Kett in rural New England for a slightly earlier period.[7] As one of the local superintendents in York County pointed out, "in summer seasons those children who are too young to labour

4

Trends in Female School Attendance

are sent to school, and those whose labour is valuable are kept at home: in the winter this order is reversed, thus making two distinct sets of pupils in the year."[8] The shortage and high price of agricultural labour necessitated children, particularly boys, working on the family farm in the busy seasons, and many local superintendents reported that the schools were virtually emptied "at the times of hay, wheat, oat, apple and potato harvests."[9] Whereas large numbers of rural boys attended only in the winter months, it would seem that many of the girls were kept home in winter to care for the younger members of the family who were unable to attend because of the distance from the school house and the severity of the weather.

Table 2—AVERAGE ATTENDANCE AT COMMON SCHOOLS, 1850-1854

YEAR	UPPER CANADA			COUNTIES			CITY		
	Total	Boys	Girls	Total	Boys	Girls	Total	Boys	Girls
1850 Summer	76,824	41784	35040	70,644	37940	32704	2,248	1495	753
Winter	81,469	48308	33161	75,215	44385	30830	2,163	1375	788
1851 Summer	83,390	44647	38743	74,438	39541	34897	2,581	1423	1158
Winter	84,981	49060	35921	76,389	44076	32313	2,376	1377	999
1852 Summer	85,161	45409	39752	75,762	40253	35509	2,730	1482	1248
Winter	86,756	49867	36889	77,656	44620	33036	2,580	1448	1132
1853 Summer	90,096	48668	41428	78,043	41955	36088	4,391	2337	2054
Winter	89,659	52252	37407	78,830	45380	33450	3,919	2259	1660
1854 Summer	91,880	49475	42405	77,682	41859	35823	4,368	2615	1753
Winter	92,925	52696	40229	79,306	44694	34612	4,542	2671	1871

Source: *Annual Report...Schools* 1850-1854.

Distance from school, inclement weather and quagmire road conditions also were reasons for non-attendance of pupils in certain seasons in the cities. Other reasons for variable attendance patterns that were shared by both rural and urban areas of Ontario were the incidence of epidemics like smallpox and measles in particular areas, dissatisfaction with the local teaching standards and the parents' inability to provide adequate clothing and footwear for their children, especially in winter. This latter reason, a consequence of poverty, was almost certainly a major contributing factor to the fall off in attendance in the urban areas in winter for, as we shall see, there was an inverse relationship between poverty and school attendance.[10]

The Social Structure of Urban Attendance: The Case of Hamilton

There are basically two ways of approaching the quantitative analysis of the social structure of school attendance. One is to use the school registers which were routinely generated by the public schools from the mid-nineteenth century and list such information as student's name, age, sex, date of entering and leaving the school and occupation and address of parent. The major problems associated with the use of registers is that rarely have complete sets of them survived, especially those from the earlier years, and consequently, it is often impossible to construct a complete picture of school attendance patterns in any one community at any one time. The second method, using the information contained on the manuscript census records, allows the researcher to analyse the pattern of attendance across the whole community and to relate the information about individual students to the wealth of socio-economic data about their parents. A major drawback of this approach is that it is not possible to distinguish between the types of school, be they public or private, that the students attended. Nor is it possible to analyse the regularity with which students attended. In this paper both types of records are drawn on, but the basis for the study is the manuscript census records for the city of Hamilton in 1851 and 1861.[11]

In 1851, 1,226 of the 4,339 children between three and twenty-one listed on the census were recorded as attending school in Hamilton (see Table 3). Of these, 683 or 55.7% were boys and 543 were girls. The vast majority, over 96%, of both the male and female students fell within Ryerson's definition of school age, five to sixteen. However, it is significant that those recorded as attending school accounted for only 39% of those five to sixteen and 28.3% of those between three and twenty-one. Remarkably, of the 3,113 children not in school, only 287 listed an occupation, of which only 75 or 26.1% were girls. That is, only 4.6% of the 1,617 girls who lived at home and did not attend school in Hamilton in 1851 were gainfully employed and more than a dozen were employed in only two types of occupations, dressmaking and millinery and domestic service. Of course many more girls lived in other households as domestic servants, but the fact remains that over 1,500 girls helped their

Trends in Female School Attendance

parents at home or work by running errands, doing housework or minding younger children or else wandered the streets of the city.

Table 3—SCHOOL ATTENDANCE IN HAMILTON, 1851

Age Group	BOYS		GIRLS		TOTAL	
	In School	Total	In School	Total	In School	Total
3-21	683	2179	543	2160	1226	4339
%	31.3		25.1		28.3	
5-16	657	1563	525	1464	1182	3027
%	42.0		35.9		39.0	
7-12	444	821	368	792	812	1613
%	54.1		46.5		50.3	

Source: Census Manuscripts, Hamilton, 1851.

What then was the social structure of those attending school? First, if you were a child, male or female, of wealthy parents then you were more likely to attend school. Whereas barely more than 25% of the children from the poorest 40% of the city's households attended school, well over 50% of children whose parents were in the wealthiest 20% did. Moreover, it helped if you were a boy. For at no one age did more girls than boys attend school, nor in any age group did a majority of girls attend. Even in the years of heaviest school attendance, ages seven through twelve, only 46.5% of the girls attended compared to 54.1% of the boys. An examination of the age-sex structure of school attendance by parent's occupation illuminates this imbalance between boys and girls.

Of course, the overall attendance pattern for occupation was closely related to that for wealth—many more children from non-manual backgrounds attended school than did those whose fathers were labourers (see Table 4). But the analysis of the occupational background of the male and female students reveals that girls from some occupational backgrounds were much less likely to attend school than their brothers.[12] If you were the daughter of a merchant or professional, a shopkeeper or clerk or a skilled artisan you were more likely to attend school than if your father was a semi-skilled worker or labourer or your mother a widow. However, unless you were the daughter of a labourer or, perhaps, a skilled artisan or widow, your chance of attending school was nowhere near as good as your brother's. This was particularly the case during the years of greatest school attendance, seven through twelve. While merchants and professionals sent more of their seven- to twelve-year-old girls to school (over 58%) than any other occupational group, they sent almost 73% of their sons of the same ages. Only 30.8% of the labourers' daughters of the same ages were in school but, then, only 32.1% of their sons were also. The semi-skilled workers differed from their unskilled counterparts dramatically as, although they sent only marginally more of their daughters to school, they sent about two-thirds of their seven- to twelve-year-old sons, an even greater proportion than the skilled artisans did. The two groups with the proportionately greatest divergence between male and female attendance, the "petite bourgeoisie" and the semi-skilled workers, may have harboured ambitions for their sons, ambitions they attempted to fulfil at the expense of their daughters.

At the bottom end of the social scale ethnic background reflected the class relationships (see Table 5). The Irish Catholics, many of whom were poor labourers, sent almost the same proportion of boys and girls to school that the labourers did. No ethnic group sent more of their daughters to school than their sons in the years of heaviest school attendance, seven to twelve. However, the Canadian Protestants, a very wealthy group, sent more of their school-age daughters to school than sons, suggesting that the lack of suitable employment opportunities for their daughters meant that they stayed in school longer than their brothers. Nonetheless, the overall picture of attendance that emerges from the analysis of the occupational and ethnic background of students in 1851, is one of limited opportunities for schooling for all children in Hamilton and for girls in particular.

At the time of the census in 1851, Hamilton's public schools were not a dominant feature in the city's educational landscape. No less than 25 private schools and the Burlington Ladies Academy competed with the seven public schools for the chance to educate the city's children, and about one-half of those who did attend went to these private schools. In 1853, large-scale public education commenced with the opening of the centralized school system which aimed at providing the city with a systematic, graded education for the majority of school-age children.[13] The establishment of the new system of public schooling had important ramifications for attendance patterns in the city because it effectively destroyed most of the alternatives to public schooling in the city. Moreover, it removed the stigma associated with attendance at the public schools and, although the number of girls enrolled remained less than the number of boys, their proportionate representation increased. The educational landscape was also altered in the fifties by the establishment of two Roman Catholic separate schools in 1856 which provided an avenue of education for the many Catholic children of the city. Both of these factors

Trends in Female School Attendance

Table 4 — SCHOOL ATTENDANCE BY PARENT'S OCCUPATION, HAMILTON 1851

Age Group	PROFESSIONAL & PROPRIETOR		SHOPKEEPER, CLERK ETC		SKILLED ARTISAN		SEMI-SKILLED WORKER		LABOURER		WIDOW, ETC	
	Boys	Girls	Boys	Girls	Boys	Girls	Boys	Girls	Boys	Girls	Boys	Girls
3-21	162	210	315	280	802	815	122	132	454	439	214	180
Total in School	64	69	143	75	249	223	55	25	80	80	60	38
%	39.5	32.9	45.4	26.8	31.0	27.4	45.1	18.9	17.6	18.2	28.0	21.1
5-16	109	143	235	166	545	560	92	92	353	315	158	111
Total in School	59	66	140	69	241	220	51	25	79	77	58	37
%	54.1	46.2	59.6	41.6	44.2	39.3	55.4	27.2	22.4	24.4	36.7	33.3
7-12	48	77	121	83	283	307	53	52	196	169	88	62
Total in School	35	45	88	47	160	159	35	20	63	52	45	24
%	72.9	58.4	72.7	56.6	56.5	51.8	66.0	38.5	32.1	30.8	51.1	38.7

Source: Census Manuscripts, Hamilton, 1851.

Table 5 — SCHOOL ATTENDANCE BY PARENT'S ETHNICITY, HAMILTON, 1851

Age-Group	IRISH CATHOLIC		IRISH PROTESTANT		SCOTTISH PRESBYTERIAN		ENGLISH ANGLICAN		ENGLISH METHODIST		CANADIAN PROTESTANT		U.S. PROTESTANT	
	Boys	Girls	Boys	Girls	Boys	Girls	Boys	Girls	Boys	Girls	Boys	Girls	Boys	Girls
3-21	521	469	394	404	268	220	264	284	108	152	148	155	92	105
Total in School	97	82	130	97	114	70	102	67	37	50	49	51	37	36
%	18.6	17.5	33.0	24.0	42.5	31.8	38.6	23.6	34.3	32.9	33.1	32.9	40.2	34.3
5-16	402	324	292	270	191	137	188	199	69	107	105	105	66	73
Total in School	92	80	126	94	111	66	99	67	34	49	48	49	35	34
%	22.9	24.7	43.2	34.8	58.1	48.2	52.7	33.7	49.3	45.8	45.7	46.7	53.0	46.6
7-12	224	178	151	147	98	79	107	95	23	59	51	62	32	37
Total in School	72	53	80	70	71	52	69	40	17	36	30	30	24	20
%	32.1	29.8	53.0	47.6	72.4	65.8	64.5	42.1	73.9	61.0	58.8	48.4	75.0	54.1

Source: Census Manuscripts, Hamilton, 1861.

Trends in Female School Attendance

influenced female attendance patterns considerably as the analysis of the students in 1861 demonstrates.

Table 6—SCHOOL ATTENDANCE IN HAMILTON, 1861

Age Group	BOYS		GIRLS		TOTAL	
	In School	Total	In School	Total	In School	Total
3-21	1371	3343	1243	3231	2615	6577*
%	41.0		38.5		39.8	
15-16	1314	2290	1198	2153	2513	4446*
%	57.4		55.6		56.5	
7-12	846	1165	793	1120	1639	2285
%	72.6		70.8		71.7	

*No sex given for 3 children, including 1 in school
Source: Census Manuscripts, Hamilton, 1861.

Although the relationship between wealth and school attendance still existed in 1861, it was not as strong as in 1851 because a larger proportion of the school-age children of the city had been drawn into the schools. Whereas in 1851 only about 28% of all children between three and twenty-one attended school, in 1861 the percentage was almost 40%, 2,615 of 6,577 (see Table 6). Like the students of 1851 though, over 96% of those attending school fell within the five to sixteen age range and only a small number of those listed as not attending, 372, indicated that they had jobs. Similarly, the proportion of girls among those who listed an occupation was very low, 75 of the 372 or just over 20%. However, a much greater proportion of girls attended school than in 1851. While the proportion of boys age five to sixteen who attended school increased from 42% to 57.4% in the decade, the proportion of girls rose from 35.9% to 55.6%. Similarly, the proportion of seven- to twelve-year-old girls attending school rose by more than 24% to 70.8% in 1861 whereas the proportion of boys rose by less than 17% to 72.6%. Significantly, the proportion of thirteen- to sixteen-year-old girls attending school was slightly greater than the proportion of boys. Clearly, a large part of the increase in school attendance between 1851 and 1861 was the result of more girls coming into the schools and staying there longer.

11

Table 7 — School Attendance by Parent's Occupation, Hamilton 1861

Age Group	Professional & Proprietor		Shopkeeper, Clerk, etc		Skilled Artisan		Semi-skilled Worker		Labourer		Widow, etc	
	Boys	Girls	Boys	Girls	Boys	Girls	Boys	Girls	Boys	Girls	Boys	Girls
3-21	318	298	502	512	1142	1161	141	134	677	617	338	322
Total in School	164	127	225	226	513	513	45	44	208	163	129	104
%	51.6	42.6	44.8	44.1	44.9	44.2	31.9	32.8	30.7	26.4	38.2	32.3
5-16	224	185	343	352	781	788	100	86	469	410	224	214
Total in School	153	113	211	215	494	498	45	43	207	162	123	102
%	68.3	61.1	61.5	61.1	63.3	63.2	45.0	50.0	44.1	39.5	54.9	47.7
7-12	116	93	169	182	409	432	46	40	229	211	115	107
Total in School	96	71	130	145	324	331	28	23	132	114	81	67
%	82.8	76.3	76.9	79.7	79.2	76.6	60.9	57.5	57.6	54.0	70.4	62.6

Source: Census Manuscripts, Hamilton, 1861.

Trends in Female School Attendance

These changes were reflected in the occupational and ethnic backgrounds of the students. Among household heads, only professionals and merchants and widows sent more than 5% more boys of school age to school than girls (see Table 7). Contrary to the situation in 1851, the small businessmen and the semi-skilled workers sent proportionately as many and more of their school-age daughters to school than their sons. The artisans sent the highest proportion of girls of any occupational group, over 63% of those of school age, while the labourers were as far behind as in 1851 sending fewer boys and girls than any other occupational group, although the proportion of school-age males in school from labouring homes had virtually doubled and females had increased by 15%. Among the ethnic groups only the Blacks and the Irish Catholics sent less than half of their school-age children, male and female, to school (see Table 8). However, the Irish Catholics had increased their attendance dramatically, reflecting the opening of the separate schools. The Blacks sent more girls than boys as did the U.S. Protestants and the English Methodists, who sent two-thirds of their school-age girls, more than any other group. The groups who had sent markedly fewer girls than boys in 1851 sent proportionately equal numbers in 1861: the proportion of students among the school-age daughters of the English Anglicans, for example, increased by 26% in the decade while the proportion of their sons in school only increased by 7%.

Certainly, the most significant feature of the occupational and ethnic distribution in 1861 was the relative balance between the proportion of males and females in school. The establishment of the centralized public school system and the separate schools was accompanied by a rapid influx of girls into the schools. By 1871, proportionately more school-age girls than boys were in school, particularly in early adolescence as many more girls stayed in school into their teen-age years.[14]

The Changing Function of the Private Female Academy

The rapid increase in the proportion of girls attending school in Hamilton in the fifties coincided with the establishment of the centralized, tax-supported public system of education and the subsequent demise of most of the private institutions in the city. That is, most of the new female students attended the common schools and, to a lesser extent, the newly established Roman Catholic separate schools. This had not been the case at mid-century. Then, it was believed, there was a lack of government support for female education as the District Grammar School accepted boys only and the local common schools

13

Table 8 — SCHOOL ATTENDANCE BY PARENT'S ETHNICITY, HAMILTON, 1861

Age Group	IRISH CATHOLIC		IRISH PROTESTANT		SCOTTISH PRESBYTERIAN		ENGLISH ANGLICAN		ENGLISH METHODIST		CANADIAN PROTESTANT		U.S. PROTESTANT		BLACKS*	
	Boys	Girls	Boys	Girls	Boys	Girls	Boys	Girls	Boys	Girls	Boys	Girls	Boys	Girls	Boys	Girls
3-21	710	684	489	522	534	506	516	472	214	234	220	225	118	115	59	55
Total in School	229	194	206	208	246	217	218	201	93	104	103	92	51	47	18	18
%	32.3	28.4	42.1	39.8	46.1	42.9	42.2	42.6	43.5	44.4	46.8	40.9	43.2	40.9	30.5	32.7
5-16	490	458	338	364	362	324	350	330	146	152	155	148	86	76	42	33
Total in School	224	192	199	199	237	210	209	197	89	101	99	86	45	43	18	16
%	45.7	41.9	58.9	54.7	65.5	64.8	59.7	59.7	61.0	66.4	63.9	58.1	52.3	56.6	42.9	48.5
7-12	239	225	164	197	194	169	172	181	75	80	84	77	41	39	21	22
Total in School	148	130	126	134	156	137	130	129	57	64	63	56	27	30	10	11
%	61.9	57.8	76.8	68.0	80.4	81.1	75.6	71.3	76.0	80.0	75.0	72.7	65.8	76.9	47.6	50.0

*In 1851 the number of black children recorded on the current census was only 52 and only six were in school
Source: Census Manuscripts, Hamilton, 1861.

Trends in Female School Attendance

were not considered the places to educate your daughters if you could afford otherwise. For example, the editor of the *Hamilton Spectator*, suggesting that the government should give financial support to the Burlington Ladies Academy, declared that "we hope that the government, which provides amply for the education of youth of the rougher sex, will take into consideration the propriety of assisting to train in a suitable manner, those who contribute so much to the happiness, virtue and welfare of mankind."[15]

Recently, R.D. Gidney has argued that in the period prior to the introduction of Ryerson's reform program, numerous private institutions flourished which catered to the educational wants of most classes of society and only from the middle decades of the nineteenth century did private schooling take on its current meaning—denoting "a conscious (and expensive) rejection of the state system."[16] The proliferation of private schools and academies in Hamilton prior to the centralization of the public school system lends credence to his argument, for they ranged from large institutions with extensive boarding facilities to groups of children taught by men and women in their own homes. Unfortunately, few enrolment lists appear to have survived, making it difficult to discover who actually attended which school. Nevertheless, lists of students are existant for the prestigious and relatively expensive Burlington Ladies Academy.

This institution was the first in a line of Methodist-run institutions offering a "solid and ornamental" education to "young ladies." After its demise in the early fifties, it was replaced by its sister school, the Adelaide Academy, which was removed from Toronto, and the latter was succeeded by the Wesleyan Female College, which opened in 1861. These schools were not representative of the majority of private institutions in the city in that they were relatively expensive, had large boarding facilities for out-of-town students and offered broad curricula far beyond that found in the common schools. However, a brief analysis of the social structure of the students of the Burlington Ladies Academy in 1849 and the Wesleyan Female College in 1861 indicates the changing nature of their clientele.[17]

In 1849 eighty-four of the 197 girls attending the Burlington Ladies Academy were listed as residents of Hamilton, the remainder mostly coming from the southern area of Upper Canada, some from upstate New York and others from Montreal. Forty-five of the eighty-four girls from Hamilton were linked to their parents on the 1851 Census of the city. An important insight into the role of this school in the community can be gleaned from the age range of the pupils, this being determined as their census age minus two years. Although the pupils ranged in age from eight to twenty-three, the vast majority of them, almost 75%, were over twelve years old and fully 44.4% were over sixteen years. Obviously, as adolescent students, their educational experience differed dramatically from other girls in the city. They were the daughters of those citizens who could afford, and deemed it desirable, to keep their girls in school throughout their teenage years.

The most significant feature of the parents' social structure is that certain large groups within the city were conspicuously absent—notably semi-skilled and unskilled labourers, Roman Catholics and the poorer household heads of the city (see Table 9). However, the school was not as exclusive as the age structure of the students initially suggests, for the daughters of the above groups were largely absent from all schools in the city. The parents' birthplaces reflected the immigrant nature of the city although those born in England and Canada predominated. Moreover, although Methodists made up the largest single group, in keeping with the advertised non-sectarian nature of the school, the parents came from all major Protestant denominations.Occupationally, they were evenly divided between entrepreneurs (be they agents, merchants or manufacturers) and professionals on the one hand and skilled artisans on the other. As a group the parents were much more likely to have servants and own property than Hamilton's heads of household as a whole. And, not surprisingly, they were more wealthy, almost 36% of them being in the wealthiest 10% in the city. Nevertheless, twelve of the parents fell in the middle income ranks of the city and eight of these were artisans. It would seem that some of Hamilton's artisans must have sacrificed financially to enable their teenage daughters to attend the most prestigious educational institution in the city as tuition for day pupils in the "common English branches" was 6£ per quarter or four times the amount at the public common schools.

The Wesleyan Female College, a proprietary institution under the auspices of the Wesleyan Methodist Church, opened in September 1861. It was situated in what had been a large hotel, located in the heart of Hamilton's commercial district, the school's proprietors having bought the building during the Depression for less than a quarter of its construction price. It flourished for many years offering tuition in three departments, preparatory, academic and collegiate and awarding, to successful students in the latter department, diplomas of Mistress of Liberal Arts and Mistress of English Literature. Like its predecessor, the Burlington Ladies Academy, it charged for basic tuition and levied extra rates for the "ornamental" subjects and board. Also like the earlier institution it was "free from sectarian bias" although under Methodist control. The Wesleyan Female College also attracted large numbers of boarders, seventy-two of the 136 students in its opening year coming from outside Hamilton, including one from Nova Scotia and another from the Hudson's Bay Territory.

Trends in Female School Attendance

Of the sixty-four students listed as residents of Hamilton in 1861, two were boarders, and forty-three of the remaining sixty-two were linked to thirty-three families in the city. The girls ranged in age from four to sixteen with three under seven years, twenty-one between seven and twelve and the same number between thirteen and sixteen. They were, as a group, significantly younger than

Table 9—SOCIAL CHARACTERISTICS OF PARENTS OF STUDENTS AT THE BURLINGTON LADIES ACADEMY, 1849

Occupation	Professional & Proprietor	Shopkeeper, Clerk, etc.	Skilled Artisan	Widow	
Total	6	10	15	3	
%	17.6	29.4	44.1	8.8	
Birthplace	England	Scotland	Ireland	Canada	U.S.
Total	13	3	6	7	5
%	38.2	8.8	17.6	20.6	14.7
Religion	Anglican	Presbyterian	Methodist	Baptist	"Protestant"
Total	10	4	11	3	4
%	31.3	12.5	34.4	9.4	12.5
Servants	None	One	Two or More		
Total	15	13	6		
%	44.1	38.2	17.6		
Property Ownership*	Owner	Renter	Board		
Total	14	12	2		
%	50.0	42.9	7.1		
Wealth*	0—10	40—60	60—80	80—90	90—100
Total	1	5	6	6	10
%	3.6	17.9	21.4	21.4	35.7
Age of Pupils	7—12	13—16	17+		
Total = 45	10	15	20		
%	22.2	33.3	44.4		

Only 28 of the parents were linked to the 1852 Assessment.

Source: *Catalogue of Burlington Ladies Academy* 1849, Census Manuscripts, Hamilton, 1851, Assessment Rolls, Hamilton, 1852.

those in the Burlington Ladies Academy. Thus, unlike the earlier school, the Wesleyan Female College was in direct competition with the public schools in the city.

The students' parents were not as representative of the household heads of the city as their counterparts in 1851. While their birthplaces still reflected the immigrant character of the community, a much larger proportion of the parents were Methodists, although there were a number of Anglicans and Presbyterians (see Table 10). The parents of the students attending the Wesleyan Female College were also wealthier than their counterparts a decade earlier. A greater proportion of them had servants even though the percentage of households with servants in the city dropped during the decade. Similarly, more of them owned property and fully 62.5% of them (compared to under 36% of the parents of students at the Burlington Ladies Academy) were among the wealthiest 10% of household heads in the city. The greater wealth of the 1861 parents was reflected in their occupational structure. Twenty-one of the thirty-three parents were in the non-manual categories and fifteen of these were merchants, manufacturers or professionals. The proportion of artisans was considerably less and they only differed from the other parents in that they were less likely to have servants. The majority of them owned property and were among the wealthiest 10% in the city. In short, those who sent their daughters to the Wesleyan Female College were drawn from a much more exclusive and wealthy segment of Hamilton society than those whose daughters attended the Burlington Ladies Academy. This latter private institution must certainly have carried with it connotations of wealth and class prejudice in a period when class divisions were becoming increasingly apparent in Hamilton.[18]

Conclusion

The middle decades of the nineteenth century saw a remarkable transformation of female educational opportunity in Ontario. Throughout the fifties and sixties the number and proportion of girls enrolled in school steadily increased so that they approximated those of the boys in 1871. Certainly, their contact with the schools remained limited as average attendance figures remained low, parents dispensed with their daughter's education first in times of crisis and many girls were kept home to mind younger children at certain seasons of the year. But, without doubt, the following lines were less true in 1871 than when they were penned in 1855:

Trends in Female School Attendance

[N]ot a few sisters are depriving themselves of privileges to render possible the education of their brothers. In too many instances are daughters and sisters passing their equally precious years at home amid never ended toils in the nursery, the kitchen and dairy—their mental faculties undeveloped and undisciplined: their opportunities for study few and imperfect...[19]

Table 10—SOCIAL CHARACTERISTICS OF PARENTS OF STUDENTS AT THE WESLEYAN FEMALE COLLEGE, 1861

Occupation	Professional & Proprietor	Shopkeeper, Clerk, etc.	Skilled Artisan	Widow	
Total	15	6	9	3	
%	45.5	18.2	27.3	9.1	
Birthplace	England	Scotland	Ireland	Canada	US
Total	12	7	4	5	5
%	36.4	21.2	12.1	15.2	15.2
Religion	Anglican	Presbyterian	Methodist	Congregational	Other
Total	5	8	18	1	1
%	15.2	24.2	54.5	3.0	3.0
Servants	None	One	Two or More		
Total	13	11	9		
%	39.4	33.3	27.3		
Property Ownership*	Owner	Renter			
Total	18	14			
%	56.3	43.8			
Wealth*	40—60	60—80	80—90	90—100	
Total	2	6	4	20	
%	6.3	18.8	12.5	62.5	
Age of Pupils	Under 7	7—12	13—16		
Total = 45	3	21	21		
%	6.7	46.7	46.7		

32 of the parents were linked to the 1861 Assessment.

Source: *Catalogue of Burlington Ladies Academy* 1861, Census Manuscripts, Hamilton, 1851, Assessment Rolls, Hamilton, 1861.

Gender And Education In Ontario: An Historical Reader

It is important to stress that the influx of girls to the schools coincided with the transformation of public schooling in Ontario spearheaded by Ryerson. Throughout the period the common schools were being welded into a cohesive system of free and non-sectarian schools supervised by a centralized administration. The vast majority of girls who entered the schools enrolled in these public institutions, for the number of students at private schools and academies barely increased from 1850 to 1871. Moreover, those private institutions which did survive, or were established, no longer catered to the majority of children. They became more exclusive, providing education for the children of the wealthy and further entrenching the class differential in educational opportunity.

It would appear that the accessibility of free public schools played a significant part in the expansion of female school attendance in Ontario. However, we know little of the effects such exposure to increased schooling had on those girls who did attend, although the values of obedience, conformity and regularity inculcated in the classroom may have been important in shaping the attitudes of female students to their role in society. Certainly, schooling bore little relationship to future occupations outside of the home for girls, because, apart from the traditional jobs in domestic service and dressmaking, teaching provided the only new avenue for employment.[20] In Hamilton, most of the girls entering the schools were from middle-class backgrounds, which probably reflects the congruence of lack of suitable employment opportunities and increased respectability of the reformed public schools. Whatever the reasons for the increase in the proportion of girls in school, the improving sex ratio among students in the fifties and sixties ameliorated one of the two gross inequalities in educational opportunity. The other, class, remained the single most important determinant of school attendance because, although an increasing proportion of both the daughters and sons of the labouring poor attended school, they remained just as far behind the other groups as at the beginning.

Trends in Female School Attendance

Notes

1. A version of this paper was presented at the Canadian Association for American Studies Conference on Women in North America in Ottawa, October 1974. I would like to thank Harvey J. Graff and Professor Ian Winchester for their comments on the paper.

2. Examples of some recent studies in school attendance patterns in North America include Michael B. Katz, "Who went to school?" *History of Education Quarterly,* 12, No. 3 (1972): 432-54; Maris A. Vinoskis, "Trends in Massachusetts Education, 1826-1860." *HEQ,* 12, No. 4 (1972): 501-529; Selwyn K. Troen, "Popular Education in Nineteenth Century St. Louis." *HEQ,* 13, No. 1 (1973): 23-40; Carl F. Kaestle's excellent study, "The Evolution of an Urban School System: New York 1750-1850," (Cambridge, Mass: Harvard University Press 1973) analyses attendance patterns in the 1790s and 1850s; Alison Prentice, "The School Promoters." (Ph. D. dissertation, University of Toronto, Ch. 7) discussed trends in attendance in Ontario in the mid-nineteenth century.

3. For a discussion of geographic mobility in a Canadian city, see Michael B. Katz, "The people of a Canadian city: 1851-2." *Canadian Historical Review*, 53, No. 4, (1972): 402-426. See also David P. Gagan and Herbert Mays, "Historical Demography and Canadian Social History: Families and Land in Peel County, Ontario," CHR, 54, No. 1, (1973): 27-47, and Stephan Thernstrom and Peter R. Knights, "Men in Motion: Some Data and Speculations about Urban Population Mobility in Nineteenth Century America," *Journal of Interdisciplinary History*, 1, (1970): 7-36.

4. See, for example, *The Annual Report of the Normal, Model, Grammar and Common Schools in Upper Canada* (hereinafter referred to as *Annual Report*) 1851, 4. Ryerson states that a "much larger number of girls than boys attend private schools, as the law makes no provision for the higher class of girls schools."

5. Ibid., 1867, Appendix, 41.

6. Ibid., 1861, 180.

7. Joseph Kett, "Growing Up in Rural New England," In Tamara K. Hareven, ed., *Anonymous Americans.* (Englewood Cliffs, N.J.: Prentice-Hall, 1971) 1-14.

8. *Annual Report,* 1859, 167.

9. See, for example, ibid., 1861, 176.

10. Poverty affected both the likelihood that children would attend and the regularity with which they attended. Seasonal and cyclical unemployment and employment by the week or day meant that economic insecurity was

a basic fact of working class life in the period. For a discussion of these factors and their relation to school attendance, see Ian E. Davey, "Education Reform and the Working Class: School Attendance in Hamilton, Ontario, 1851-1891," (Ph.D. dissertation, University of Toronto, in progress) Ch. 3.

11. Katz, "Who went to school?" contains an excellent discussion of the possibilities and methodology of quantitative analysis of school attendance. The following analysis was made possible by access to the data bank of the Canadian Social History Project, Dept. of History and Philosophy, Ontario Institute for Studies in Education.

12. The occupational categories employed here account for over 95% of the children's parents who were heads of households in 1851.

13. For an analysis of the impact of the central school on Hamilton's schools attendance see Ian E. Davey, "School Reform and School Attendance: The Hamilton Central School 1853-61," in Michael B. Katz, ed., *Education and History: The English Canadian Experience,* forthcoming (New York University Press: 1975). See also my M.A. thesis of the same title, University of Toronto, 1971.

14. This conclusion is drawn from the analysis of social structure of school attendance in Hamilton. See Ibid., Ch. 4.

15. *The Hamilton Spectator and Journal of Commerce,* August 21st, 1847, 3.

16. R.D. Gidney, "Elementary Education in Upper Canada: A Reassessment," *Ontario History,* 65, No. 3, (1973): 169-185.

17. Lists of students are existant for the Burlington Ladies Academy in 1847 and 1849 and for the Wesleyan Female College from its inception in 1861 to its demise in 1897. They are to be found in the catalogues of the schools, located in the Reference Department of the Hamilton Public Library. The following analysis is based on the linkage of those students from Hamilton to their parents on the Census and Assessment rolls. As the latest list of students for the Burlington Ladies Academy is for 1849 and the Census was not taken until late 1851 and as the only information given about each student was her name, the number who could be positively identified was limited. I am indebted to Marion Royce, Research Officer in the Department of History and Philosophy at O.I.S.E., for background information on the schools.

18. Michael B. Katz, *Family and Class in a Canadian City: Mid-Nineteenth Century Hamilton*, forthcoming (Harvard University Press: 1975) especially "The Structure of Inequality."

19. From "How Long Shall the Education of the Daughters of Canada be Neglected?" in *The Christian Guardian,* Oct. 31st, 1855.

Trends in Female School Attendance

20. For a discussion of the increase in female teachers in the period, see Alison Prentice, "The Feminization of Teaching in British North America and Canada, 1845-1875." A paper presented to the Canadian Association for American Studies Conference on Women in North America, Ottawa, October 1974. For an analysis of job opportunities for girls in Hamilton in 1851, 1861 and 1871, see Davey, "Educational Reform and the Working Class," Ch. 4.

From Household to School House: The Emergence of the Teacher as Servant of the State*

Alison Prentice

Abstract: *This paper explores the relationships between school teaching and changes in the material and social environment in which the work of teaching occurred, and between both of these and the changing social structure of the teaching force. First, nineteenth-century pedagogy and working conditions for teachers (chiefly in Upper Canada and Ontario) are analysed in terms of state-promoted innovations and debates affecting attendance, school building and classroom design, teaching tools and who should clean the school. This is followed by a brief discussion, drawing on the work of Marta Danylewycz on Quebec and Alison Prentice and Beth Light on Ontario, of the social structure of teaching and how changes in this structure might be related to the material environment and tools of teachers' work in schools. The paper concludes with a suggested periodization for the history of teachers.*

Mary O'Brien and Anne Langton were early Upper Canadians who "kept school." During one period of her life in Canada, Anne Langton, a spinster who devoted her life chiefly to housekeeping for brothers in Canada and

* Originally presented in January 1983 at "Industrious in Their Habits: Rediscovering the World of Work," a Heritage Conference jointly sponsored by the Ontario Museum Association and the Ontario Institute for Studies in Education. The Ontario research reported in this paper has been sponsored by the Ontario Institute for Studies in Education, while the research on teachers in Quebec was supported by a Social Sciences and Humanities Research Council grant to my colleague in the study of teachers, Marta Danylewycz. I am grateful for this support and as well to Beth Light, who assisted with the study of teachers' characteristics using the manuscript census. My thanks also to John Abbott and Marta Danylewycz for careful and extremely helpful critical readings of earlier versions of the paper.

25

England, took in neighbours' children to teach a few days a week. Not all that enamoured of her "untutored children of the forest," she nevertheless believed it her duty to spread British culture to the inhabitants of the Canadian backwoods. Mary O'Brien's motives were rather different. She took in a pupil in order to have, in exchange, the young woman's help with her own children and the housework. Mary's pupil lived with her teacher's family and she and the O'Brien daughters were taught together.[1]

Domestic schools of the sort run by Mary O'Brien and Anne Langton were not uncommon in British North America. They clearly had long roots in a past which did not distinguish very sharply between pupils and servants or between the mistresses and masters of households and the mistresses and masters of schools. To examine the shift from the kind of teacher represented by Langton and O'Brien to the modern teacher is to explore a major shift in the nature of work in schools: a transition encompassing not only the work itself, but the workplace and the social characteristics of the workers.

North American studies in the history of teaching have unveiled many aspects of the shift. Studies of the ideology surrounding the movement of women from domestic or private into public school teaching followed earlier work which focussed on the quest for professionalism in an occupation that was relatively poorly paid and tended to attract large numbers of transient or temporary workers.[2] More recently, research and writing in the history of teachers have focussed on the teachers themselves: on the organization of teacher associations, sexual divisions of labour in the occupation, and cultural and regional variations in its history.[3] What follows is in part a summary of some Canadian findings in this research. In part it is also an attempt to open up a new approach to this history of teaching, one which focusses on the relationships that can be traced between the teachers—who they were, where they came from, and how they were seen in the community—and the work that they did in and out of schools.

I

To begin with the work is to consider the workplace. One of the most significant transitions that has occurred between Mary O'Brien and Anne Langton's time and our own clearly has been the shift from the private or family school, conducted in the household of its teacher or teachers, to the non-domestic or public institution, conducted in a building now formally identified as a school house or, eventually, simply as a school. In terms of their own numbers, the vast majority of schools continued to be carried on in the rooms

From Household to School House

of private dwellings or in the transitional one-room schools that dotted the Canadian landscape for most of the nineteenth century. In terms of numbers of pupils and teachers, however, by the end of that century and certainly by the first quarter of the twentieth, more and more of those involved in schooling were spending their working days in larger structures: the two- or three-room schools of villages or the even more grand, graded institutions of towns and cities. The latter, of course, were the prototypes of the future. By the mid-twentieth century it is certain that the majority of teachers and pupils alike were to be found in such institutions, despite the persistence in some locations and the continuing mystique of the one-room rural school.

On the grounds that the physical environment in which schooling took place necessarily affected (and was affected by) the teacher's work, it is worth examining in some detail. In traditional domestic or family schools, pupils were instructed in kitchens, in parlours, or in upstairs rooms set aside for the purpose. Somewhat untypically, perhaps, an Ancaster, Upper Canada, schoolmistress even proposed in 1828 to conduct her school in a neighbour's ballroom. The furnishings in such schools were essentially the chairs and tables or, in more simple surroundings, the stools and benches that the household possessed, multiplied according to the number of scholars to be accommodated. In the early one-room school house, benches or "forms" provided the most common seating for pupils, while the teacher was usually provided with a chair or a stool. Although writing desks were increasingly thought necessary, they were often placed along the walls and were rarely sufficient to accommodate all the scholars at any one time. Nor did every teacher enjoy the privilege of a desk in the first school houses.[4]

It is interesting to speculate on the probable relationship between these physical surroundings and the teacher's work. Chairs and the ordinary furnishings of houses suggest the possibility of a mobile, fairly flexible atmosphere. With benches we are already moving toward the immobilization of the pupils who typically now would be lined up in rows facing the teacher. Yet the bench was still a potentially flexible piece of furniture compared with what was to come, as an elderly schoolmaster from the District of Gore, Canada West, proved to the school superintendent of that district in the late 1840s. The superintendent, Patrick Thornton, reported to the province's Chief Superintendent of Schools that he had found the teacher using the school bench to relax. Comfortably lying on it, the aged pedagogue had permitted the children to read to him as they gradually drifted into the school house during the course of the morning. This was an old-fashioned and far too grandfatherly approach for Thornton. When all of the scholars were assembled, he gave both the old man and the pupils a lecture on punctuality. Later he saw to it that the government grant was denied to this teacher.[5]

Figure 1

Entitled "March of Intellect," this 1845 sketch of a common school in Adelaide Township, Upper Canada, was the work of school superintendent William Elliott. The open fire, single window, and low ceilings—even the relaxed posture of the schoolmaster—were all features of mid-nineteenth-century common schooling that critics like Elliott ultimately condemned. (Metropolitan Toronto Library, JRR 3338.)

The casual approach that Thornton so deplored begins to suggest not only the relationship between the physical environment of the school and the character of the teacher's work, but the importance of the social environment as well. In the early household and family schools and even in the first one-room community schools, the attendance of the pupils was not only extremely unpunctual by modern standards, but also highly sporadic. No teacher knew which of his or her registered pupils would be in attendance on any given day or for what period of time they might stay once they did come to school. As late as 1882 schoolmaster D. Farquhar McLennan of Charlottenburgh, Ontario, noted in his diary the pupils who left at recess or noon and did not return. The delightful diary of Maggie Beattie, who taught near Morrisburg, Ontario, in 1898, records a constantly fluctuating number of scholars in attendance and, as well, the changeable weather conditions that could prevent school trustees from meeting in the same way that they often kept children at home.[6]

Figure 2

The work of a Toronto firm enjoying the sanction of the Upper Canadian Department of Education, these desks were nevertheless held by Deputy Superintendent of Schools John George Hodgins to be less than ideal. The hinged lids caused unnecessary noise when they were being opened and shut. Pupils could also hide behind them and thus perform "acts...which would not be openly attempted." (John George Hodgins. 1857. The School House: Its Architecture, External and Internal Arrangements, with Additional Papers....Toronto: Department of Public Instruction for Upper Canada, 75.)

Of course weather was only one of the factors affecting school attendance. Both enrolment and daily attendance[7] were also dictated by the length and character of the journey to school, by the numbers of children in a family, and by their parents' or guardians' ability to clothe them. Most importantly, they were dictated by the other work that children and young people had to do. Thus, on a particular September day in 1852, the teacher of a small country school in West Gwillimbury, Canada West, had no doubts whatsoever about why some of his pupils had stayed away. They were involved in the potato harvest.[8]

As Canadians were increasingly sold on the idea of regular schooling for their children and as more and more people left farm or bush to take up residence in towns, these material conditions of the teacher's work gradually changed. Although poor families continued to need the labour of their children and resisted regular and extended bouts of schooling for them, the general trend was toward increasing school attendance, both in terms of a lengthening school year and in terms of a growing number of days and years that any given child might continue in school. The promoters of increased and more regular schooling agonized over the "idleness" of the young and one suspects that it was chiefly urban youth that concerned them, as fears were expressed about the potential for juvenile delinquency that existed among the idle and unschooled in cities. Whatever their reasoning, by the end of the nineteenth century most provinces had enacted compulsory school laws to try to ensure that children under twelve years of age received several years in school. While these laws may not, in fact, have altered either rates of enrolment or attendance, they symbolized new attitudes to schooling and new conditions of work for teachers. Increasingly, the expectation was that most children would attend school for five days a week and for all of the school days of the year.[9]

In the course of the nineteenth century, school "government" or the maintenance of order in school was also both an increasing concern and a growing expectation. Clearly, in the early household or private schools, pupil numbers were so small that order was rarely a problem. Older scholars helped out with younger ones and parental discipline, even if this was frequently harsh, was the order of the day. But as teaching moved out of the household and into the public school, problems of control often developed. Numbers in any given school were larger. Indeed classes were frequently huge by modern standards. There were older children in attendance who had never experienced confinement in a school before; occasionally pupils were even older than the teacher. In these circumstances questions were increasingly raised about how best to keep order and systems developed for doing so. Students filed in and out of classrooms; individual seats, screwed to the floor, replaced benches and made it easier to keep pupils apart (Figures 2, 3); teachers introduced government-produced merit cards and other rewards to encourage orderly behaviour in their pupils.[10]

From Household to School House

Figure 3

The author of The School House believed that this arrangement of desks was well designed for the purposes of school government. Pupils seated diagonally could not see each others' faces and were prevented from "playing and whispering." Furthermore, in a space that normally seated only 36, this arrangement permitted the accommodation of as many as 46 children. (John George Hodgins. 1857. The School House: Its Architecture, External and Internal Arrangements, with Additional Papers....Toronto: Department of Public Instruction for Upper Canada, 78.)

Other shifts occurred in the tools of the teacher's trade. Instead of allowing pupils to bring their own books, often texts which had been handed down from child to child in the family, provincial and local school authorities began to insist on uniform classroom sets of books. They also insisted that schools acquire blackboards, globes, and other technologies unknown to the traditional

Figure 4

Catalogues like that of the E.N. Moyer Company, "Canada's School Furnishers," urged boards of trustees to provide their schools with the best and the latest in school furnishings and teaching aids. Along with their products, they promoted less tangible items as well: the virtues of competition and the thrill of consumerism. (E.N. Moyer Company. 1912. Catalogue, p. 10. Hodgins Rare Book Room, Ontario Institute for Studies in Education.)

domestic or even the early one-room schoolteacher (Figures 4, 5). From a pedagogy which focussed on individual, if rote, recitations from the pupil's own book, teachers were urged to move to the "simultaneous" method of teaching. In this method, whole classes were instructed at the same time, a pedagogy that was suited to the larger, graded schools and also to more regular attendance, for it depended on entire classes of children being kept at the same place in the same book at the same time. The desire to create this kind of learning environment, indeed, was behind the building of larger schools and the intense campaigns to promote regular attendance among pupils. Simultaneous teaching, the method school reformers believed to be the most efficient, was impossible

From Household to School House

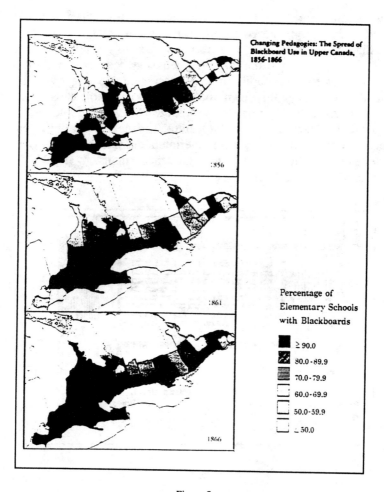

Figure 5

Upper Canadian teachers and trustees appear to have responded with amazing speed to Education Department pressure favouring blackboards in the 1850s and 1860s. By fixing pupils' attention collectively on an object and on the written rather than the spoken word, blackboards must have assisted teachers in the shift to the highly regarded "simultaneous" mode of teaching and altered schoolroom relations in the direction of greater silence, collectivity, and control. (Courtesy of The Historical Atlas of Canada, Vol. 2. Research for the maps was carried out by Susan Kaskin and funded by the Social Sciences and Humanities Research Council of Canada.)

if students came irregularly or were unpunctual, or if children of all ages and stages of learning were mixed together and used a great variety of different books. Simultaneous teaching was also supposed to be more stimulating to children and, according to the reformed pedagogy, teachers were not only to instruct and control their pupils but to interest them. No longer wending their individual ways through their own books and lessons, whole classes were now expected to rivet their attention on the teacher, or on the increasingly ubiquitous blackboard, and to work together. The ideal, according to one late-nineteenth-century American school superintendent, was that at any given time any given grade of children throughout the schools in his city should be on the same page of the same book at the same time.[11]

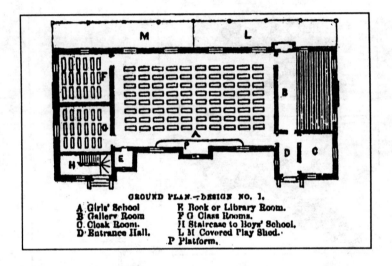

GROUND PLAN.—DESIGN NO. 1.

A Girls' School
B Gallery Room
C Cloak Room.
D Entrance Hall.
E Book or Library Room.
F G Class Rooms.
H Staircase to Boys' School.
L M Covered Play Shed.
P Platform.

Figure 6

The ground floor of a two-storey brick school house, designed by Toronto architects for the town of Simcoe, Norfolk County, Upper Canada, to hold from 500 to 600 pupils. Schoolroom "A" alone was intended to accommodate 160. (John George Hodgins. 1857. The School House: Its Architecture, External and Internal Arrangements, with Additional Papers....Toronto: Department of Public Instruction for Upper Canada, 211.)

Thus the more structured learning environments that gradually developed in the course of the nineteenth century both dictated and made possible more formal and distanced approaches to the teacher's work. Early nineteenth-century teachers and many who followed them probably maintained whatever

distance they could from their pupils with the use o.
1860s, Toronto Normal School students were still learnin
to "flog," according to the notes of one of them, while 1.
McClennan reported the need to "whip" his pupils with an.
But formal pedagogies, larger schools and, perhaps, the pre
numbers of women teachers created a new kind of distance b   ~ders
and taught. And as teachers were increasingly urged to strive for   ~ressional
status superior to that of their scholars, social class factors were involved as
well. The ideal teacher by 1900 was hardly an old gentlewoman quietly going
about her business in her own household and instructing the young at the same
time. The new teacher was a person who stood at the front of the room,
actively pursuing the attention and allegiance of his or her pupils. The latter
were, in theory and increasingly in practice, fixed in individual seats that were
firmly screwed to the floor and were organized according to age and academic
level in classrooms that were inside large buildings containing many other
classrooms similarly organized (Figure 6).

Over both teachers and taught loomed the authority of a whole new set of
educators whose presence gradually altered the conditions of work for the
ordinary classroom teacher: principals, school board trustees, superintendents
and inspectors and, ultimately, the provincial officials who ran the ever-growing
bureaucracies known as provincial departments of education. Much that was
new in nineteenth-century teachers' work was promoted by these authorities
and the new often was hotly debated. Parents and trustees objected to the new
subjects as they were introduced or to the new pedagogies. Some had no use
for grammar; others had no intention of supplying the local teacher with a
blackboard. In some rural Ontario communities at least, grammar and
blackboards appear to have symbolized an alien culture, the unnecessary and
offensive trappings of an all-too-distant metropolitan power.[13]

Another vigorously debated question involved what might best be described
as the housework of the school, the laying of fires and the cleaning of the
schoolroom. In 1848, the Chief Superintendent of Schools for Canada West,
Egerton Ryerson, wrote that these matters were subject to negotiation between
teachers and the trustees who employed them, the law not specifying who was
responsible for the work of school maintenance. But arguments on the subject
continued. One gathers that most local school trustees thought that the
housework of the school was part of the teacher's job, while a good many
teachers increasingly objected to doing it. Finally, in 1861, the *Journal of
Education for Upper Canada* pronounced on the subject. The question was no
longer one to be settled locally, at least in theory. According to the Department

education, teachers were not required to make fires or to clean, much less repair, the school house. Teachers were employed only to teach school.[14]

Figure 7

An aspect of the schoolroom environment much disliked by turn-of-the century teachers was the dust and dirt, particularly associated with oily school floors. The transition to janitors meant that urban teachers at least, no longer had to clean their own schools. E.N. Moyer's "New Dustless Floor Brush" was designed to take the irritation away even from being present while the janitor was doing his work. School boards were responding, in this period, to the efficiency movement in industry and Moyer's description of schoolroom cleaning also attempted to capitalize on this trend. (E.N. Moyer Company. 1912. Catalogue, p. 31. Hodgins Rare Book Room, Ontario Institute for Studies in Education.)

With the development of larger schools and more sophisticated methods of cleaning and heating, a separate category of caretakers evolved who specialized in the maintenance of schools and these debates eventually came to an end. Yet defining the boundaries of the teacher's work has continued to be a problem to this day. If teachers trying to establish themselves in nineteenth-century communities felt undermined or overworked if asked to perform the housekeeping tasks of the school, many contemporary teachers have felt the supervision of lunchrooms equally beneath their dignity as educators or, more mundanely, simply beyond their capacities in terms of time and energy.

Perhaps nowadays, however, it is the ever-increasing mountains of paperwork that most irritate the people who work in schools. This condition

From Household to School House

too can be traced to the nineteenth century. From the ubiquitous school register, which had to be filled in at least twice a day, to the growing numbers of tests and exams to mark, forms to fill out and reports to make, teachers even in one-room rural schools were more and more involved in written work, as were their pupils.[15] Gradually spelling bees, mental arithmetic contests, and public examinations, and the oral culture which sustained these activities, gave way to the culture of the written word, once again substantially altering the conditions of the teacher's work. The hard work of keeping fires going and cleaning school houses may have disappeared, but only to be replaced by what many teachers would see as a different sort of drudgery.

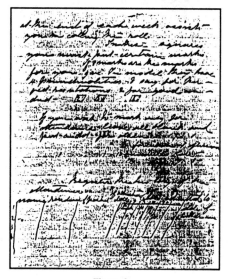

Figure 8

Normal School students learned the importance of school government both by the example of their own training and by precept. Maria Payne's notes, made at the Normal School in Toronto in the late 1860s, record her reaction to instruction in the keeping of school registers. "In these squares," she notes with apparent mystification, "you must put certain marks." Although she could not keep up with the speed of the lecture, she attempted to get down, at the very least, what was done at the model school attached to Toronto Normal. In the "model," marks were given not only for punctual attendance (evidently four times a day) but for "perfect recitations" and "good conduct." The keeping of such records marked the beginning of a trend toward ever-increasing amounts of paperwork for teachers. (Maria Payne Notebooks, Toronto Normal School, Education Records, General Collection, 1860-69, Mu 975, Box 5, no. 6, Archives of Ontario.)

II

Figure 9

This plan of a school house measuring 24 feet by 26 feet, with 10-foot ceilings, appears to have been submitted in 1882 by the school commissioners of St. Gabriel de Brandon-Berthier to the Quebec superintendent of schools, Gideon Ouimet, for his approval. Its designers assumed both that the teacher would be a single woman and that she would live in the school house. (M. O'Keir to the Honourable Gideon Ouimet, 14 January 1882, Education Records E 13, Archives Nationales du Québec.)

One can imagine public examinations conducted by gentlemen teachers who, by virtue of their age, status, and gender, had the potential to exercise the kind of authority and showmanship appropriate to such occasions. Christmas recitals, on the other hand, may have seemed more suitable tasks for the young women who increasingly came to staff Canada's one-room rural, as well as larger urban, schools. This is only one of many possible illustrations of the relationships that may exist between the perceived characteristics of workers and the nature of the work they perform. When it came to the manual work associated with nineteenth-century rural schools, it may have seemed proper for male teachers to split the firewood for the school but not quite right for them to take on the cleaning. For young women, the opposite likely would have been the case, although one must beware of applying modern stereotypes to a pioneer society. Nevertheless it is clear that this reasoning applied to the use of the birch rod, which was gradually replaced, as teaching forces feminized, by

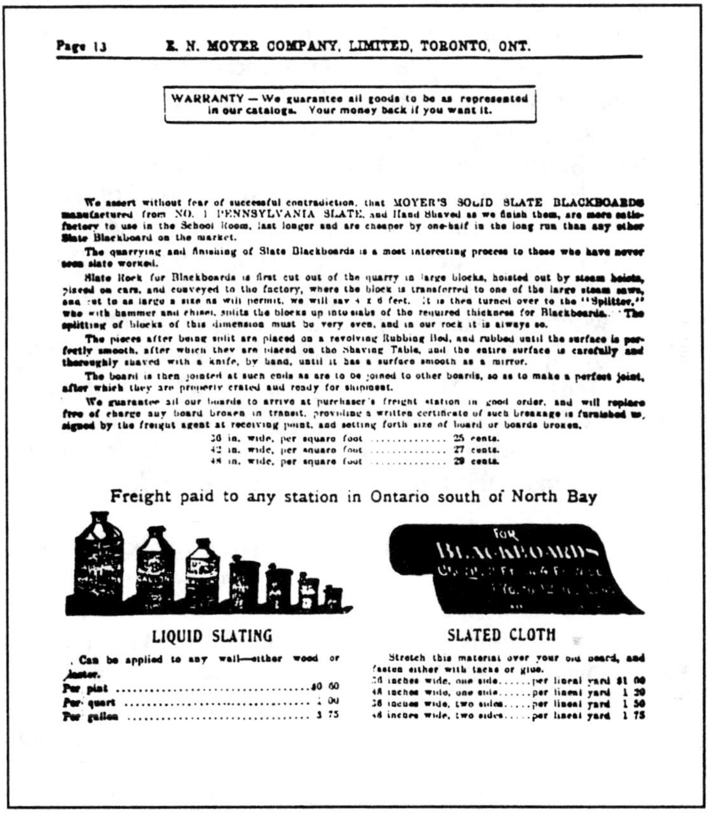

From Household to School House

Figure 10

Hodgins' 1857 school manual had described the construction of a modest blackboard that could be accommodated on an easel. Not so the school supplier of 1912, who imagined school room walls almost entirely covered with boards. (E.N. Moyer Company. 1912. Catalogue, p. 13. Hodgins Rare Book Room, Ontario Institute for Studies in Education.)

the "strap" which, in its turn, was recommended for sparing use and, eventually, only by principals. In the large, graded schools where these same principals held sway, it was assumed that kindergarten and early grade schools teachers

39

would be women. The principals themselves and the teachers of the higher grades, on the other hand, seemed more appropriately male.[16]

Yet that the social structure of teaching has been a more complex and changeable phenomenon than such statements would imply is revealed when we examine questions such as gender more minutely. Statistical profiles of nineteenth-century teachers compiled from manuscript census returns currently available to researchers for the years 1851, 1861, 1871, and 1881, make such detailed examination possible for at least one brief but important period of Canadian history. Marta Danylewycz, Beth Light, and I have analysed the changing characteristics of teachers during the third quarter of the nineteenth century for selected rural counties of Quebec and Ontario and for the cities of Montreal and Toronto, using these sources in conjunction with the records of local school boards and the provincial departments of education.[17]

If we begin with the two cities, we find that in Toronto feminization proceeded rapidly, especially in the schools controlled by the Public School Board until, by 1881, over 80 percent of the teachers were women. In Montreal, the opposite occurred. Gradually, among the lay teachers employed by the Roman Catholic School Commission in the city, the men increased in proportion to the women until, by the end of our period, they were in the majority.

In Montreal, in fact, large numbers of Roman Catholic women teachers continued in private or domestic teaching well beyond the period when most other Canadian teachers were abandoning this traditional form of educational work. An alternative, of course, was to join a teaching order and this was the path that many Quebec Catholic women chose. Convent schools multiplied rapidly in the second half of the nineteenth century and became preferred workplaces for many middle-class and urban Francophone women teachers.[18]

Young lay women, however, continued to staff the poorer schools of rural districts in Quebec. Indeed, they did so in far greater proportions and from an earlier date than was the case for most parts of rural Ontario. In Quebec as a whole women were already the majority of teachers by the 1850s. Although certain eastern counties of Ontario followed the Quebec pattern of early female majorities among teachers, in rural Ontario as a whole male teachers continued to be numerically dominant for several decades longer.

We believe that the different rates and patterns of feminization in the two provinces can be explained by a combination of factors. Ontario, first of all, seems to have had a larger and more persistent pool of cash-hungry immigrant men who wanted teaching jobs than was the case in Quebec. The fact that young women were hired in disproportionate numbers in the poorer primary resource frontier regions of both provinces, where men were likely to be employed at least part of the time in industries such as lumbering and the fishery and where spare cash for teachers' salaries was in short supply, suggests that local economic conditions also played an important role. Finally, the persistence of the sexual segregation of pupils in the schools of Montreal—and its gradual disappearance in Toronto—may explain at least in part the different patterns which developed in these two cities. In Montreal, the Catholic School Commission was able to focus not only on boys' schooling to the almost virtual exclusion of girls', but also on the professional advancement of male teachers by choosing not to support many women's schools. The Public School Board in Toronto, on the other hand, paid more attention to the education of girls and also hired far more women; in Toronto, male career patterns and professional interests were nevertheless promoted, but through the creation of gender-based hierarchies within a rapidly growing and increasingly co-educational system.

If larger proportions of non-Canadian-born individuals among the male teachers of Ontario suggest a possible correlation between ethnicity and the sexual division of labour in teaching, the average ages and household positions of teachers also prove to have explanatory power. Men teachers were older than women on the average, in both Quebec and Ontario, and were far more likely to be either boarders or heads of their own households in all four census years. In Ontario the growing number of rural schoolmistresses meant not only an increase in the proportion of Canadian-born teachers but an increase in the proportion who were dependent young people living in the households of their parents. Evidently as rural trustees found that they were less and less able to afford the salaries of male teachers or that fewer immigrant men were available for hire, they increasingly turned to the girls of their own communities in their search for teachers. In Quebec, where country districts adopted this pattern even earlier, an even greater need for economy evidently dictated that some 25 percent of rural schoolmistresses not only had to teach but to live in the frequently inadequate school houses that were also the locations of their daily work.

From the social characteristics of the teachers we thus come full circle to be confronted once again with the character of the workplace and the work. Where boarding with different families in the community, being head of one's household or living in the school house were actually requirements of the job—and all of these at different times and places evidently were—such living arrangements must be treated as aspects of the teachers' work as well as of their private lives. In the nineteenth century, indeed, when public and private lives may have been more integrated than is the case today, household and employment status may well have seemed all of a piece. Women teachers, who tended to be young and dependent members of families, understandably had less status and earned lower salaries than male teachers, who tended to be older and heads of their households. Only those women who stayed in teaching for more than a few years and were making careers in the occupation began to feel the injustice of their admitted and, in some cases, growing inequality.[19]

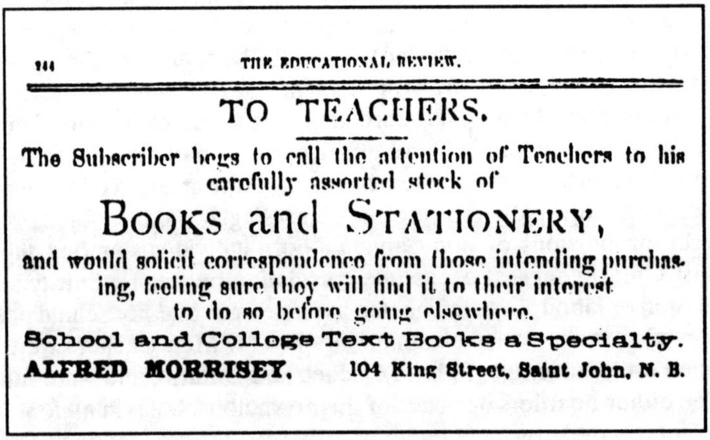

144   THE EDUCATIONAL REVIEW.

TO TEACHERS.

The Subscriber begs to call the attention of Teachers to his carefully assorted stock of

Books and Stationery,

and would solicit correspondence from those intending purchasing, feeling sure they will find it to their interest to do so before going elsewhere.

School and College Text Books a Specialty.

ALFRED MORRISEY.   104 King Street, Saint John, N. B.

Figure 11

Teachers as well as school boards were seen as eager consumers of new educational products. Potential customers for books and stationery in New Brunswick were urged to correspond with this company concerning their requirements. (The Educational Review. 2[May 1888]. New Brunswick, 244.)

III

Three overlapping periods can be discerned in the history of Canadian teachers, periods whose boundaries shift as one moves away from central places to thinly settled or remote regions where traditional forms have tended to persist. The first was the period of the domestic or private teacher, who predominated in most parts of Canada until at least the middle of the nineteenth century. During the second period, one-room public schoolteachers were probably the majority. Again, in most regions of the country this condition prevailed until at least World War I when one-room teachers, if no longer numerically dominant, were still often symbolically so. The vast majority of such teachers by the turn of the century were women and whether women or men, like their domestic predecessors, they often seem to have combined school teaching with other work. Male teachers were most often farmers, but they were also clergymen, surveyors, storekeepers, and clerks, while a late nineteenth-century Quebec woman teacher recorded in her diary long sessions of weaving in addition to her work in the school.[20] For many teachers of this period, whether female or male, the one-room school was not only a part-time job, but a temporary one as well, to be abandoned to other schoolmasters and mistresses at marriage or when other occupations beckoned.

Already evident in the latter part of the nineteenth century was the beginning of a new era and a third type of teacher, a person more likely than his or her predecessors to be engaged in teaching full-time and as a life-long career. No longer either inhabiting or working in one-room schools, these teachers were increasingly urban dwellers and the employees of large, bureaucratically organized school systems.

While this sketch of the transition from the keepers of private or domestic schools, through one-room schoolmistresses and masters to the career teachers of the twentieth century, can be suggestive only of the relationships between the characteristics of teachers and the character of their work, it has tried at least to raise some of the key questions that such a study should probe. From the domestic and literary skills that Mary O'Brien and Anne Langton imparted to their pupils to the grade school work of today may not seem an enormous leap. What has clearly changed, however, are both the workplace and the larger social environment within which teaching takes place. More subtle to trace or assess in its effects, perhaps, is the shifting character of the teaching force, as old men lying on benches, housekeepers working at home, and teenage boys and girls have gradually been ruled out as appropriate instructors of the young, at least as far as public, tax-supported schooling is concerned. One need not idealize these teachers of the past to recognize that a great change has occurred between their time and our own.

Notes

1.   A.S. Miller, ed., *The Journals of Mary O'Brien* (Toronto: Macmillan, 1968); and H.H. Langton, ed., *A Gentlewoman in Upper Canada: The Journals of Anne Langton* (Toronto: Clarke, Irwin, 1950) especially 143.

2.   The words "private" and "public" when applied to schools in the early nineteenth century generally referred to whether they were conducted in private (that is domestic) or in public places. The more modern meaning, referring to the sources of funding, developed only gradually in the course of the nineteenth century. Studies dealing with the ideology which promoted the employment of women teachers include: Glenda Riley, "Origins of the Argument for Improved Female Education," *History of Education Quarterly* 9, no. 4 (Winter 1969); Keith Melder, "Women's High Calling: The Teaching Profession in America, 1830-1860," *American Quarterly* 13 (Fall 1972); Joan N. Burstyn, "Catharine Beecher and the Education of American Women," *New England Quarterly* 47 (September 1974); Kathryn Kish Sklar, *Catharine Beecher: A Study in American Domesticity* (New Haven: Yale University Press, 1972); Alison Prentice, "The Feminization of Teaching in British North America and Canada, 1845-1875," *Histoire sociale/Social History* 8 (May 1975). Canadian studies in the history of teacher professionalism are J.G. Althouse, *The Ontario Teacher: A Historical Account of Progress, 1800-1910* (Toronto: Ontario Teachers' Federation, 1967); and André Labarrère-Paulé, *Les Instituteurs laïques au Canada français, 1836-1900* (Québec: Les Presses de l'université Laval, 1965).

3.   Myra H. Strober and David Tyack, "Why Do Women Teach and Men Manage?" *Signs* 5, no. 3 (Spring 1980); David B. Tyack and Myra H. Strober, "Jobs and Gender: A History of the Structuring of Educational Employment by Sex," in Patricia Schmuck and W.W. Charles. eds., *Educational Policy and Management: Sex Differentials* (San Diego: Academic Press, 1981); Myra H. Strober and Laura Best, "The Female/Male Salary Differential in Public Schools: Some Lessons From San Francisco, 1879," *Economic Inquiry* 17, no. 2 (April 1979); Marta, Danylewycz, Beth Light and Alison Prentice, "The Evolution of the Sexual Division of Labour in Teaching: A Nineteenth Century Ontario and Quebec Case Study," *Histoire sociale/Social History* 15, no. 30 (Spring 1983); Marta Danylewycz and Alison Prentice, "Teachers, Gender and Bureaucratizing School Systems in Nineteenth Century Montreal and Toronto," *History of Education Quarterly* 24, no. 1 (Spring 1984): 75-100; Myra H. Strober and Audri Gordon Lanford, "The Percentages of Women in Public School Teaching: A Cross-Section Analysis, 1850-1880," paper presented at the annual meeting of the

Social Science History Association, Nashville, Tennessee, October 1981; Wayne J. Urban, *Why Teachers Organized* (Detroit: Wayne State University Press, 1982).

4. *Gore Gazette*, 12 July 1828. Descriptions of early Canadian common and parish schools may be found in Charles E. Phillips, *The Development of Education in Canada* (Toronto: W.J. Gage & Co. Ltd., 1957).

5. Patrick Thornton to Egerton Ryerson, 22 January 1849, RG 2 (Education Records) C-6-C, Archives of Ontario.

6. D. Farquhar McLennan Diary, 1882, Diaries Collection, Mu 1962, Archives of Ontario; Maggie Beattie Diary, 1898, courtesy of her daughter, Mrs. Harvey Barkley, Morrisburg, Ontario, and now in the Archives of Ontario.

7. The importance of distinguishing between enrolment and attendance becomes clear on the examination of attendance records for almost any constituency in the nineteenth century. The vast majority of children who enrolled attended far fewer than the number of days that schools were open. On school attendance and enrolment, see Michael B. Katz, "Who Went to School?," Ian E. Davey, "School Reform and School Attendance: The Hamilton Central School, 1853-1861," and Haley P. Bamman, "Patterns of School Attendance in Toronto, 1840-1878: Some Spatial Considerations," in Michael B. Katz and Paul H. Mattingly, eds., *Education and Social Change: Themes from Ontario's Past* (New York: New York University Press, 1975); Ian E. Davey, "The Rhythm of Work and the Rhythm of School," in Neil McDonald and Alf Chaiton, eds., *Egerton Ryerson and His Times* (Toronto: Macmillan); Chad Gaffield and David Levine, "Dependency and Adolescence on the Canadian Frontier: Orillia, Ontario in the Mid-Nineteenth Century," *History of Education Quarterly* 18 (Spring 1978).

8. West Gwillimbury School Register, 1844-49, Mu 972, Archives of Ontario, entry dated Saturday, 2 September 1844.

9. On the question of compulsory schooling, see Susan E. Houston, "Social Reform and Education: The Issue of Compulsory Schooling," in McDonald and Chaiton eds., *Egerton Ryerson and His Times*.

10. Alison Prentice, *The School Promoters: Education and Social Class in Mid-Nineteenth Century Upper Canada* (Toronto: McClelland & Stewart, 1977) especially chapters 5 and 6. On the question of women teachers or very young teachers and order in the schoolroom, see Prentice, "The Feminization of Teaching," and "Difficulties of Young Teachers," *Journal of Education for Upper Canada* 18 (October 1865), 156.

11. Prentice. *The School Promoters*; David B. Tyack, *The One Best System: A History of American Urban Education* (Cambridge, Mass.: Harvard University Press, 1974) 48.

12. Maria Payne Notebooks, Toronto Normal School, Box 5, Mu 975, Education: General Collection, 1860-69, no. 6, Archives of Ontario; D. Farquhar McLennan Diary, 1882, Diaries Collection, Mu 1962, Archives of Ontario.

13. For a discussion of the movement to teach English grammar in nineteenth-century Ontario schools and some reactions against it, see Prentice. *The School Promoters*, 75-81.

14. Egerton Ryerson to Mr. John Monger, 26 December 1848, RG 2 C 1 Letterbook D, p. 360, Archives of Ontario. For enquiries to the Department of Education on the subject, see C.W.D. de L'Armitage to Ryerson, 27 June 1849; Meade N. Wright to Ryerson, 26 June 1859; and Teacher to Ryerson, 1 April 1859, RG 2 C-6-C. The Education Department policy statement appeared in "Official Replies of the Chief Superintendent of Schools to Local School Authorities in Upper Canada," *Journal of Education for Upper Canada* 14, no. 3 (March 1861) 40.

15. The proliferation of paperwork generated by the Ontario Department of Education under Ryerson is described in my article, "The Public Instructor: Ryerson and the Role of the Public School Administrator," in McDonald and Chaiton eds., *Egerton Ryerson and His Times*, 144-47.

16. Prentice, "The Feminization of Teaching," 52-56 and 61-62.

17. Marta Danylewycz, Beth Light and Alison Prentice, "The Evolution of the Sexual Division of Labour in Teaching: A Nineteenth Century Ontario and Quebec Case Study," *Histoire sociale/Social History* 15, no. 30 (Spring 1983); Marta Danylewycz and Alison Prentice, "Teachers, Gender and Bureaucratizing School Systems in Nineteenth Century Montreal and Toronto," *History of Education Quarterly* 24, no. 1 (Spring 1984) 75-100.

18. Marta Danylewycz, "Taking the Veil in Montreal: An Alternative to Marriage, Motherhood and Spinsterhood," (Ph.D. thesis, University of Toronto, 1981).

19. Prentice, "The Feminization of Teaching," 62-64.

20. Bell and Laing School Papers. Lennox and Addington History Society, *Papers*, Vols. 5-9 (1914-17), 29-37, describe an early Upper Canadian schoolmaster who combined teaching with surveying and clerical work. The schoolmistress/weaver was Ruth Pearson. Ruth Pearson Diary, 1881, courtesy of Althea Douglas.

Part Two:

The Different Worlds of Turn of the Century Teachers

Accomplishing "a Man's Task": Rural Women Teachers, Male Culture, and the School Inspectorate in Turn of the Century Ontario

John Abbott

Late nineteenth- and early twentieth-century public school inspectors were men in the middle: top men in the local administrative hierarchy, responsible for the educational efficiency of teachers, principals, and trustees; and low men in the central administrative hierarchy, accountable to the chief inspector, the deputy minister, and the Minister of Education. Their position was somewhat analogous to that of the Lieutenant-Governor in the old province of Upper Canada. Both linked policy-making and policy-implementing bodies at the local and the metropolitan levels. They initiated and functioned as conduits for a vast correspondence. Neither was safe from appeals that local authorities might make over his head to metropolitan referees. Each was liable to be embarrassed should his superiors uphold the appeal.

The evolution of the supervisor's status and role, from that of an amateur visitor in schools to that of a professional inspector, reflected the changes that had occurred in the culture of schooling in the last half of the nineteenth century. During those years an enterprise formerly characterized by local predilection and financed by the users was transformed into a provincial school system, financed by the taxpayers in general and governed by a myriad of regulations centrally framed by the Department of Education and enforced by a corps of inspectors whose career prospects were increasingly determined by the hierarchy's assessment of their worth.[1]

Meanwhile a system demanding many more teachers at economical rates found a ready supply of female applicants at salaries substantially lower than those of their male counterparts. Within the teaching ranks the ratio of men to women shrank rapidly. As early as the late '50s the Toronto board employed four women for each man. By the late 1880s the ratio was nine to one. The men who remained in the Toronto ranks tended to be older and the heads of families, whereas the women tended to be younger and single. Young as these Toronto female teachers were, however, they were substantially older than their rural sisters.[2] In the countryside, male inspectors, usually heads of families and well advanced in their careers, superintended a very young, inexperienced, minimally trained, and transient female teaching force in the employ of boards more responsive to financial than pedagogical stimuli.

Gender And Education In Ontario: An Historical Reader

Under the circumstances a school inspector's career was often arduous and sometimes eventful, as illustrated by Assistant Chief Inspector MacDougall's campaign to improve the appearance of Ontario educational statistics in the late summer of 1920. In his exhortation he suggested that his district supervisors reduce their complements of teachers on district and temporary certificates. He conceded that there were rural sections in Northern Ontario to which few if any qualified teaches would go, particularly in that time of short supply. Yet, as a sturdy believer in the gospel of girding up the loins, he added that "much may be done by an increase of salaries, careful and systematic direction of Boards, a wise classification of schools, judicious advice to teachers and a vigorous and well-directed oversight, to bring the schools to a higher plan of efficiency through an upward move in the standard of teachers." It was, he concluded, "a man's task to carry out the diverse duties that devolve upon our leaders under the adverse conditions that prevail in the north, but we have every faith that by active effort and loyal co-operation the desired end will be achieved."[3]

If the quality of the profession could be assessed on the basis of certification, it could also be defined in terms of sex. "The demand here is so great that the best teachers have secured places already. There seems to be a great scarcity of teachers, especially of male teachers of the better class." So spoke the principal of the Toronto Normal School when he was unable to recommend a principal for service in a small but progressive Northern Ontario town in 1910. School trustees expressed similar misgivings. "If men cannot be got to teach our boys and hence leave their training to girls I fear it will tend towards effeminacy and eventually breed a generation more fit to be apparelled in petticoats than pants." So wrote William Corbett, the secretary-treasurer of a backwoods school, after failing to secure a male teacher.[4]

Old as they are, the records still exude a pungent aroma of fear; fear that the unwillingness or inability of funding authorities to compete with commerce and the professions for male recruits entailed the subversion of patriarchal civilization. Female domination of the teaching ranks threatened the cult of true manhood. That Secretary Corbett and his inspector feared for the future of civilization, that they believed that the school was the crucible of the socialization process, is evident in Inspector Leslie Green's annual report for 1919. Of the thirty-nine candidates who had achieved middle and upper school matriculation in the Algoma inspectorate that year, only six had applied for normal entrance. Of the six, none had obtained first-class standing. Ominous as the numbers were, they did not in themselves reveal the full significance of the situation. "The tragedy of this whole business," he informed his immediate superior,

50

Accomplishing "a Man's Task"

is that not one young man has entered the teaching profession and does not intend to...And this would not be so tragic were it not the recurrence of a yearly affair—no young men from this district entering the teaching profession and getting in line to claim the higher positions that will be theirs in due course. We have imported every man we have had in the last 20 years. Must we continue to do so? Is this state of affairs widespread? Are we going to lose the vitalizing effect of good manhood on the growing young men of today?[5]

The assumptions ring loud and clear. If men, for financial reasons, could not dominate the teaching staff by their numbers, some promising candidates had to be recruited, seasoned in the classroom, and advanced to positions of patriarchal authority in educational administration. The dearth of men teachers, he continued, should be of deep concern to the Department of Education, for it was from the supervisory staff in the schools that it drew its own personnel. "If our young men do not rise to the need of the hour in these respects what is to become of the greatest of callings? What kind of citizenship are we going to produce? I fear it will be a citizenship without a vision, and untrained to the great responsibility of caring for the heritage that will be theirs in the years to come."[6]

The suppositions that fuelled Leslie Green's fears were embedded in the culture of nineteenth- and early twentieth-century schooling. Explorations of this culture have shown that nineteenth-century schoolmen in Ontario, as elsewhere, formulated educational hierarchies from prescriptions based on age and ethnicity, certification and wages, training and sex. Recent studies suggest that an especially significant—perhaps even the most significant—ingredient in the formula was sex. Women taught; men managed. And at first, few challenged the formulary that shaped public school organization.[7]

By the turn of the century, however, some were finding this "natural" state of affairs clearly unacceptable. We now know from studies of women teachers' organizations—particularly those centred in large North American cities—that women teachers were profoundly disturbed by the evidence of sex discrimination. Wages and working conditions were a primary concern, but their campaigns for improvement also stressed the need to elect women as trustees and, particularly in the first two decades of the twentieth century, to promote their appointment to inspectorships.[8]

Figure 1

J.B. MacDougall—educator, orator, and visionary. (Courtesy Archives of Ontario, J.B. MacDougall, Building the North, *Toronto: McClelland and Stewart, 1917.)*

To date, however, little detailed attention has been paid to the relationship between teachers and inspectors or to the specific grievances that women teachers entertained about the men who supervised their work. Yet the relationship was a potent one, especially in rural districts, where distance and isolation added a special dimension to the visits of the inspector and the work of the inspected. If inspectors felt hard pressed, given the difficulties of carrying out their tasks, so too did the teachers. Though usually silent and unable to organize for mutual support or protection, rural women teachers nevertheless sometimes expressed their discontent. The occasional vehemence of that protest only served to highlight the ambiguousness of their power. Although the rural school economy was dependent upon a continuing supply of willing women teachers, the overall direction of the provincial education enterprise, as the all-male, turn-of-the-century inspectors amply demonstrated, was in the hands of the men.

I

The strategy that Inspector Green of Algoma devised to solve the problem he had outlined in his 1919 report seems somewhat contradictory. While he hoped that the policy of raising salaries would net some of the young men who were "drifting aimlessly into law and other schools and colleges," he also argued that the educational authorities should wage the war of moral man against the destructive forces of materialism. The processes of post-war construction needed to be informed, Green concluded, by "the old school master spirit" that carried the conviction that "the sterner qualities" were worth inculcating. The "real business" of life was not to be found in making money, but rather in living.[9]

To live, in these terms, was to function in part as members of a brotherhood that might act as a protective and benevolent society, as it did in 1909. In that year the government decided to terminate the careers of a number of inspectors, ancient pedagogies from an earlier, easier age who owed their appointments to county friends rather than certificated merit. The younger brethren, while recognizing that "the interest of the children" might well require the government to discharge "some of the older men," argued that many of their elders had subsisted so long on salaries so mean that they had been unable to save for their retirement. Accordingly, they requested the government to grant gratuities of one thousand dollars to each of the retirees. The committee that had prepared the memorial counselled solidarity:

> It is absolutely necessary that we show united action, and that every possible pressure be brought to bear if we are to be successful in obtaining for the aged inspectors the consideration that they have earned from the country, instead of allowing them to be turned adrift in their old age to eke out an existence as best they may. This appeal is made especially to inspectors under sixty. As you hope for comfort in your old age, help us. Inspectors Waugh, Campbell and Mills will present the case to the Cabinet.[10]

Gender And Education In Ontario: An Historical Reader

But there was more to the brotherhood than benevolence: it was an organized professional "communion" with its own appointed ritual. Until recently, no ceremony associated with schooling was more sacred than the services celebrating final examinations. Indeed, the authority to examine was to the educational vatican what ordination is to the priesthood. How ironic it was then, that an innocent decision on the part of a clergyman, the Rev. George Grant, inspector for the Districts of Parry Sound and Nipissing in 1891-2, to hire female acolytes should have forced the deputy minister to record an assumption revealing the rich underworld of male administrative culture.

In the course of perusing expense accounts associated with the administration of annual examinations in Grant's inspectorate, the Deputy Minister of Education discovered that the former had hired a female reader—Miss A.J. Merrett—to assist with entrance and third-class papers. While covering Grant's breach of custom by graciously suspending the prohibition against female participation in her specific case, he was careful to add that his forgiveness represented only a suspension, not a dispensation, of the appropriate convention: "In future, ladies must not be appointed to take any part in the exams. This is a long established rule of the Dept." Furthermore, his suspicions fully aroused and probably confirmed by an examination of personnel rolls maintained at the department, he added that the Minister of Education wished to know the identity of T.C. Grant, to whom some twenty dollars had been paid.[11]

In his reply Grant pointed out that the Minister, when granting permission to hire help in 1889, had not specified sex as a qualifying consideration for examination readers. Nor was he aware until the receipt of Millar's letter that hiring women violated the rules of the department. "As the person or persons assisting me were not members of the Examining Board, and as I alone was responsible for the proper conduct of the whole work, I supposed that a generous latitude was given to use my judgment and common sense, so as, to secure the best results possible." Given the pioneer conditions prevalent in the districts, he concluded that examiners would be forced to hire from a very small pool of qualified persons and supervise those individuals closely. If the department found this unsatisfactory, it was welcome to offer solutions. For his part, he could "do no better."

Neither, it seems, had he thought the department would object to a reader on grounds of consanguinity. After conceding that T.C. Grant shared Miss Merrett's defective sex, he proudly pronounced her the holder of First Class Literary and Second Class Professional Certificates. Not only was she an experienced teacher then in the employ of the Toronto public school system,

Accomplishing "a Man's Task"

she was indeed his daughter: a person "in all respects impartial, trustworthy and competent for the work of reading papers."

Figure 2

The Rev. George Grant: "It is painful...in the extreme to enter upon a defence of my conduct." (Courtesy Archives of Ontario, J.B. MacDougall, Building the North, Toronto: McClelland and Stewart, 1917.)

Tone and content both suggest that Grant considered himself dishonoured by the department. Since under the circumstances we may assume he made the strongest possible case for his actions, it is worth noting where the inspector established the limits of female responsibility. By implication, he would neither place a woman on the Board of Examiners nor permit her to exercise supervisory power in the examination process. Furthermore, he conceded the authority of the department to regulate sexual roles in these matters. "I beg of you," he concluded, "to give me some definite instructions that I can follow without hesitation. It is painful for me in the extreme, after having done my level best, to have to enter upon a defence of my conduct."[12]

In light of these revelations, it may be useful to ask what characteristics the department sought in its inspectors. Officially, candidates probably did not have to be male: the regulations governing eligibility for Public School Inspectors' Certificates in 1908 and 1918 do not mention sex. Yet educational, professional, and experience requirements could be to middle-echelon educational administration what literacy tests were to potential black voters in the era of Jim Crow. In 1918 only a very small proportion of the population received a university education, and of those who did, the vast majority were men. One list of candidates capable of meeting the regulations proposed for 1918 contained eighty-seven names, of which only three were women. Furthermore, though the legislation did not specify sex, even as late as 1918, custom did. The author of a "Synoptical View of the Requirements of the Regulations for Public School Inspectors for 1908 and those now Proposed [for 1918]" declared, under the first head, that "the Inspector should be a *man* of good general academic culture, and should be the, or at least an, educational leader in his district [emphasis mine]."[14]

II

In his examination of inspectors during 1918, Assistant Chief Inspector Chisholm invariably expected his men to be sympathetic, kindly, friendly, helpful, and frank. The profile that emerges from the accumulating evidence suggests that the ideal candidate for the job was an exquisite combination of father, father confessor, and commissioned educational officer. In his examination of 1918 Chisholm found the incumbents up to standard, though he suggested that one had been insufficiently frank when discussing the results of his inspection with his teachers. It is important to remember that these assessments were compiled during the course of multiple evaluations, with the assistant chief assessing his inspectors at the same time as they were measuring the worth of teachers and trustees.[15] Given the peculiar set of environments that characterize any kind of inquisitional activity, it may be useful to observe how "officers" and "men," "fathers" and "children," related to each other under field and confessional conditions. Some routine—and some not-so-routine—correspondence may imply an even more complex relationship than this typology suggests.

Inspector Leslie A. Green had been born and reared within the prosperous environs of Oxford and Brant counties, educated at the University of Toronto, and appointed supervising principal of the Sault Ste. Marie public schools in 1896. For someone as well educated, as ambitious, and as "energetic and thoroughly up-to-date" as L.A. Green, the Sault was a certain magnet. That sleepy little administrative town had become the Pittsburg of the north, thanks to the efforts of Francis Hector Clergue, the American miracle maker, who was then approaching the height of his powers in a meteoric career that saw him turn water into electricity, trees into paper, and earth into steel.

And Green had risen with the town. Within five years he had witnessed the evolution of the continuation and model schools, the establishment of separate facilities for post-public school work, and his appointment as principal of the new high school. When Green took up his appointment as resident inspector for the District of Algoma on January 1, 1904, he was thirty-six years old, in "robust health," and ready to administer the district "without fear or favour of anyone...in a fair and businesslike manner."[16]

One of his abiding problems was finding teachers willing to fill positions in the more remote sections of the Algoma inspectorate. In times of acute shortage, rural northern Ontario boards had no choice but to hire where and whom they could. What they often hired were the dregs from southern Ontario normal schools, loose fish shaken out of southern Ontario boards, or unqualified local candidates. Twenty-seven—or approximately half—of Green's rural schools suffered from inadequate supply in March of 1920. The list of unqualified and barely qualified teachers that he submitted to the department was peppered with explanations strung on a common thread: isolation. "Small school remote, lonely for teacher; one term enough" or "Only the bravest will go in here. Have been trying all year to get a teacher."[17]

Such circumstances occasioned a good deal of anxiety. Local ratepayers whose schools remained closed for weeks or months might well question his stewardship. His superior officer, the assistant chief inspector, was busy drawing up and circulating statistical tables that ranked inspectoral districts on the basis of teaching certificates. If he did not keep the number of temporaries and district thirds to a bare minimum, the hierarchy might question his "efficiency." Then there were untold numbers of young women teachers, born and reared in southern Ontario, who found themselves facing the triple trauma of seeking employment, leaving home, and living in a northern wilderness, all for the first time. Consider the case of Grace Holmes, who lived in Ripley, a village some twenty-five miles northeast of Goderich.

In the summer of 1916 Miss Holmes had agreed to take charge of the school in Goulais Bay, a lumbering and small-scale farming community on Lake Superior north of Sault Ste. Marie. Sometime after she had accepted the position but before she began her journey, her parents' protective instincts were aroused by fear of the remote and unknown. They denied her permission to travel until the trustees at the Goulais Bay had described the "character" of the community. When they failed to write, she failed to appear. At the last moment she wrote to Green, explaining her parents' attitude and asking whether, since she had to travel some eighteen to thirty miles by stage, the road was much travelled or "lonesome."

Green was very harsh and not completely honest with her. Addressing her as "Dear Miss," he charged that she had broken faith with her employers and delayed the opening of the school for a week. Why had she not investigated the school and community by examining the reference books available to every teacher? Did she not have "sufficient confidence in an official that he would not send a teacher where it [was] not safe or where conditions [were] not fit to go into?" Goulais Bay was only twenty miles from Sault Ste. Marie on a road suitable for automobiles. The stage—always well patronized—was managed by a driver "of excellent character" who made the journey twice a week. "There were," Green stated categorically, "no wolves bears or other wild animals on the road or in the country." As for the school, it was up-to-date, attended by about twenty-five children, "nearly all of Canadian parentage—three or four Russians." In conclusion, he intimated that he had other candidates waiting for the position and informed her that, in the event she refused to come, she would be charged $1.05 for the telegrams and be liable to have her certificate cancelled for withdrawing after accepting a position.[18]

Green's tone has the strident edge of one whose patience had long been tried. A district chronically short of teachers attracted female candidates from Old Ontario who, underqualified for schools in their own communities, required an income. Some who had mustered the courage to think about a wilderness adventure found themselves unable to act when faced with the moment of truth. Nevertheless, his letter does constitute a cruel assault on someone he considered a girl-woman, whom he clearly hoped to coerce by a show of authority and pique.

The school in question was almost certainly #2 Fenwick, which appears repeatedly on the lists of schools requiring the deputy minister's permission to hire teachers on permanent or limited third class certificates. On October 28, 1916, Green had informed Chief Inspector Waugh that #2 Fenwick had operated as a summer school but that the ratepayers were "self-sacrificing" and, even though their assessment base was under ten thousand dollars, they had, with the assistance of a special grant (secured by their inspector), furnished their school for winter operation. In 1917 the section was described as "very small...not capable of much expansion...very remote." In 1919 he listed it as a school that had been unable to obtain a teacher of any standing. By 1920 the future was uncertain, and in 1921 it operated only half the year. But in 1916 Green had obviously taken a strong personal interest in it, believed he had made a breakthrough, and felt personally affronted that his efforts had been endangered by the timid young woman from Ripley.[19]

Accomplishing "a Man's Task"

The routine manuscript record so far suggests that teachers tended to endure such chastisement in silence. If they protested, they rarely made their cases official by committing them to paper and submitting them to the inspector or his superiors. Yet there were exceptions, some startling in their boldness, many the products of outraged womanhood.

Take the case of Lizzie Campbell and her "magnificent cheek." In July 1886, Miss Campbell of Duntroon wrote the examinations for her third class certificate in Collingwood. On August 23 she paid two dollars to have her paper in French grammar reread. At the same time, she informed Alex Marling, secretary of the department, that in her own estimation she deserved to receive the certificate. Five days later the department sent out the certificate, which Lizzie failed to receive. On September 18 she informed the department that, although Mr. Williams, the head master of Collingwood Collegiate Institute, had called in at College Street to pick up her certificate, he had been told that it had been sent by mail. He also informed her that she had been passed on the basis of her high aggregate scores.

Meanwhile an interdepartmental memo reveals that, contrary to standard practice, the letter had not been registered. The Post Office had no record, and a duplicate had been sent on October 6. On October 30 Lizzie requested the return of her two-dollar fee, which she thought her due since the department had revised its opinion. This letter contained the fatal statement: "I received my Second Class non-professional Certificate and would please ask you to send me the two dollars and oblige."

Two notes appear on the above letter: $2.00 omitted by H.I.K. 28 Aug. sent on 5 Nov./86..." and "Miss Lizzie Campbell should return her II Class Certif issued by mistake for a III." In a letter of November 17, 1886, Marling ordered her to return her II Class Certificate "for correction at once. As you were previously informed, the certificate awarded is for Class III." Three days later Miss Campbell composed what must be one of the most cooly impertinent letters on record.

Sir—Your letter of the 17th and No. 10752 reached me in due time with an acknowledgement of the magnificent blunder which the worthy gentlemen managing the affairs of the Education Department made in sending me a Second Class Certificate instead of a Third. Truly, they deserve our implicit confidence in all affairs of trust. I feel very thankful that the mistake is discovered so early for it would not be desirable to go to the Normal School and find out then that a Second Class Certificate—(Non Professional) had not been awarded to me as I fully believed. It was extremely kind, very generous to let me enjoy a few

59

blissful months in the thought that I was the happy possessor of a Second. When I received the Certificate, I was surprised for I expected only a Third. But I supposed that my Second Class papers had been reconsidered also and therefore had no doubts as to my being rightfully entitled to the document which declared me to be Second Class. But your letter informed me of the fact that I was acting a false part. Therefore I enclose that Certificate to have exchanged for my Third Class Certificate which I hope to be able to keep in unmolested peace and quiet.

Your humble and grateful servant
Miss Lizzie Campbell

Instead of confronting a solitary inspector, Lizzie Campbell had taken on the Toronto-based, male bureaucratic establishment. If there is an element of outrage here, there is something else more subtle and subversive. A humble female candidate for a teaching certificate of the lowest level had noted that the educational emperors wore no clothes. Marling's underlining of her phrase "magnificent blunder" in red ink is evidence that her flash of inspired insight had penetrating power. We are not told what happened to Miss Campbell. We only know that on her letter is pencilled the note: "III Cert sent by R.L. [or R.C., the last letter is hastily—perhaps angrily—scrawled]." The chances are that he was an inspector, under instruction to coach Miss Campbell in manners appropriate to her station.[20]

Yet teachers could censure their inspectors' deportment as well. In the preliminaries leading up to the publication of Regulation 17, Green of Algoma had, on a number of instances, to evict teachers certified in Quebec from classrooms where francophone boards had placed them. Toward the end of 1908 Green had decided to replace, with a model school graduate, one such teacher who had been holding school in Mond, a settlement just outside of Sudbury.

Accomplishing "a Man's Task"

Figure 3

Inspector Leslie A. Green: "No wolves, bears or other wild animals." (Courtesy Archives of Ontario, J.B. MacDougall, Building the North, *Toronto: McClelland and Stewart, 1917.)*

The incumbent, signing herself "A Quebec Teacher," asked the inspector how the needs of children whose first language was French would be satisfied by one of his model schoolteachers. She condemned his use of an "overbearing deceptive authority" and accused him of hypocrisy (on the ground that he had recommended two other Quebec teachers), of favouring inferior Ontario teachers whom he had placed "in schools where they...failed in their exams," and of disregarding the wishes of residents and school boards, as well as the "interests of those poor little French and Foreign children," who had progressed under her guidance.

Remember, Mr. Green, I do not stoop to my inferiors, as I am as independent as the sun that shines, and I assure you, if you think you have done Justice to me, you are sadly mistaken, and sooner or later, your overbearing authority may prosper to a certain extent in this world; but in the next your feeble tongue shall no longer have its earthly power, and you will moan forth for a Quebec Teacher to sympathise with you in your agonies.

Gender And Education In Ontario: An Historical Reader

She defended her qualifications, her experience, and her work with the students and argued that she was more than qualified to teach "from letters up [to] the Third reader up here in shanty town." Did she not have her model school certificate? Had she not taught three terms in Ontario, and also at the Ottawa Business College where "they were just as smart a people as you'll find at the Soo?" She hoped that his "remorse of conscience" would give him pause and moderate his "undermining [*sic*] deceptive, and overbearing disposition, and learn a lesson from a Quebec Teacher."

"Now," she concluded, "I am satisfied, so you can satisfy yourself." Although the record is silent in the matter—Green did not deign even to annotate the letter—the chances are that the Inspector welcomed the opportunity to replace her.[21]

One of the most extraordinary exchanges between inspector and teacher was initiated by Miss Kathleen McCallum, B.A., assistant teacher in the Tara Continuation School just outside Stratford. On December 17, 1916, she informed Dr. Pyne, the Minister of Education, that Mr. J.P. Hoag had acted "most ungentlemanly" in inspecting her classroom. She charged that he had virtually accused her of lying when she told him her lesson in ancient history for that day was "Alexander the Great." After seeking confirmation from the class and finding that he had been wrong, he proceeded to make sport of her publicly, speaking "in...an insulting manner," scorning a student's suggestion "that Shakespeare introduced the drunken porter scene in Macbeth, to make a laugh," in spite of the fact that she had offered that interpretation, based on the opinion of Professor Alexander, Toronto University. Furthermore, he had questioned her placement of accents in rhetoric, specifically in "The Island of the Scot," a subject and exercise which she believed she knew better than he.

Finally, Mr. Hoag had completed his work by delivering a devastating report to the board, blaming the low grade that the school had received on the work of the assistant teacher. To that Kathleen McCallum took strong exception, affirming that her work had been graded as well as the principal's, that some of the board thought the high failure rate could be laid at his door, that she had arrived only in September of that year, and that she had had "scarcely a failure" in a dozen years of teaching. Indeed, the inspector would do well to curb his insulting and impertinent tongue, leave the profession, "...fight for his country and let willing women workers keep on working."

Have we teachers to stand such an imposition? We went to Model and Normal College, and received our high standing, just as much as Hoag did. Why should he be such a god? I would thank him more if he had looked after the Heating of the school, as we have to endure a temperature of less than 50 every day, and the day Inspector Hoag was here, my teeth chattered while I was teaching.

I have taught *well* and can do *so* and defy any man like Hoag to insult me. I hope you will inquire into the matter Dr. Pyne.[22]

On December 21 Inspector Hoag, responding to the department's request for information, cited the portion of his report that bore on Miss McCallum's teaching. Under "character of teaching" he had noted that the grading in English III and History III was "due to the character of the work of the Assistant." Without offering the board specific evidence for his charges, he expressed regret that his "impression" of Miss McCallum's teaching was "not good"; nor did her "influence on the school...appear...to be helpful." He concluded by suggesting that the Minister contact Inspectors Wetherell and Spotten, men who had observed her performance in other jurisdictions.[23]

On December 26 J.E. Wetherell, a Toronto high school inspector, posted the following brief response:

The woman whose very hysterical letter you enclose is a well-known Scold. Some years ago I was so unfortunate as to be one of her victims. Her letter of December 17 was evidently written on one of her bad days and therefore it should not be taken seriously.[24]

The following day H.B. Spotten, likewise a Toronto high school inspector, responded in a similar vein:

Inspector Wetherell's letter very well expresses my own opinion about Miss McCallum. She made complaints about me when I inspected her work some years ago, and I felt that she was more or less eccentric, and, as Inspector Wetherell says, should not be taken too seriously.[25]

On January 11, 1917, the deputy minister informed Kathleen McCallum that he had investigated her charges and been assured by a number of "inspectors" that Mr. Hoag had neither shown her "discourtesy" nor treated her with "undue severity." For his own part, Colqhoun urged her to accept their judgment "as satisfactory."[26]

One senses that Kathleen McCallum burned for a week before sending a heated letter to the Minister of Education. It is a remarkable document, a furious compendium of charges implying or alleging departmental collusion and fraud, a vindictive animus on the part of the chairman of her school board, the subversion of standard pedagogical procedures and the violation of normal codes of human behaviour by Inspector Hoag, and departmental failure to select inspectors for their knowledge of curriculum and pedagogy or to prune those who disgraced themselves and the profession.

Dear Sir,

I received your letter, stating that the Inspectors and yourself had decided that there was no undue severity, in the Report sent by Inspector Hoag re, my work in Tara School.

Well let me inquire who were the *Inspectors*? Inspector Hoag is the only one who came to inspect my work there, and I have had *no* inspection for five years, as I have not been teaching, on account of illness in the family, except for four months two years ago, and I certainly had a good record as we passed four times as many pupils as next year, when I was not there. I had accepted only a temporary position.

I told Inspector Hoag that there were three or four pupils in Form 1 Tara, who had never studied History before. He flatly contradicted me, and Mr. Gilmour was present and told him what I said, was correct. Now what is the good of the Department, when they tolerate such? What are their Inspectors doing? Inspector Hoag certainly was prejudiced by the chairman of the Board...who has one girl in Form II Tara, who has been in the Form two years already, and he could not stand to see other pupils get ahead of her, who were in the room only this year. All the other Pupils complimented my teaching most highly.

Inspector Hoag used no judgment or common sense, also he tried to terrify and intimidate the pupils Why they learned just fine for me and I had not the slightest trouble with Discipline Inspector Hoag was informed there was some trouble with a boy but he was in the Entrance class. Why the absurdity Discipline II. Why it was almost perfect as far as I Know.

Then too Mr. Gilmore Principal said that Inspector Hoag got all "mixed up" on some work he was taking in chemistry, the same time. I have a Record that would stand against yours or his any day. I headed every list in my Public and High School Work & also in my teaching I have [been] told I was a *perfect* Grammar Teacher. Inspector Hoag marked *Art,* my best work, and I know I can teach anything else, *ten times as well,* though I Know I can teach Art also, much better than *most* teachers who try. They get no ideas from your summer school, they tell me. Mr. Gilmour and the Pupils of Tara, said my teaching of Art was *far* ahead of the last teacher's, and she was marked good. I think Inspector Hoag Knows very little about half the work he inspects. I would like to meet him in a school again. I would ridicule him.

Accomplishing "a Man's Task"

I am independent of means and do not *have* to teach but do so for the *love* of teaching and I certainly Know *how to teach* and intend to show Inspector Hoag he had better get out. His big back might stop a few German Bullets. What Kind of a Family Compact are you having in the Department? You had better look after P.S. Inspector...of...he is reported here as being so indecent, no decent teacher wishes to teach in his Inspectorate. Good teachers in this township report he tried to throw his arms around them this Fall, while inspecting the school. You are a queer Bunch of "Boodlers" you Tory Department of Ed. You are running the Education System, as the Bookseller in Tara, Mr....said, "That Know-Nothing Dr. Pyne," and he is a Tory too You see where you are coming to. You had better waken up.

There has been no decent inspection ever since you got in power. The country can easily see it. Mr. Crowley commended my work most highly and so did Mr. Spotten and Mr. Wetherell. I was teaching Reading in Tillsonburg H.S. two years ago now. The Inspector was not there while I was, but the next time he inspected the school, the Pupils wrote and told me, he said that they must have had a fine teacher of Reading, for they read splendidly.

Of course, I have not had the marking I should for I have changed my position so frequently as I have been ill so many winters with Pleurisy. I had to for instance take Inspector Wetherells' marking of Latin though I taught only a couple of months and was judged from Pronunciation alone almost. That is not a fair marking. I hope the Department will let me Know more accurately what they meant. Yours Truly

Kathleen McCallum B.A.[27]

This letter is notable as an act of open rebellion. It is not a well-composed, cogently argued case. It buzzes with indignation, stutters with special pleading, stings with insults, sweeps in gossip. How markedly her letter contrasts with the reports of Hoag, Wetherell, and Spotten, which are short, terse, magisterial, calculated in tone and substance to stand as the final word! They are the work of men long accustomed to the habit of authority, easy in their relationship one with another, comfortable in the knowledge that they know their brothers' minds in such matters.

Kathleen McCallum's outrageous language is both measure and acknowledgement of her impotence. She must have known, the moment she read the deputy minister's letter, that her charges had been placed before a Sanhedrin of inspectors, and the outcome could not be in doubt. In educational attainments, teaching ability, and general culture she thought herself superior to J. Hoag. The fact that the department coolly confirmed the substance of his indictment while implying that the inspector's assessment was dispassionate, clinical, scientific—unalloyed by "discourtesy or undue severity"—triggered a display on her part that could only have confirmed Spotten and Wetherell in their diagnoses. Predictably, not only did the Minister refuse to comment further on "the treatment meted out" by Inspector Hoag but "so extraordinary" was the nature of her letter, and "so unsuitable" the terms she "thought fit to employ" that he considered taking "further action" against her.[28]

At this point the record ends. One wonders about the subsequent lives of Kathleen McCallum, the "Quebec Teacher," and Lizzie Campbell. They were exceptional to the same degree that their inspectors appear to have been standard issue. We suspect that the Greens, Hoags, and Wetherells continued to function in relatively predictable ways. Why should they have questioned their motives or altered their behaviour? From the beginning of their careers in the classroom they had observed the proportion of women in teaching increasing while turnover within the youthful female ranks remained high. Thus they tended to associate maleness with a commitment to teaching as a way of life and as a profession. In graded schools men tended to teach advanced classes at the upper levels.[29] Although this translation to a higher sphere was in part a function of those patriarchal assumptions that informed our culture, it must have conveyed the impression that men were more capable of dispensing not only discipline but also the elements of the more advanced knowledge essential to civilized existence. Along with smaller classes and higher salaries, these considerations combined to enforce the assumption that positions of command within the profession ought to be occupied by men. This assumption, and the attitudes and actions to which it gave rise, earned the resentment of many a woman teacher and occasioned impassioned outbursts on the part of a few.

There is more than a modicum of truth in Kathleen McCallum's charge that the inspectorate constituted a Family Compact. While seeking to insult Pyne by linking his conservatives with an early nineteenth-century Tory clique, she made a shrewd point, for our early twentieth-century administrative hierarchy was no less committed to the perpetuation of male administrative culture than John Strachan's Tories were the advocates of a distinctive political culture nurtured by ideas peculiar to traditional, deferential, eighteenth-century Anglo-American society. Powerful cultures are sustained by assumptions so deeply rooted as to defy, not only eradication, but even examination.

Recall the words of William Corbett, secretary-treasurer of the Wharncliffe school section. "If men cannot be got to teach our boys and hence leave their training to girls I fear it will tend towards effeminacy and eventually breed a generation more fit to be apparelled in petticoats than pants." Presumably, the assumption of the teacher's role automatically turned a sixteen-year-old boy

Accomplishing "a Man's Task"

into a man, but did not transform a sixteen-year-old girl into a woman. His unconscious choice of words reveals in a flash the existence of a male manitou that continued to inform patriarchal images, precepts, and practices even down into our own time. If the Department of Education fostered a male administrative culture, it was ultimately sustained, as Corbett's words show, by powerful spiritual currents in the society at large.

Gender And Education In Ontario: An Historical Reader

Notes

The author wishes to express his appreciation for the financial assistance rendered by the Social Science and Humanities Research Council of Canada, and Algoma University College.

1. For contemporary impressions of the Regulations and their enforcement, see Robert M. Stamp, *The Schools of Ontario, 1876-1976* (Toronto: University of Toronto Press, 1982) 47.
2. Alison Prentice, "Themes in the Early History of the Women Teachers' Association of Toronto," in Paula Bourne, ed., *Women's Paid and Unpaid Work, Historical and Contemporary Perspectives* (Toronto: New Hogtown Press, 1985) 102-3.
3. Archives of Ontario [hereafter AO], RG 2, F-3-E, J.B. MacDougall to L.A. Green, North Bay, Aug. 10, 1920.
4. AO, RG 2, F-3-E, A. Mackintosh to L.A. Green, Toronto, Mar. 16, 1910; Wm. Corbett to L.A. Green, Wharncliffe, Aug. 29, 1912.
5. AO, RG 2, F-3-E, L.A. Green to Chief Inspector John Waugh, Sault Ste. Marie, Dec. 27, 1919.
6. Ibid.
7. Among the studies investigating sex roles and the history of teaching in the nineteenth and early twentieth centuries, the following are useful introductions to the subject: Alison Prentice, "The Feminization of Teaching in British North America and Canada, 1845-1875," *Social History/histoire sociale* 8 (May 1975) 5 20; Marta Danylewycz, Beth Light and Alison Prentice, "The Evolution of the Sexual Division of Labour in Teaching: A Nineteenth Century Ontario and Quebec Study," *Social History/histoire sociale* 31 (May 1983), 80-109; Marta Danylewycz, "Sexes et classes sociales dans l'enseignement: le cas du Montréal à la fin du 19ᶜ siècle," in Micheline Dumont, et Nadia Fahmy-Eid, eds., *Maîtresses de maison, maîtresses d'école* (Montreal: Boreal Express, 1983); Alison Prentice and Marta Danylewycz, "Teachers, Gender and Bureaucratizing School Systems in Nineteenth Century Montreal and Toronto," *History of Education Quarterly* 24 (Spring 1984) 75-100; Myra Strober and Laura Best, "The Female-Male Salary Differential in Public Schools: Some Lessons from San Francisco, 1879," *Economic Inquiry* 17, no. 2 (April 1979); Myra Strober and David B. Tyack, "Why Do Women Teach and Men Manage?" *Signs* 5, no. 3 (Spring 1980).
8. Wayne Urban, *Why Teachers Organized* (Detroit: Wayne State University Press, 1982); Alison Prentice, "Themes in the History of the Women

Accomplishing "a Man's Task"

Teachers' Association of Toronto," in Paula Bourne, ed., *Women's Paid and Unpaid Work* (Toronto: New Hogtown Press, 1985); Alison Prentice with Marta Danylewycz, "Teachers' Work: Changing Patterns and Perceptions in the Emerging School Systems of 19th and Early 20th Century Central Canada," *Labour/le travail* (Spring 1986).

9.   AO, RG 2, F-3-E, L. A. Green to Chief Inspector John Waugh, Sault Ste. Marie, Dec. 27, 1919.

10. AO, RG 2, P-2, Selected Files, G.K. Mills to Inspectors, Collingwood, Dec. 21, 1909. The file contained no record as to the outcome of their campaign.

11. AO, RG 2, P-2, Selected Files, John Millar, Deputy Ministry of Education, to Rev. George Grant, Toronto, Dec. 30, 1891.

12. AO, RG 2, P-2, Selected Files, Rev. George Grant to John Millar, Orillia, Lindecrest, Jan. 12, 1892.

13. AO, RG 2, P-3, *Review of Qualifications of Public School Inspectors from 1878 on, with Proposed Regulations for 1918.*

14. Ibid.

15. AO, RG 2, P-3. Reports of the work of various inspectors, made by Assistant Chief Inspector Chisholm, 1918.

16. AO, RG 2, D-7, L.A. Green to Richard Harcourt, Sault Ste. Marie, Oct. 20, 1903 and Nov. 28, 1903; Dr. J.A. Shannon, Chairman, Sault Ste. Marie Board of Education, to Richard Harcourt, Sault Ste. Marie, Oct. 28, 1903.

17. AO, RG 2, F-3-E. Rationales justifying hiring teachers with Third Class certificates, addressed to the Deputy Ministry of Education.

18. AO, RG 2, F-3-E, Grace Holmes to L.A. Green, Ripley, Ont., Aug. 7, 1916; Green to Holmes, Sault Ste. Marie, Sept., 1916.

19. AO, RG 17, P-2, Lizzie Campbell to Hon. Alex Marling, Duntroon, Aug. 23, 1886; Marling to Campbell, Aug. 28, Draft Letter; Campbell to Marling, Sept. 18, Oct. 30; Marling to Campbell, Nov. 17; Campbell to Marling, Barrie, Nov. 20, 1886.

21. AO, RG 2, F-3-E, "A Quebec Teacher" to L.A. Green, Mond, Ont., Dec. 1, 1908.

22. AO, RG 2, P-3, Kathleen McCallum to Dr. Pyne, Minister of Education, Tara, Dec. 1, 1916.

23. AO, RG 2, P-3, J.P. Hoag to Deputy Minister of Education, Dec. 21, 1916. Inspector Hoag began: "In my report re Tara Continuation School I reported the facts as I found them. The parts of the report dealing with Miss McCallum are as follows..."

24. AO, RG 2, P-3, J. Wetherell to Deputy Minister, Toronto, Dec. 26, 1916.

25. AO, RG 2, P-3, H.B. Spotten to Deputy Minister, Toronto, Dec. 27, 1916.

26. AO, RG 2, P-3, Deputy Minister to Kathleen McCallum, Toronto, Jan. 11, 1917.

27. AO, RG 2, P-3, Kathleen McCallum to Minister of Education, Jan. 22, 1917.

28. AO, RG 2, P-3, Deputy Minister to Kathleen McCallum, Jan. 30, 1917.

29. In her essay on the Women Teachers' Association of Toronto, Alison Prentice details some of the frustrations that prompted female teachers to organize. Among them were heavier workloads, lower salaries, and slower promotions than those experienced by men. Another was the anxiety occasioned by the enhanced levels of supervision required in a system increasingly governed by method and saddled by regulations. Their frustration was increased by a growing conviction that male supervisors did not understand the problems of teaching in the junior grades. In 1912 the organization petitioned the Toronto Board to select a women inspector, though it was not until 1919 that Aletta E. Marty, Toronto's first woman inspector, was appointed. Prentice, "The Women Teachers' Association of Toronto," in Bourne, 102-7.

The "Feminization" of the High School: Women Secondary Schoolteachers in Toronto: 1871-1930[*]

Susan Gelman

In August 1871, Mrs. Howe was engaged as "Lady Superintendent" of the new "Female Department" of the Toronto High School. Mrs. Howe, widow of the previous headmaster, Rev. Michael C. Howe,[1] was hired on a six-month term at the rate of $500 a year. Early in the following year, Madame Dely was appointed on probation, at $30.00 a month, to teach French and German. In February 1872, the headmaster of the High School, Dr. Wickson, reported to the High School Board of Education regarding the "efficiency" of his two female staff members and the classics teacher Mr. Crawford. The three teachers were put on suspension until the school's headmaster, known as the rector, would see fit to have them reinstated. In May, Crawford was rehired as a temporary classics teacher at $2.00 a day. The following month, Madame Dely resigned, at which time she was given a "certificate of approval for her services."[2]

A subcommittee was appointed to investigate the complaints that had been brought against Mrs. Howe. They resolved that Mrs. Howe "must subject herself to the rector in reference to the management of the school." The subcommittee further stated that in order to create an atmosphere of proper discipline within the school "the rector must have full power and authority over the management of the school." They recommended that a Code of Rules be drawn up by the rector and submitted to the Board for approval. In September of the following year, Mrs. Howe was advised by the High School Board of

---

[*] This paper is based on my M.A. thesis, "The 'Feminization' of the High Schools? Female Public High Schoolteachers in Toronto: 1871-1930," (University of Toronto, 1988), and on a previous version presented at the Canadian History of Education Association biennial conference, October 1988. I wish to express my thanks and appreciation to Alison Prentice for her guidance and support. I would also like to thank Wyn Millar for her helpful editorial suggestions. To the archivists and staff at the Toronto Board of Education many thanks for their assistance. I should also like to thank Jill Given-King for her help preparing the disk for this paper.

Gender And Education In Ontario: An Historical Reader

Education that they could no longer employ an assistant high schoolteacher who did not have either a first- or second-class teaching certificate. She was instructed that unless she took the teacher's examination to obtain legal qualification to teach she would be discharged by Christmas vacation. In November 1873, Mrs. Howe resigned her post at the Toronto High School (which had been renamed the Toronto Collegiate Institute) and on December 17 of that year, Miss Charlotte E. Thompson was appointed "Head Female Teacher" at $600 a year.[3]

Mrs. Howe's short and rocky career at the Toronto Collegiate stands out for several reasons. She was the first woman teacher hired in a school which had previously been an all-boys' grammar school. Her appointment was tied to changes in the structure of state-provided secondary education in Ontario as a result of the School Act of 1871, and the subsequent expanding provision of public secondary schooling for girls. The problems Mrs. Howe faced with the rector were largely the result of the way in which the Toronto High School Board of Education dealt with the changes in public secondary education; but the incident also points to the relationship between the development of public secondary schooling and the opportunities for women in public secondary school teaching. As the secondary school system in Toronto expanded, the number of women teachers increased. One objective of this paper is to examine the way in which this change occurred, and how women teachers established themselves in the system from 1871 to 1930.

During the late nineteenth and early twentieth centuries, Toronto's women secondary schoolteachers were part of an equally small but noticeable number who were pioneering this new public occupation for women in Ontario. At this time, not only were more women entering the paid work-force, but many were taking on non-traditional occupations.[4] Public secondary school teaching was considered such an occupation. The Provincial Department of Education records do not contain any evidence that women had been teaching in the province's grammar schools.[5] This is not to suggest that women were not teaching at advanced levels. A large number of women were teachers in the denominational private girls' academies that had been operating in the province since the middle of the century, where they were teaching advanced academic subjects in a formal setting.[6] Therefore, as was the case with elementary school teaching, the entrance of women into high school and collegiate institute teaching must be seen as the entrance of women into *public* secondary school teaching,[7] rather than something entirely new. Yet, from the onset, male educators were concerned with the number of women in collegiate and high school teaching jobs and, as the number of women multiplied, they became the object of increasing attention. A second objective of this paper, therefore, is to examine the reaction of leading male educators to the role of women in secondary school teaching.

I

The School Act of 1871 reflected several decades of change in the structure of the province's grammar schools and the secondary education of girls in Ontario. Traditionally a girl's education emphasized learning the three Rs and the various skills that a woman would need for her role as a wife and mother. In Upper Canada during the late eighteenth and early nineteenth centuries, girls were educated in domestic situations, either by their parents, or employers. Early in the nineteenth century, private girls' schools, or dame schools, and convent schools were opening to meet the demand of parents for a more sound and formal education for their daughters. As common schools became more popular by the 1820s and 1830s, girls in rural areas could be found attending these schools for an elementary education.[8] By mid-century, private girls' academies, which had grown out of the smaller dame schools, were increasing in number throughout the province. These schools offered girls a formal education in advanced academic subjects, along with the traditional social and domestic pursuits.[9] Girls were also attending grammar schools, which provided a way to educate girls that was less expensive than the academies.[10] Formal schooling gave girls the necessary education to train for teaching and fill the increasing number of common school positions being made available to women past the mid-nineteenth century.[11]

By the 1860s, the fact of girls attending grammar schools became problematic. Grammar schools in Upper Canada had originally been designed as separate from the common schools, to provide boys with a classical education in preparation for university and the public sphere, but many appeared not to be fulfilling this purpose as they admitted increasing numbers of young women.[12] The Ontario School act of 1871 was designed to resolve this problem. It gave official sanction to the public secondary education of girls in the newly created high schools and collegiate institutes. High schools were to provide an English and commercial education with Latin and Greek optional upon parental choice. An additional grant of $750 a year would, however, be issued from the Superior Education Fund to high schools with a daily average attendance of sixty boys studying Latin and Greek under a minimum of four masters. High schools receiving this extra funding were to be classified as collegiate institutes. Girls were not restricted from attending the collegiates.

However, Ryerson hoped that they would be encouraged to attend the non-classical high schools.[13]

In the case of Toronto, the School Act of 1871 marked a significant change in both the secondary education of girls and the employment of women in public secondary school teaching. The Toronto Grammar School had been one of only two grammar schools in the province that had not admitted girls prior to 1871, and the Toronto school was particularly proud of the standard of education they upheld because girls were not admitted.[14] With the passing of the 1871 School Act, the Toronto Grammar School, now the Toronto High School, was forced to admit girls for the first time. The Toronto High School Board decided to issue five scholarships to girls attending the city's public schools, but this and the admission of girls to the High School had to be delayed until a "Lady Superintendent" could be hired. An advertisement was put in the *Globe* and Mrs. Howe was employed.[15]

To further accommodate girls within the school, a separate "Female Department" was established. Indeed the Toronto High School was an extreme example of sexually segregated co-education. The girls were taught in classrooms located in a separate wing of the building, which was partitioned from the boys' department by a set of double doors. When higher form classes had to be shared with the boys, because of the small number of students at this level, the girls were accompanied by a chaperon. Any further competition was avoided by continuing to issue scholarships separately, and by conducting extracurricular activities in separate groups. Social contact between boys and girls on school property was also avoided by means of a tall fence that divided the two-acre playground behind the school in half. "The only break in the fence was a pump with handles and spouts on each side."[16]

It was largely the sexually segregated structure of the school that determined the problem Mrs. Howe faced in her short time there. The expansion of the high school in this *ad hoc* manner by the High School Board in order to accommodate girls created problems of authority between the rector and the new Lady Superintendent, resulting in a breakdown in authority based on gender. In his analysis of developing bureaucracies, Michael Katz has argued that when positions are added piecemeal within an institution, confusion arises over the definition of roles. As a result, the designation of duties within the hierarchical structure becomes blurred and tension results from overlapping functions.[17] In the case of the Toronto High School, the addition of a new and physically separate department within the traditional boys' school, and the title of Lady Superintendent, could have suggested to Mrs. Howe that her authority was autonomous. Any authority Mrs. Howe assumed within the school would no doubt have posed a threat to the long-standing male power figure, the

The "Feminization" of the High School

rector. It is interesting to note that when Charlotte Thompson was hired by the new headmaster, Archibald MacMurchy (who had taken over the position of rector in 1872), Thompson was given the title of Head Female Teacher and not Superintendent. The new title would have eliminated any confusion over her position within the school hierarchy.[18]

Charlotte Thompson remained at the Toronto Collegiate Institute, which was renamed Jarvis Collegiate Institute in 1889,[19] for twenty-two years.[20] At the beginning, she taught the entire female student body, which at times numbered over fifty, every subject with the exception of French and drawing. French was taught by Richard Baigent, who was also on staff at Upper Canada College.[21] Thompson's duties were no doubt relieved somewhat when Helen MacMurchy was hired in 1880, and a third woman teacher, Janie Thomas, was taken on staff in 1888.[22] While the school remained sexually segregated until 1896, it was evidently possible for a male teacher to teach the girls. It is unlikely, however, that the women ever taught the boys in the school.

Expanding urbanization and an increasing demand for secondary schooling during the late nineteenth century[23] brought two new collegiate institutes under the jurisdiction of the city of Toronto by the early 1890s. When the Village of Parkdale was annexed to the City of Toronto in 1889, the newly built Jameson Collegiate came under the umbrella of the Toronto Collegiate Institute Board. Three women teachers—Nellie Spence,[24] Madge Robertson,[25] and Louise L. Rychman—were added to Jameson's staff during the first three years after the school opened. Robertson left Jameson in 1892,[26] and a third woman teacher was not hired at the school until the early twentieth century. When Harbord Collegiate opened in 1892,[27] two women teachers were appointed: Gertrude Lawler as English "Master" and Eliza May Balmer as Modern Language "Master."[28] Unlike Jarvis Collegiate, neither Jameson nor Harbord were sexually segregated; therefore, it is likely that the women teachers may have taught the boys as well as the girls. In the case of Toronto, the opening of public secondary schooling to girls, and especially the segregated co-educational structure of the first school, created the need for the first women teachers in the new public high school. As the secondary school system in the city expanded more teaching opportunities were made available to women at this level in non-sexually segregated co-educational environments. But despite the expanding system, women were slow to enter secondary school teaching in Toronto. From 1871 to 1892, the number of women secondary schoolteachers in the city had increased from one to seven, representing only 21.9% of the total teaching staff of 32 (Table 2). Provincially a similar expansion had occurred, but at a slightly different pace. In 1872, several high school boards had successfully applied to the province for approval to hire "female" teachers.[29] J.G. Althouse, in his history of teachers in Ontario, notes that in 1874 there were 15 women secondary schoolteachers in the province.[30] By 1881, the number of women had only increased to 16, which represented 8.5% of the secondary schoolteachers in Ontario. In 1892, there were 89 women secondary schoolteachers representing 17% of the total secondary school teaching population of 522 in Ontario (Table 1).

There are several possible explanations that can be offered for this generally slow rate of entry of women into public secondary school teaching during the late nineteenth century. Firstly, the traditional image of the grammar school master as a male scholar made it difficult for women to qualify as public secondary schoolteachers. Most grammar school masters had been university educated, and many had been clerics. During the late nineteenth century, many educators continued to feel that a university education was sufficient preparation for teaching at the secondary level. Until 1895, an assistant could be employed with either a university degree or a teaching certificate.[31] Three years later, it became mandatory for an assistant to hold a university degree to qualify as a specialist, but it was not until 1920 that a B.A. was required for entrance into the secondary school assistant's teacher training program.[32] Nevertheless, during the late nineteenth century the majority of secondary schoolteachers in the province did hold university degrees.[33]

Table 1—NUMBER AND PERCENTAGE OF WOMEN AND MEN SECONDARY SCHOOLTEACHERS IN ONTARIO: 1881 - 1930

	1881	1892	1900	1910	1920	1930
Women Teachers	16	89	98	288	594	1589
Percentage of Total	8.4	17	17.3	35.1	50.9	49.8
Male Teachers	175	433	470	532	574	1600
Percentage of Total	91.6	83	82.7	64.9	49.1	50.2
Total Teachers	191	522	568	820	1168	3189

Note: The figures for 1920 do not include 177 day vocational schoolteachers as they were not reported by gender in the *Annual Report* for 1919.

Sources: *Annual Report* (1880-81), 100-101; (1892), 306; (1899), 210; (1909), 608; (1919), 352; (1931); 91, 298.

It was the opening of university education to women in Canada during the late nineteenth century that gave them the ability to compete both academically and professionally for secondary school teaching positions. Toronto's early

The "Feminization" of the High School

women secondary schoolteachers were part of a new generation of university-educated women, representing some of the first women to have graduated from the University of Toronto. The university had allowed women to write matriculation exams in 1875, but it was not until 1884 that they could officially register as undergraduate students and thereby receive degrees.[34] In addition to teaching certificates, Nellie Spence, Louise Rychman, and Eliza Balmer had B.A.s, and Gertrude Lawler and Madge Robertson had Master's degrees when they began teaching.[35] In contrast to the women teachers at Jameson and Harbord, Thomas and MacMurchy earned their degrees after they began teaching. Janie Thomas was hired with a Professional Teaching Certificate and earned a B.A. by 1900, and an M.A. by 1910,[36] both from the University of Toronto.[37] Helen MacMurchy was hired without a degree or certification to teach. A year later, she was given a two-month leave of absence to take a "high professional certificate," at which time she was required to provide her own substitute for the period that she was absent from the school. MacMurchy gave up teaching in 1901 to pursue a career in medicine.[38] Charlotte Thompson was the only woman in this early group of secondary schoolteachers who did not earn a university degree. She taught for over twenty years at Jarvis with a teaching certificate.[39] Although women had attained access to university education during the late nineteenth century, they accounted for only a small percentage of university students in Canada. In 1881-2 women represented .1% of students in Canadian universities; this increased to 12.2% by 1891.[40]

Secondly, secondary school teaching was viewed as a male occupation because the primary role of the secondary school was still seen as the education of boys. Despite the opening of public secondary schooling to girls, the concern remained to create a stable male teaching force. This, in turn, was to secure the best possible level of instruction to educate "the leading men of the next generation." The Chief Superintendent of Education, Egerton Ryerson, repeatedly drew the connection between secondary schooling and male concerns. In 1872 he designated the collegiate institute as a school that would

> prepare youths for certain professions, and especially for the universities, where will be completed the education of men for the learned professions, and for the Professorships in Colleges, and Masterships in the Collegiate Institutes and High Schools.[41]

Although girls were being admitted into secondary schools, including the classical program, this education was not to prepare them for the profession of secondary school teaching.

Despite these views, it was Ryerson who in 1872 had approved of the "employment of a qualified female as the second teacher" in several of the secondary schools in Ontario.[42] But he was still primarily concerned with providing an adequate number of male teachers to facilitate the expansion of the secondary schools, to ensure the "quality of instruction" for the boys in attendance. In 1873 he stipulated that schools with an average attendance of less than 35 pupils could operate sufficiently with two teachers. When attendance reached between 35 and 60, three teachers had to be employed, and for each "successive increment of 25" an additional teacher should be hired. But this policy did not extend to the hiring of women teachers, for Ryerson went on to state that trustees should allow for the hiring of "one Female Teacher in every mixed school," increasing their number according to the proportion of female pupils only. There was no indication as to how many women teachers were to be hired per number of girls, possibly leaving this to the discretion of the individual school headmaster or principal. Ryerson's hiring policy for secondary schoolteachers reflected the traditional role of women as teachers of girls at the secondary level, specifying two separate procedures, one for male teachers and a second for the women.[43]

II

During the first decade of the twentieth century the number of women in secondary school teaching in the province increased greatly. In 1910 there were 288 women teachers, representing 35.1% of the total secondary school teaching population of 820 and double the percentage of 17.3% in 1900. By 1920 the proportion of women secondary schoolteachers had increased again, representing 50.9% or 594 compared to 574 men teachers. The proportion of women did however, remain stable by 1930, at 49.8% (Table 1). Ontario educators were alarmed by this rapid increase in women secondary schoolteachers. They blamed low salaries and a shortage of qualified teachers.

In 1904, Richard Harcourt, Minister of Education, noted that since 1896 there had been increasingly fewer students attending County Model Schools in Ontario, and recently the numbers preparing for secondary school teaching had been decreasing as well. To meet their need for teachers many county school boards were issuing temporary certificates. Concerned with declining standards, Harcourt felt that the low salaries being paid to teachers had caused the shortage. He argued that in an era of general prosperity within the province, teachers' salaries had to be increased to attract more numbers to the profession.[44]

The "Feminization" of the High School

The following year, R.A. Pyne, the new Minister of Education, repeated the observation that many school boards were issuing temporary certificates in order to meet their need for secondary schoolteachers. Although teachers' salaries had increased, he argued, they were still the lowest salaries of all professions in the province. This not only discouraged many young people from entering teaching, but held back many new teachers from qualifying for first-class certification. As a result teachers holding second-class certificates, renewed third-class certificates, and "Old Country Board certificates" far outnumbered those with first-class certification. The solution, he felt, lay with the province. Legislative grants had to be given less freely to schools that continued to hire secondary schoolteachers who were not adequately qualified.[45]

But Pyne's attention had also been drawn to the number of women employed in secondary school teaching. In 1904, the Mosley Commission, which had been sent to the United States during the previous year to investigate education there, reported its findings to the Department of Education. The commissioners found that elementary schools in the United States, as in Canada, were mostly staffed by women. However, they also found that the number of male teachers in American high schools and universities was decreasing yearly. On receiving the Commission's report, Pyne became concerned with the fact that many urban secondary schools in Ontario were of "too great a disposition to employ, even for the more advanced pupils, women teachers." Still, the proportion of women secondary schoolteachers was not so great as to cause "alarm." He proposed that the poor salaries being paid to teachers could not attract male teachers to the secondary schools. The problem arose from "false views of economy," he stated. "If trustees were willing to give proper salaries, the difficulty would be readily met."[46]

Pyne argued that if the objective of education was merely to impart knowledge then he would be willing to agree with the "frequently" heard statement that "the work of the woman [was] as good in the school as that of the man." But since an essential goal of education was character building, women were not suitable teachers for older boys.

> It is unreasonable to think that for large boys a woman is as competent as a man.... If proper discipline is to be exercised, that force of character which a well trained male teacher should possess is essential.

Women were necessary in the secondary schools, but only because of the large number of girls in attendance. He therefore recommended that secondary schools not employ more than one woman teacher for every two men on staff.[47]

Gender And Education In Ontario: An Historical Reader

Writing in the *Queen's Quarterly* in 1909, J.F. Macdonald was concerned that many secondary schools in the province had started the school year understaffed. The greater demand for teachers, he stated, had resulted in an increase in the starting salaries of secondary schoolteachers since the late nineteenth century, and a general increase in the average salary earned over the last five years. But Macdonald contended that the reported shortages were localized, and that in fact over the last decade the number of secondary schoolteachers had nearly doubled. The real teacher shortage, Macdonald stated, was a decrease in the number of male specialists available. From 1900 to 1908, the number of specialists had declined from 51 to 32. Collegiates were required to have five specialists on staff, one in mathematics, science, classics, moderns, and English and history, and often to fill this need, school boards were promoting women teachers with "the lowest assistants' certificates" to fill the specialist positions. But what concerned Macdonald even more was that while the number of women secondary schoolteachers had increased between 1903 and 1909, the proportions holding university degrees and specialist qualifications had actually decreased. With the general increase in the average secondary schoolteachers' salary during this same time period, women secondary teachers on average were, therefore, earning $150 more in 1909 compared to 1904, while their qualifications had in fact declined.[48]

Macdonald cited two reasons for the shortage of male specialists. Firstly, few "college men" were willing to complete the "grind" of the specialists' course, which was the hardest university program, and then go on to a fifth year at the Faculty of Education in order to teach, when they could earn higher salaries in business and in engineering. Since 1900 especially, an increasing number of men were choosing engineering, which, he stated, offered higher starting salaries to science graduates than they could possibly hope to achieve in teaching. Secondly, Macdonald argued that there had always been a "leakage of trained teachers" out of the profession. After working for a few years women left to marry, while men took higher-paying jobs as insurance agents or inspectors in public schools in the Northwest. But recently the problem had intensified. Since 1904, at least half of the public school inspectors and high schoolteachers in Alberta and Saskatchewan had once been teachers in Ontario's high schools. Macdonald doubted that the number of male graduates seeking first-class certification for high school teaching would ever increase. In the last year, only 20 of the 112 women specialists were in mathematics, science, and the classics. With most women specialists "crowded" into history, English, and moderns, Macdonald felt confident that the larger schools would "continue to need male assistants for a good many years to come."[49] In 1911, the province attempted to address the teacher shortage problem by requiring

The "Feminization" of the High School

normal and model school graduates to sign an agreement promising to spend their first year of teaching in Ontario.[50]

Macdonald predicted that the trend towards hiring more women secondary schoolteachers could continue, having already increased from 21% in 1903 to 32% in 1908. "Let the experts worry as much as they please over what they call the 'feminization' of the high schools, it is coming in Ontario," he stated. But he hoped that the secondary schoolteachers' salary figures quoted for the years 1904 to 1908, which showed the average male teacher's salary as having increased steadily above that of women, would serve to attract more men to the profession. When women held positions as department heads, they were paid at the same rate as men in these positions, but Macdonald claimed that the recent policy of many school boards to hire only those women with the "lowest grade of assistant's certificate" for junior positions in smaller secondary schools had resulted in keeping the average salary of women secondary schoolteachers $400 below that of the average male teacher's salary. Many school boards were "prejudiced in favour" of hiring male secondary schoolteachers; hence, given a choice, they would hire a man over a woman for secondary school teaching. This was carried out, he stated, in order to maintain proper discipline within the secondary schools. Although Macdonald was not willing to discuss the validity of the opinions behind these actions, he clearly supported them, for he believed that this would arrest what had been an "abnormally rapid increase" in women secondary schoolteachers.[51]

Macdonald's use of the term "feminization" must be addressed within its historical context, for he was clearly referring to more than the numerical dominance of women teachers in the secondary schools. Unlike Pyne, Macdonald was less concerned with women teachers' inability to provide the proper discipline to educate older boys as with the fact that women were posing a threat to the status of the teaching profession. While Pyne and Harcourt both addressed declining standards generally as the shortage of teachers increased, it was Macdonald who recognized that the increasing number of women being hired as specialists was pulling "standards" down within the profession. Unlike Pyne, Macdonald was resigned to the fact that women would continue to increase in secondary school teaching. However, he contended that if the *number* of women could not be limited in the long run, then women had at least to be kept out of the higher-paying positions and schools. Over the next decade the campaign to limit women in secondary school teaching gained greater momentum, as the efforts to increase salaries and improve standards within the profession were directed at men, with the hope of attracting more men to teaching.

Gender And Education In Ontario: An Historical Reader

Writing in the journal *The School* in 1914, Peter Sandiford, a member of the Faculty of Education at the University of Toronto, also argued that the average salaries of women secondary schoolteachers were below those of male teachers in these schools. Years of experience determined the rate of pay, and since women did not stay in teaching as long as men, their salaries were being kept, on average, below those of men. By calculating the distribution of the province's secondary schoolteachers' salaries by years of experience and gender, he concluded that during the early years of teaching women earned on average lower salaries than men; however, "after fourteen years there are so few women left in the profession that to all intents and purposes the [salary distribution] curve for men and women is the same as for men teachers alone." Sandiford stated that the "facts probably indicated that in many cases there must be unequal pay for equal work"; however, he argued that the major reason for the generally low salaries earned by women teachers was the high rate at which they left the profession. Men left teaching to take up other professions, but women left at an even higher rate for marriage, causing a great "leakage of women teachers" in the province. Male secondary schoolteachers, Sandiford claimed, had an average professional life of 14.2 years, whereas women on average taught for only 5.85 years. Although it was to be expected that women give up teaching upon marriage, it was still of value to the community to train women for teaching. He maintained that school boards had to realize that since 1882, considering both public and secondary school teaching, women had been crowding men out of the profession. He concluded by stating that since many people felt that children should not be taught exclusively by women, "there is a premium put upon the services of men teachers...[and this] is probably a deciding factor in favour of higher salaries for men."[52]

At the end of World War I, Macdonald again addressed the problem of the shortage of male secondary schoolteachers. He maintained that men returning from the war were still choosing professions which offered more freedom than teaching, such as business, law, medicine, and engineering. "The Ontario educational system is the most thoroughly regulated and beruled on earth," he stated. Bureaucratic regulations were chasing bright young men to other professions, where they would have "more elbow room." He continued that men on the whole did not work well under the "rigid Paternalism" characteristic of the Department of Education, while "women seemed to suffer it more gladly, whether from great docility of nature or because three out of four of them have no intention of staying in the profession." To attract more men to the profession, Macdonald demanded that secondary schoolteachers be granted greater professional responsibility.[53]

The "Feminization" of the High School

Macdonald also argued that men would not be attracted to a profession where women were being paid equal salaries when initially hired. Urban schools made no distinction in salaries paid to both men and women secondary schoolteachers. Any differences in salaries were due to variations in individual qualifications. Macdonald warned that equal pay for apparently equal work would continue to result in fewer men entering secondary school teaching, as well as forcing many more to leave.

> Let us get the main point clear; if women receive the same pay as men, men will not go into the profession. Moreover, many men will leave it and the feminization of the schools, as someone has called it, will be rapidly completed.

Questioning what was meant by equal work, he proposed that, on the surface, the work of men and women teachers appeared equal, whereas in reality men performed two services and women only one. Men not only served the school board by teaching, they also provided a service to the state by marrying and rearing children. Most women teachers were spinsters and constituted "practically a celibate teaching order, though not under vows." They therefore provided only one service, that of teaching.[54]

In 1920, school inspector I.M. Levan reported that many secondary schools were staffed with only one male teacher, if indeed they had any. He argued that many boys, having never studied under a male teacher in public school, should for this very reason at least have the influence of a male teacher in secondary school. He was willing to concede that generally women teachers were "quite as effective" as men, but the "stronger personality" and "refined manners" of the male teacher were still essential to the education of boys. Particularly alarmed by the fact that more girls than boys were attending secondary school, he felt that male teachers were essential to keep boys in school by encouraging them in sports. Appealing to the Department of Education to attract more men to secondary school teaching, Levan proposed that the Department influence school boards and trustees to pay higher salaries to men as opposed to women in secondary school teaching.[55]

In 1922, when the Department of Education reported an increase in men enrolled in teacher training courses, especially the high school assistants' program,[56] the change was attributed to an increase in salaries, and the consequent reduction in the movement of teachers to other provinces, and to commerce and industry. R.H. Grant, the Minister of Education, felt certain that this trend would continue and that the number of certified male teachers would increase; and that within a short period of time the "supply" of male teachers in this province would "restore the former proportion of men and women teachers."[57] In 1926, the shortage of teachers was reported to be over, the Department of Education stating that in fact there was a surplus for the elementary and secondary schools.[58]

III

During the early twentieth century Toronto's secondary school system grew in both size and structure. The increasing number of schools and courses offered demanded that more teachers staff the collegiates and high schools. With the pressing shortage of male teachers in the province, women were increasingly relied upon to fill the available positions. An examination of women secondary schoolteachers in Toronto between 1900 and 1930 shows that they did not increase at the same rate as within the province as a whole.[59] The percentage of women teachers in the province's secondary schools had doubled during the first decade of the century from 17.3% to 35.1%, increasing again during the following decade to 50.9% by 1920 (Table 1). In contrast, the percentage of women teachers in Toronto's secondary schools increased only during the 1910s. In 1900 and 1910 the percentage of women teachers compared to the total number of secondary schoolteachers in Toronto was 19.4% and 18.4% respectively. During the 1910s the proportion of women teachers increased by the highest amount, accounting for 32.7% of the total in 1920. By 1930, the percentage of women had changed very little, reading 33.4% in that year. Women teachers held approximately one in three teaching positions in Toronto's secondary schools in 1920 and 1930, compared to one in four in 1900 and 1910 (Table 2).

Between 1900 and 1930, increasing urban expansion and changes in provincial educational policy can be seen to have affected both the size and structure of the secondary school system in Toronto. At the beginning of the century there were three collegiate institutes: Jarvis, Jameson (Parkdale), and Harbord. Expansion occurred primarily with the addition of five existing high schools that were brought under the jurisdiction of Toronto's secondary school system by 1910. With the annexation of surrounding areas to the city of Toronto, North West High School (renamed Oakwood), Humberside, East Toronto High School (renamed Malvern), and Riverdale High school became part of the Toronto system.[60] In 1910, the Technical School, which had been operating under business and labour interest since 1891,[61] was brought within the control of the Toronto Board of Education as the Technical High School.

The "Feminization" of the High School

Table 2—NUMBER AND PERCENTAGE OF WOMEN AND MEN SECONDARY
SCHOOLTEACHERS IN TORONTO: 1881 - 1930

	1881	1892	1900	1910	1920	1930
Women Teachers	1	7	6	19	73	230
Percentage of Total	11.1	21.9	19.4	18.4	32.7	33.4
Male Teachers	8	25	25	84	150	458
Percentage of Total	88.9	78.1	80.6	81.6	67.3	66.6
Total Teachers	9	32	31	103	223	688

Note: The number of teachers reported for Toronto in the *Annual Report* for 1880-81,
unlike the Collegiate Institute Minutes, does not reflect the presence of a second
woman teacher.

Sources: *Annual Reports* (1880-81), 100; (1892), 299; The Toronto Collegiate Institute
Board Minutes, 1900; Toronto Board of Education Handbooks, 1910, 1920, and
1930.

The addition of the Toronto Technical School in 1910 was the most important change in the structure of the public secondary school system in the city to occur during the early twentieth century and was to mark the beginning of a trend in the expansion of vocational schooling during the following two decades. In 1915, the Technical School was relocated in larger premises and renamed the Central Technical High School. In the following year a second specialized school was opened, the Central High School of Commerce.[62] During the 1920s, nine new secondary schools were built within the Toronto system; eight were vocational high schools—two technical, three commercial, and three auxiliary/vocational.[63] The Eastern High school of Commerce and the Danforth Branch Technical School were opened in 1925. Western Branch Technical School was built in 1928 and housed in the same building as the newly established Western High School of Commerce. They operated as two schools under the same roof until they were separated in 1930. Northern Vocational High School opened in 1930 as a commercial school, offering a program of technical, commercial, and academic courses. In comparison to the growth of the vocational high schools during the 1910s and 1920s, only two new collegiates appeared in the city. In 1912, North Toronto High School (renamed Malvern) was annexed to the city's system; and in 1925, Bloor Collegiate opened the same year that Jarvis Collegiate expanded to accommodate more students.[64]

In the late 1920s, three auxiliary/vocational high schools were opened in the city. These schools were promoted by Mrs. Edith L. Groves,[65] a member of the

Toronto Board of Education, who had been sent to the United States to investigate vocational schools there. Toronto's auxiliary schools offered a two-year program designed to train "subnormal adolescent children" over the age of thirteen. These youths had either attended auxiliary training classes in public school or were selected from regular elementary schools by a board consisting of the school principal, an inspector, and a health officer.[66] The students were segregated by gender in separate schools. The Edith L. Groves School for girls and the Junior Vocational School for boys offered academic and vocational courses for adolescents who, school officials felt, were not being adequately educated within the existing system. Educators considered that the auxiliary program would do more to train these adolescents "to become useful and self-supporting citizens."[67] The Bolton Avenue School for Girls offered a similar curriculum as the Edith L. Groves School, but it was designed to give troublesome girls, who did not fit into the regular school program, a vocationally "corrective" education. To channel problem thirteen-year-old girls out of the regular schools and into Bolton Avenue, school principals and Board psychiatrists worked together to convince the parents of these adolescents of the benefits that this school had to offer their daughters. Educators saw Bolton Avenue as providing an alternative to the home environment rather than working in conjunction with it.[68]

The introduction of vocational high schools within the Toronto public school system between 1910 and 1920 was largely the result of provincial efforts to make public secondary schooling responsible for providing youths with job-related skills training. In 1904, there had been seven possible courses available in the collegiate institutes and high schools: general, commercial, manual training, household science, agriculture, university matriculation, and normal school entrance.[69] Harcourt noted that the objective of manual training and technical classes in the high schools was to prepare adolescents for the changes in the mechanical sciences. Foreseeing the disappearance of unskilled labourers, Harcourt felt it was necessary for the high schools to offer non-academic courses to prepare students for industrial work.[70] The Industrial Education Act of 1911 opened the way for a more theoretical application of vocational education, whether technical, commercial, or agricultural, within specialized commercial, technical, and vocational high schools.[71]

During the 1910s and 1920s, the secondary school curriculum in Toronto became increasingly diversified, largely as a result of the introduction of the vocational high schools. In 1910, the Technical High School taught commerce and finance along with industrial and technical subjects including architecture. By 1930, the technical schools were offering a wider variety of subjects such as engineering and courses relating to the construction industry. The boys'

The "Feminization" of the High School

auxiliary/vocational school primarily taught skilled trades such as barbering, shoe repair, painting, and typewriting. With the opening of the commercial high school the technical school no longer taught commerce. Although several of the collegiates continued to teach commerce and finance, and bookkeeping,[72] by 1910, they were no longer teaching stenography and typing as they had been earlier.[73] The commercial high schools were able to offer a wider variety of clerical, secretarial, and business subjects including economics, salesmanship, and advertising. Domestic or household science was first taught in the Technical High School in 1910. During the following two decades domestic science was more widely offered in the technical high schools, although several collegiates and one commercial high school did teach household science. Besides teaching household science, the vocational curriculum of the girls' auxiliary high schools was largely made up of subjects designed to prepare the students for jobs in the needle trade, in the service industry, and as clerical typists.[74]

Expansion of the secondary school system during the 1920s occurred in response to a greater demand for vocational education as an increasingly greater number of adolescents were attending these high schools. In 1900, enrolment in the city's collegiates was 1,298; this increased to 4,446 in 1910. By 1930, secondary school enrolment had reached 22,367, which included 12,778 students attending the technical, commercial, and auxiliary high schools. This was a substantial increase of 13,997 over the total enrolment figure of 8,370 reported for 1920, the majority of this increase having taken place in the vocational high schools, where enrolment rose by 8,727 from 1920. In 1930, enrolment in the vocational high schools accounted for 57.1% of the total secondary school enrolment, compared to 48.4% in 1920 and 25.3% in 1910. Girls made up 59.1% of the Technical High School enrolment in 1910. With the opening of the commercial high school this changed, and girls represented 37.9% of the technical school enrolment in 1920 and 34.4% in 1930, while making up 70% of the commercial high school student body in both these years.[75] The trend towards commercial education for girls probably reflected the fact that since the late nineteenth century the number of women employed in clerical jobs had been steadily increasing; by 1911, they represented 32.6% of all clerical workers, increasing to 41.8% in 1921.[76]

In 1922, the Department of Education reported that secondary school attendance in the province had increased by 22.5% for the year 1921-22, compared to 1920-21, and was the highest it had ever been in Ontario.[7] Credit for the increase in attendance was attributed to the Adolescent School Attendance Act of 1921, which extended the compulsory school-leaving age from fourteen to sixteen.[78] Since fourteen was the customary age of public school completion, there had been no means to enforce secondary school

Table 3—DISTRIBUTION BY SCHOOL OF WOMEN AND MEN SECONDARY SCHOOLTEACHERS IN TORONTO: 1900-1930

Name of School	1900			1910			1920			1930		
	W	%W	M	W	%W	M	W	%W	M	W	%W	M
Collegiate Institutes												
Jarvis	2	20.0	8	4	25.0	12	5	29.4	12	10	29.4	24
Parkdale	2	22.0	7	3	21.4	11	6	33.3	12	11	37.9	18
Harbord	2	16.6	10	2	13.3	13	6	27.3	16	12	36.4	21
Oakwood				1	10.0	9	12	44.4	15	16	43.2	21
Humberside				1	11.1	8	6	35.3	11	14	38.9	22
Malvern				1	33.3	2	3	30.0	7	8	30.8	18
Riverdale				1	12.5	7	8	42.1	11	10	30.3	23
North Toronto							2	11.1	7	13	33.3	26
Bloor										8	36.4	14
Vocational High Schools												
Central Tech.				6	21.4	22	16	28.6	40	27	30.0	63
Danforth Tech.										10	24.4	31
Western Tech.										7	19.4	29
Central Comm.							9	32.1	19	19	31.7	41
Eastern Comm.										17	39.0	29
Western Comm.										9	25.0	27
Northern Voc.										16	12.8	31
Auxiliary High Schools												
Junior Voc.										1	4.8	20
E.L. Groves										13	100	--
Bolton Ave.										9	100	--
Total Teachers	6		25	19		84	73		150	230		458

Sources: Toronto Collegiate Institute Board Minutes, 1900; Toronto Board of Education Handbooks, 1910, 1920, and 1930.

The "Feminization" of the High School

attendance in the province. The Adolescent School Attendance Act would make secondary school attendance compulsory for the first time in Ontario.[79]

Robert Stamp concludes that the School Act of 1921 was a symptom rather than a cause of change, for many contemporary educators had observed that school attendance had been increasing before the beginning of the First World War. After the war, the economic and social conditions that had been developing before 1914 were accentuated, and secondary school attendance continued to grow at a higher rate. Parents recognized that with increasing industrialization, jobs for those without a secondary school education were declining, and they were therefore encouraging their adolescent children to attend secondary school.[80]

The demand for compulsory adolescent school attendance had largely come from the appeal to expand vocational education after the First World War. Ontario educators were concerned with the fact that a large number of adolescents were not continuing on to secondary school. In 1919, F.W. Merchant, Director of Technical Education for the province, stated that at least 80% of young people were not attending secondary school after completing the elementary grades.[81] Merchant wanted high schools to play a large role in Ontario's post-war reconstruction program by training skilled labour. Educators felt that with the decreasing demand for adolescent labour and the collapse of the apprenticeship system, greater responsibility had to be placed on the secondary school to train working-class youths who might have otherwise gone directly from elementary school to industry without attending high school.[82] The vocational high school program would provide the job-related training they needed. Adolescents between the ages of fourteen and sixteen, who could prove the need to work, would be issued employment certificates, and those who were needed by their parents at home to do "household tasks" would be issued home permits. The government, recognizing that working youth was largely an urban problem, stipulated in the School Act that municipalities with a population of 5,000 and over were required to provide part-time classes for these adolescents, who would have to attend school for 400 hours a year.[83] Secondary school fees were also abolished in schools still charging them.[84] The Toronto Board of Education had stopped charging fees for first form ten years earlier.[85]

What was the distribution of women teachers in the expanding secondary school system in Toronto during these years? As Table 3 shows, in 1900 each of the three schools employed two of the six women teachers in the city. With the exception of Julia Hillock, who had been appointed to Jameson Collegiate in that year, the remaining five teachers were all original women staff members. By 1910, despite the addition of six secondary schools, only a small number of new women teachers appeared within the system. Only four schools had more than one woman teacher on staff, and only in three of them did women represent between 21% and 25% of the total staff. The Technical High School had both the largest staff of teachers and the largest number of women teachers of the city's secondary schools, representing 21.4% of the total women teachers in the school. The decade between 1910 and 1920 was the period of the greatest expansion in the proportion of women teachers during this thirty-year period. In 1920, women represented between 27.3% and 44.4% of the teaching staff in all of the secondary schools but one. During the 1910s, collegiate expansion was accomplished with the hiring of more women than men teachers. This pattern was visible in the seven schools that had existed in 1910. In contrast, the technical high school expanded by hiring almost double the number of men to women teachers. Between 1920 and 1930, although almost twice as many male teachers were hired to staff the expanding system, women still retained as high a percentage of the teaching staff in the same schools as had existed in 1920, as six schools doubled their number of women teachers. In only one secondary school did the percentage of women teachers on staff in 1930 show a substantial decline from 1920. The proportion of women teachers on staff in twelve secondary schools in 1930 ranged between 29.4% and 43.2% and in only one school did the proportion of women fall below 25%. The three auxiliary schools presented a different teaching environment for women during the 1920s. The two girls' schools, Edith L. Groves School and Bolton Avenue, both had a teaching staff totally composed of women, whereas the boys' Junior Vocational School was staffed by twenty male teachers and one woman (Table 3).

By 1930, the collegiates no longer claimed a majority of secondary schoolteachers in the city, either men or women, as in 1910 and 1920. In 1910, 68.4%, and in 1920, 65.6% of the women secondary schoolteachers in the city taught in the collegiates; this declined to 44.4% in 1930. With commercial school expansion during the 1920s, 26.5% of the women secondary schoolteachers in 1930 were now teaching in these four high schools, compared to 12.3% in 1920. In contrast, the percentage of women teaching in the technical schools declined from 21.9% in 1920 to 19.1% in 1930. Lastly, 10% of the women secondary schoolteachers in 1930 taught in the three auxiliary high schools.[86]

The figures in Table 4 represent the numbers and relative percentages of women teachers who taught each subject; but they do not correspond with the total number of women teachers on staff in each particular year of this study as the majority of women teachers employed during this period taught more than one subject. In 1900, all of the women secondary schoolteachers taught

The "Feminization" of the High School

either English or a language such as French or German. Only one woman taught history and one mathematics, both as a second subject. With collegiate expansion during the first decade the majority of women taught English, representing 73.7% of the women teachers in 1910. The second largest number of women teachers in 1910 taught a language and English, or history, or the new collegiate subject of calisthenics, representing 57.9% of the total number of women teachers that year. The demand for more teachers during the 1910s to staff the expanding secondary schools, especially the collegiates, found a smaller percentage of women teaching English, languages, and history. In 1920, 46.6% of the women secondary schoolteachers taught English, 27.4% taught one or more language, and 13.6% taught history. Women were now teaching a large number of collegiate arts subjects that had previously been taught by men, such as Latin, commerce, art, geography, and science. With collegiate expansion more women were teaching physical training in 1920 compared to 1910, resulting in a proportional increase of these teachers from 21.1% to 27.4%, 80% of whom were employed in the collegiates. In 1910, the majority of women in the technical school taught English and/or a language, whereas in 1920 ten of the sixteen women teachers in the technical school were now teaching one subject, domestic science (and an eleventh taught art and design and embroidery) (Table 4).

There were more women teaching the same arts subjects in 1930 than in 1920, but there was a decrease in the percentages of women teaching most of these subjects. By 1930, the percentage of women teaching English and languages had decreased to 40% and 21.7% respectively. A proportional decrease can be particularly noted in the case of physical training, where the percentage of women teaching this subject declined from 27.4% in 1920 to 10.4% in 1930. Although the majority of women employed in all the secondary schools were still teaching arts subjects in 1930, the increasing number of vocational high schools provided more opportunities for women teaching the expanding gender-related vocational subjects. In 1930, 23% of the women teachers in the secondary schools taught domestic science (and the varied vocational subjects offered for girls in the technical and auxiliary schools), compared to 17.8% in 1920. All of the women teaching domestic science were employed in the technical and vocational schools, with the exception of one in 1920 and two in 1930 who taught household science in the collegiates. Expansion of the commercial high schools found more women teaching commercial subjects, which had largely been taught by men just ten years earlier. The percentage of women teaching commercial subjects represented 11.3% in 1930, compared to 4.1% in 1920 (Table 4), which accounted for 45% of the women teaching in the commercial and auxiliary high schools. Despite

Table 4—SUBJECTS TAUGHT BY WOMEN SECONDARY SCHOOLTEACHERS IN TORONTO: 1900-1930

Subject	1900 #	1900 %	1910 #	1910 %	1920 #	1920 %	1930 #	1930 %
English	3	50.0	14	73.7	34	46.6	92	40.0
Languages	3	50.0	11	57.9	20	27.4	50	21.7
History	1	16.6	4	21.1	10	13.6	33	14.3
Mathematics	1	16.6			6	8.2	14	6.1
Latin					5	6.8	21	9.1
Science					4	5.5	5	2.2
Geography					2	2.7	7	3.0
General Subjects					2	2.7	2	0.9
Art					4	5.5	10	4.3
Music							4	1.7
Library							1	0.4
Health							1	0.4
Drama							1	0.4
Current Events							1	0.4
Physical Tr.			4	21.1	20	27.4	24	10.4
Domestic Sci.			3	15.8	13	17.8	53	23.0
Commerce					3	4.1	26	11.3
Industrial Art							1	0.4
Horticulture							1	0.4
Total Women Teachers	6		19		73		230	

Note: Vocational subjects such as sewing, dressmaking, embroidery, millinery, handicrafts, laundry, cooking, and home nursing have been included with domestic science. In 1900, 66.7% of the women teachers taught two subjects; in 1910, 63.2% taught between two and four subjects, with one woman teaching seven subjects; in 1920, 75.3% and in 1930, 50.9% of the women taught between two and four subjects.

Sources: Toronto Collegiate Institute Board of Education Minutes, 1900; Toronto Board of Education Handbooks, 1910, 1920, and 1930.

The "Feminization" of the High School

the large percentage of girls who were attending the commercial high school in 1920, and the Technical High School in 1910 when it taught commerce, women had been slow to be accepted as teachers of commerce. One possible explanation is that this trend followed the generally slow acceptance of women in clerical work, for it was not until the 1920s that clerical work became identified as acceptable women's work.[87] By 1930 the large number of women teaching high school commercial subjects reflected the changing attitude regarding women's work. In 1930, over half of the women teachers in the city were employed in the vocational high schools, but only one-third of these teachers taught arts subjects, while the remainder taught the wide variety of gender-related vocational subjects being offered for girls.

In 1900 the majority of all collegiate teachers, both men and women, held positions as specialists. Only two categories of teachers were noted in 1910, principal and assistant, thus making it impossible to draw a comparison between the positions held by men and women until 1920 and 1930. Table 4 shows that in 1920, there were six women department heads and four directors (three in the Technical School), which represented 4.5% of the teaching population that year. In the next decade year there were seventeen women department heads and nine directors (two in the Technical School). The two gender-segregated auxiliary/vocational high schools provided a different opportunity for women teachers, for it was in these two schools that women were employed for the first time in the city as secondary school principals. While a larger proportion of male teachers held positions as principals, directors, department heads, and specialists in both 1920 and 1930, the number of women in these positions increased proportionally during the decade, representing 4.5% and 17.7% of the total number of teachers in 1920 and 1930 respectively (Table 5).

From 1900 to 1930, the largest number of teachers, including both women and men, held academic degrees. By 1930, there were an increasing number of teachers with pedagogical degrees, but no woman held one until 1930, when there were four women with a Bachelor of Pedagogy. Table 6 indicates that between 1900 and 1930 there was a slowly declining percentage of teachers with degrees, which was especially true for the male teachers by 1920. In 1920, there was a substantially larger percentage of men than women teachers holding teaching certificates. Approximately half of these men held only a teaching certificate and were employed in the Central High School of Commerce teaching commercial subjects, representing three-quarters of the male commercial teachers in the school. In 1930, there was a considerably larger percentage of women teachers than men who held teaching certificates

(Table 6). The majority of their certificates were either household science, manual training, or auxiliary and vocational teaching, in comparison to 1920,

Table 5—POSITIONS HELD BY WOMEN AND MEN SECONDARY SCHOOLTEACHERS IN TORONTO: 1900-1930

Position	1900		1910		1920		1930	
	W	M	W	M	W	M	W	M
Principal		3		8		10	2	17
Assistant Principal						1		1
Director					4	5	9	29
Department Head					6	42	17	62
Specialist	4	14					94	129
Sub-total	4	17		8	10	58	122	238
%	12.9	54.8		7.8	4.5	26.0	17.7	34.6
Assistant	2	8	19	76	62	85	80	166
Male Industrial Teachers						6		33
Teachers							21	19
Temporary					1	1	7	2
Sub-total	2	8	19	76	63	92	108	220
%	6.5	25.8	18.4	73.8	28.8	41.2	15.7	32.0
Total Teachers	6	25	19	84	73	150	230	458
%	19.4	80.6	18.4	81.6	32.7	67.3	33.4	66.6

Sources: Toronto Collegiate Institute Board Minutes, 1900; Toronto Board of Education Handbooks, 1910, 1920, and 1930.

when all of the certificates held were either first-class or specialist, with the exception of one in manual training.[88] The auxiliary schools employed a larger percentage of women teachers holding these certificates, 73.3%, compared to 57.1% of the male teachers. All of these teachers, with the exception of four women and three men, held only teaching certificates, and not a university degree.[89]

Table 6—DEGREES AND CERTIFICATES HELD BY WOMEN AND MEN SECONDARY SCHOOLTEACHERS IN TORONTO: 1900-1930

	1900		1910		1920		1930	
	W	M	W	M	W	M	W	M
Degrees	5	23	17	74	63	117	178	360
%	83.3	92.0	89.5	88.0	86.3	78.0	77.4	78.6
Teaching Cert.	1	1	2	5	6	20	29	28
%	16.7	4.0	10.5	5.9	8.2	13.3	12.6	6.1
No Degree or Cert.		1		6	5	13	29	71
%		4.0		7.1	6.8	9.3	12.6	15.5
Total Teachers	6	25	19	84	73	150	230	458

Note: Totals for some years will exceed the total number of teachers, as several teachers held both a degree and a teaching certificate. Where teachers held more than one degree or certificate only one was counted.

Sources: Toronto Collegiate Institute Board Minutes, 1900; Toronto Board of Education Handbooks, 1910, 1920, and 1930.

From 1920 to 1930, the percentage of teachers who did not hold either a university degree or a teaching certificate increased from 6.8% to 12.6% for women and 9.3% to 15.5% for men (Table 6). A closer examination of the data reveals that 71% of the teachers who were not certified staffed the three technical schools in 1930. The number of uncertified women teachers in the technical high schools represented 52.3% of the total women teaching in these schools. In contrast, uncertified male teachers accounted for only 39% of the total male technical high school teaching staff. Twenty-one of the twenty-three uncertified women technical high schoolteachers taught household science, including sewing and millinery, representing 37.7% of the household science teachers in 1930. The technical high schools had been able to expand during the 1920s by employing a large number of vocational teachers, especially women, who did not hold teaching qualifications.[90]

Gender And Education In Ontario: An Historical Reader

Conclusion

During the first two decades of the twentieth century there was a shortage of teachers in Ontario's public schools which was acutely felt in the secondary schools. Educators were concerned that this shortage of secondary schoolteachers had led many school boards to hire an increasing number of women teachers. They were not prepared to accept the increase of women in secondary school teaching, arguing that if more than one-third of any secondary school was staffed by women teachers, the quality of education received by older boys would be compromised. It was the responsibility of the school boards, these educators argued, to attract more men into secondary schoolteaching by offering them higher salaries than were paid to women. By 1910, the percentage of women teachers in the province's secondary schools had increased to 35.1%, double that of 1900. In contrast, the percentage of women teachers in Toronto's secondary schools increased only during the 1910s, representing 32.7% in 1920, compared to 19.4% and 18.4% in 1900 and 1910 respectively. The Toronto Board may have been trying to prevent the trend toward a large number of women secondary schoolteachers that educators saw and deplored in the province as a whole.

The history of women in public secondary school teaching is the history of women entering a non-traditional aspect of public teaching. The evidence drawn from Toronto indicates that, prior to 1871, no woman had ever taught in the grammar school in the city, but with the extension of financial and moral support to the secondary schooling of girls we find women gradually entering this new public occupation during the late nineteenth and early twentieth centuries. And as university training was extended to women they were able to compete both academically and professionally for teaching positions. The data in this study tell us how women fitted into this occupation in Toronto as the secondary school system in the city expanded in size and scope. The percentage of women teachers increased greatly during the 1910s as they were filling an increasing demand for secondary schoolteachers in the collegiates that men could not meet. And by 1920, women were teaching a greater variety of arts subjects that had previously been taught by men. By the next decade, despite the fact that more men were available for more secondary school positions, women were able to compete for the growing number of vocational and collegiate teaching positions. The increasing number of vocational schools created more positions for women to teach the gender-related vocational subjects being taught to girls. Although the trend towards women teaching these subjects had been visible a decade earlier, by 1930 both the expanding system and changing social factors increased the secondary school teaching

The "Feminization" of the High School

opportunities for women. An increasing number of women who did not hold university degrees were hired to fill many of the vocational teaching positions. As the school structure and bureaucracy expanded, women took their place with men, although not always on equal grounds. Women had been represented in all positions except that of principal until 1930, when the gender-segregated auxiliary schools, devised by a woman, provided the first two secondary school principalships for women in the city. The expansion of the gender-related vocational high school courses during the 1920s made it possible for women to retain their foothold in secondary school teaching and not lose their ground proportionally.

Gender And Education In Ontario: An Historical Reader

Notes

1. Toronto Board of Education Archives, Jarvis Collegiate File, *The Telegram,* 29 Sept. 1922.
2. Collegiate Institute Board Minutes (hereafter Collegiate Minutes), 14 and 21 Aug. 1871, 19 Jan., 7 Feb., 6 Mar., 10 May, and 27 June 1872.
3. Ibid., 10 May, 27 June, 26 Feb., 6 Mar. 1872.
4. Alison Prentice, et al., *Canadian Women: A History* (Toronto: Harcourt Brace Jovanovich, 1988) 113-41.
5. Susan Houston and Alison Prentice have noted that Letitia Youmans was listed in the 1861 census as an assistant at the Colborne Grammar School in Northumberland County: Susan E. Houston and Alison Prentice, *Schooling and Scholars in Nineteenth-Century Ontario* (Toronto: University of Toronto Press, 1988) 11; 347-48, note 5. However, as the Colborne school was a union grammar and common school, she may have been in charge of the common school department. W. Millar and R. Gidney suggest that in the few cases in which women taught in grammar schools during this period, they were the teachers of the common school departments in such union schools, although they might very well have taught some subjects to the grammar school pupils. Private communication, W. Millar to author, 18 Dec. 1989.
6. Kate Rousmaniere, "To Prepare the Ideal Woman: Private Denominational Girls' Schooling in Late Nineteenth Century Ontario," (M.A., University of Toronto, 1984) 42-43.
7. Alison Prentice states that the entrance of women into common or elementary school teaching during the mid-nineteenth century was not the entrance of women into teaching as such, but into public school teaching, for there were many women teachers in the numerous "small private schools" that had been operating in the province since the early nineteenth century. See Susan Mann Trofimenkoff and Alison Prentice, eds., "The Feminization of Teaching," in *The Neglected Majority* (Toronto: McClelland and Stewart, 1977).
8. Beth Light and Alison Prentice, *Pioneer And Gentlewomen of British North America, 1713-1867* (Toronto: Hogtown Press, 1980) 63-64.
9. Rousmaniere, "To Prepare the Ideal Woman," 38-47.
10. Marion V. Royce, "Arguments Over the Education of Girls—Their Admission to Grammar Schools in This Province," *Ontario History* LXVII, 1 (Mar. 1975), 3-13.
11. Prentice, "The Feminization of Teaching," 49-65.

12. For a discussion of grammar schools in Ontario, the issue of girls attending these schools, and the background to the 1871 legislation, see Royce, "Arguments Over the Education of Girls"; R.D. Gidney and D.A. Lawr, "Egerton Ryerson and the Origins of the Ontario Secondary School," *Canadian Historical Review* LX, 4 (Dec. 1979), 442-65; Houston and Prentice, *Schooling and Scholars*, 310-37.

13. J.G. Hodgins, *Documentary History of Education in Upper Canada.* (Toronto, 1894-1910) [*DHE*], 1871, 112-13. In 1883 the Collegiates lost their original gender designation and were classified as such according to the provisions and structure of the schools and the qualifications of the teaching staff. Robert M. Stamp, *The Schools of Ontario, 1867-1967* (Toronto: University of Toronto Press, 1979) 7.

14. The second grammar school in the province that did not admit girls prior to 1871 was in Galt. Ann Margaret Gray, "Continuity in Change: the Effects on Girls of Co-Educational Secondary Schooling in Ontario 1860-1910," (M.A., University of Toronto, 1979) 23-24, 36.

15. Collegiate Minutes, 20 May, 14 and 21 Aug. 1871.

16. Gray, "Continuity in Change," 36-37.

17. Michael B. Katz, "The Emergence of Bureaucracy in Urban Education: The Boston Case, 1850-1885," *History of Education Quarterly* (Summer 1968) 155-87.

18. Collegiate Minutes, 17 Dec. 1873.

19. Honora M. Cochrane, ed., *Centennial Story, The Board of Education for The City of Toronto, 1850-1950* (Toronto: Nelson, 1950) 145.

20. Toronto Board of Education Archives, Jarvis Collegiate File, *The Telegram* (Toronto) 9 Sept. 1922.

21. Ibid.

22. Collegiate Minutes, 14 Dec. 1880, and 1888. Both women were students at the Toronto Collegiate, and Helen MacMurchy was the daughter of the headmaster, Dr. Archibald MacMurchy. Cochrane, *Centennial Story*, 145, and W. Stewart Wallace, ed., *The Dictionary of Canadian Biography*, 4th ed. (Toronto: MacMillan of Canada, 1978) 541.

23. Stamp, *The Schools of Ontario*, 38.

24. Cochrane, *Centennial Story*, 145.

25. Collegiate Minutes, 7 Jan. 1890.

26. *Annual Reports of The Minister of Education of Ontario* [hereafter *Annual Report*], 1891, 342, and 1892, 299.

27. Cochrane, *Centennial Story*, 148.

28. Collegiate Minutes, 6 Oct. 1891.

29. *DHE*, 1872, 179.

30. J.G. Althouse, *The Ontario Teacher: A Historical Account of Progress, 1800-1910* (Toronto: The Ontario Teachers' Federation, 1967) 140; (D.Paed diss., University of Toronto, 1929).

31. Robin S. Harris, *Quiet Evolution, A Study of The Educational System of Ontario* (Toronto: University of Toronto Press, 1967) 78, 80-81.

32. *Annual Report*, 1892, notes that 326 of the 522 secondary schoolteachers employed that year held university degrees. In Toronto 24 of the 32 teachers held degrees: 296-306.

34. Nancy Ramsay Thompson, "The Controversy Over the Admission of Women to University," (M.A., University of Toronto, 1973) 50-53.

35. *Annual Report*, 1899, 200. Eliza Balmer had been one of the women responsible for exerting pressure on the University of Toronto administration to allow women into lectures: Thompson, "Controversy," 50-53. Gertrude Lawler remained at Harbord as Head of the English Department until 1919, at which time she left to teach at the Faculty of Education at the University of Toronto, having been a member of the University Senate since 1910. In 1927 she was granted a Doctor of Law Degree. Lawler was also a member of the Women's Voters' League. "Our New Doctors of Law," *Teachers' Bulletin*, OSSTF, 7, 2 (June 1927) 49.

36. Collegiate Minutes, 7 Dec. 1881.

37. *Annual Report*, 1910, 428.

38. For more on the life of Helen MacMurchy see Kathleen McConnachie, "Methodology in the Study of Women in History: A Case Study of Helen MacMurchy, M.D.," *Ontario History* LXXV, 1 (Mar. 1983) 61-70. The Department of Education Annual Report shows Helen MacMurchy on the list of teachers at Jarvis for January 1900, whereas the *Dictionary of Canadian Biography* and McConnachie's article both state that MacMurchy graduated with a medical degree in 1901.

39. Cochrane, *Centennial Story*, 145; *Annual Report*, 1888, 326.

40. Gray, "Continuity in Change," 158.

41. *DHE*, 1871-72, 260.

42. *DHE*, 1872, 179.

43. *Annual Report*, 1873, 9-10.

44. *Annual Report*, 1903, xliv, xlv.

45. *Annual Report*, 1904, xliv.

46. *Annual Report*, 1904, xxxvii-xxxviii.

47. Ibid., xxxvii.

48. J.F. Macdonald, "Salaries in Ontario High Schools," *Queen's Quarterly* XXII, 2 (Oct., Nov., Dec. 1909) 132-34.

49. Ibid., 134-35.
50. *Annual Report,* 1911, x.
51. Macdonald, "Salaries in Ontario High Schools."
52. Peter Sandiford, "Salaries of Teachers in Ontario," *The School* III, 2 (Oct. 1914) 176-82; III, 4 (Dec. 1914) 250-54.
53. J.F. Macdonald, "Salaries in Ontario High Schools."
54. Ibid.
55. *Annual Report,* 1920, 49-51.
56. *Annual Report,* 1922, 97.
57. *Annual Report,* 1922, xii.
58. *Annual Report,* 1926, 2.
59. The data presented in this section of the paper were taken from three main sources: The Toronto Collegiate Institute Board Minutes for 1900, the Toronto Board of Education Handbooks for 1910, 1920, and 1930 (following the amalgamation of both boards in 1904), and the Department of Education *Annual Reports* from 1900 to 1930. The handbooks and minutes provide a list of all teachers employed in the city's collegiate institutes, and commercial, technical, and vocational high schools. The Department of Education *Reports* include a schedule of teachers listed by collegiate institute and high school for each municipality from 1889 until 1921, as well as the total number of teachers by gender. But the *Reports* do not offer as complete a source of information for secondary schoolteachers in comparison to the handbooks, which for the purpose of this study consistently provide more information on Toronto's secondary schoolteachers, including the positions they held, the subjects they taught, and their education. In addition, the names of the teachers employed in the technical schools were not included in the Department of Education *Reports* in 1910 and 1920. And in 1910, the total number of teachers in the province's technical schools was not provided by gender.
60. Cochrane, *Centennial Story,* 120-21.
61. Stamp, *The Schools of Ontario,* 44.
62. The Central High School of Commerce was the first commercial high school in Ontario. Cochrane, *Centennial Story,* 120-21.
63. Toronto Board of Education Handbooks (hereafter Handbooks), 1920, 1930.
64. Cochrane, *Centennial Story,* 120, 150, 210.
65. Edith Groves, a former teacher at Ryerson Public School, sat on the Board of Education for eleven years and was elected as chairman in

      1929. "Toronto's First Woman Chairman," *Teacher's Bulletin,* OSSTF, 9, 1 (Feb. 1929) 29.

66.   *Annual Report,* 1924, 50-51.
67.   "Edith L. Groves School," *Canadian School Board Journal* VI, 9 (Aug. 1927) 6.
68.   Miss C.I. Mackenzie, "Vocational Training for the Adolescent Girl," *Canadian School Board Journal* IX, 6 (June 1930) 15.
69.   Stamp, *The Schools of Ontario,* 80.
70.   *Annual Report,* 1903, xix.
71.   *Annual Report,* 1921, 24.
72.   Toronto Collegiate Institute Board Minutes, 1900; Handbooks, 1910, 1920, 1930.
73.   Cochrane, *Centennial Story,* 210.
74.   Handbooks, 1910, 1920, 1930.
75.   *Annual Report,* 1901, 36; 1911, 70, 78; 1920, 242, 250, 258; 1931, 232, 298. In contrast to the percentage of girls enrolled in the technical and commercial high schools in 1910, 1920, and 1930, the percentage of girls enrolled in the collegiate in 1910 and 1920 was 51.7% and 49.1% respectively, declining to 42.8% in 1930.
76.   Prentice, *Canadian Women: A History,* 113, 423.
77.   *Annual Report,* 1922, ix, xi, 34-35.
78.   *Annual Report,* 191, 17-18.
79.   *Annual Report,,* 1921, 39.
80.   Stamp, *The Schools of Ontario,* 110.
81.   *Annual Report,* 1919, 15.
82.   *Annual Report,* 1918, 20, 23, 26.
83.   *Annual Report,* 1919, 17.
84.   Stamp, *The Schools of Ontario,* 107.
85.   Cochrane, *Centennial Story,* 121.
86.   Gelman, "The 'Feminization' of the High Schools?" Table 2, 85.
87.   Prentice, *Canadian Women: A History,* 128.
88.   Gelman, "The 'Feminization' of the High Schools?" Table 10, 94.
89.   Handbooks, 1930.
90.   Ibid.

"A Room of One's Own": The Early Years of the Toronto Women Teachers' Association

Harry Smaller[*]

Introduction

In 1876 Egerton Ryerson, the Chief Superintendent of Education for Ontario, retired from his post, one which he had held continuously for thirty-two years. No successor was appointed. Rather, his office was abolished and a new position of Minister of Education was established in the provincial cabinet—an event which clearly signalled the advent of a number of significant, and intended, changes in the Ontario educational system.

Among many other schooling matters affected by these shifting political winds, there was an abrupt move to increase dramatically the involvement of the provincial state in local teachers' organizations. Within the year, regulations were passed, stating that "[i]n each County or Inspectoral Division a Teachers' Association shall be formed," giving the hours of their operation, and making it clear that "all questions and discussion foreign to the teachers' work should be avoided."[1] In 1884, these regulations were strengthened, by placing "the Education Department, on consultation with the Inspector or Inspectors of the county or divisional Institute" in charge of setting the time, place and content of each annual meeting. Among other additions, these new regulations stated that

> It shall be the duty of every teacher to attend continuously all the meetings of the Institute held in his county or inspectoral division...and in the event of his inability so to attend, he shall report to his Inspector, giving reasons for his absence.

The 1884 Act also mandated the hiring of a Provincial Director of Teachers' Institutes, who, among other things, was required to "attend the annual meeting of each [county] Institute, and...discuss at least three subjects on the program."[2]

---

[*] An earlier draft of this paper was presented at the 1988 Biennial Conference of the Canadian History of Education Association, London, Ontario, October 1988.

Gender And Education In Ontario: An Historical Reader

These actions had wide ranging effects on all teachers across the province, as well as on their local associations which, where they existed, had been voluntary in nature and somewhat independent of direction by state officials. Of particular significance were the effects of these regulations on women teachers in the province, and especially those in the highly feminized teaching staffs of the larger towns and cities. In fact, it was probably no coincidence that, directly following this legislative incursion, the province's first women teachers' organization emerged, the Women Teachers' Association of Toronto. It is the purpose of this paper, then, both to explore the effects on women teachers of the state's attempts to regulate teacher associations, as well as to examine the first twenty-five years of the Women Teachers' Association of Toronto. As I hope to demonstrate, state regulation over these early teacher unions, implemented by and clearly benefitting male board trustees and, indeed, male teachers, served to provide a strong "double bind"—and impetus—for women in their struggle to improve conditions in their workplace.

The Toronto Women Teachers' Association has been the subject of several analyses. Historians are fortunate in having at their disposal a history of the organization written by three of its founding members. It is an informative, first-hand account, especially rich in its descriptions of conditions and events over a forty-five year period, not to mention the attitudes, values and feelings expressed by the authors themselves.[3] More recently, Wendy Bryans has examined the overall development of the association, and placed it within the larger economic and political context of the time.[4] Alison Prentice has explored a number of underlying themes—the family backgrounds of Toronto women teachers during this era, their working conditions, the relation of the WTA to other groups, the overall image and reality of the WTA itself, and especially the problems associated with an organization attempting to meet the needs of a membership which represented a variety of backgrounds and interests.[5] Related studies in other jurisdictions provide a comparative framework. Wayne Urban's analysis of three urban teachers' unions in the United States compares approaches in New York, Chicago and Atlanta to issues such as affiliation with labour, the suffrage movement, and internal bureaucratization, while the historical studies of Andrew Spaull in Australia and Jenny Ozga and Martin Lawn in England[6] also raise questions about sectional and ideological tensions in central teachers' unions.

On the one hand, the overall history of the WTA proved to be very similar to those of many other male and/or female teachers' protective associations, then and since—struggling against great odds, within the context of a membership which, while basically in agreement on the overall goals, often differed greatly (because of individual differences in backgrounds, values and family/work situations) on the most appropriate strategies to achieve these goals. However, what is significantly different about the WTA, as compared to most teacher unions, and what guides the main exploration in this paper, is the gendering of their struggles. In this light, I would argue that an examination of the internal processes, interactions, and events surrounding this association (to whatever extent they can be uncovered and displayed) adds significantly to an overall analysis of teachers' protective organizations. Such an exploration forms the core of this paper.

The Toronto Teachers' Association

Unfortunately, little is known of the nature of gender relations within teachers' associations in Toronto during the voluntary membership years, before the onset of the 1877 and 1884 legislation that mandated compulsory attendance. After that time, however, it is clear that the dominance of female teachers by male authority spilled over from the classroom and the school into the domain of the association as well. Twice a year, usually in February and again in October, regular meetings, consisting of two full-day sessions on a Friday and Saturday, were held in one of the city's elementary schools. During each session, after opening exercises involving local dignitaries, prayers and anthems, teachers were required to listen to lectures and presentations. For the most part, these talks were based either on "inspirational" themes, like one in 1882 entitled *The Moral Power and Duty of Teachers,*[7] or on more practical topics, such as *Mental Arithmetic,*[8] *How to Direct the Private Reading of Scholars*[9] and *Auziliary [sic] Verbs of Mood.*[10] During the shorter "business" section of each session, items pertaining to the school system were often raised and discussed. For example, at a meeting in 1881, a motion was passed extending

> warm appreciation to the enlightened and benevolent efforts of Mr. W.H. Howland [mayor of Toronto] to bring the City Arab [sic] Children under the influence of our Public School System,

as well as a subsidiary motion asking the Minister of Education to do his part in dealing with the "27,409 children [across the province], who according to his last Report, attended no School."[11] On occasion, time would also be spent dealing with requests from the Ontario Teachers' Association for local opinion on matters considered pertinent, such as whether "the Bible [should] be retained in our Public Schools, or [whether] the Scripture selections fully answer in all respects and fully compensate for the Bible itself."[12] At some point during one of the two meetings each year, elections were also held to select a new executive for the ensuing term.

There are a number of indications to suggest that these meetings left a lot to be desired for many teachers. Attendance at meetings became problematic, and elaborate procedures were instituted to record, and enforce, teachers' participation. For example, at the February 1883 meeting, "a roll of teachers was called [and] 164 answered to their names."[13] In 1886, the minute book states that the "roll of teachers was called and absentees noted";[14] again the next year the "absentees [were] noted."[15] While these absentees, or attendance figures generally, were never recorded in the official minutes, one certainly gets the impression that not only those with "legitimate" excuses absented themselves from the affair. At one session in February 1885, for example, the minutes note that "the attendance of teachers [was] over that of yesterday."[16]

Collecting membership fees also seems to have proven difficult over the years, in spite of an early decision to encourage participation by subsidizing subscriptions to the *Canada School Journal* for paid-up TTA members.[17] In 1890 one association official "called the attention of the Convention to the fact that a large percentage of the teachers do not pay Annual Fees."[18] At the spring meeting in 1892, there was considerable discussion on whether eligibility to vote in executive elections required payment of membership fees, a matter which was finally resolved with the decision that everyone present would be allowed to participate "whether paid up members or not."[19]

Clearly however, provincial regulation governing association structure and process was not the only, or even main reason for dissatisfaction within the Toronto Teachers' Association. Rather, in assessing the overall events of the period, it is safe to conclude that the patriarchal nature of the organization played a major role in developing frustration among many of its members. During this era, the Toronto Board was in the process of feminizing its work force. By 1885, of a total of 230 elementary schoolteachers employed in the city, 203 were women, 192 of whom were classroom teachers with titles such as "Female Assistants," "Female Junior Assistants," "Senior Female Assistants" and "Female Teachers." By comparison, not one male teacher held a position less than assistant master, and most (23 of 27) were principals.[20] It was then a simple matter for the Board to ensure differential salaries for men and women, by assigning pay based on these various job titles—even for those males who were still in the classroom. To make matters worse, teachers were not given salary increments on the basis of years of teaching experience, but rather on the level of the classes they taught. In the words of the co-authors of the Association's first history, "advancement [could be] made only on the retirement or death of some teacher who had taught a higher grade."[21] The

106

overall result was a clear difference in income for men and women. In 1870, for example, salaries of women in the Board ranged from $220-400, those of men from $600-700. By 1881, these differences had actually increased: $200-600 for women and $750-1,100 for men.[22] In addition, salaries were by no means the only area in which gender discrimination was in evidence. As will be shown below, the work of a women teacher in the Toronto Board was, in many ways, very different from that of her male colleague.

The activities of the TTA also reflected this masculine dominance. Male teachers and principals, in spite of their relatively few numbers, were able to extend their workplace authority into the association, and control the structure, content and proceedings of the meetings. To be sure, they were very interested in promoting the attendance and participation of their female counterparts. Over the years a number of attempts were made to correct this "problem," ranging from short diversions, such as choral singing and poetry reading, between the speeches on each day's agenda,[23] to evening social gatherings.[24] However, judging by the minutes, attendance and overall disinterest continued to be problematic, at least to those in charge. On the odd occasion when "a large attendance of teachers" was reported in the minutes, the meeting involved, not carefully orchestrated "entertainment," but matters such as the discussion of a controversial proposal for a new pension plan, presented by the male executive of the association.[25] Overall, however, it was rare that such topics as pension plans, organization of students into classes,[26] and teacher certification[27]—matters relating directly to the material working conditions of women teachers—were discussed, or allowed to be discussed, at the regular TTA meetings.

It thus became increasingly apparent to women teachers that the Toronto Teachers' Association was of little value to them in dealing with the grave inequities they experienced in salaries, benefits, job tenure and working conditions. Given that the executive was dominated each year, not only by men, but men who occupied management positions in the Board, it was quite clear that material improvements would be very slow in coming. On a number of occasions, the women attempted to convince their male colleagues that their cause should be supported,[28] but generally to little or no avail.[29] In fact, it is interesting to note that nowhere in the official minutes of the TTA for the nineteenth century is there any indication that salary matters were ever discussed formally at their meetings, even though it is clear from other sources that this often occurred, perhaps spontaneously after the formal end of a session.[30]

Founding of the Women Teachers' Association

Buffeted by their lack of status, both in the workplace and in their "own" association, women teachers soon began to organize among themselves. At first, these activities occurred among small, informal groups. In 1879, for example, some women refused to comply with a Board demand that they "muster with their classes"[31] for a civic parade being held in honour of the Governor-General. It was an action which, after much attention from the Board and the local press,[32] proved successful—this, in spite of criticism in at least one journal that their actions posed the

> danger...of encouraging a disregard of constituted authority, and of weakening the claims of school discipline in the case of those who should be the first to respect and maintain them;...[and of] placing oneself heedlessly out of accord with one's professional brethren [sic].[33]

At an 1882 meeting, attended by many women teachers, called to discuss salaries,

> a petition was circulated and signed by most of those present, stating that they were not satisfied with the twenty-five dollar increase, given in February of that year, and asking for further consideration of this matter.

In this particular case, the Board response was anything but sympathetic. As the account of this case, told by WTA members themselves, continued,

> The result was that every teacher on the staff received a letter from the secretary of the Board intimating that if her position was not to her liking, the board would accept her resignation.[34]

By the following year, however, women teachers reassumed their organizing strategies. A number of them attended a meeting of the Toronto Board *en masse*, in order to request a raise in salary. While they were once again not successful in meeting their objective, they did gain some publicity in the press for their actions.[35]

In 1885, a formative step was taken. During the spring meeting of the Toronto Teachers' Association, women had again attempted to raise the issue of salary inequalities in the Board, in the hopes of formulating strategies for alleviating the problem. When their male colleagues refused once again to take their concerns seriously, several women "lingered after the meeting." In the words of one participant, we

> realiz[ed] that our point of view would receive no consideration until we united in some definite way...[We] discussed ways and means [and] the nucleus of the first association of women teachers in Canada was formed.[36]

Thus was founded the Women Teachers' Association of Toronto.

While the minutes of the first six years of the Women Teachers' Association of Toronto are no longer available, there is considerable evidence to suggest that the members were active, and the organization effective, from the outset. For example, in 1886, within a year of the formation of the WTA, the Toronto Board changed its long-standing method of determining salaries, from level of grade taught to that of seniority. This was a change which could only have benefitted women teachers, and, given the Board's previous intransigence, probably resulted from concerted lobbying on the part of women.[37] Soon afterwards, another motion was passed by the Board, allowing women teachers extra years of seniority towards calculation of salary if they had previously been employed by the Board, and subsequently been reinstated—another indication of the leverage which the new association was able to wield.[38]

Another immediate success for the new union was a campaign to change the composition of the TTA executive. Since its founding in 1877, the three senior positions in the TTA had been, without exception, held by males, along with three of the five places on the "management committee." Invariably as well, the presidential position was held by a man with at least the rank of a principal or school inspector. In fact, over a number of years from 1880 to 1900, the chief inspector for the city, J.L. Hughes, held the post. Women, who numerically dominated the Toronto Board teaching staff, held only two of eight positions on the executive of the association. Beginning in 1886, however, this situation changed. In that year, four of the eight positions, including that of the vice-president, were taken by WTA members, and in ensuing years women continued to maintain a stronger presence on the executive—a clear result of WTA's ability to muster forces at TTA meetings when required.[39]

In the spring of 1888, the women teachers further solidified their structure.[40] The organization was named "The Lady Teachers' Association," its constitution and bylaws were printed up, and a self-financed sick-leave plan was established. In April a letter was sent to the Board asking for the use of its board room "to hold semi-monthly meetings."[41] While the women teachers were not allowed the use of this room,[42] they were given the use of alternative space for their meetings in one of the local schools.[43] Judging from another Board minute two years later, teachers' concern about adequate meeting space remained, for a motion was passed by the Board at that time, asking for the Sites and Buildings Committee to consider "the advisability of fitting up a room in Elizabeth Street School for the purpose mentioned by the Secretary of the Lady Teachers' Association."[44] No action, however, appears to have been taken on this motion, or on an identical proposal passed by the Board a year later.[45] Similarly, no action seems to have been taken on a motion (passed by the Board soon after the women reorganized formally in the spring of 1888) stating that Board officials should

> consider the propriety of promoting the most competent of our female teachers to the position of head teachers in some of our larger schools, whenever suitable opportunities present themselves for so doing.[46]

This all-too-common tactic by politicians of providing the appearance, but not the substance, of action was not lost on the women. After another frustrating encounter over salaries in November of 1891, involving a petition to the Board signed by 361 women,[47] some members of the association became directly involved with the municipal elections taking place that winter. In conjunction with the Women's Enfranchisement Association, they were successful in assisting three women to be elected to the Toronto Public School Board for the first time.[48] Fresh from these victories, the women launched another appeal to increase their wages. During the annual salary deliberations in the spring of 1892, they attended a number of Board meetings, supported by at least one newspaper in the city.

> The plucky representatives of the women teachers employed in the Public schools of Toronto who on Monday interviewed a committee of the School Board with respect to their salaries have right and reason on their side when they ask for an increase in pay.[49]

In spite of this support, and in spite of their presence in large numbers when the matter was discussed at the Board meeting the following week, the women teachers' requests were again rejected. Indeed, their cause was by no means popular with everyone. The *Toronto News* for example, in an editorial entitled "Well Enough Paid Now," stated that

> The lady teachers do not seem to have any just ground for complaint with their lot as it is...[They] have nothing to complain of. And even if

they had a substantial grievance, their case would be less strong because of the gross indelicacy shown in attempting to terrorize the members of the board by attending the meetings en masse when the salary question is up.[50]

A Room of Their Own

Once again, however, these defeats did not seem to affect the women adversely. In fact, judging by the ensuing events, these set-backs served only to stiffen their resolve. Within the space of one week at the end of March 1892, two important meetings of the women teachers were held to discuss three main issues: first, planning further action on securing the municipal franchise for women; secondly, restructuring the organization under a new title, the "Women Teachers' Association"; finally, investigating the possibility of acquiring their own quarters. As the minutes indicate, groundwork on this last matter had already been undertaken.

> The committee appointed to see about the rental of a room suitable as a meeting place then presented a detailed report of the location, rent, seating capacity etc., of a number of rooms.[51]

At the follow-up meeting, held within the week, the planning continued. A new constitution was adopted, one which incorporated three main objects for the association:

(1)   to encourage social and professional union of women teachers that the standing of women teachers shall be duly recognized;
(2)   to encourage professional esprit-de-corps;
(3)   the free discussion of all questions affecting the profession.[52]

While at first glance this constitution seems to suggest a membership interest solely in "professional" matters, the fact that this reorganization was occurring precisely because of material concerns suggests that something quite different underlay the words on the paper. Certainly the matter of *"free discussion of all questions"*[53] is suggestive, considering the teachers' recent dealings with the Board over salary matters. It is highly likely that their interest in acquiring their own room for meetings was based at least partly on the need for some privacy in these affairs. The fact was surely not lost on the women that, only the year before, the Board had passed a motion to investigate the possibility of firing a teacher because of comments he had purportedly made at a meeting of the Toronto Teachers' Association.[54] Control by the dominant groups in the Board (principals, inspectors and trustees) of physical space and the activities within it, must have been a factor in the minds of the women, especially as they had been meeting on Board property since the birth of their organization. The expressed need for separate accommodation reflected an understanding of the nature of this control.

> During the second meeting, once again the advisability of having a furnished room downtown for the use of members was...discussed. It was deemed best to leave the matter over for a time till the Ass'n was stronger, and on a good financial basis.[55]

Even though it was felt propitious to delay action on renting outside premises for permanent use, a definite decision was reached that no further meetings would occur on Board property. The next meeting of the WTA was held in the Sunday School room of the Carleton Street Methodist Church, where the main agenda item involved discussion of a recent Board move to consider merit pay for teachers. Other matters discussed included a plan to "write articles for the press to bring us before the public," and the development of procedures to promote membership in the organization among the teachers in the Toronto schools.[56] The remaining meetings that spring, held in a room provided by the Young Women's Christian Guild, included a talk by Dr. Augusta Stowe-Gullen, a leading suffragist and one of the three women trustees recently elected, and three different travelogues, given by members themselves.[57]

In the fall of 1892, new plans were taken up by the group. The minutes of the first meeting in October, stated that a

> communication from Queen Victoria School was read. Its contents were discussed. Moved...That the trustees nominated for St. Alban's Ward be interviewed on the salary question, and that those who pledge themselves in support of an increase in salary have the influence and vote of the W.T.A. and their friends.[58]

By this time as well, one can assume that members saw their organization as indeed "stronger, and on a good financial basis," for the matter of quarters was raised again. This time, a committee was formed on the spot, and sent "to interview the secretary of the Guild"[59] while the remaining members went on with other business. After the committee returned and reported, the

"A Room of One's Own"

"advisability of having a permanent room was taken, and found to be strongly favourable." A decision was then reached to rent the room at least "till Christmas" at a cost "not to exceed eight dollars a month."[60] Within three weeks, the group had acquired possession and had called a special session "to open the room and to discuss the furnishing thereof."[61] One can assume that the task was completed by the middle of November, for a follow-up session was held on the fifteenth of that month to inaugurate their centre with a literary lecture.[62]

Events which occurred only a week later served to remind members about the importance of having control of their own space. At the outset of a meeting, according to the minutes, a Board trustee "presented himself and asked to be allowed to remain throughout the meeting." He was informed that he could speak to the group if he wished, but then he would have to "retire" from the room. As a result he left "without addressing the meeting" first, even though he had been given the opportunity to do so.[63] General discussion began, and a number of issues relating to salaries and work load were resolved. Agreement was reached that, "in order to equalize the labour of teaching, all classes should be mixed (boys and girls)." Following this, the matter of monthly reports made on women teachers by principals and officials of the Board was taken up. By Board policy, these reports had been kept secret from the teachers themselves. As a result, they had no idea what was being said about their competence—a crucial matter, especially given that there was little security of tenure at that time: teachers could be, and were, fired without notice or reason given. At this meeting, a resolution was passed, requesting that teachers be given a copy in writing of any reports made on them.[64] This request was received by the Board in short order, although not promptly acted upon.[65]

At the December 1892 and January 1893 meetings, new executive elections were held, and the matter of the Board's newly reorganized supervisory structure discussed at length. In its continuing efforts to further bureaucratize the school system, streamline the methods of supervision, and at the same time save money, the Board had promoted four men to the newly created position of "supervising principal," and assigned them to assist, inspect, and report on teachers in the city.[66] While it seems clear, judging from the "heartburning and dissatisfaction" reported by women teachers,[67] that these new officials were busy carrying out their inspection and reporting tasks, it is highly unlikely that they were interested in, or capable of, "assisting" teachers along the way. At the December 1892 meeting of the WTA, a large committee was appointed to look into the matter. At the following meeting, a straw vote was taken of members to determine how many, of those present, had "received help from supervisors." As the minutes curtly indicate, "There were eighty to a hundred present; three [said they had] received help." A letter was subsequently fired off to the Board stating the women's position on the matter, including appropriate comments on the inspectors' suggestion that an additional eight "supervising principals" be appointed. Within a few months the Board voted to discontinue the plan entirely, and to return the principals to their respective schools.[68]

Unfortunately, however, while progress in negotiations was being made by women teachers at the Board level, problems were developing in relation to the financial situation of their own organization, especially as it pertained to their newly acquired premises. Although the original motion stated clearly that the room would be rented only "till Christmas," the December minutes record agreement to continue the rent on the room until January 18. While no further mention of quarters is made in these months, the minutes for February indicate a payment of $14.00 for rent, presumably for the two months up to that time. This month-by-month existence clearly foreshadowed serious problems. At the February meeting, an ominous motion was passed, requiring

> that a committee of three be appointed to interview the management of the YWCG to see if the rent can be reduced....[They] appointed a committee and went at once. On their return, the chairwoman reported that the Secretary of the Guild had promised to lay the matter before the proper authorities.[69]

At the next regular meeting a month later,

> [t]here followed a discussion as to the availability of retaining the club-room. Finally it was moved by Miss Cruise, seconded by Miss Semple, that as the room had not been used it be given up, and one hired when needed.[70]

Four short months after opening up "their room," the door was once again closed.

Examination of "the room" helps provide insight into some of the underlying dynamics of the WTA. First, it sheds light on underlying economic factors bearing on the existence and effectiveness of the Women Teachers' Association. There is no doubt that finances remained a serious problem during this entire period. Annual membership fees were set at 50 cents in 1892 but were then lowered to 25 and then to 10 cents in 1894 and 1898 respectively.[71] These actions were undoubtedly taken to encourage teachers to join, as well as to retain ongoing members. The WTA's collectively written account of their history indicates that the ranks swelled "immediately" from 114 to 275 members, after the second decrease.[72] From the incidental reporting of the straw vote at the January 1893 meeting, referred to above, it would seem that something over a hundred members, and thus an annual income of approximately $50.00, might be a realistic calculation for the finances of 1892-3. At that level, the "good financial basis" desired at the outset for maintaining permanent quarters was uncertain, at best.

Secondly, uncovering events around the renting of "the room" helps to shed light on some aspects of women teachers' lives, in relation to the level of their involvement in association activities. For example, it is difficult to determine precisely if, or how often, the room actually was utilized, even for the monthly meetings. While the minutes clearly state that the November literary meeting was held there, no other meeting is so described; the minutes mention only the YWCG building. It is difficult to imagine the 80 to 100 women referred to at the January meeting being accommodated on the borrowed "set of furniture" or even physically in the room, in spite of its designation as the "regular meeting-place." Perhaps the room was big enough and that extra chairs were borrowed when necessary. More important, however, its other intended use, "for rest or social purpose"[73] seems not to have materialized at all. It soon became clear to the union activists that women teachers generally, certainly the vast majority of them, had little time for such activities, even if they were interested. Indeed, one can infer that attendance at regular monthly meetings was difficult for many members, even when matters of obvious concern were being discussed. The executive had learned early, as the result of one ill-fated meeting which had been scheduled for an evening hour, that most of the members were not able to attend meetings held during that part of the day. Many women were able to participate, if at all, only by going to meetings directly from school in the afternoon.[74] While it was true that few married women were hired by the Board during this era, the stereotype of unmarried teachers being totally independent, and responsible only for themselves, was probably far from the reality.[75] A survey conducted by the women teachers in Toronto a decade later, in 1907, indicated that 76% of them had "more to do with their salaries than support only themselves."[76] On many occasions, the minutes reported absences from meetings, and even resignations in mid-term from executive and committee positions, as a result of illness and other pressures in the home.[77] Toronto Board minutes are also replete with requests for leaves of absence for similar reasons.[78]

Whatever the reasons were for not making use of the room, and for the decision to close it, there is no doubt that having a space of their own continued to be a preoccupation of many of those involved with the association.

Particularly disappointing was a decision the union was forced to make in 1904. After much discussion, members finally rejected the idea of subscribing to the *Women Workers'* magazine, in spite of the fact that it contained much desired "reports of the work of women's associations," because the association had "no library, nor other provision for keeping books."[79]

Indeed, it is surmisable that the delays in disposing of the furnishings from the room spoke to the continued harbouring of hopes that the situation might improve. The "subject of the disposal of the leftover furniture" was not dealt with immediately after the decision to surrender the room, but left until the next meeting. At that time, it was decided "that the furniture be stored until it can be sold, leaving the Executive Committee to decide prices."[80] Clearly neither the executive nor anyone else was anxious to act on the matter, for over a year was to pass before the issue was raised again, only to be deferred on two occasions for a further six months.[81] Finally, at a meeting in October of 1894, it was decided "to allow Miss E. Langton to purchase the curtains for $2.75."[82] Clearly, however, the matter was never laid to rest, at least in the minds of women who saw "the room" as a desirable, or even necessary space for encouraging and supporting union activity. The idea of acquiring a new set of quarters for the members was raised on a number of occasions subsequently,[83] even though it was financially impossible to act on these wishes until well after the end of the First World War.[84]

Room or no room, the WTA continued to do battle for its members. During the remainder of the 1890s, the Board was lobbied frequently over matters of salary,[85] school organization,[86] job tenure,[87] and inspection by school board or provincial officials,[88] among other issues. In addition, pension schemes were discussed on a number of occasions,[89] and strategising over the annual issue of basic salaries consumed much time and energy each winter. Over these years, the union was also engaged in a number of matters of wider concern to women, including support for women's suffrage[90] and the decision to affiliate with the National Council of Women and the Toronto Local Council of Women.[91]

Even after 1900, and for at least the first decade of the new century, the WTA continued to pursue the original goals of the organization, actively working to improve the material lives of its members. In November of 1900, for example, the Toronto women surveyed teachers' associations in eighteen U.S. cities in order to prepare a brief to the Board requesting salary improvements for women teachers. A "large number of teachers [were] out and interested" for a special meeting held two months later to discuss the matter.[92] As part of the salary campaign of 1905, "every trustee in town was visited once and many several times."[93] During this time, some women teachers also began looking towards new sources of support in their dealings with their employers. In 1901, a committee was appointed to meet with the Toronto Trades and Labour Council to discuss items of mutual interest;[94] during the following year, a motion considering the advisability of affiliating with that body was discussed.[95] While this action was never actually taken, the WTA was able to draw on the Labour Council for support in their salary struggles, and on a number of occasions one of the Council's leaders, James Simpson (who was also a member of the Toronto School Board, later to become its Chairman, and later still the mayor of Toronto) was invited to speak at WTA meetings. Other issues remained high priorities as well during the first decade of the twentieth century. Within the Board, for example, the WTA continued to take a strong stand in opposing the increased bureaucratization and control measures being imposed by school officials, while at the same time promoting issues of women's rights and political enfranchisement in the larger community.[96]

Conclusion

By 1910, the Women Teachers' Association of Toronto had completed its first quarter century. It had been a period of strenuous struggle by a union dedicated to improving the material conditions of its members. Its efforts had met with both success and failure. These conditions were not unlike that of other Canadian workers across many occupations, communities and decades, especially where the structure and activities of their protective associations were shaped by government regulation. For women teachers in Toronto and other centres, however, their struggles were further hindered by the "double bind" of gender difference in their workplace. Male employers (the elected trustees of the Board) worked in conjunction with their male supervisory employees (principals and assistant masters) to ensure that a hierarchically gendered system remained in place, one which allowed much better material conditions for male teachers, at the direct expense of their female "colleagues."

The history of the WTA was not unique in the annals of women teachers organizing. During this same period, in Chicago, New York, Melbourne and Sidney (to cite but four examples) separate teacher unions had also been formed to defend and improve women's employment conditions. Moreover, in Melbourne and Chicago, women teachers' unions or teacher unions dominated by women, were the first teachers' unions to be so formed, and as a result, contributed directly to the re-formation of teachers associations into central unions in their respective jurisdictions.[97]

Wayne Urban, in his volume *Why Teachers Organized*, raises two important matters in relation to the female (or largely female) teachers' organizations which were active during this era in Chicago and New York City. First, he claims that the strength with which feminist issues were raised at that time has "not assumed a comparable significance for contemporary [male/female] teachers' organizations." Indeed, he suggests that "contemporary feminist teachers might conclude that they are battling the same male dominance within their own organizations, that exists in school systems and in the larger society."[98] One could similarly argue that this is also the case for most teachers' organizations in Canada. But female elementary schoolteachers in Ontario occupy a distinctive position in this regard. Since 1918 they have been represented by their own province-wide organization, the Federation of Women Teachers' Associations, which assumes responsibility for all protective and "professional" matters.[99] There is no doubt that the FWTAO owes much of its existence to those women who had cut their first organizational teeth as members of the Women Teachers' Association of Toronto.

Urban's second point relates to his observation that the "stirrings of an independent teachers' consciousness in the early decades of the century [were, by the 1920s]...short-circuited by...[school] administrators [who] then assumed full control" of teachers associations.[100] There is no doubt that the early years of the Toronto WTA also reflected these same "stirrings" of "consciousness." Women teachers, almost all of whom occupied basically the same (low) level of the Toronto Board hierarchy, banded together and agitated for change in their material conditions. As this paper has attempted to demonstrate, the WTA's activities reflected to a large extent a consensus of both purpose and strategy, at least among those who joined the organization and participated in it. Gender and class (that is, position in the workplace) combined to enhance this unity of purpose in women teachers' struggles against male employers and supervisors.

By the 1920s, it would appear that the WTA, too, had become much less forceful, and less successful, in its advocacy work. Further, there is evidence to indicate that serious internal divisions within the membership began to appear during this time.[101] Certainly, economic and social conditions had shifted on a variety of planes. However, the nature of women's work in the Toronto Board had begun to change as well—at least to the extent that more women were now being promoted to administrative positions within schools, and even within the Board itself. These women remained eligible for membership in the WTA.[102] It will take further exploration of the association, and its internal processes, to determine the extent to which this reduced activism, and increased internal conflict, resulted from increasing hierarchical divisions within the membership of the organization. This question is especially intriguing now that boards of education in Ontario are being required to implement affirmative action

"A Room of One's Own"

promotion plans for their female employees. One is left to speculate how the direction and strategies of the provincial women teachers' union might change in the future, given the potential for increasing class divisiveness within its own membership.

In any event, the early years of the Women Teachers' Association of Toronto, whether or not affected by class difference among the membership, were certainly marked by constant struggle against male employers and male "colleagues." Both in terms of improvements in material conditions during that time, and providing groundwork for the further development in teachers' organizations, there is no doubt that the members of this organization achieved considerable success—even if they were unable to enjoy, for more than a brief four months, a room of their own.

Notes

1. Ontario Department of Education, Annual Report of the Chief Superintendent of Education (hereafter *Provincial Report*), 266. *Canada School Journal* 1, n. 2 (February 1877), 24.

2. *Provincial Report*, 1884.

3. Harriet Johnston, Jessie P. Semple and A.A. Gray, *The Story of the Women Teachers' Association of Toronto* (Toronto: Thomas Nelson and Sons, 1932).

4. Wendy Bryans, "Virtuous Women at Half the Price: The Feminization of the Teaching Force and Early Women Teachers' Organization in Ontario," (M.A. diss., University of Toronto, 1974).

5. Alison Prentice, "Themes in the Early History of the Women Teachers' Association of Toronto," in Paula Bourne, ed., *Women's Paid and Unpaid Work* (Toronto: New Hogtown Press, 1985).

6. Wayne Urban, *Why Teachers Organized* (Detroit: Wayne State University Press, 1982); Andrew Spaull, "The Origins and Formation of Teachers' Unions in Nineteenth Century Australia," in *Melbourne Studies in Education* (Melbourne: Melbourne University Press, 1984); Jennifer Ozga and Martin Lawn, *Teachers, Professionalism and Class: A Study of Organized Teachers* (London: Falmer Press, 1981).

7. Toronto Board of Education Archives, Minute Book of the Toronto Teachers' Association (hereafter *TTA Minutes*). 1882, 18. "The moral education of the people had not sufficient prominence and attention in a School System. The condition of the world, its vices and crimes, were referred to as evidence of the necessity for more attention on the subject, and the use of the Bible as a basis for religious and moral culture was strongly urged."

8. *TTA Minutes*, 1884, 59.

9. Ibid. 60.

10. Ibid. 1883, 53.

11. Ibid. 1881, 10, 11.

12. Ibid. 1885, 93.

13. Ibid. 1883, 39.

14. Ibid. 1886, 96.

15. Ibid. 1887, 129.

16. Ibid. 1885, 81. Another common euphemism of the day was the comment, such as that describing a 1878 session, that the "attendance of teachers was very credible." (*Canada School Journal* 2, n. 9 [March, 1878], 37.)

17. Ibid. 1881, 8.
18. Ibid. 1890, 177.
19. Ibid. 1892, 203.
20. Toronto Board of Education Archives. *Toronto Board of Education Annual Report* (hereafter *Toronto Report*) 1880, 49; Bryans, "Virtuous Women," 42.
21. Quoted in Johnston, *Story*, 7-8.
22. *Toronto Report* 1870, 56-57; 1881, App., 10-15.
23. Ibid. 1881, 9.
24. Ibid. 1885, 88.
25. Ibid. 1881, 1; 1895, 226.
26. *TTA Minutes*. 1882, 27; 1883, 41.
27. See, for example, ibid. 1886, 111; 1895, 224; 1898, 450.
28. See, for example, Johnston, *Story*, 8, 11.
29. There is no doubt that the entire structure of the Toronto Board, and other urban boards during this time, was based on a few highly paid males supervising many lower-paid females. To the extent that the strength of male salaries was based on the paucity of women's pay, it is no wonder that male-dominated associations would do little to promote any change in this situation. For further discussion on gender differentiation in urban school boards of the nineteenth century, see Marta Danylewycz and Alison Prentice, "Teachers' Work: Changing Patterns and Perceptions in the Emerging School Systems of Nineteenth and Early Twentieth Century Central Canada," *Labour/Le Travail*, (Spring, 1986), 17; and Alison Prentice, "The Feminization of Teaching," in Susan Mann Trofimenkoff and Alison Prentice, eds., *The Neglected Majority: Essays in Canadian Women's History* (Toronto: McClelland and Stewart, 1977).
30. See, for example, Johnston, *Story*, 8, 10.
31. *Canadian Educational Monthly* 1, n. 10 (October, 1879), 528.
32. *Toronto Globe*, Sept. 18, Oct. 2, Nov. 6, 1879.
33. *Canadian Educational Monthly* 1, n. 10 (October, 1879), 529.
34. Johnston. *Story*, 9; Honora Cochrane, *Centennial Story. The Board of Education for the City of Toronto, 1850-1950* (Toronto: Thomas Nelson and Sons, 1950) 171-2.
35. *Toronto Telegram*, Feb. 22, 1883.
36. Johnston, *Story*, 10.
37. *TBE Minutes*, 1886, Appendix, 45; Johnston, *Story*, 8.
38. *TBE Minutes*, 1886, Appendix, 53.

39. The issue concerning leadership of these early teachers' associations is one which affected both the TTA and the WTA. For example, it is interesting to note that the women teachers in Toronto decided in 1892 that it would be in their interests to have one of their members as president of the TTA—a feat which was simple to accomplish, given their numbers, once the decision was made. However, this lasted for only one year, and for the rest of the decade, no women even ran for the office. Unfortunately, very little evidence is available to explain why this routine was not repeated. It is possible that teachers felt that having school officials as head of that organization would assist in their overall bargaining with school board trustees for salaries, and/or would improve the status of the organization, and themselves. Federation of Women Teachers' Associations of Ontario Archives, Minutes of the Women Teachers' Association General Meetings (hereafter *WTA Minutes*). 1894, 31; *TTA Minutes*, 1894, 218.

40. Johnston, *Story*, 11.

41. *TBE Minutes*, 1888, 59.

42. As compared to the Provincial Association of School Trustees, for example, who were often allowed this privilege. See for example, *TBE Minutes*, 1888, 129; 1891, 92.

43. Ibid. 1888, 78.

44. Ibid. 1890, 127.

45. Ibid. 1891, 7.

46. Ibid. 1888, 46.

47. Ibid. 1891, 133-134.

48. For the relation of these women teachers, and their organization, to the organizations and activities of the contemporary women's movement, see Prentice, *Themes*; and Bryans, *Virtuous Women*.

49. *Mail,* March 17, 1892.

50. *Toronto News,* Feb. 25, 1892.

51. *WTA Minutes*, 1892, 1.

52. *WTA Minutes*, 1892, 3.

53. Emphasis added.

54. *TBE Minutes*, 1891, 35.

55. *WTA Minutes*, 1892, 5.

56. Ibid. 1892, 8.

57. Ibid.

58. Ibid. 1892, 11-12.

59. Presumably the Y.W.C.G. where they were meeting.

60. Ibid.

61. Ibid. 13.
62. Ibid. 14.
63. Ibid. 1892, 14.
64. Ibid. 17.
65. *TBE Minutes*, 1892, 165. It is interesting to note that the Board minutes state that this resolution was received from the "Secretary of the Women's Temperance Association."
66. *TBE Minutes*, 1890.
67. Johnston, *Story*, 18.
68. *WTA Minutes*, 1893, 18-20; *TBE Minutes*. 1893, 5; Johnston. *Story*, 18-19.
69. *WTA Minutes*, 1893, 21.
70. Ibid. 23.
71. Another 14 years were to pass before the fees were again raised, even to 25 cents, in 1912. *WTA Minutes*, 1892, 4; 1894, 30-31; Johnston. *Story*, 22, 34.
72. Johnston, *Story*, 22.
73. Johnston, *Story*, 19.
74. *WTA Minutes*, 1892, 5-6.
75. It was, however, a stereotype which those responsible for maintaining the depressed wages of women teachers probably did little to change.
76. *WTA Minutes*. 1907, 209. In response to a request from the Toronto Local Council of Women in 1908 for volunteers, the association found itself unable to assist because "Saturday was the only day [available]...and that day usually filled with other duties." (*WTA Minutes*, 1908, 221.) This same situation has also been demonstrated for the period 1861-1881 in Marta Danylewycz and Alison Prentice, "Teachers, Gender and Bureaucratizing School Systems in Nineteenth Century Montreal and Toronto," *History of Education Quarterly*, 24 (1984) 75-100.
77. See, for example, *WTA Minutes*, 1892, 8; 1893, 24, 26; 1895, 46; 1896, 54; 1899, 90; 1903, 125.
78. See, for example, *TBE Minutes*. 1894, 157, 160, 170, Appendix, p. 170.
79. Ibid. 1904, 137.
80. Ibid. 1893, 24.
81. Ibid. 1894, 33, 39.
82. Ibid. 1894, 39.
83. See, for example, *WTA Minutes*, 1902, 121-2; 1903, 131; 1906, 182.
84. In fact, a full thirty years were to pass from the time of the Women Teachers' Association's initial venture into establishing its own centre, before it was again in the position of being able to rent and furnish its

own space—rooms in the Mulberry Tea Room on Bloor Street. (Ibid., Vol. 2, 1924, 132.)

85. Ibid. 1895, 53-54; 1897, 65, 75-76.
86. Ibid. 1894, 39; 1895, 40.
87. Ibid. 1895, 45, 50.
88. Ibid. 1895, 50.
89. Ibid. 1895, 44; 1896, 60.
90. Ibid. 1896, 55, 58.
91. Ibid. 1899, 88; 1900, 102.
92. Ibid. 1900, 105; 1901, 111.
93. Ibid. 1905, 177.
94. Ibid. 1901, 118.
95. Ibid. 1902.
96. See, for example, *WTA Minutes*, 1907, 192; and 1908, 219.
97. Urban, *Why Teachers Organized*; Spaull, *Origins,* 148 and 166.
98. Urban, *Why Teachers Organized,* 176-7.
99. From well before the end of the nineteenth century, women teachers have formed themselves into separate unions in many parts of (at least the "Western") world. From 1890 to 1920, such groups were formed in Germany and France, as well as the Scandinavian countries. Separate unions for women teachers became a reality in England and Wales with the formation of the National Union of Women Teachers in 1902; similar groups in Australia included the Women Assistant Teachers' Association in Victoria State (1918) and the Women Teachers' Guild in South Australia (1936). In Quebec, the FCIV was to dominate in the era from 1937 to 1946. (Personal discussions with Andy Spaull, November, 1989.)
100. Ibid. 177.
101. Bryans, *Virtuous Women.*
102. School board administrators, such as principals, vice-principals, co-ordinators and consultants, have remained as members of teachers' protective associations in Ontario to this day.

Part Three:

Vocationalism and Its Meaning for Girls' Schooling

Domestic Science Education in Ontario, 1900-1940[*]

Marta Danylewycz

The Ontario public school system, like its counterparts in Quebec, underwent a major transformation at the turn of the century. Integral to this process of change was the lengthening of the number of years children spent in school, the expansion and revision of the curriculum, and the introduction of alternatives to classical education at the secondary level. Technological advances in agriculture and industry set the stage for this transformation, while the emergence of an influential and growing body of social reformers committed to practical education and less abstract schooling ensured its realization.[1]

As the Ontario reform movement began to take shape, Adelaide Hoodless, wife of a Hamilton manufacturer and Conservative politician, joined its ranks. She entered public life in 1889 with the belief that scientific understanding of food preparation and home management could curb some of the evils of industrialization. By 1894 she had succeeded in opening training centres for students and prospective teachers in household science. More importantly, it was her presentation of a resolution passed by the National Council of Women of Canada (NCWC) in support of "manual training for girls" that convinced George W. Ross, Minister of Education (1883-1899), to permit local school boards to add domestic science to the curriculum. The 1894 School Act reflected the Ministry's acceptance of the recommendation of curricular reform, while subsequent acts and provisions provided the impetus for the formalization and expansion of domestic science programs.[2]

When Richard Harcourt replaced Ross as Minister of Education, Adelaide Hoodless worked through the provincial government to advance her ideas about domestic science education. In fact, during Harcourt's tenure she was the Ministry's official representative in matters dealing with the "feminine of manual training." In that capacity she won the further support of local and national feminist organizations for curricular reform and secured the assistance of the Macdonald Training Fund, established at the turn of the century for schools heeding the call of practical education.

---

[*] Editors' Note: The following text, authored by Marta Danylewycz, represents the second part of an article offering a comparative analysis of the evolution of domestic science in Ontario and Quebec at the beginning of the twentieth century. Hence the conclusion's contents. Footnoting has been edited.

Gender And Education In Ontario: An Historical Reader

Private funding and public support made a difference to girls' education. Between 1900-1904 nine school boards in Ontario had introduced domestic science into the curriculum, some in the elementary schools and others at the secondary level only. Not surprisingly, Hoodless's home town led the way in organizing instruction in this area. Stratford followed suit in 1901, not only offering courses but also making them an integral part of the school curriculum. A graduate of Hamilton's recently established Ontario Normal School of Domestic Science and Art was appointed instructor for the board. In 1902 a new building was erected next to the collegiate institute to accommodate nine classes from the public schools and one from the separate school receiving instruction in household science. Renfrew, Brantford, Belleville, London, Berlin (later Kitchener), Toronto, and Ingersoll were among the remaining seven boards to join the domestic science movement.[3]

With the expiration of the Macdonald Fund in 1904, Harcourt amended the earlier School Act to ensure the newly developed programs financial support. He also created the office of the Inspector of Manual Training and Technical Education, thus formalizing the position held by Hoodless since 1899. The new appointment, however, went to Albert Leake, former manager of the Macdonald Training Fund.

The release of public funds for practical education and the establishment of an inspectorate to centralize and survey its development concluded the process of integrating the new courses into the curriculum. As a result of these two measures, manual training was put on par with the traditional academic courses.[4]

The next step following the 1904 School Act was to make practical education compulsory; this occurred thirty years later, as educators sought solutions to problems of high unemployment and the attendant rising high school enrolment rates engendered by the Great Depression. In 1937 Education Minister Leo Simpson unveiled the McArthur Plan which reformed the public school curriculum as well as providing for a smoother transition between the two levels of schooling. To facilitate the advance from one grade to the next, it diminished the number of external exams high school students were required to take at the end of the year and turned grade 9 into a year of testing, thus delaying for one year students' choice of a matriculation, technical, or commercial program. In order to assist informed decision making, the revised grade 9 course of study acquainted students with the available practical education and career options. For boys, these fell under the category of general shop; for girls, the heading of domestic science.[5]

The fact that more adolescents were staying in school longer, but not necessarily planning to undertake university education, is an essential key to

Domestic Science Education in Ontario, 1900-1940

understanding the reforms introduced by Simpson. Given that the age of compulsory education had been raised to 16 in 1921 and that the manufacturing sector chose to rely on an older workforce than in the past, it became possible to extend the period of grace before directing adolescents into the academic or vocational streams. In turn, an increasing number of students was exposed to practical education.

According to the Department of Education, familiarity with the vocational options was intended to help students "discover in themselves any latent aptitude for practical work."[6] Noble as this intention sounds, its aim was not to undermine the prevailing class and gender divisions. Middle class youth were expected to opt for academic programs, while working class adolescents to select from courses leading to manual occupations.[7] More importantly, the vocational options to which students were introduced in grade 9 were sex-segregated. From the outset the gender-specific programs of practical education denied girls the opportunity to discover talents and develop interests that went against the accepted notions of femininity, thus barring their entry to the male-dominated occupations.

The commitment of political authorities to the retention and reinforcement of the prevailing sexual division of labour was written into the McArthur Plan. It was also expressed in the 1937 establishment of the Dominion-Provincial Training Program for men and women between the ages of 16 and 30. Like the former, the latter too was a response to shifting employment patterns during the Depression, offering women an array of household science and related sex-typed courses.[8] The creation of a wider range of educational and work opportunities in the restricted domain of household and personal service, therefore, reinstated the provincial and federal governments' defence of the male prerogative in economic life.

The reinforcement of domestic science education by provincial and federal governments during the 1930s, and then in the post-World War II period, gave the "feminine of manual training" a life force more enduring than anything conceived by the women who had organized in its favour at the turn of the century. On the other hand, it was the programs Hoodless and her contemporaries had designed that defined and shaped domestic science education for many years to come.

Training in household sciences began in the senior second grade. During that first year students mastered basting, running stitching, overcasting and cross-stitching. In the junior and senior grade three, students advanced to hemming, top-sewing, darning, feather-stitching and then were to apply these skills to mending garments, making over clothes, and sewing doilies, handkerchiefs, and shirts. Concurrently, a teacher holding a domestic science certificate instructed older students in food processing, table etiquette, laundry work, general housework, and home nursing, which included the preparation of a simple diet for the sick, bandaging, and the making of plasters and poultices.[9] In the newly built schools which boasted well-equipped manual training centres, girls apprenticed by performing actual household tasks. There the ideas of "progressive educators" had taken hold and students worked in groups, alternating in the roles that women and girls in actual family situations performed.[10]

The study of household science aimed to prepare girls for their life's work. But there was another, less gender-specific, dimension to the push for proficient homemaking. The inculcation of correct habits and uniform standards among future homemakers resembled the earlier efforts of Egerton Ryerson to instil sobriety and moral discipline through the acquisition of literacy. Indeed, considering the socio-economic factors which led to the formalization of practical education, it is clear that domestic science, like temperance, military drill and citizenship training, had a special message to the immigrant child. Loyalty to the Union Jack, as prescribed by government officials, was more than flag waving and parading on Empire day. For immigrants it was supposed to entail the discarding of their own cultural and domestic practices and the adoption of Canadian ways.

At the secondary level, household science was a continuation of the work commenced in the lower grades. Divided into hygiene, sanitation, cooking, needlework, basket and raffia work, it offered a more thorough and scientific grounding in women's domestic work. The fact that its goal was not the transmission of marketable skills but the development of "the vocational ability for housekeeping and homemaking" was made patently clear in the reports of the Minister and Inspector of Manual Training and Technical Education. Employment-oriented goals were reserved for the technical schools.[11] As high school had become a continuation of common schooling, so too advanced domestic science was an elaboration of the housewifery skills acquired at the elementary level.

The compulsory domestic science course of 1937 aimed "to develop a sound standard of living, and an appreciation of the functions of family and community life."[12] Translated into units of study, this meant further apprenticeship in cooking, sewing, and cleaning. On a social and more personal level, the course stressed the importance of appearance, deportment, and family relations. In short, the advanced course sought to impart practical skills, competence in interpersonal relations and correct attitudes toward motherhood and marriage.

Domestic Science Education in Ontario, 1900-1940

Although the campaign to raise the standards of home life continued into the post-World War II period, it had the greatest impact on classroom teaching during the height of the feminist and "New Education" movements. Between 1905 and 1925 the number of girls learning domestic science in Ontario's public schools increased by 2600%. At the beginning of this twenty-year period, only 1.6% of girls attending Ontario's public schools spent a couple of hours per school week sewing or cooking; at its end over 30% were studying domestic science. By the late 1920s the numbers stabilized and then began to decrease. In 1930, 22.8% of the female public school population was enrolled in domestic science (Table 1).

Table 1—DOMESTIC SCIENCE EDUCATION IN ONTARIO'S ELEMENTARY PUBLIC SCHOOL SYSTEM, 1905-1930

	1905-06	1910-11	1915-16	1920-21	1925-26	1930-31*
Number of Girls Attending School						
Rural schools	112,120	103,761	102,979	101,338	104,687	
City schools	35,297	45,826	65,576	92,465	101,766	108,826 - Rural **
Town schools	31,788	32,660	32,120	34,961	35,920	158,802 - Urban
Village schools	13,711	13,612	12,942	12,174	11,270	
Total	192,916	195,859	213,617	240,938	253,643	267,627
Number of Girls Enrolled in Domestic Science						
Rural schools	492	431	2,473	6,673	11,648	
City schools	2,002	11,990	32,793	64,313	72,007	27,919 - Rural **
Town schools	484	1,613	2,967	3,565	2,474	31,433 - Urban
Village schools	172	10	110	680	694	
Total	3,150	14,044	38,343	75,231	86,823	59,352
Percentage of Girls Attending School Enrolled in Domestic Science						
Rural schools	.44	.42	2.40	6.58	11.1	
City schools	5.7	26.16	50.00	69.55	70.8	25.65 - Rural
Town schools	1.5	4.94	9.24	10.20	6.9	19.79 - Urban
Village schools	1.25	.07	.85	5.59	6.2	
Total	1.63	7.17	17.95	31.22	34.2	22.18

* The number of students enrolled in domestic science courses cannot be determined on the basis of the later reports.
** The four categories of schools are collapsed into rural and urban.
Source: The Ontario Department of Education Annual Reports

A similar pattern emerged at the secondary level. Within this sector the proportion of girls taking domestic science in high schools and collegiate institutes[13] increased from 10% in 1905 to 19% in 1920. A downward trend began in the early 1920s, about five years before this occurred at the elementary level, and continued into the period of the McArthur reforms. Although after 1937 figures on girls registered in domestic science courses were not published in the annual reports of the Department of Education, one would expect (because of compulsion) an upward swing, raising the proportion by the 1940s to about 25 to 30% of the female high school and collegiate population (Table 2).

Table 2—DOMESTIC SCIENCE EDUCATION IN ONTARIO'S COLLEGIATE INSTITUTES AND HIGH SCHOOLS, 1905-30

	1905-06	1910-11	1915-16	1920-21	1925-26	1930-31
Number of Girls Attending High Schools and Collegiate Institutes						
Collegiate Ins.	8,207	9,152	11,630	10,320	15,501	17,001
High Schools	7,419	8,264	9,091	8,605	12,086	12,466
Total	15,626	17,416	20,721	18,905	27,587	29,467
Number of Girls Enrolled in Domestic Science Classes						
Collegiate Ins.	1,192	1,628	3,108	3,277	2,997	1,726
High Schools	358	533	171	301	452	169
Total	1,550	2,161	3,279	3,578	3,449	1,895
Percentage of Total High School and Collegiate Female Population Enrolled in Domestic Science						
Collegiate Ins.	14.5	17.8	26.7	31.8	19.3	10.1
High Schools	4.8	6.5	1.8	3.5	3.7	1.5
Total	9.9	12.4	15.8	18.9	12.5	6.4

Source: The Ontario Department of Education Annual Reports

Domestic Science Education in Ontario, 1900-1940

It is clear from Table 2 that, as far as the secondary schools were concerned, domestic science courses were offered mainly in the collegiate institutes. Continuation schools did not provide training in this area and only a handful of high schools (4 out of the 127 in 1930) made domestic science available to their students. This discrepancy was a function of the ranking within the secondary system and a manifestation of regional inequalities. Continuation schools, a remnant of the age of the ungraded and more informal school, were the poor cousins of the modern secondary institutions, the high school and the collegiate institute. Located in rural communities, these schools suffered from provincial neglect and local indifference to turn of the century reforms. Neither as poor as continuation schools nor as well endowed as collegiate institutes, high schools held the middle ground. Even their students could not lay claim to a first-rate education, as could those in the collegiate institutes. Nor could they expect equal access to costly equipment and pedagogical materials.

In addition to reflecting inequality within the school system, the uneven spread of domestic science education was no doubt related to teacher supply and demand. While the preference of rural parents for "education along the old traditional lines" might have been an obstacle, as school inspectors claimed,[14] to the implementation of reform in country schools, the reluctance of certified domestic science teachers to seek employment in the economically backward regions of the province also held back the tide of change. Aware of the differences in status and funding among the schools within the secondary system, they opted for the more lucrative positions in the prestigious institutions, hence facilitating the more rapid spread of domestic science into the collegiate institutes.

An explanation for the profound regional differences in the numbers of elementary school girls learning homemaking skills also must take into account the broader context of family, community support, and the circumstances of teachers. Like the continuation schools, most rural elementary schools could not afford to install manual training centres. If financing them was not the impediment, then the inconvenience of transporting small children over long distances to the properly equipped central schools acted as a deterrent to their installation. Finally, the attitudes of individual teachers and the circumstances under which they worked contributed to the uneven spread of domestic science. Whether products of the "dry husks of a formal curriculum"[15] or graduates of the supposedly more progressive and engaging programs, teachers would embrace innovation only if the basic needs of schooling had been met. These were a long way from being realized. As historians are beginning to discover, in many regions of Ontario the struggle for higher salaries and battles against overcrowded classrooms, damp and insufficiently ventilated rooms were very much the abiding and overriding concerns of most schoolmistresses and masters well into the twentieth century.[16]

Clearly, then, the availability of domestic science education in individual school districts depended on more than the mere endorsement and financial assistance of the Minister of Education. In essence equality of opportunity was contingent upon equal social conditions and the latter was slow in coming. Yet the Minister's stamp of approval marked a turning point in the history of girls' education in Ontario for without it schooling in housewifery could not have become part of official pedagogical praxis. Similarly, had the provincial government shelved the recommendation of the NCWC on behalf of manual training for girls, household science would have acquired a less prominent place in academic and vocational schooling.

The age of vocational education in Ontario dawned with the passing of the 1911 Industrial Education Act by the province and the subsequent drafting of the Technical Education Act in 1919 by the federal government. Under the patronage of the two levels of government, the number of technical schools in Ontario rose from 1 in 1901 to 13 in 1921 to 63 in 1935. By the latter date 32% of the secondary school population was in the vocational stream.

Of those enrolled in technical schools half were girls by the 1920s and by the next decade both sexes attended for the same number of years (Table 3). What set the male and female students apart were the programs into which they were registered.

Table 3—FULL-TIME STUDENTS IN TECHNICAL SCHOOLS

	Total Number	Female	Male	% Female
1920-21	2,600	673	1,927	25.88
1925-26	15,201	7,797	7,404	51.29
1930-31	29,470	15,172	14,298	51.48
1935-36	34,406	16,890	17,516	49.09
1940-41	30,921*	15,475	15,446	50.00

* Decline in enrolment due to involvement of technical school students in war industries.
Source: Annual Reports of the Minister of Education

Girls who attended vocational schools specialized in either household science or business and commercial training. The former prepared them for domestic service, practical nursing, clothing design, and seamstressing, and the latter for clerical and secretarial work. Courses within the household science department were divided into domestic science, which included housekeeping, home economics, home nursing, hygiene, dietetics, and domestic arts, which consisted of sewing, and dress making, millinery, embroidery and lace making, textiles, design, and knitting. During the 1920s and 30s over two-thirds of the girls attending technical schools were registered in these two programs. The remaining one-third specialized in business.[17]

In 1927 the Faculty of Household Science at the University of Toronto established a matriculation course for technical school graduates wishing to enter its program. Prior to that date only collegiate institute and high school graduates were eligible for admission to the Faculty.

The Faculty of Household Science opened its door to technical high school graduates after it had been in existence for over twenty years. Established in 1906 at the behest of Lillian Massey Treble, it formalized the degree in household science the university had been offering since 1902. Acceptance into the new faculty was contingent upon the candidates' successful completion of the junior matriculation examination from a high school or a collegiate institute. Its four-year program consisted of a general arts course, which included study of Latin, modern languages, mathematics, English, history, philosophy, and general science. The household science component encompassed the study of the history of home life, food and nutrition, household management, hygiene and sanitary service, nutrition, and dietetics. In 1910-11 a Physiology and Household Science option was introduced which allowed the substitution of general arts with science courses. This option was discontinued following the establishment of the Household Science General Course in 1915-16, renamed Home Economics in 1919. The new course included the B.A. program as well as a wide assortment of science and household science courses. The final modification in the period 1900-1940 was the development of a pass and honour course for the degree of Bachelor of Household Science. Both were four years in length but acceptance into the honours program required honour matriculation in mathematics, French or German, history and science. Moreover, the course of study was much more exacting, demanding a total of 115 hours as opposed to the 88 for the Bachelor of Household Science pass. Much of the additional time was devoted to the study of home economics.[18]

The university's confirmation of their expertise in "scientific homemaking" allowed graduates to enter the professional world as well as to create new occupations in the area of nutrition and dietetics. Indeed, the Faculty's survey of women who had completed their degrees between 1911 and 1931 shows that of those who entered the work force one-third were employed as dieticians or food services experts in hospitals, factories, and cafeterias.[19]

Gender And Education In Ontario: An Historical Reader

The professionalization of food services was the end result of the integration of domestic science courses into the vocational stream and particularly of the establishment of the Faculty of Household Science. The various women's groups involved in promoting the scientific approach to homemaking anticipated this development, although in building up their forces the professionally minded allied themselves with those who held conservative and domestically oriented assumptions about the meaning of household science. President Burwash, who presided over the introduction of this course of study into the university, explained his interest and co-operation as an effort to establish a course "pre-eminently fitted for women, for women's work, and for a true woman's noblest and most beautiful personal life."[20] In other words, the entry of women into the university necessitated the creation of programs appropriate for their future roles as wives and mothers. Household science clearly filled the bill.

While the combination of a supply of highly educated home-scientists and a demand for their services as teachers, nutritionists, and dieticians by public and private institutions thwarted the domestically oriented intentions of traditional university administrators, this subversion did not threaten the prevailing sexual division of labour. The participation of university certified homemakers in the workforce merely widened the range of activity open to women within their prescribed sphere.

If the combined effect of supply and demand favoured the development of new career opportunities within the feminine sphere, it also led to changes in the curriculum. The Faculty of Household Science introduced the study of Latin into its program so that its graduates could qualify for admission into the Faculty of Education. Several years later, more science courses were incorporated into the program for those wishing to become nutritionists and dieticians. Normal schools implemented similar curricular reforms and, as might be expected, their initiators were Adelaide Hoodless, Lillian Massey and Richard Harcourt.

Hoodless's concern for teacher training was an extension of her preoccupation with the integration of domestic science courses into the elementary and secondary levels. In 1896 she convinced the National Council of Women to pass her second resolution, which committed its members to promote the training of teachers in domestic science in their respective provinces.[21] The following year the Ontario Department of Education's guidelines for introducing domestic science into the public schools contained regulations concerning the preparation of domestic science teachers. The rapidity with which they were implemented is evident in the observation made by Harcourt to Massey Treble in 1903: "I have so arranged that the girls

Domestic Science Education in Ontario, 1900-1940

attending the Ottawa, Toronto, London and Hamilton Normal Schools must take up this course (domestic science) this term."[22] As all normal schools began to offer training in the teaching of domestic science, summer school courses in home economics as well as Saturday classes between the months of October and June were organized for teachers already in service to acquire expertise in this area.[23]

Hoodless's concern for teacher training did not end with her overtures to the Department of Education. She secured a grant from Lord Strathcona to help found the Ontario Normal School of Domestic Science and Art in Hamilton, which, from 1900 until its incorporation in 1903 into the Macdonald Institute, offered a two-year teacher training program.

The year the Hamilton school opened, Lillian Massey Treble founded the Victor School of Household Science and Art in Toronto. Established to provide training for homemakers, mistress and servant alike, it evolved quickly into a normal school. Renamed the Lillian Massey Training School of Household Science in 1901, it offered a two-year course for women with no teacher training, and a one-year program for normal school graduates. With the introduction of domestic science into the university, the teacher training section in Massey's school was phased out and its staff and facilities became the basis of the Faculty of Household Science at the University of Toronto.[24]

In a mere decade domestic science became an integral part of Ontario's educational system. The rapidity with which this occurred testified to the success and popularity of the attempts of social reformers, women's groups, and Ministers of Education to introduce practical training into the schools. At the same time, it demonstrates how "natural" and automatic was the assumption that preparation for life's work had to be gender-specific and how pervasive the acceptance of the prevailing sexual division of labour.

But the apparent consensus regarding the needs for domestic science education conceals particularistic tendencies and perspectives within the movement. The writings of turn of the century women make clear that domestic science was seen as an antidote by middle-class women to the social and personal problems confronting their sex. Having witnessed illness and death caused by containable contagion, Hoodless, Massey Treble and countless others in the NCWC promoted domestic science in an effort to eliminate unnecessary human suffering. "Creating a strong and healthy race," a call with a particular message to women, was certainly one of the factors leading to the organization of the domestic science movement.

By the same token, the campaign for domestic science education arose out of the related concern of providing a scientific underpinning to housework and thus elevating its status in society. While altering the nature of housework, the

137

progressive removal of productive activity from the home did not undermine the ideology of the separate spheres. The contradictory result of this process of erosion engendered a redefinition of housework, one which stressed the psychological and intellectual, as opposed to the manual, character of women's work. Domestic science prepared women for this task, for as Adelaide Hoodless explained:

> The training of the up-to-date housewife must rest upon a working knowledge of chemistry, physics, psychology and other fundamental sciences.... It must now include a fair knowledge of social and political economics and of ethical and economical standards of values of goods, of labour and of time in relation to human efficiency.[25]

Despite the fact that women's work was to be performed in the home, it was held to require as much formal preparation as men's within the public domain. "The men have their engineering schools, their schools of practical sciences.... We have a profession as grand and as important as any; we need training for it—and we will have it," proclaimed one of Hoodless's ardent supporters.[26] Inherent in this demand for the recognition of housework as a *bona fide* profession that required appropriate training was the condemnation of male neglect of female schooling. It was Dr. Emily Stowe, a leader in the struggle for women's rights, who levelled an attack against the male bias in education.

> Why has not the state legislated in favour of women's education in so justly prized and valuable an art? This neglect on the part of our Governments is conclusively convincing that men cannot and do not legislate in and for the best interests of women....[27]

Part of her solution to the problem of male control was women's suffrage and political equality. Although in this regard she parted ways with the more conservative social feminism of Hoodless, she nevertheless joined her in the campaign for domestic science education.

If middle-class women sought to raise the image and prestige of housework through domestic science education, they also viewed it as a means of upgrading the work and status of domestic servants. The evident decline in the numbers of women entering domestic service as well as the supposed poor quality of service provided by this waning occupational class troubled many upper-class Ontario women. Personal documents like correspondence and diaries as well as public ones like minutes of the annual meetings of the NCWC

Domestic Science Education in Ontario, 1900-1940

attest to their preoccupation with the service class. In one of the many sessions devoted to the "domestic problem," Stowe made clear the connection between domestic science education and the need of hired help: "if we ever expect to secure good and competent help in the department of homemaking, we will have first to make it respectable, give it a standing that belongs only to the skilled...."[28] Not surprisingly then, when the Royal Commission on Industrial Training of 1913 solicited the advice of women's groups, the brief isolated the training of servants as the most important aspect of vocational training for girls and young women.[29]

Thus, to understand the appeal of domestic science education, one must take into account the concern for both a better skilled servant class and a more competent and confident class of homemakers. Although the connection between domestic science education and the middle-class demand for hired help has frequently been made, the fact that home economics filtered into every stream and level of Ontario's educational system makes clear the need for a less class-specific explanation as well. Like their lower-class counterparts, daughters of the elite were exposed to domestic science education. And when such training was unavailable in Canada, they acquired it in the United States, as did Hoodless's daughter. Thus, what divided the two social classes in this instance was not the content of the course per se, but the intentions underlying it. The acquisition of homemaking skills was seen as a necessity for all women. Such training among women of less prosperous backgrounds, however, was expected to produce a body of workers prepared to serve in the homes of the rich.

The uneven spread of domestic science education (Tables 1 and 2) suggests that, despite the preoccupation of the NCWC and other upper-class women's associations with "vocational" training for prospective servants, the servant problem would be addressed only after domestic science had become part of the curriculum in the more prosperous boards and regions of the province. Ironically, the combined effect of unequal educational opportunity and differing class attitudes towards adolescent schooling was the earlier and greater exposure of the middle-class girls to domestic science education. In other words, domestic science became part of the general curriculum before it became a component of working-class schooling in technical schools.

To conclude, then, domestic science education was a product of the social and familial concerns of turn of the century middle- and upper-class women. Its integration into the curriculum of Ontario schools, however, was also subject to factors outside the control of the programs' female initiators and supporters. Just as the actions of Adelaide Hoodless and Massey Treble are part of the history of domestic science education, so too the priorities of school boards, policies of the Department of Education, decisions of parents regarding the schooling of their children, and attitudes and aspirations of girls and young women belong to this chapter of Ontario's past. The examination of these factors, separately and in relation to one another, illuminates the processes whereby the curriculum became more gender-specific in the first half of the twentieth century.

Comparative Conclusion: Quebec and Ontario

The timing of and reasons for the formalization and institutionalization of domestic science education in Ontario and Quebec are striking in their similarities. Taking place at the turn of the century, these processes occurred in response to the demands of educators, social activists, and reformers for a more practical and socially responsive curriculum. Yet despite the similarities in timing and context and the analogous constraints of insufficient funding and regional inequality, important differences emerge from our comparative study of programs and their impact on formal education in these two provinces.

The Ontario public school system, like its Protestant counterpart in Quebec, was more successful than the francophone Catholic one in integrating domestic science education into the primary level. Although the Council of Public Instruction supported this area of study, the learning of cookery, sewing and housewifery rarely took place at the elementary level of the public Catholic school system. It occurred with greater regularity and frequency in the private sector, particularly in the *classico-ménager* schools, which were designed to provide students with the basics of homemaking.

At the secondary level, the Catholic public system in Quebec and the public one in Ontario, in contrast to the Protestant system in Quebec, offered home economics in grade 9. It should be noted, however, that instruction in domestic science in French Quebec took place at the *post-primaire* level which structurally resembled Ontario's continuation schools. Both were extensions of the common school. In the private sector, the *écoles ménageres supérieures* offered a commercial as well as a domestic science course. The former option was not available in the *écoles ménageres supérieures*.

At the normal school and the university level, home economics courses prepared students for professional work. In both provinces, teacher training in domestic science was seen as essential to the successful introduction of practical training into the public school curriculum. University programs were designed to train teachers as well, but the demands of industry and public service institutions for dieticians, nutritionists and food science experts broadened their

Domestic Science Education in Ontario, 1900-1940

scope. French Quebec was much slower than the two English societies under study to establish Faculties of Household Science in its universities. It was not until 1943 that Laval University founded one.

While an explanation for this delay requires a study of economic and cultural factors beyond the scope of this comparative discussion, the reasons for the differences that have been noted on the elementary and secondary levels between the three cultural groups are more within our grasp. At least in part, they were a consequence of the contrasting organizational structures that enveloped the educational systems of the two Central Canadian provinces.

Ontario's highly centralized bureaucracy favoured a more uniform spread of domestic science education. The jurisdiction of the Catholic section of the Council of Public Instruction in Quebec was limited to the Catholic public school system. Protestant schools, private Catholic academies and boarding schools, and educational institutions under the supervision of the Department of Agriculture and Colonisation were outside its purview. A further splintering of command took place in the private sector. Religious teaching communities retained control over the curriculum and staffing of the schools they administered.

If by its very nature a centralized system accelerated the pace of integration, it also facilitated a more even spread of domestic science education. The preference of French Canada's elite for private schooling, and its subsequent development into a formidable rival of public schooling, deprived the children attending free schools of the educational crumbs that would have fallen their way in a more unified system. The sharp division along class lines of Catholic education in Quebec contributed to the unevenness in the integration of domestic science education. Like the other amenities ushered in by the "New Education Movement," manual training centres were affordable only if the more essential needs of schooling had been met. Poorer than its two counterparts, Quebec's Catholic public system understandably lagged behind in the realization of the goals of turn of the century educational reform.

Co-educational schooling in the English societies, as opposed to sex-segregated education in the French one, adds further complexity to this comparative study. Generally in North America the introduction of domestic science was part of a broader campaign staged by "progressive" educators, industrialists, and labour groups to reform the curriculum, rendering it less abstract and more practical. Despite common origins, it seems that the implementation of reform in sex-segregated schools took a slightly different route from the trajectory followed by co-educational institutions. As the feminine of manual training, domestic science became part of the school program at the time shop or woodworking for boys was introduced. In sex-segregated schools the causal relationship between these two modes of practical training need not have been as direct as in co-educational ones. Catholic schools in Quebec could modify the curriculum in boys' schools and equip them with manual training centres, without making equivalent changes in girls' schools. It is very likely that in a system that tended to spend more public funds on male schooling the greater unavailability of domestic science education in the Catholic public schools reflected yet another form of social inequality, that of gender.

There is an ironic twist to this seeming inequality. By favouring male schools it not only had the obvious effect of subjecting female students in state schools to difficult conditions of intellectual work but also deprived them of an education devised to fit them for their future roles as wives and mothers. Ironies such as this, of course, are one measure of the effectiveness of reform and an illustration of the extent and ways in which reformers' intentions can be thwarted by social factors outside their control.

But anomalies and unforeseen consequences should not make us lose sight of the ultimate success of the domestic science movement. Despite its uneven spread in Ontario and Quebec, it reached a large proportion of the female school age population. Directed and overseen by provincial and federal authorities domestic science became an effective means of reinforcing the existing sexual division of labour at a time when women seemed to be breaking the barriers against their entry into the workforce and especially into male-dominated occupations.

Domestic Science Education in Ontario, 1900-1940

Notes

1.   For a thorough discussion of turn of the century educational reform movements see Neil Sutherland, *Children in English-Canadian Society: Framing the Twentieth Century Consensus* (Toronto: University of Toronto Press, 1978).

2.   Edith Rowles, *Home Economics in Canada* (Saskatoon: Modern Press, 1964) 11. In addition to Rowles' study, see Robert M. Stamp, "Teaching Girls Their 'God-given Place in Life'—The Introduction of Home Economics in the Schools," *Atlantis* 2, 2 (Spring 1977), 18-34; Ruth Howes, "Adelaide Hoodless," in Mary Quayle Innis, ed., *The Clear Spirit*, (Toronto: University of Toronto Press, 1966) 103-119.

3.   Adelaide Hoodless, "Household Science Report," *The Report of the Minister of Education, Province of Ontario* [hereafter RMEPO] (1903), 158-162.

4.   Ibid., 162.

5.   Robert M. Stamp, *The Schools of Ontario, 1876-1976* (Toronto: University of Toronto Press, 1982) 155-163.

6.   RMEPO (1939), 18.

7.   T.R. Morrison, "Reform as Social Tracking: The Case of Industrial Education in Ontario, 1870-1900," *The Journal of Educational Thought*, 8 (1974), 87-110; Marvin Lazerson and Timothy Dunn, "Schools and the Work Crisis: Vocationalism in Canadian Education," in H.A. Stevenson and J.D. Wilson, eds., *Precepts, Policy, and Process: Perspectives on Contemporary Canadian Education*, (London: Alexander, Blake and Associates, 1977).

8.   Ruth Roach Pierson and Marjorie Cohen, "Educating Women for Work: Government Training Programs for Women Before, During and After World War II," in M. Cross and G.S. Kealey, eds., *Modern Canada, 1930-1980s* (Toronto: McClelland and Stewart, 1984). The role of provincial and federal governments in reinforcing the sexual division of labour in Canadian society is also discussed in Veronica Strong-Boag, "Working Women and the State: The Case of Canada, 1880-1945," *Atlantis* 6, 2 (Spring 1981), 1-9.

9.   Ida M. Hunter, "Report of the Supervisor of Household Science," *Annual Report of the Board of Education of Toronto (1906, 1912, 1913)*. See also Draft of proposed changes in public and high school courses of study and organization, 1903. Department of Education, Government Documents, Ontario Public Archives [hereafter OPA].

10. Albert Leake often reported on schools which were exemplary in their implementation of the principles of the "New Education" movement. See, for example, his discussion of Memorial Public School in Hamilton in "Report of the Inspector of Manual Training and Household Science," *RMEPO* (1929) 47.

11. RMEPO (1937) 18.

12. F.S. Rutherford, "Report of the Director of Vocational Education," *RMEPO* (1938) 19.

13. Collegiate institutes were intended to be "the link between the public school and the university." Hence they were to cater to the more intelligent and serious student, while high schools were to serve the average one. Collegiate institutes were also given additional funding by the provincial government. The history of these institutions is outlined in J.M. McCutcheon, *Public Education in Ontario* (Toronto: T.H. Best Publishing Co., 1941).

14. See Stamp's discussion of parental attitudes in rural communities toward practical education: *The Schools of Ontario*, 125. The remarks of school inspectors also make clear the reluctance of rural communities to accept the various curriculum reforms proposed by the Ministry.

15. *RMEPO* (1905), xxv. Richard Harcourt was in fact quite damning of "new education" opponents, labelling them reactionary.

16. Recent work on the history of teaching makes clear the extent to which teachers were preoccupied with their working conditions because they were so dismal. For a discussion of Ontario teachers see: Alison Prentice, "The School Promoters: Education and Social Class in Mid-Nineteenth Century Upper Canada," (Ph.D. thesis, University of Toronto, 1974). For Quebec see: Maryse Thivierge, "Les institutrices laiques à l'école primaire catholique au Québec de 1900 à 1964," (Thèse de Ph.D., Université Laval, 1981) and Marta Danylewycz, "Sexes et classes sociales dans l'enseignement: le cas de Montréal à la fin du 19e siècle," in N. Fahmy-Eid and Micheline Dumont, *Maîtresses de maison, maîtresses d'école* (Montréal: Boréal Express, 1983).

17. This is a rough estimate based on the numbers of students registered in courses listed under the domestic science or commercial category.

18. The university calendars for the years 1902-1936 have been used for this general outline of program changes. They may be consulted at the University of Toronto Archives.

19. Sample of Professions of University of Toronto Faculty of Household Science Graduates, University of Toronto Archives.

20. N. Burwash, "Views of Prominent Educators on Household Science," *Lillian Massey School of Household Science and Arts Calendar, 1903-04,* University of Toronto Archives, B80-0024.

21. Rowles, *Home Economics in Canada,* 16.

22. Richard Harcourt to Mrs. Treble, February 1903, RG 2 Series D 7, Box 3, OPA.

23. *RMEPO* (1921), 50, 315-326, and (1926), 36-38.

24. Rowles, *Home Economics in Canada,* 14-22, discusses the establishment of these forerunners to the Macdonald Institute and the University of Toronto Faculty of Household Science. For primary sources dealing with the founding of these two institutes, see correspondence and documents in Series RG2, P-2, Boxes 59-62, OPA. See also Victor School of Household Science and Art Calendars in the University of Toronto Archives, B80-0024.

25. Quoted in Ann Margaret Gray, "Continuity in Change: The Effects on Girls of Co-Educational Secondary Schooling in Ontario, 1860-1910," (M.A. Thesis, University of Toronto, 1979) 134.

26. Helen Parker, "Technical Schools for Work," *The Canadian Magazine* (1893), 34-37, reprinted in Ramsay Cook and Wendy Mitchinson, eds., *Their Proper Sphere: Women's Place in Canadian Society* (Toronto: Oxford University Press, 1976).

27. Mrs. Stowe, "Domestic Problems, Cause and Cure," in *Proceedings of the Meeting of the National Council of Women of Canada* (1894) 164.

28. Ibid., 167.

29. *Royal Commission on Industrial Training and Technical Education,* Vol. 1, Part II (Ottawa 1913) 336.

For Intelligent Motherhood and National Efficiency: The Toronto Home and School Council, 1916-1930[1]

Kari Dehli

To start little children on the right road of general efficiency seems to me the greatest thing women can do.[2]

In her recent book on truancy in Scotland, Fiona Paterson has argued that schools not only "school" children (or teachers), but families as well.[3] She suggests that with compulsory, state schooling, a number of techniques were put in place to regulate the lives of children, within and beyond the schoolhouse. Indeed, during the second half of the 19th century, legal definitions of and responsibility for children came increasingly to refer to schooling as an obvious and necessary "stage" of transition to adulthood. In state education and legal discourses, "child" and a "pupil" became synonymous. To be absent from those buildings defined as school during the prescribed hours of organized teaching, was to be "truant," or as Paterson says, to be "out of place." Parents, and especially mothers, were held legally and morally responsible for ensuring that their children would be in the right place at the right times. Indeed, their ability and willingness to do so became a mark of good mothering.

But there was and is more to this responsibility vested in mothers to ensure that children attend school. The regulatory practices which compulsory attendance legislation made possible have been changed and elaborated since the 19th century. Today's schooling discourses and practices in North America explicitly tell us, or tacitly assume, that children not only have to be present in the classroom, they must be ready to adjust to its routines and relations, they must be able and willing to learn, and they ought to be happy and content, as well. That mothers are largely held responsible for children's adjustment to schooling, as well as for their successes and failures, has become taken for granted and embedded in the talk and work practices of teachers, school social workers, administrators, and often, mothers themselves. Women who mother children must negotiate relations with schools as part of their ordinary work of mothering.

In this paper I want to trace how some of the ordinary and apparently "normal" and "natural" relations between mothers and schools were put in place in one Ontario city.[4] I want to explore how practices and relations which "school the family" were organized over time, in one place. I do not assume that women were (or are) simply passive victims in this process, nor that "woman" can be taken to signify a coherent and unitary category. Thus I am

147

especially interested in how groups of women took part in debating and shaping relations between mothers and schools, and how these features of schooling had (and continue to have) different effects on different groups of women. In order to look at these questions here, I will consider some of the debates and organizational work of one middle-class Toronto school reform organization from 1916 to 1930.

The Toronto Home and School Council was an organization in which many "ordinary" middle-class women met with, listened and talked to professionals and "experts" from several fields related to education, such as social science, social work, psychology, public health, juvenile justice and urban planning. The Council also produced and circulated pamphlets, organized study groups and recommended readings to interested mothers. Reading their organizational documents can therefore tell us something about how discourses of school, family and child became part of the everyday organizational practices of middle-class women in the inter-war period. Although the documents of this kind of organization can allude to how its members wrestled with often conflicting ideas and advice presented to them, the documents tell us little about middle-class women's own approaches to child rearing, or their personal worries for their children. Therefore, this paper is not an attempt to tell a story of "the reality" of women's childrearing experiences. It is about how an organization of women engaged with discourses and practices regulating "families." One of the effects of Home and School organizations' engagement with such discourses and practices was to help produce and normalize certain meanings of the categories of "home" and "school," as well as women's roles in managing the relations between them. While other chapters in this book focus on the lives and work of women teachers, I will discuss the other half, as it were, in the relation between schools and families.

The first Home and School associations in Toronto were organized by middle-class women as Art Leagues or Mothers' Clubs in the 1890s. Similar clubs had been organized elsewhere in North America and Western Europe, and in this city these groups had overlapping memberships with the Women's Christian Temperance Union, the YWCA, and the Toronto Local Council of Women. In 1916 Ada Mary Brown Courtice called together a meeting as convenor of the Education Committee of the Local Council of Women. The widow of a Methodist minister and editor of the *Christian Guardian,* Ada Courtice had ambitions to become a trustee of the Toronto Board of Education, having been defeated in her first attempt in 1914.[5] One of the purposes of the meeting she called was therefore to create an organization which would become actively involved in local educational politics, finding and assisting women to run for office. With the help of the newly created Toronto

148

The Toronto Home and School Council, 1916-1930

Home and School Council, Courtice was elected to Toronto's School Board in 1917, where she became a vociferous advocate for women teachers and pushed for a number of reforms, including expansion of public school kindergartens and domestic science.

Nine Art Leagues and Mothers' Clubs formed the first Home and School Council in 1916. In 1921 there were 33 member organizations, and by 1930 the Council had 70 local clubs, which together counted a membership in the thousands. Although not formally a part of the school system, Home and School clubs (or parent-teacher associations) were actively encouraged by school authorities as a means of fostering "intelligent sympathy" between teachers and parents.[6] Their proponents thought that Home and School clubs could bring the work of mothers into closer relation and harmony with the work of teachers, thus aiding the latter in their tasks. On the other hand, mothers were invited to join an organization which claimed to represent "the home view" in discussions with teachers and in public and political debates of educational issues.[7]

Meetings of the central Home and School Council were advertised and reported on in Toronto newspapers. During the 1920s and 1930s, this organization became a venue where Toronto school reformers discussed a wide range of educational questions. Monthly meetings of the Council were well attended, often in the hundreds, mostly by "lay" women who made up the majority of members, but also by male "experts" and professionals from Toronto and other cities in Canada, the United States and England. It had been the intention of Ada Courtice to involve fathers as well as mothers in local Home and School clubs and in the Council, but men tended to participate not as fathers, but as experts and scientists giving women advice and providing glimpses into the latest educational and psychological research. The gender asymmetry in the division of organizational labour was striking: women administered the organization and spoke on its behalf, while male experts were provided with a podium from which to present their positions on educational reform or child welfare. Very few men appear to have taken part in any other capacity, as ordinary members of the Council or even less in the more anonymous local clubs. The everyday organizational work was clearly marked as a feminine domain, while public events and debates positioned men as possessors of knowledge and expertise.

While the sexual division of organizational labour is unsurprising, and in many ways parallels prevalent divisions of domestic and childrearing labour, the Home and School Council challenged other taken-for-granted notions of "proper" spheres for women and men. Women's entry into local educational politics, for example, was highly controversial and tenuous. Small groups of single women (who paid property taxes in their own name) had been able to vote and run for office in school board elections since the 19th century. However, women's participation as voters and candidates, as political subjects, in such contests was caught up in arguments around general suffrage for women. Some suffragists argued that women could demonstrate their political competence and moral virtue by participating as voters and candidates in school board elections. Such elections were therefore promoted as a way of preparing and educating women for their rights and duties as citizens.[8] But another type of argument was also put forward, modifying the broader claims for women to suffrage and citizenship. The work of school boards was seen as especially important and "naturally" suited to women, since their business was to make decisions about children. Thus it was "in the interest of children" that the Toronto Local Council of Women joined forces with the Home and School to "nominate more women as school trustees" for the 1918 election.[9] In this sense, the politics of school board elections were seen as apolitical, an arena where in fact the innocent interests of the child should not be contaminated with politics.

Although they helped elect a few women to the Toronto Board of Education, the Home and School Council's self-proclaimed position as representative of women voters was not, and could not be, attained. Council records from the 1920s lament the "apathy" of women, and their poor turnout at the polls. To make matters even more difficult, the Home and School Council often encountered opponents in the press as well as on the School Board itself. Accusing the Council of playing "the game of sex politics," a 1925 editorial in *The Toronto Telegram* argued that, " ' the women of Toronto' are not represented or controlled by the busybody organizations that represent nobody outside of the ranks of an extremely limited membership."[10] This kind of reaction from men towards women's organizations that were critical of dominant institutions and beliefs was (and still is) not unusual. It was a response which met Home and School members and other women whenever they crossed the boundaries of acceptable feminine behaviour in the public domain. Perhaps in response to *The Toronto Telegram*'s sentiment, the Council abandoned its practice of publicly supporting candidates in school board elections in November 1925.[11]

The political and organizational space created for women through the Home and School Council, then, was at once empowering and confining. Women could and did come together to discuss educational issues, and to take concerted action, as participants in public debates and official politics about education and childrearing. Some of the women who were elected through the Council's efforts, such as Ada Courtice, Edith Groves and Ida Siegel, made important contributions to the School Board. However, the Council's focus on education and mothering confirmed childrearing and schooling as women's responsibilities. Whenever women went beyond "proper" expression of opinion (as in the example above), appeals to women's moral responsibility for children was contrasted with politics on behalf of women. Somehow the "interest of children" could be detached from the personal or political interest of adults, be they parents, teachers or school trustees. It should be noted that this notion of apolitical or innocent politics continues to be very pervasive. When the New Democratic Party began to field candidates in Toronto School Board elections in the 1970s, the move was met with outrage and condemned in the press and by fellow trustees.

While women had to negotiate a difficult course in electoral politics, they were actively sought out by prominent male educators as potential supporters of the latest innovations in education policy, child psychology, juvenile justice, health care and social work. The constant parade of male experts positioned women as consumers of men's knowledge, although I would not venture to claim how or even whether women accepted and practised what they heard and read. Leaving that issue aside, the forms and content of knowledge which women were exposed to in Council meetings and literature were forever changing, forever requiring more study and learning. With the active support of school administrators, the organization of Home and School clubs became a model for how women could learn mothering. Indeed, being a member of such a club signified "intelligent motherhood," thus constructing a norm to which all women could be compared.

The Council's claim to represent "all women" or "the home view" was therefore more problematic than the sexist responses to their political forays, or the "apathy" of women, bespeak. In several ways, by presenting itself as speaking on behalf of all women, the Home and School Council was drawn into constructing an ideal or "normal" model for relations within and between schools and families. A full-time mother and homemaker, a wage-earning husband and dependent children were clearly presumed to constitute a family or a home. Actual families who differed from this model were seen to require particular attention and reform, including organized intervention by Home and School. Early Council documents described Home and School clubs as especially important in schools attended by poor and "foreign" working-class children, as a vehicle to educate their mothers in "Canadian" and middle-class practices of homemaking and childrearing.[12] The difficulties which these children represented to school reformers arose in the context and organization of schooling itself, where many children did not adjust to rigid regulation of time, space, behaviour and appearance (to mention only some of the major

Gender And Education In Ontario: An Historical Reader

issues). Extension and enforcement of compulsory schooling to include ever larger and older populations defined as "children" only increased these problems. Although they manifested themselves as difficulties for teachers in the classroom, the causes of children's problems were often sought in children themselves, or in their families and neighbourhoods. Lack of knowledge and understanding on the part of mothers was (and remains) a popular explanation of school failure.

In this context, an obvious role presented itself for Home and School clubs, whose purpose it was to build precisely the kind of knowledge among mothers which would produce "harmony" and "understanding" between families and schools. Certain families were seen to need special attention. A special committee was established by the Toronto Home and School Council in 1917 to "study the question of interesting the non-English speaking parents in Home and School work."[13] However, Home and School meetings in "foreign districts" were poorly attended, and with the exception of an active mothers' club of working-class Jewish women in the city core, most efforts to create and sustain local clubs outside Anglo-Saxon, middle-class neighbourhoods failed.

This lack of response did not stop the Toronto Home and School Council from discussing and proposing actions in response to any number of problems arising in the schooling of poor and working-class children, "foreign" or otherwise. On the contrary, the Council spent numerous meetings discussing "other" children and their mothers, drawing on psychological concepts of normality and deviance, and notions of efficiency in school management. At the Council's meeting in December 1917 Dr. Horace Britton, Director of Toronto's Bureau of Municipal Research, was invited to speak. He urged, and the secretary who recorded his comments noted that those present agreed, that "the classification of children is most essential," and that school classes "should be divided according to the ability of children and the ability of teachers."[14] I was not able to discover any further references in Council documents to the intriguing notion of organizing classes according to the ability of teachers. Classifying children according to their "ability," on the other hand, was a topic which received substantial attention. Classifying practices drew directly on the emerging science of psychology, and techniques of intelligence testing. The "problems" which such tests and classifications claimed to solve were themselves produced through the organization and practices of schooling; they were displayed by children who did not "adjust" to school discipline, who were in the wrong place at the wrong time, who rejected or ignored school knowledge, or whose behaviour did not conform to dominant codes of morality.

Psychological testing made it possible to identify tensions between the different social sites inhabited by children as though these conflicts were fixed

The Toronto Home and School Council, 1916-1930

properties of individual children themselves. Once identified, "different" children could be segregated into separate classes and schools, where they would no longer endanger or slow the progress of "normal" children.

The Home and School Council was not satisfied with discussing the dangers of "defective" children among themselves. Shortly after Britton's speech, three Council members (who were also Toronto School Board trustees) spoke before the Hodgins Commission which was investigating "The Care and Control of the Mentally Defective and Feeble-minded in Ontario."[15] Hodgins devoted a long discussion to the role of schools in discovering and preventing "defect." He urged his readers to see that "the future solution of the major part of this great problem lies in the schools. They are not only a source of information but the only place where the mental status of the large majority of the children can be definitely and authoritatively settled."[16] To this explicit rationale for the sorting functions of schooling, Hodgins added that measures should be taken to ensure the co-operation of parents, including, if necessary, legal compulsion to submit children to tests and to "special" classes and schools. More useful, however, was the active support of organizations representing parents, such as the Home and School Council. Another suggestion by Hodgins was to change the language used to describe the purposes of testing and segregated schooling. Rather than terms such as "defective" or "feeble-minded," Hodgins suggested that "the desired end" could just as well be attained by using a "neutral term to describe classes formed for this purpose."[17] Describing a practice, such as segregated classes, as "special" no doubt sounds more attractive than referring to the same practice as "classes for defectives."

The Home and School Council, for its part, continued to discuss and support various measures to discover and deal with "different" children in the schools. A proposal that the School Board establish psychological clinics to "pick out children capable of going ahead," was applauded by those who listened to principal Richardson speaking at a Council meeting in 1920. As for the children who were not selected for promotion, or who "would otherwise be a drag on the class," Richardson recommended a "farm school," where "rigid kindly discipline would hold sway."[18] Council meetings in January 1918, November 1919, December 1922, March 1926, September and October 1927 and March 1928 were devoted to discussions of children variously described as "defective," "sub-normal" or "dull." More often than not, these terms were linked to others such as "underprivileged," "poor" or "foreign," or used while discussing particular problems facing teachers in downtown schools attended by working-class students.

Although they consistently supported measures to institute what we now describe as special education, one speaker at a Council meeting in 1928 warned that enough had been done for "sub-normal" children. It was time, she argued, to "give fair play to the average," by creating a differentiated curriculum and improving school buildings.[19] As the Home and School Council developed during the 1920s, their attention began to shift from a strong preoccupation with "problem" children and reforms which they thought would benefit them. Although they never completely abandoned their interest in such children or their mothers, this work was more and more taken over by the expanding departments of school social work, special education and school nursing. Moreover, as I have suggested above, the Council's attempts to organize working-class women into Home and School clubs were not successful. The Council launched a home visiting campaign among "new Canadian" women in 1923, to introduce them to "Canadian ideals" and to the benefits of Home and School clubs.[20] The enthusiastic claim that "visitors were most delightfully received and found the work a great inspiration" was not matched by participation of "new Canadian" women in Home and School affairs.[21] Indeed, a speaker at the Annual Meeting of the Ontario Federation of Home and School Associations complained in 1925 that, "the people who need it the most could not be induced to attend a meeting of that sort at all. It is very difficult to get them; we have to have a tea-party or a special program to get them at all."[22] The only accounts of participation by "new Canadian" women that I could find took the form of performances, during which the Council's white, Anglo-Saxon members were entertained by watching "other" women and children put their cultures on display.[23]

Middle-class women's debates about "problem" children and their mothers in the early 20th century were shot through with tensions around class, race, ethnicity and sexuality. While ostensibly talking and worrying about different "others," members of the Toronto Home and School Council were positioning themselves and their own children as the "efficient," "intelligent" and "normal" referents to which "problem" children and mothers were compared. Although often presented in terms which claimed to represent the best interest of "different" children, worries about their effect on Council members' own children and their progress in school, were also expressed. We should not assume, therefore, that the position of normality was one which middle-class women could take for granted, or one which their children could automatically assume. A great deal of effort, and a great deal of talk, were expended on how to ensure all children's "happy adjustment" to school life in particular and social life in general. The threat of failure lurked not just among "others," it was present everywhere and required diligent application of scientific childrearing methods by all mothers.[24]

The Toronto Home and School Council, 1916-1930

In March 1922 the Council debated the question "Are Parents Fitted for their Responsibilities?"[25] No conclusive answer seemed to be given, but much activity and talk was devoted to this question in the years to come. Committees were established to teach nutrition, health care, cleanliness, budgeting, home gardening and crafts to women. Other topics included finding the "proper" balance between work, rest and recreation; how to promote music and beauty in the home; principles of home life; children's mental development; and rights, duties and privileges of parents and children. In case there could be any misunderstanding of the moral duty involved in "home science" and "parent education," the chair of one such committee, Kate J. MacTavish, declared that educating adult women for these tasks was crucial in order to enable "our Canadian home to become the source of all that is noble, pure and capable in private, public and national life."[26]

It is impossible to separate the skills and knowledge which women might need (or, which organizations such as Home and School thought they needed) from the social and moral regulation implied in these educational efforts. Like many other such initiatives in this period, the Home and School Council's forays into "home science" for women promoted a nuclear family form, with a wage-earning husband/father and a full-time mother/homemaker. The curriculum stressed the ideal of a well-ordered, predictable and harmonious household, with lines of authority between parents and children matching those of teachers and pupils. Nevertheless, it was not until the mid-1920s that the Council's adult education efforts obtained a consistent focus and a coherent curriculum. From then on it was "parent education" rather than "home science" which came to dominate their efforts, and increasingly it was the middle-class members of Home and School clubs who participated, and it was their "normal" children who were the objects of discussion.

One event which made this shift possible was the establishment of the St. George's School for Child Study (later the Institute for Child Study) at the University of Toronto.[27] Psychologist William Blatz was appointed as director of the new Institute, and became a frequent speaker at Home and School Council meetings, as in November 1925, when he addressed the topic of "child development."[28] But it was through study groups organized jointly by the Institute for Child Study and the Home and School Council, that the discourses of developmental child psychology were transmitted to middle-class women. Most of these study groups took the "pre-school child"—in itself a concept which depends on the elaboration of compulsory schooling—as their topic. The version of developmental psychology put forward by Blatz and his colleagues argued that "the foundation of the child's health and character development is laid during the first six years of his [sic] life." It was crucial to focus educational efforts on mothers, because "the child accepts without question, his manner, his habits, and his normal standards from his parents, and more especially from his mother."[29]

Building their theories of childhood on the idea that children move through stages of mental and physical growth, each with observable characteristic behaviours and problems, developmental psychologists emphasized the role of early training and education. Blatz favoured nursery education run by trained teachers, and Home and School leaders were among the few who supported him when he faced critics of nursery education in the Toronto press in 1925. Speaking in his defence, Kate J. MacTavish claimed that working-class children in particular could benefit from this innovation, suggesting that "parents whose lives are composed of manual labour have neither the time nor the patience, neither the training nor the proper environment to give their runabout children attention."[30] Aside from presenting patronizing assumptions as facts, it turned out that the children who attended Blatz' nursery school were not those of manual labourers at all, but rather the children of professors, managers and civil servants.[31] These children became the objects of detailed and longitudinal psychological research: their behaviour was carefully observed and recorded by student-teachers according to pre-defined categories on detailed charts.

The import of these records extended beyond these particular children, since they were organized and analysed so as to "arrange a system of habit rules in order that advice may be given to parents who have the responsibility of raising children."[32] Advice to parents, then, was to be based on observed behaviours of middle-class children in a carefully regulated environment, constructed so as to produce, discover and describe a "system of habits and rules" in children. There was an obvious tautology in this procedure: a system of habits was presumed to exist, latently in each child, and the methods of observation were designed to assemble instances or behaviours in such a way as to fit the system's characteristics. The role of mothers and teachers was to organize children's environments so that they could "develop" through each "stage." Evidence that "development" was taking place could in turn be garnered from observations of children's behaviours, wherein evidence of habits and rules could be discovered. So, it was not the case that "child development" was already there, simply waiting for the psychologist, teacher or mother's discovery: it was actively produced in the explicitly organized relations between adults and children. An important implication of this employment of psychology, and of pedagogy and mothering, was therefore to construct and promote notions of "normal" childhood and of "normal" teaching and mothering.[33]

The Toronto Home and School Council, 1916-1930

Since the number of children who could attend nursery school was small, it was necessary to educate mothers in the principles and practices of "child development." Home and School members joined together in study groups to learn the do's and dont's of scientific mothering. Even mothers whose children were enrolled in nursery school had to be trained, so as to provide the necessary consistency for the child. In contrast to earlier efforts to educate "other" women for motherhood, child study groups presumed that Council members themselves were wanting in their knowledge. William Blatz' colleague, Elizabeth Bott, remarked to a meeting of the Ontario Federation of Home and School Associations in 1926 that, "we must abandon the old idea that parents, by virtue of their parentage, know exactly what they do...it is as important to have an expert opinion in regard to the behaviour of the child as in regard to the physical health of the child."[34]

One of the mistakes made by most mothers, in Blatz' and Bott's view, was that they indulged children and did not apply consistent rules of behaviour in their childrearing.[35] To integrate the kind of observation described above demanded a detached sort of mothering. One pamphlet used in Toronto child study groups in 1930 stated as fact that, "we regard children from a more scientific attitude. We are more restrained in our love and don't pamper children because we know it will be better for them when they grow up."[36] The kind of mothering demanded by child study experts—incessant activity, ceaseless monitoring, consistent rules and discipline—constructed mothers as a kind of professional carrying out work that required scientific knowledge and training. Judging from the widespread popularity of child study groups in Toronto (and elsewhere), middle-class women were ready to perceive themselves in this way.[37] However, the short-lived "success" of child study groups also bespeaks the difficulty women encountered when attempting to put the advice into practice.

In many ways, the very form of organization in the Home and School—groups of women inviting mostly male speakers to address issues facing mothers and teachers, study groups to discuss "scientific" childrearing—presumed and reinforced the position of male "experts" in relation to middle-class women. In particular, the new science and profession of psychology came to obtain an important position for North American middle-class women, and to organizations such as the Home and School in the 1920s.[38] But, as I have shown, the advice given to women by psychologists or other "experts" was not consistent, and it changed over time, addressing different issues and anxieties, presuming different women (and children) as their objects. Some early pioneers of Home and School, such as Ada Courtice, wanted the organization to promote "intelligent mothering," but in her terms this would be based on practices which closely resembled the child-centred kindergarten.[39] Here "the child" was constructed as a bearer of unlimited potential for good, a potential which mothers (and teachers) could bring to fruition through selfless love and nurturing. Ironically, a "passive" woman/mother/teacher was considered especially suited to produce an "active" child/worker/ citizen, at a time when women themselves were only beginning to obtain the rights and responsibilities of citizenship.

The psychology of intelligence testing and measurement made quite different assumptions about "the child" and "the mother." Here the emphasis was not on developing potential, or on loving and nurturing relations between adults and children. Arising out of problems in school and classroom management, intelligence testing aimed, and claimed, to discover and classify "differences" inherent in each child. A repertoire of fixed categories such as "mentally defective," "feeble-minded" and "abnormal" were made available and popularized through interactions between psychologists, social workers, teachers and middle-class women's organizations such as the Home and School. While rarely using such terms to discuss their own children (at least not in the documented, public domain which I have had access to), Home and School women engaged in lively debates and school reform initiatives which took such categories to be factual, and which embedded them in the practices of schools and teachers.

Developmental psychology and child study groups made different assumptions again, and involved middle-class women's mothering much more directly. Here a more detached, planned and organized mothering was favoured, where "too much love" was seen to interfere with children's development. Throughout the short period I have discussed, we can see that different and seemingly contradictory theories of childhood and mothering were advanced by representatives of psychology, education and social science in the Home and School Council. Male "experts" not only shaped the ways in which certain patterns of behaviours or characteristics of population groups were discovered and described, they also suggested courses of action to address the "problems" they identified. One field of such action was the compulsory state school system, and its relation to families.

I have tried to show that women were not passive consumers of "new" knowledges of childhood, or passive victims of state regulation through schooling. In the short period which I have discussed, one middle-class women's organization in Toronto took up several different, and at times inconsistent, discourses of childhood, schooling and mothering. Initially an organization with a strong social reform agenda—promoting women as candidates for School Board elections, supporting kindergartens and domestic science, backing women

The Toronto Home and School Council, 1916-1930

teachers, and endorsing social welfare measures for the poor—the Home and School gradually confined its activities to self-education for middle-class women and support for school administrators. While intentional or not, their claims to represent the "home view" and "all women" helped to elaborate pervasive notions of good mothering, notions which continue to influence school policy and practice, with different effects for different groups of women.

Home and School organizations have received little attention from historians of education in Canada. If they are discussed at all, they are dismissed as rather trivial or ineffectual. Robert Stamp, who at least mentions them, suggests that "Home and Schoolers were co-opted by the educational bureaucracy to serve the latter's own ends," and that their "talk had little impact on the Ontario classroom of the 1920s."[40] In my research on the Toronto Home and School Council I initially had a very similar interpretation of their work. There was a lot of talk about reforms which were never incorporated into classroom practice. It seemed that the Council was used by male school administrators to provide a public platform and support for their reform initiatives, or to defend the school against others. For quite a while, I searched for instances where the Home and School Council had made an observable difference in terms of School Board decisions. I did find that Home and School leaders influenced official debates about kindergartens, domestic science curriculum and the promotion of women teachers. But I was dissatisfied with adding up a list of such accomplishments as "proof" that this neglected organization of women had "really" been more important in school policy and practice than historians had given them credit for.

Instead of attempting to measure the Council's effectiveness in putting forward and implementing its proposals for school reform, I began to think about Home and School Council debates in a different way. Rather than reading the documents as windows into a reality behind their talk, I began to focus on the talk itself—on their debates, minute books, pamphlets and speeches—as integral to and constitutive of the social relations in which members of the Home and School Council were embedded.[41] Thus my interest in the participation of women in this organization, and the consequences of their work, is not so much about measuring observable accomplishments. Rather, the organization itself and the discourses its members engaged in, tell us something about how middle-class women aimed to shape the social relations in which they and their children were embedded. In the early 20th century, these social relations were rapidly changing, seemingly chaotic and threatening, as forms and relations of production and reproduction were being transformed. In many ways, this was the period when the middle-class came to be formed as a class in North America. Organized forms of schooling and "scientific" knowledge were crucial to this process. Industrial capitalism and the modern state elaborated and required new forms of knowledge, modes of representation and administration, creating opportunities for middle-class careers. The positions of women (and children) in these relations were not given in advance, they had to be worked for or they had to be regulated. Home and School organizations were one site where these positions were debated and worked out, with consequences for the women who participated in them, and for "other" women who became targets for the regulatory practices they helped to shape.

The Toronto Home and School Council, 1916-1930

Notes

1. An earlier version of this paper was given at the Biennial Conference of the Canadian History of Education Association in Halifax, 1986. I want to thank Wally Seccombe, Philip Corrigan and the editors of this book for their comments and suggestions, and the Social Sciences and Humanities Research Council of Canada for funding my doctoral research.

2. Ada Mary Brown Courtice, quoted in *The Story of the Toronto Home and School Council through the Years 1916 - 1936* (Toronto: The Council, 1935) p. 4.

3. Fiona Paterson, *Out of Place: Public Policy and the Emergence of Truancy* (Barcombe, Lewes: Falmer, 1989).

4. This paper is part of a larger research project for my Ph. D. thesis. Kari Dehli, "Women and Class: The Social Organization of Mothers' Relations to Schools in Toronto, 1915 to 1940," (Unpublished Ph.D. dissertation, University Of Toronto (OISE), 1988).

5. For a biographical history of Ada Courtice, see Terry Crowley, "Ada Mary Brown Courtice: Pacifist, Feminist and Educational Reformer in Early Twentieth-Century Canada," *Studies in History and Politics*, 1980: 75-114.

6. Toronto Home and School Council, *The Story of the Toronto Home and School Council through the Years 1916–1936* (Toronto: The Council, 1935) p. 7.

7. Dehli, 1988, Chapter 4.

8. Carol Bacchi, *Liberation Deferred? The Ideas of English-Canadian Suffragists, 1877–1919* (Toronto: University of Toronto Press, 1983).

9. Toronto Local Council of Women, Executive Committee Minutes, 16 October 1917. Public Archives of Ontario, MU 6362.

10. *Toronto Telegram*, 2 January 1925.

11. Toronto Home and School Council, Civics Committee, 12 November 1925. Board of Education for the City of Toronto Archives, Toronto Home and School Council Collection, Cab. 8-1. Hereafter referred to as TBE/THSC.

12. It should be noted that the term "foreign" had a specific meaning in dominant English Canadian discourse of the early 20th century. It referred to non-English-speaking immigrants, and especially those from southern and eastern Europe.

13. TBE/THSC, Minutes, 11 June 1917.

14. TBE/THSC, Minutes, 3 December 1917.

15. Ada Courtice, Caroline Brown and Edith L. Groves appeared before the Hodgins Commission. F.E. Hodgins, "Report on the Care and Control of the Mentally Defective and the Feeble-minded," *Ontario Sessional Papers*, 52(5), 1920, Appendix.

16. Ibid., p. 99.

17. Ibid., p. 95.

18. TBE/THSC, Minutes, 9 March 1920.

19. "Council Entertains Overseas Teachers. Mrs. Plumptree Gives Brilliant Address." *Home and School*. 1(1) December 1928: 8. Adabel Plumptree was a trustee on the Board of Education. She was later elected to the Toronto City Council.

20. TBE/THSC, "Plan for Home Visiting," Toronto Home and School Council, Education Department, not dated, but likely 1923.

21. Ibid.

22. Mrs. Frederick Hosmer, "The Parent and the School," Ontario Educational Association, Home and School Section, *Proceedings*, 1925: 224.

23. TBE/THSC, Scrapbooks, 1920-1930.

24. Katherine Arnup, "Educating Mothers: Government Advice for Women in the Inter-War Years," in *Delivering Motherhood. Maternal Ideologies and Practices in the 19th and 20th Centuries*, Katherine Arnup, Andreé Lévesque and Ruth Roach Pierson eds., (London: Routledge, 1990) pp. 190-210.

25. TBE/THSC, Minutes, 8 March 1922.

26. TBE/THSC, Kate J. MacTavish, "Letter to Presidents," Ontario Federation of Home and School Associations, Home Science Committee, 3 October 1924.

27. Mary L. Northway, "Child Study in Canada: A Casual History," in *Child Development: Selected Readings*, L. M. Brockman et al. eds., (Toronto: McClelland and Stewart, 1973). For a history of institutes for child study in North American universities, see Steven L. Schlossman, "Philanthropy and the Gospel of Child Development," *History of Education Quarterly*, 21, Fall 1981: 275-299.

28. TBE/THSC, Minutes, 8 March 1925.

29. "Parent Education," *The Ontario Home and School Review* 6(3) May 1931: 14.

30. "First Five Years Children Learn Definitive Habits," TBE/THSC, Newsclips, no source, no date, but likely late 1925, on occasion of the opening of the St. George's School for Child Study at the University of Toronto.

The Toronto Home and School Council, 1916-1930

31.   Veronica Strong-Boag, "Intruders in the Nursery: Childcare Professionals Reshape the Years One to Five," in *Childhood and Family in Canadian History*, Joy Parr ed., (Toronto: McClelland and Stewart, 1982) p. 167.

32.   *Ontario Home and School Review* 2(1) September—November 1925: 7.

33.   For an elaboration of a similar argument about how developmental psychology actively construct the object it claims to discover, see Valerie Walkerdine, "Developmental Psychology and the Child-centred Pedagogy: the Insertion of Piaget into Early Education," in *Changing the Subject. Psychology, Social Regulation and Subjectivity*, Julian Henriques et al., eds., (London: Methuen, 1984) pp. 153-202.

34.   Ontario Educational Association, Home and School Section, Proceedings, 1926, p. 249.

35.   W.E. Blatz and E. Bott, *Parents and the Pre-school Child* (Toronto: J.M. Dent and Sons, 1929).

36.   St. George's School for Child Study, Parent Education Division, Study Course No. U. Extension Groups, "The Appetites and Habit Formation 1930–31," (Toronto; University of Toronto Press, 1930) p. 2.

37.   Steven L. Schlossman, "The Formative Era in American Parent Education: Overview and Interpretation," in *Parent Education and Public Policy*, Ron Haskins and Diane Adams eds., (Norwood, N.J.: Ablex Publishing, 1983).

38.   Schlossman, 1983, pp. 32-34.

39.   Dehli, 1988, chapter 7.

40.   Robert Stamp, *The Schools of Ontario, 1876–1976* (Toronto: University of Toronto Press, 1983).

41.   For an elaboration of this approach to text, discourse and social relations, see Dorothy Smith, *The Everyday World as Problematic. A Feminist Sociology*, (Toronto: University of Toronto Press, 1987).

White Collar Vocationalism: The Rise of Commercial Education in Ontario and British Columbia, 1870-1920*

Nancy S. Jackson and Jane S. Gaskell

Abstract: The authors trace the origins of commercial education in nineteenth-century middle-class schooling and examine its relation to the vocational reform movements of the twentieth century. They explore the role of practical education in middle-class support for secondary education, the significance for commercial instruction of the proliferation, fragmentation and feminization of office employment, and the impact on school reform of the intense competition between private and public business educators. Attention is drawn to the dynamics of gender as well as class in the emergence of vocationalism and the shaping of public education.

Debates about vocational schooling at the turn of the century have generated a good deal of historical attention. The "triumph of vocationalism" by about 1920 has been interpreted as a defeat for working-class interests and a turning point in the evolution of school systems from a democratic to a vocational ideal. As Hogan puts it:

> The triumph of vocationalism marked the victory of the market revolution in education and the defeat of Whig and radical republican conceptions of society and education premised on visions of a 'classless society and common schooling'...(It) made possible the transformation of public education into an adjunct of the labour process and the labour market...(it)...stratified educational credentials in a wholly new way and strengthened the connection between schooling and the system of stratification (1985, 193).

Or as Katznelson and Weir phrase their similar concern:

---

* This research has been supported by the Social Sciences and Humanities Research Council of Canada, Grant No. 410-83-0535R2.

Gender And Education In Ontario: An Historical Reader

The conflicts over vocational education proved to be the last site where a class-based battle was fought over whether the ideal of the common school would be replaced by a highly stratified and differentiated system of public education (1985, 151).

Interpretations of vocational education in the public school system have been dominated by the study of manual training, industrial education and domestic science. These were new subjects, hailed by progressive reformers at the turn of the century, resisted by academic traditionalists and debated widely by organized labour, business and civic reformers. Analysis of the claims and counterclaims as well as explanations for the changes that did take place have fuelled many theoretical debates about the relations between school and work, the meaning of progressive education, the role of the working-class in school reform and the reproduction of the relations of the workplace in the school (Lazerson and Grubb 1974; Oakes 1985; Kliebard 1986). The issue of class is front and centre in all the analysis. Gender issues are ignored.

The attention received by the new vocational subjects has obscured the importance of another, more well-established vocational tradition in the public schools: commercial or business education. Basic commercial instruction, such as bookkeeping, business transactions, and even stenography, was part of the school curriculum for several decades before the era of vocational reform, and before the now-familiar subject areas of typing, office machines and procedures, marketing and general business were added around the turn of the century. Significantly, commercial education has been overwhelmingly associated with females by most interested observers, and in fact has served from the turn of the century to the present as the predominant form of labour market preparation for girls. Indeed, few developments in secondary curriculum have had a greater influence on the education of women. The fact that it has been overlooked in the development of a general interpretation of vocationalism is yet another example of sexism in educational scholarship, and has contributed to the gender-blindness of the dominant understandings of vocationalism which we will address in this article.

In the literature on vocationalism, commercial education has been treated variously as insignificant (Lazerson and Grubb 1974; Stamp 1972, 1970), as a female equivalent to industrial education (Hogan 1986; Katznelson and Weir 1985), as a part of the movement for social reform (Weiss 1981, 1978; Kantor and Tyack 1982) and as a response to changing labour market demands (Rury 1984, 1982; Carter and Prus 1982; Rotella 1981). However, all of these approaches leave unanswered questions about the role of gender as a feature of the social and educational changes taking place at the turn of the century,

White Collar Vocationalism

about the particular experience of women in the context of those changes, and about the significance for women of the emergence of commercial courses. These silences undoubtedly reflect in part the climate of public interest and concerns that existed at the turn of the century: the education and training of women were generally considered to be of less public significance than that of men; women's interests in education and training were not as well represented by vocal interest groups such as trade unions; and commercial education was already an established part of the curriculum. Thus the growth of commercial education offered little to attract fundamental controversy. On the other hand, the silence of present day scholarship on women's experience and interest in education is being widely noted and increasingly challenged, and this paper re-examines commercial education in light of these concerns. We want not only to reclaim women's past, but also to lay the basis for a re-evaluation of the dominant educational concepts, like "vocationalism" which have overgeneralized men's experience to represent the experiences of all, and have failed to look seriously at the impact of gender as well as class on the structure and the development of public education.

We will argue that many of the characteristics of vocationalism as it is traditionally understood do not apply to commercial education. The campaigns for vocational reform in the early twentieth century were largely a product of middle- and upper-class interests in improving public morality and industrial productivity through schooling. They were characterized by a variety of charitable and social reforming themes, mostly concerning the education of the children of the masses, with objectives that were distinct by gender. Reformers who were interested in the education of girls focussed their attention almost exclusively on women's role in the home, recommending domestic science education as the one true way to prepare young girls for womanhood.[1] For boys, the focus was on industrial and technical education as a means to achieve a better trained and disciplined workforce and greater industrial productivity.[2] Both sets of objectives were supported by many social reformers who saw vocational training as a means to save the urban poor from conditions of poverty, disease and crime. In Canada they included such powerful lobby groups as the Canadian Manufacturers Association, the Ottawa Board of Trade, the National Council of Women and the Young Women's Christian Association. Their efforts culminated in the Technical Education Act of 1919.

The roots of commercial education, on the other hand, are to be found in the traditions of middle-class schooling in the last half of the nineteenth century. During these formative years, commercial classes enrolled primarily males and taught basic commercial skills such as penmanship, bookkeeping, and business law which were useful in commerce and industry as well as in

167

agricultural pursuits. They enjoyed broad popular support in rural as well as urban communities because they satisfied a widely held desire for education of practical value for youth (largely males) of the middle class. Around the turn of the century, significant changes took place in commercial education, including a dramatic expansion in commercial subjects and enrolments, and a shift to predominantly female students. These changes occurred as a result of the interests of middle-class parents in maintaining the practical and respectable character of secondary schooling, for both sons and daughters, and in the context of the rapid expansion and feminization of clerical employment which continued to be seen as a respectable occupational pursuit for the middle-class. Contributing to this expansion was the self-interest of educators in the public sector in defending their professional territory from the rapid advance of private business colleges which began as early as the 1860s in Ontario. In these circumstances, commercial programs in the public secondary schools were successfully established around the turn of the century, without an atmosphere of reform or rehabilitation, and largely without the enrolment of working-class students. Commercial education thus became the first curriculum specialty in the public secondary school to define itself in primarily vocational terms, in the years when other "modern" vocational subjects were still struggling for a recognized place in the curriculum, although its significance in this respect largely has been overlooked because of its gender and class character.

In this article, we explore the emergence of business education in two regions of Canada, Ontario and British Columbia, between 1870 and 1920. In section one we examine secondary schooling in the last half of the nineteenth century, with emphasis on the place of commercial studies and the enrolment of girls. In section two, our focus shifts to changes in commercial life in the decades surrounding the turn of the century and the response of private as well as public educators to the new demands of commercial life. In the final section we consider the implications of this process of development in commercial studies for an understanding of the advent of vocationalism in the twentieth century and its implications for women.

I. Commercial Education and the Traditions of Secondary Schooling

Public secondary schools in English Canada in the last half of the nineteenth century have been represented as elitist institutions whose primary, if not exclusive, concern was for classical studies and the preparation of boys for university entrance. This conception of the secondary curriculum is supported

White Collar Vocationalism

by public documents such as the annual reports of the ministers of education and the leading education journal of the period, the *Canada Educational Monthly*. However, upon closer examination, neither the grammar schools of the 1860s and 1870s, nor the high schools and collegiate institutes of later years turn out to be strictly classical in program or primarily male in enrolment. Instead, we find that they addressed a variety of vocational concerns and that the attendance of girls was integral to their survival, particularly in rural areas. Since these circumstances were central to the inclusion of commercial education in the curriculum and were critical to its later character and development, we examine them here in some detail.

In Ontario before 1870, the only publicly subsidized form of secondary education was the grammar school. These were locally controlled institutions, often with one or two teachers who were called on to teach a wide variety of subjects as local needs dictated. In 1867, there were 103 such schools and 159 teachers. (Ontario Annual Reports 1887: xi; hereafter *Ont. A.R.*) and they took a variety of forms. A very few fulfilled the classical idea of the grammar school, stressing classical studies and an academic curriculum. However, as Gidney and Lawr (1979) have shown in some detail, most grammar schools taught some classics, especially Latin, along with the more advanced stages of an English and commercial education. There was no one prescribed course of study. Students could choose the subjects that they wanted from among English, Mathematics, Geography, History, Latin, Commercial Arithmetic, Bookkeeping, Penmanship, Mensuration, Physical Science, and so on. Many students would pick up some Latin as a sign of their educated status, but the schools served primarily as vocational preparation for a range of occupational pursuits. The schools prepared young people for first and second class teachers' examinations, for some apprenticeships, for commercial life, and for the examinations of medical and legal societies, at the same time as they prepared a small handful of students for university matriculation. The grammar schools had become by the 1860s "the vocational and prevocational schools of the broad spectrum of the middling portions of society of farmers, merchants, independent artisans and small town professional men" (Gidney and Lawr 1979, 454).

Intense public controversy over this character of grammar schools arose in the mid-1860s when Egerton Ryerson began a campaign to upgrade the state-aided grammar schools and focus them exclusively on classical education. This he attempted to do by introducing regulations in 1865 that tied funding to the average attendance of students learning Greek and Latin, prohibiting the enrolment of girls, imposing a minimum school size, instituting centralized inspection of examinations and banning course options and partial courses.

While his actions were a de facto recognition of the diverse, practical and ad hoc curriculum that was actually in use in the schools, his objective was to change this situation by imposing a strict hierarchy between English subjects and classical education. Under the proposed regulations, English and commercial subjects would be taught through "superior" classes in the common schools wherever the demand existed. Classical studies would become the strict preserve of the grammar school (Gidney and Lawr 1979).

The proposed changes evoked a storm of protest from local communities. Irate letters poured in to Ryerson and the Council of Public Instruction accusing them of "going back to the Dark Ages when nothing was taught but classics" and of "palpable unfairness," "tyranny" and "despotism" for the attempt "to eject girls from the Grammar Schools" (Royce 1975, 7, 11; Gidney and Lawr 1979, 455). Teachers, parents and trustees alike argued that with these measures attendance at secondary schools would be substantially reduced, undermining the broad base of support which publicly funded secondary schooling enjoyed. When local boards ignored the regulations prohibiting the enrolment of girls, Ryerson rewrote the regulations to make two girls studying Latin the equivalent of one boy for the purposes of funding. When this failed to discourage the enrolment of girls, he sought a legal interpretation excluding girls altogether from eligibility for funding under the Grammar School Act. Neither action succeeded in quelling the rebellion of local boards.

Ryerson was eventually forced to compromise on his plans for secondary education, although he conceded as little as he could. With the introduction of the new School Act of 1871, he attempted to accommodate the demand for a diverse curriculum through the creation of separate but parallel institutions for classical scholarship and other higher learning. High schools would be designated for the instruction of both boys and girls in the higher branches of English and commercial education, including mathematics and the natural sciences. Collegiate institutes were to be reserved for the classical education of boys. In principle this innovation was intended to satisfy both the elitist educator, who wanted to purify and raise the standards of the academic curriculum, as well as the local communities and practically minded educators, who wanted to keep enrolments up and maintain a place in schooling for the essential concerns of everyday life. However, in practice the new act did not successfully accomplish the kind of educational hierarchy that Ryerson had envisioned. Within a short period, both the collegiate institutes and the high schools were offering a wide variety of educational programs for both males and females headed for professional, white collar, and agricultural occupations as well as university entrance.[3]

White Collar Vocationalism

The heated public response to Ryerson's proposed regulations reveals the depth of popular support for practically oriented education and the firmly entrenched position of girls in secondary education. In 1865, approximately 2000 of the 5600 pupils registered in Ontario secondary schools were female (Gray 1979). Despite their importance numerically, girls' presence had long been officially overlooked, as was pointed out by the chairman of the Board of the Newmarket Grammar School in a letter to Ryerson in 1865:

> You have never taken any notice of girls attending the grammar schools, they were never intended to be instituted for girls, nevertheless their attendance has always been allowed or winked at; in the country such permission is the greatest possible boon (quoted in Gidney and Lawr 1979, 455).

Winking at the attendance of girls covered up a host of contradictions for the late nineteenth-century educator. The elitist image of the grammar schools was aided by the public emphasis on the "education of the boy." At the same time, the attendance of girls was necessary in order for the schools to be financially viable. Separate girls' academies, which were officially prescribed for girls' education, were rarely made available by local boards, and admission to grammar schools made up for this lack of provision. Furthermore, grammar schooling had become a common educational route for the increasing numbers of middle-class women entering teaching as a vocation, and their exclusion would have interfered with this generally popular development. Even Ryerson was on record as regarding the increase in female teachers as "a...circumstance favourable to the diffusion of good elementary instruction" (Prentice 1977, 56). Thus, access to secondary schooling served not only as an important vocational route for middle-class girls,[4] but was seen to be in the interests of the education system as a whole.

Preparation for commercial occupations was also deeply rooted in the prevocational character of secondary schools in this period. Bookkeeping had been taught as part of mathematics as far back as 1850. Along with penmanship, it was considered part of what every educated person needed to know. It satisfied a commonplace vocational need for middle-class boys in the same way that teaching provided for middle-class girls. The uses of a commercial education were increasingly varied, as the need expanded for farmers, lawyers, merchants, and others to have a knowledge of how to keep books and engage in commercial transactions. But it was the growth of office work which had the greatest impact on education. The traditions of clerical work strongly linked it to the children of the middle-class, who predominated

171

in the public secondary schools of Ontario. From the earliest records of the "black coat worker" to the twentieth century concept of "white collar" work, employment in clerical work carried with it a tradition of genteel respectability. In Great Britain, the U.S. and in Canada, it was children of professional, managerial and white collar parents who entered clerical employment (Coombs 1978; Lowe 1980; Lockwood 1958; Davin 1976; Aron 1981; Rury 1982; Davies 1982). Their training was done on-the-job through apprenticeships but included, as one British advertisement put it in 1878:

> ...a little instruction in Latin and probably a very little in Greek, a little in geography, a little in science, a little in arithmetic and bookkeeping, a little in French, with such a sprinkling in English reading as may enable a lad to distinguish Milton from Shakespeare (Lockwood 1958, 20).

These requirements closely reflect the secondary school curriculum in Canada in the late nineteenth century. This kind of education prepared young middle-class males to enter office employment as clerks, with the hope of working their way upward into positions of increasing responsibility and sometimes into eventual partnership in the firm (Davies 1982; Lowe 1980; Coombs 1978). But as commercial life changed, so did both the substance and the organization of training for clerical employment, and it is to a discussion of these changes that we will now turn.

II. Changes in Commercial Work and Education

In the last decades of the nineteenth century, tremendous changes were taking place in the organization of commercial life in Canada. The reorganization of financial structures, the expansion of manufacturing, and the elaboration of marketing and distributive mechanisms resulted in the exponential growth and reorganization of clerical work processes (Lowe 1980; Coombs 1978). The total number of clerical workers in the Canadian labour force grew from 33,017 or 2.0% of the workforce in 1891 to 216,691 or 6.8% in 1921 (Lowe 1982). The overall growth of clerical occupations depended upon a complex process of reorganization and rationalization of work. As the volume of work expanded, tasks became more specialized and jobs became more clearly differentiated from one another. The typewriter was invented, shorthand increased in popularity, and filing systems, bookkeeping machines and other office equipment and techniques came into common use (Davies 1982; Rotella 1981;

White Collar Vocationalism

Lowe 1980; Braverman 1974). Lowe (1980) characterizes these changes in Canada as an "administrative revolution" in which office procedures were drastically restructured in order to secure greater managerial control and increase efficiency. This involved the increasing centralization of power and authority, and the creation of a new subordinate class of clerical functionaries. The possibility of advancement from these jobs into more senior clerical or administrative positions diminished drastically.

These changes were gradual and uneven, but they had consistent implications for who went into office jobs. Employees became younger on average, they came from a broader sector of society; and they became female (Lowe 1980; Aron 1981; Coombs 1978). In Canada, women's share of clerical employment grew from 14.3% in 1891 to 41.8% in 1921. These figures represent an increase in female clerical workers from 4710 in 1891 to 90,577 in 1921, an increase of more than 18-fold in 30 years (Lowe 1980).

Women were hired into the lower ranks of clerical work. A study of Toronto workers showed that by 1911 women represented 53% of junior clerical positions and only 12% of general clerks, with little or no growth of female employment in supervisory or managerial white collar positions (Coombs 1978).[5] But much of the image of middle-class respectability of traditional male clerical jobs carried over to the new subordinated positions into which women were hired (Coombs 1978; Lowe 1980). The first women who went into clerical positions in the U.S. and in England tended to be respectable ladies from native-born, white, middle-class families that could afford to keep their daughters in school, or middle-class wives who had been forced "out to work" through economic misfortune or family tragedy. Such women sought out clerical employment in order to preserve their social status and to maintain a middle-class way of life (Aron 1981; McNally 1979; Davin 1976). No comparable data has been published on early female clerical workers in Canada but the circumstances of Canadian women were similar in many important respects (Light and Parr 1983), and the desirability of clerical employment on the basis of its status was commonly recognized (Coombs 1978; Canada, Royal Commission 1913; National Council of Women 1910).

Wages for clerical work, which had traditionally been marginally adequate to support a middle-class lifestyle for nineteenth-century British male clerks (Lockwood 1958; Klingender 1935) deteriorated over the period 1880-1920. In Canada they remained higher than the average production wage for men until 1931, and higher than the labour force average until 1941 (Lowe 1980, Coombs 1978). Women were hired at lower wages than men, but the wages for female clerical workers remained good relative to other women's jobs. For example, in 1920, the Minimum Wage Board of British Columbia found that the category

173

of "clerical work" comprised of "typist, billing clerks, filing clerks, cashiers, cash girls, checkers, invoicing auditors, attendants in physicians' and dentists' offices, and all kinds of clerical help," "stands out above all others as offering the best wages to the greatest number of employees" (British Columbia Department of Labour 1923, 3, 8). Teachers were excluded from this survey, but it gives an indication of the relatively good position of clerical work.

The proliferation and reorganization of clerical occupations had enormous implications for education. A demand was created for a growing number of subordinate workers to perform relatively routinized and standardized tasks in an office environment. Many of these skills could be learned as easily in the classroom as on the job. At first, these skills were centred around bookkeeping and penmanship, and later increasingly around typewriting, shorthand, and the use of standardized business forms and machines. Growing interest in commercial education led to a proliferation of courses in a variety of settings and commercial education soon became a thriving arena of educational entrepreneurship.

The first large scale educational response to the changes at work took place not in the public schools, but in the private sector. Alternatives to the commercial instruction offered in the grammar schools had existed in urban centres across Canada since the 1860s, in private religious schools, in the Mechanics' Institutes and in the Young Men's Christian Association (Foster 1970; Stamp 1970; Down 1966; Moreland[6] 1977). But it was private entrepreneurs who developed the most successful commercial courses. The first private business college in Ontario opened in 1860 in Toronto. The British American Commercial College offered instruction in penmanship, phonography (shorthand), commercial arithmetic, commercial law and bookkeeping. By 1868, five more colleges had opened in Toronto, London, Hamilton, Ottawa and Belleville, and in 1887 the opening of Central Business College in Toronto marked the beginning of the chain of Shaw Business Colleges which exist to the present (Moreland 1977). In B.C. the only business college to open its doors before the turn of the century was Pitman Business College, which opened in 1898 in Vancouver. By 1910, however, Vancouver had the Western School of Commerce, the Duffus School of Commerce, the Fenton Commercial School, the New Westminster Business College, the Trail Business College, and a chain of five Sprott-Shaw schools in Vancouver and Victoria (Moreland 1977).

Business Colleges played up their differences from, and advantages over, the public schools. In 1903, the principal of Toronto's Central Business College wrote that his courses emphasized not "the development of mental power," as in the public secondary school, but "work...of real practical value" to the student "who would qualify...for a particular calling" (McIntosh 1903, 316). The colleges boasted that they were business enterprises run by successful entrepreneurs who had caught "the spirit with which all successful businessmen and women are imbued." They stayed open during the summer, "like any other place of business," unlike the "average school [which] is closed during July and August" (Central Business College 1905, 43). Their programs were short and flexible, and they required no entrance exam. They boasted of better facilities, teachers and texts than the public schools, where they claimed, "too often we hear complaints [about] texts and school equipment."

They promised specialist teachers who taught only business subjects, and made assurances that "No theory is learned that is not made a subject of actual business practice" (Shaw 1903, 6). Perhaps most importantly, the business colleges promised jobs to their students. Shaw's advertising is full of testimonials from former students about their job placements, and they note, "The Employment Department is one of the important features of our office." They allocated resources to contacting employers and placing their students. They assured students that "every dollar of tuition money paid to us will be refunded to any graduate whom we fail to place in a position" (Central Business College 1910, 42).

The popularity of this approach to commercial education is evidenced by the proliferation of colleges. Canadian statistics on private college enrolments are not published in government statistics for the early years, but by 1921, 14,547 students were enrolled in private business schools in Ontario, and 30,034 were enrolled in Canada as a whole (Moreland 1977).[7] The entrepreneurial, profit-making character of the private colleges, and their lack of traditional academic material soon aroused the concern of both public educators and employers (Ontario, Commission on Unemployment 1916). The result was considerable public debate, even scandal, about the legitimacy of private business colleges. These early debates led the business schools to form the Business Educators' Association in 1896 and to attempt to standardize courses, examinations, and diplomas (Moreland 1977). This move gave the business colleges a more professional image and limited the variety of programs they could offer, but it did not end the controversy over whether such colleges served "the public interest." On the contrary, there was a growing sense of conflict and competition between public and private educators that carried on into the new century, mostly taking the form of debates about the adequacy of various approaches to training. Employers got involved in the struggle, complaining that the occupation was "overcrowded with young, inefficient, poorly trained workers," that some "schools" were just an excuse for free labour, and that virtually anyone could "rent a room and start a business college" (Ontario, Commission on Unemployment 1916, 181-182). Employment agencies (many of them maintained by typewriter companies) took the position that even "three years at a secondary school is too short a time to fit a girl to become an efficient stenographer." They recommended instead "...in order to secure the best advantages for the occupation...university matriculation, or three years in a high school, and nine months or a year's training in a business college" (Ontario, Commission on Unemployment 1916, 181-182).

Public school educators, on the other hand, were neither as quick nor as pragmatic as their counterparts in the private sector in responding to the changing demands of commercial life. Much of the attention of public educators was occupied with an ongoing debate about the relative merits of classical and practical education. In this context, those who were sympathetic to commercial studies couched their support in very traditional terms, emphasizing the importance of character building and development of the mind. The following excerpt from an article in the *Canadian Educational Monthly* is a typical example of this emphasis:

> ...the qualifications of the man of commerce...coincide in large measure with those which we associate with the ideal citizen...honesty and integrity of character must be from first to last the distinguishing feature of the business man. Preparation for commerce will, therefore insist with special force on all those elements in education which are closely bound up with the formation of character (Kahn 1900, 216).

A less typical but more pragmatic approach to support for commercial education is found in the Minister's report of 1886 in Ontario. He wrote:

> ...during the last fifteen years...the importance of the commercial department has grown. The cheapness of the equipment and the comparative ease with which students of the course can qualify themselves for wage-earning positions have conduced to the same end. Moreover, as the subjects of a commercial course are practical, many parents believe that if their children take them at school, they will be in a better position to earn a livelihood (quoted in Moreland 1977, 121).

However, this straightforward view of the merits of commercial studies was not universally shared, and it was several decades before the public schools began to catch up with the private colleges by offering a more diverse and practical commercial curriculum.

Bookkeeping instruction had been common in the public schools of Ontario as far back as the 1850s. In 1882 it was made compulsory for all students in the

White Collar Vocationalism

lower forms of the secondary school. The prescribed course was described as giving instruction in matters relating to commercial and business transactions including familiarity with: "...Single and Double Entry; Commercial Forms, and Usages; Banking, Custom House and General Business Transactions" (*Ont. A.R.* 1882, 35). A new authorized text published in 1887, entitled *High School Bookkeeping* also included chapters on banking, partnership (business law), business forms, correspondence and abbreviations, as well as precise writing and indexing which were "added so that the book might cover the commercial course prescribed for the High Schools and Collegiate Institutes" (MacLean 1887, ii).

A Commercial Diploma Course was introduced for the first time in 1885 in Ontario secondary schools, calling for commercial subjects to be taken in a one-year program along with the academic course of instruction. The initial response was enthusiastic, with 1643 students, or 3.4% of the total student population, enrolled in the first year and 1733 students in the second year. Thereafter, the number of diplomas granted grew steadily, to 2247 or 11.6% of total enrolment in 1890, and to a high of 3592 or 15.3% of students in 1894. When the commercial diploma course was expanded to a two-year program in 1896, the number of diplomas granted plummeted to less than 1% of students, where it remained for a decade (*Ont. A.R.* 1885-1910). Meanwhile, in 1891 the requirement was introduced for the training of special commercial teachers and the granting of Commercial Specialist Certificates, which was an important step in creating a separation between commercial courses and other forms of instruction (Hewson 1940). In 1901, stenography (theory and dictation) was added to the diploma course, followed in 1903 by typewriting. In 1904, provincial examinations were dropped and authority for examinations and diplomas shifted to local school boards and to the Commercial Section of the Ontario Educational Association, which had been organized in 1895 (Hewson 1940). Enrolment bounced back to 3006 or 10.8% of students in 1904, fell to 5.9% in 1912, and then climbed again to 12.0% in 1920, which amounted to little overall gain in percentage terms over three decades. The stenography course attracted a much smaller enrolment than the general commercial diploma program until 1896 when the diploma enrolment fell off and stenography began to gain steadily, to a high of 17.3% by 1904, and finally settled to around 12% until 1920. Typewriting enrolment also jumped to an early high of 11.5% of students in 1904, and then levelled off between 9% and 10% until 1920 (*Ont. A.R.* 1900-1920), (see Table 1).

Table 1—COMMERCIAL ENROLMENTS IN ONTARIO, 1885-1920,
PUBLIC HIGH SCHOOLS AND COLLEGIATE INSTITUTES

Year	Stenography %	Typewriting %	Commercial Diploma[b] %	Total Secondary Enrolment
1885	3.4	[a]	11.5	14,250
1886	2.6	[a]	11.3	15,344
1888	3.8	[a]	[a]	17,742
1890	2.2	[a]	11.6	19,395
1892	3.8	[a]	11.6	22,837
1894	6.2	[a]	15.3	23,523
1896	5.6	[a]	1.4	24,567
1898	9.2	[a]	0.4	23,301
1900	12.4	4.5	0.2	21,723
1902	15.0	8.0	0.4	24,472
1904	17.3	11.5	10.8	27,709
1906	13.9	10.6	8.7	29,392
1908	12.2	9.1	9.0	31,912
1910	11.4	9.4	7.3	32,612
1912	11.4	9.7	6.9	32,273
1914	10.2	9.6	8.3	36,466
1917[c]	11.2	9.2	9.9	28,833
1918	11.9	10.1	10.9	29,097
1920	12.8	10.4	12.0	33,036

[a] No statistics reported
[b] Up to 1903, figures reported were the number of commercial diplomas granted; Beginning in 1904, they represent enrolment. [c] Statistics for 1916 not available.
Source: Ontario, Department of Education, Annual Reports, 1885-1921.

In 1904, the first centralization of commercial courses in Ontario took place in the new Toronto Technical High School, and in 1916, the Central High School of Commerce opened in Toronto as the first exclusively commercial high school in Canada. In 1911, the Ontario government adopted the recommendations of John Seath, Superintendent of Education, to divide the commercial program into two main streams in order to better meet "the requirements of the different kinds and grades of business." He proposed a four-year General Business Course for those who intended to enter business "in some of the more responsible positions, eventually becoming travellers, buyers, managers, etc." and a three-year Office Course for "bookkeepers, accountants, stenographers, secretaries, etc." (Seath 1911, 347, 328). The Office Course was further subdivided into an Accountancy course and a Shorthand course. In addition, Seath recommended the establishment of Advisory Committees which were assigned the responsibility for managing commercial departments, including the power to prescribe courses and to set exams and diplomas. These changes had a major, long range impact on the organization of commercial studies and on its marginal position within the secondary curriculum.

Table 2—COMMERCIAL ENROLMENTS IN BRITISH COLUMBIA HIGH SCHOOLS, 1910-1920

Year	Commercial Subjects %	Total Secondary Enrolment
1910[a]	4.8	2,041
1912	5.6	2,151
1914	7.8	3,007
1916	9.3	4,770
1918	15.6	5,150
1920	14.2	6,636

[a] No statistics for commercial subjects are recorded before this date.
Source: British Columbia, Superintendent of Education, Annual Reports, 1900-1920.

In British Columbia, bookkeeping was included in the first prescribed course of studies for the high school in 1879. In 1885, a one-year Commercial Diploma was introduced which called for all students entering the high school to receive instruction in the English course for the first six months and then to make a choice between either the Commercial Course or the Classical Course. The Commercial Course included single and double entry bookkeeping, banking, commercial correspondence, and commercial law. The Diploma Course met with little success until 1906, when it became a two-year option and was expanded to include typewriting, shorthand theory and practice, business forms and laws of business (Green 1944; McLaurin 1936). Department examinations were set the following year in these subjects. The first official record of enrolment in commercial subjects is in 1910, when 98 students were enrolled or 4.8% of the high school population (British Columbia Annual Reports 1910-1920; hereafter *B.C.A.R.*). This figure increased steadily to a high of 14.9% in 1919 (see Table 2).

Thus, by the time of the federal Technical Education Act of 1919, commercial education was already well established in the schools of Ontario and British Columbia. The curriculum had been revised to include the "modern" and "practical" commercial subjects that were the boast of the private commercial colleges, and they had enjoyed two or three decades of growing support. By the mid-1920s, public educators expressed pride and optimism that "there is no more thorough office training to be obtained anywhere" and that "the high school course should not be seen as preparatory to a business course elsewhere" (*B.C.A.R.* 1924-1925, 58). By the early 1930s it was clear that the tide had turned on the competition between private and public commercial educators. During the years 1921-1934 enrolment in private business colleges declined by 68% in Ontario and by 40% across Canada (Moreland 1977). However, two important aspects of commercial education in these early decades remain to be clarified; the gender and class character of the students who were enrolled. These features of commercial education are particularly important in establishing its relationship to the wider movement for vocational education.

III. Gender and Class: Vocational Education Reconsidered

We have argued that the emergence of commercial education in the public secondary schools involved several quite distinct historical phases. The first consisted of the establishment of commercial subjects as a legitimate area of instruction in the high school, both formally and in practice. This took place throughout the last half of the nineteenth century and was advocated at the grass roots level primarily by local parents and educators who wanted to make the secondary curriculum relevant to middle-class youth in their communities. This early expansion of commercial instruction was fuelled by the expanding importance of commercial knowledge, primarily for educated males in a variety of occupations, and it was this clientele which educators originally hoped to serve. This solidly middle-class base was central to the successful entrenchment of commercial education in the secondary curriculum, well ahead of the cries for educational reform directed at working-class youth.

The second phase of development in public commercial education began just around the turn of the century, and brought a profound transformation in

White Collar Vocationalism

commercial instruction. Public secondary schools revised and expanded their programs of commercial instruction in response to the reorganization and feminization of office work itself, and in order to take advantage of the thriving market for clerical skills training that was emerging. In responding to these changes, business educators were in the forefront of the movement to bring secondary schooling into line with the demands of the waged labour markets of twentieth-century capitalism. However the results were major and contradictory for both teachers and students. For teachers, the introduction of "modern" commercial subjects to the curriculum, which was the sine qua non of expansion, considerably reduced the scope and content of instruction, and the new waves of commercial enrolment brought a less prestigious student clientele, i.e., females. For the students, the changing focus of commercial education meant that the skills and knowledge which they acquired were a mere fragment of those associated with the "clerk" of the past. The positions for which women were being trained, while respectable, nevertheless promised low wages (compared to males) and little opportunity for advancement. Yet both parties saw their prospects rising with the tide of commercial prosperity that was sweeping urban centres of Canada.

The shift in commercial enrolment from male to female students is relatively obscured in most courses of information about commercial education in Canada.[8] Well into the twentieth century, the most common public statements of educators continued to be about "preparing the boy for commercial life," but it is evident that this predominantly male image was maintained long after the clientele for commercial education was in fact largely female. Neither the existing histories of commercial education nor the major, official documents of the period, including the annual reports of the provincial ministers of education, report the gender of commercial students or discuss gender as a factor in the development of commercial education. The best evidence regarding the process of feminization is to be found in unofficial sources and by reading "between the lines" of various public statements.

In Ontario, the earliest figures on the gender of commercial students are found in an unpublished study of the Central High School of Commerce in Toronto, which suggests that as far back as 1911 the proportion of females in commercial education was high, and that it changed very little over three decades: from 74.2% in 1911-1920, to 75.4% in 1921-1930, to 73.9% in 1931-1940 (Posen 1980). Posen's data also show the gender segregation of different courses within the commercial program, and indicate that the different "kinds and grades of business" to which Seath referred in his 1911 report were already highly gender-specific. In the decade 1911-1920, 71% of males were enrolled in the General Business course and 60% of females were enrolled in

Stenography. In the following decade, female enrolment expanded into the Secretarial stream and male enrolment increased in the area of Accounting.[9] Official statistics on gender from Ontario and elsewhere are not available until the 1920s, by which time they show that feminization was well advanced. The Central High School of Commerce in Toronto reported 69% female enrolment in 1923 and 74% in 1926 (*Ont. A.R.* 1924, 1927). The Cecil Rhodes High School of Commerce in Vancouver reported 72.2% females in 1919 and 74% in 1929-1930 (*B.C.A.R.* 1920, 1931).

These data suggest that feminization was already well under way in commercial education by the time Canadian public educators began to revise and expand their commercial course offerings around the turn of the century. A rare acknowledgement of this development is found in the following statement by J.E. Farewell, first President of the Toronto Public and High School Trustees Association in 1887:

> With the greatly increased number of positions connected with commercial pursuits which are fortunately now open to women, and considering the large number of young women who desire to fill such positions and so exchange idleness and dependence for work, usefulness, and independence, it is clearly the duty of the government to provide them the opportunity to qualify themselves to accept such positions (quoted in Moreland 1977, 122).

These comments are unusual in their explicit recognition of the expanding role of women in clerical employment, and in their endorsement of the principle of expanding employment opportunities for women through schooling. More typical public statements about changes in clerical work and education either failed to acknowledge the significant increase of women, or were generally disparaging about the nature of the changes that were taking place. Some employers frankly bemoaned the growing employment of girls despite their superior performance of clerical duties.[10] Many educators complained that the field was becoming too narrow and practical, that the growing focus on stenography and typewriting was detrimental to the education value of commercial education, and that the courses no longer provided a suitable preparation for the "man of commerce." These concerns are reflected in the Ontario Annual Report of 1900, in which the President of Harvard University is quoted as criticizing "so-called" commercial courses which were "hopelessly inferior to other courses, being made up by substituting bookkeeping, stenography, typewriting, and commercial arithmetic for [parts of] the classical

White Collar Vocationalism

or English scientific course" and which "seldom train anybody for service above that of a clerk" (*Ont. A.R.* 1900, xxxiii).

Complaints about these changes in commercial education are noteworthy because of what they do not say, which is that the narrowing and practical focus of commercial courses were directly associated with the fragmentation and feminization of clerical work itself. The clientele and raison d'être for commercial programs were increasingly restricted to women and to the limited prospects in the business world which were associated with women's employment. These changes undermined the traditional male orientation of business educators and interfered with the lofty status of their field.[11] While business educators could and did resist what they saw as an erosion of their status, they were caught in a tide of broad economic and social change that was well beyond their power to control.

The third phase of development in commercial education which remains to be examined is its identification as an educational option for working-class students. This occurred long after the shift to a female clientele and under circumstances that were significantly altered from the period being examined in this paper. Only a few basic indicators of this change will be considered here.

Data on the class backgrounds of Canadian secondary school students are limited and often difficult to interpret, but the available evidence suggests that wealth remained the primary determinant of school participation throughout the nineteenth century (Gray 1979; Davey 1975; Katz 1975). It was largely children of the middle-class and of professional families who could afford to remain in school until high school age. High school participation rates for Ontario youth suggest that this situation remained relatively unchanged throughout the formative years of commercial education, as reflected in the very modest increase in participation over three decades, from 12.8% in 1891 to 16.8% in 1921.[12] Participation began to increase substantially only in the 1920s after the passing of the Adolescent School Act of 1919, which eliminated high school fees and extended the compulsory school age to 16 years, and the Industrial Education Act of 1921 which facilitated rapid expansion of secondary schooling in Ontario.[13] Between 1921 and 1931, the proportion of 15-18-year-old youth enrolled in secondary education in Ontario more than doubled, from 16.8% in 1921 to 34.6% in 1931, and one-third of the number enrolled in 1931 were in the newly established vocational/technical high schools. During this period, the vast majority of commercial instruction shifted to the vocational high schools, where half of all enrolments in 1931 were commercial students as opposed to 3.4% of enrolments in the academic high schools and collegiates (*Ont. A.R.* 1932).

Gender And Education In Ontario: An Historical Reader

In British Columbia in the same years high school participation rates increased from 24% in 1921 to 32% in 1931,[14] and enrolment in vocational classes grew to one-quarter of all students, half of which were in commercial subjects (*B.C.A.R.* 1930). Although the label "working-class" has been used to describe this twentieth-century clientele of commercial education, closer examination has shown that in fact students tended to come from financially stable families of the native-born, English-speaking population, and not from the poor, industrial working-classes (Rury 1982; Aron 1981; Posen 1980; Weiss 1978).

These patterns of expansion and change suggest that an understanding of the major orientation toward working-class students in commercial education should be sought as part of the educational expansion and reforms of the 1920s and 1930s, including the introduction of streaming as a means to manage the influx of students from diverse social backgrounds (Stamp 1979, 1978). Questions about the role of commercial education in this process deserve a detailed examination beyond the scope of this article. For the present argument, the evidence sets commercial education apart from the dominant understanding of vocationalism as an educational reform for the working-class. Our findings suggest instead that commercial education failed to satisfy the interests and concerns of the promoters of vocationalism for several related reasons. Firstly, it attracted a middle-class rather than a working-class clientele. In this context it was seen as not as a new phenomenon, but part of the old tradition which reformers wanted to break. Secondly, commercial education had become predominantly female, which meant it failed to satisfy those concerned with the predominantly male industrial workforce. Furthermore it was drawing women into the labour force rather than confirming them in their domestic roles as many reformers intended. In fact, commercial education came under attack for filling girls with "false notions" that led them "to seek office and store work" rather than work in the home because it was "more genteel" (Canada, Royal Commission 1913). Thus, although commercial education was formally included in the major reports and recommendations of the period concerned with vocational education (and this may have lured historians into regarding it as part of the movement for vocational reform), it is clear that the association between them is more adequately described as an ex post facto marriage of convenience, consummated in the Technical Education Act of 1919, where they were united for the purposes of federal funding.[15]

This interpretation of commercial education emphasizes several features of vocationalism that deserve further exploration. The first is that the specific vocational relevance of schooling was not an entirely new phenomenon with the emergence of twentieth-century movements for reform. The history of

White Collar Vocationalism

commercial subjects suggests instead that vocational relevance was integral to the popular support for schooling among the middle-class in the last half of the nineteenth century.[16] Furthermore, commercial education had, from its beginnings, at least some of the features associated with modern vocationalism: it had a less academic emphasis than the regular course of studies, substituting commercial subjects for classical ones; it was oriented to labour market entry rather than higher education, and thus was "terminal" in educational terms; and it was marginalized, to varying degrees, with the introduction of special certificates, programs and instructors from a very early stage. However, at least some of these characteristics of commercial studies were consistent with the educational objectives of a middle-class school constituency, and indeed were defended by them in the face of attempted reforms, in the case of the Ryerson initiatives in Ontario.[17] Thus the practice of identifying and striving to serve diverse interests and of trying to achieve multiple outcomes through schooling should not be seen as something strictly imposed on an unsuspecting or necessarily resistant Canadian public by reformers and industrialists in the twentieth century, or even as certainly out of step with popular conceptions of democratic schooling.[18] Instead, the extension and differentiation of schooling to incorporate ever greater segments of the population needs to be examined in broad historical terms as part of the complex process of transformation in the social organization of class relations under industrial capitalism. In this process, the active part played by various classes and interests in defining and defending their needs and objectives remains to be adequately explored in many cases, particularly those involving women.

Attention to women identifies the second, and perhaps most striking, though little explored, feature of vocational schooling, its relevance to the production of gender differences and inequalities in their twentieth-century form. In the case of commercial education, the long term impact has been to channel young women toward a distinctly routinized and subordinated place in the white collar work force, and the creation of what has come to be dubbed the "pink collar ghetto." This is a form of segregation that has depended heavily on gender as the basis of differentiation, and has remained in a very ambiguous relation to class background or class affiliation.[19] In fact, throughout the period examined in this article, commercial education served to direct young women whose class backgrounds were specifically not working-class into employment situations where their work would be fundamentally circumscribed in ways that are commonly identified as "working-class" or "proletarianized" forms of labour.[20] As Gaskell (1983) has argued elsewhere, the continuous supply of trained clerical labour from the public schools has figured prominently in the assignment of low status, skill labels, and pay to clerical work and workers. In this respect, commercial education as a form of vocationalism has contributed significantly to a form of segregation and subordination which is largely disregarded by vocational theorists: that is on the basis of gender.

This brings us to a final, and more speculative, kind of observation about vocationalism in general, seen in the light of women's experience in commercial education. Vocational differentiation through schooling on the basis of gender has been part of a more generalized social process through which positions of power and privilege in twentieth-century capitalism have been reserved for men. In this regard, schools have contributed along with other forms of institutional and bureaucratic organization to the systematic production of gender differences as an integral feature of the relations of domination and subordination, in the workplace as elsewhere, in contemporary society. To the extent that this is the case, the efforts of educational theorists to describe and explain the role of vocational (or any other) schooling in the production of social inequalities, without regard to the significance of gender in that process, are doomed to inadequacy. Ongoing investigation of this proposition remains central to the feminist agenda for scholarship in education.

White Collar Vocationalism

Notes

1. See Canada, Report of the Royal Commission on Industrial Training and Technical Education (1913); National Council of Women of Canada (1910); Danylewycz et al. (1984).

2. See Canada, Report of the Royal Commission on Industrial Training and Technical Education (1913); Stamp (1970); Foster (1970); Dunn (1978).

3. The following observation in the *Canada Educational Monthly* in 1881 illustrates this point as well as the ongoing debate over the use of secondary schooling. "There were 104 high schools [includes collegiate institutes] in 1879, with an attendance of 12,036 pupils...(Of these)...248 pupils, or 8 percent of the whole number registered, matriculated; 565 or 18 percent entered mercantile life; 535 or 16 percent adopted agriculture as a pursuit; 693 or 21 percent joined the learned professions; while 37 percent went to other occupations.... The above statistics should direct the attention of the High School authorities—trustees as well as teachers—to the fact that these schools are not used by those who attend them chiefly to prepare for entering the university, but mainly to prepare for agriculture and commercial pursuits." (Vol. 3 [1881], 186-187).

4. For discussion of the vocational importance of secondary schooling for girls in the United States at the turn of the century, see Poss (1981); and Carter and Prus (1982).

5. The concentration of women in the lower ranks of clerical work has also been documented in the United States. Rotella (1981, 122) reports that by 1920, 91.8% of all stenographers and typists were female in contrast to 48.8% of bookkeepers, cashiers, and accountants, and only 32% of the general category of clerks.

6. Paul Moreland was a business educator whose published work, although poorly documented, represents one of the few comprehensive attempts to assemble the historical evidence regarding business education across Canada.

7. In the United States enrolment figures for private commercial schools are available from 1871. Weiss (1978, 38, 77) reports total enrolments of 6,640 in 1871, 26,109 in 1875, 47,146 in 1885, 96,135 in 1895, and 146,086 in 1905.

8. Weiss (1978, 38, 174) reports the following statistics on female enrolment in commercial education in the United States before the turn of the century. In private commercial schools, females were 4% of

students in 1871, 9% in 1875, 10% in 1880, 15% in 1885, 28% in 1890, 32% in 1895 and 36% in 1900. In public high school commercial programs females were 54% of graduates in 1903, 57% in 1910, 66% in 1924 and 67% in 1930.

9. Posen's (1980) data are based on information from student registration cards at Toronto's Central High School of Commerce, which may have been partially incomplete for the first half of the decade 1911-1920. Her figures appear in Table 3.

Table 3—COMMERCIAL PROGRAM ENROLMENT BY GENDER, CENTRAL HIGH SCHOOL OF COMMERCE, TORONTO, 1911-1930

Years	Total %	General Business %	Accounting %	Stenography %	Secretarial %	Other* %
1911-1920						
M	26	71	18	6	3	2
F	74	29	3	60	6	2
1921-1930						
M	25	66	28	—	2	4
F	75	25	3	49	21	2

* Other includes Salesmanship, Bookkeeping, and No Response
Source: Posen, G. 1980. *The Office Boom*. Toronto, Ontario: Institute for Studies in Education. Photocopy.

10. The British Columbia Annual Report of 1902 reflects this sentiment in the following quotation from an employer: "...my experience, which has been chiefly with boys sixteen years of age, is that nine boys out of ten write in a most slovenly manner, and that less than sixty percent of them spell correctly words in everyday use...In a word, their education is crude and too thinly spread. The boys are handicapped and so are the business houses. No little energy has to be devoted to teaching the boys the very things they should be taught at school; energy that can ill be spared in a busy office...Among other consequences, in many offices girls are preferred for minor work, because of their greater neatness and carefulness. One may not care about employing girls, but one finds in them an ambition to do their work well, which is just the spirit we should like to see in the boys (1902, A16).

11. As late as 1926, Frederick G. Nichols of Harvard University was quoted in the Canadian magazine *Vocational Education* expressing the concern that "commercial education has come to be identified with bookkeeping

and stenography in the minds of most people. This narrow conception of this field of training has led to many shortcomings both from the standpoint of education and of business training: (Canada, Department of Labour, 1926, 4).

12. These figures have been calculated from census data for the years 1891 and 1921 (using 80% of the age cohort 15-19 years to approximate school age) and Ontario Annual Reports statistics for secondary enrolment. Also, it is important to keep in mind that both secondary enrolment in general and commercial education in particular were largely urban phenomena, so provincial statistics must be interpreted with caution.

13. For a discussion of the impact of legislation on the development of vocational programs in Canada, see Stamp (1972, 1971).

14. Calculated from British Columbia Annual Reports and census data for the years 1921 and 1931. Earlier data are available only for 1901, when high school participation stood at 6.2%. See note 12.

15. In the United States, by contrast, advocates of commercial education were opposed to identifying with "blue collar" education, and commercial programs were excluded from funding under the Smith Hughes Act of 1917. For discussion, see Powers (1984).

16. On this point see also Poss (1981) and Kantor and Tyack, eds. (1982).

17. See also Powers (1984) for a discussion of advocacy of commercial education in the United States.

18. See Hogan (1985), chapter 4, for a discussion of the convergence of vocational goals and democratic ideals in Chicago.

19. See Valli (1986) for an excellent study of contemporary clerical training.

20. See Lowe (1982) for a discussion and critique of these characterizations of clerical work and their relation to gender.

References

Analysis of school leavers in Ontario headed for commerce and agriculture. *Canada Educational Monthly* 3 (1881), 185-187.

Aron, Cindy S. "To barter their souls for gold: female clerks in federal government offices, 1862-1890." *The Journal of American History* 67, no. 4 (1981): 835-853.

British Columbia, Superintendent of Education. *Annual Report of the Public Schools of the Province of British Columbia* Victoria: 1870-1930 [hereafter cited as *B.C.A.R.*).

_____. Department of Education. *One Hundred Years: Education in British Columbia.* Victoria: Supplement to the Annual Report, 1970-1971.

_____. Department of Labour. *Report of the Minimum Wage Board.* Victoria: 1923.

Braverman, Harry. 1974. *Labor and Monopoly Capital.* New York: Monthly Review Press.

Canada, Department of Labour. "Purpose and Objectives of Commercial Education." *Vocational Education,* no. 17 (1926), 2-22.

Canada. *Report of the Royal Commission on Industrial Training and Technical Education* IV. Ottawa: Kings Printer, 1913.

Carter, Susan B. and Prus, Mark. "The Labour Market and the American High School Girl, 1890-1928." *Journal of Economic History* 42, no. 1 (1982): 163-171.

Central Business College of Toronto. *Prospectus of the Central Business College of Toronto.* Toronto, 1907, 1910.

Clifford, Geraldine J. "Marry, Stitch, Die or Do Worse: Educating Women for Work." In Kantor, H. and Tyack, D.B. (Eds.). *Work, Youth and Schooling.* Stanford: Stanford University Press, 1982, 223-268.

Coombs, David S. "The Emergence of a White Collar Workforce in Toronto, 1895-1911. (Ph.D. diss., York University) 1978.

Danylewycz, Marta, Fahmy-Eid, Nadia, and Thivierge, Nicole. L'enseignement ménager et les "home economics" au Québec et en Ontario au début du 20e siècle: une analyse comparée. In Wilson, J.D. (Ed.). *An Imperfect Past: Education and Society in Canadian History.* Vancouver: University of British Columbia, Centre for the Study of Curriculum and Instruction, 1984, 67-119.

Davey, Ian E. "Trends in Female School Attendance in Mid-Nineteenth Century Ontario." *Social History* 8 (1975), 238-254.

Davies, Margery W. *Woman's Place is at the Typewriter: Office Work and Office Workers 1870-1930.* Philadelphia: Temple University Press, 1982.

White Collar Vocationalism

Davin, Anna. "Genteel Occupations in Late 19th Century London: Class and Employment for Women." London: Photocopy, 1976.

Down, Edith (Sister Mary Margaret). *A Century of Service 1858-1958: A History of the Sisters of Saint Ann.* Victoria: Sisters of Saint Ann, 1966.

Dunn, Timothy A. "Work, Class and Education: Vocationalism in British Columbia Public Schools, 1900-1929." (Master's thesis, University of British Columbia) 1978.

Foster, John K. "Education and Work in a Changing Society: British Columbia 1870-1930." (Master's thesis, University of British Columbia) 1970.

Gaskell, Jane. "Sex Inequalities in Education for Work: The Case of Business Education." *Canadian Journal of Education* 6 (1981): 54-72.

Gidney, Robert D. and Lawr, Douglas A. "Egerton Ryerson and the Origins of the Ontario Secondary School." *The Canadian Historical Review* 60, no. 4 (1979): 442-465.

Gray, Ann Margaret. "Continuity in Change: The Effects on Girls of Co-Educational Secondary Schooling in Ontario, 1860-1910." (Master's thesis, University of Toronto) 1979.

Green, George H. "Development of the Curricula in the Secondary Schools of B.C." (Ph.D. diss., University of Toronto) 1944.

Hewson, John C. "The History of Commercial Education in Canada." (Master's thesis, University of Alberta) 1940.

Hogan, David. *Class and Reform: School and Society in Chicago, 1880-1930.* Philadelphia: University of Pennsylvania Press, 1985.

Kahn, A. "Commercial Education in Secondary Schools." *Canada Education Monthly* 22 (1900): 215-221.

Kantor, Harvey and Tyack, David (Eds.). *Work, Youth and Schooling.* Stanford: Stanford University Press, 1982.

Katz, Michael. "Who Went to School?" In Mattingly, P. and Katz, M. (Eds.). *Education and Social change: Themes from Ontario's Past.* New York: New York University Press, 1975, 271-293.

Katznelson, Ira and Weir, Margaret. *Schooling for All: Race, Class and the Decline of the Democratic Ideal.* New York: Basic Books, 1985.

Kliebard, Herbert M. *The Struggle for the American Curriculum, 1893-1958.* Boston: Routledge and Kegan Paul, 1986.

Klingender, F.D. *The Condition of Clerical Labour in Britain.* New York: International Publishers, 1935.

Lazerson, Marvin and Dunn, Timothy. "Schools and the Work Crisis: Vocationalism in Canadian Education." In Stevenson, H.A. and Wilson, J.D. (Eds.) *Precepts, Policy and Process: Perspectives on Contemporary Canadian Education.* Ontario: Alexander Blake Associates, 1977, 285-303.

191

Lazerson, Marvin and Grubb, Norton. *American Education and Vocationalism: A Documentary History, 1870-1970*. New York: Teachers College Press, 1974.

Light, Beth and Parr, Joy (Eds.). *Canadian Women on the Move, 1867-1920*. Toronto: New Hogtown Press and Ontario Institute for Studies in Education, 1983.

Lockwood, David. *The Blackcoated Worker: A Study in Class Consciousness*. London: George, Allen and Unwin, 1958.

Lowe, Graham. "The Administrative Revolution: The Growth of the Clerical Occupations and Development of the Modern Office in Canada 1911-1931." (Ph.D. diss., University of Toronto) 1979.

_____. "Women, Work and the Office: The Feminization of Clerical Occupations in Canada, 1901-1931." *Canadian Journal of Sociology* 5, no. 4 (1980): 361-381.

_____. "Class, Job and Gender in the Canadian Office." *Labour/Le Travailleur* 10 (1982): 11-37.

McIntosh, P.D. "Why Business Colleges Succeed." *Canadian Magazine* 21, no. 4 (1903): 4.

_____, *The Central Business College: Accounts of its Systems and Methods*. Toronto: Central Business College of Toronto, Ltd, 1905.

McLaurin, Donald L. "The History of Education in the Crown Colonies of Vancouver Island and British Columbia and in the Provinces of British Columbia." (Ph.D. diss., University of Washington) 1936.

McNally, Fiona. *Women for Hire: A Study of the Female Office Worker*. London: Macmillan, 1979.

MacLean, H.S. *High School Bookkeeping*. Toronto: Copp Clark, 1887.

Moreland, Paul. *History of Business Education*. Toronto: Pitman Publishing, 1977.

National Council of Women of Canada. *Report of the International Congress of Women, Toronto, June 24-30, 1909*, Vol. 2. Toronto: National Council of Women, 1910.

Oakes, Jeannie. *Keeping Track: How Schools Structure Inequality*. New Haven: Yale University Press, 1985.

Ontario, Commission on Unemployment. *Report of the Ontario Commission on Unemployment*. Toronto, 1916.

_____. Department of Education. *Annual Report of the Minister of Education*. Toronto: 1870-1930 [hereafter cited as *Ont. A.R.*).

Posen, Gail. "The Office Boom: The Relationship between the Expansion of the Female Clerical Labour Force and the Response of the Public

Education System, 1900-1940." Ontario Institute for Studies in Education, Toronto: Photocopy, 1980.

Poss, Katherine J. "The Sexual Structuring of Public High School Education, 1870-1930." Paper presented at the Western Association of Women Historians, Pacific Grove, California, May 1981.

Powers, Jane B. "Feminist Politics, Pressure Groups, and Personalities: Trades Training Versus Home Economics in Smith-Hughes." Paper presented at the annual meeting of the American Educational Research Association, New Orleans, April, 1984.

Prentice, Alison. *The School Promoters.* Toronto: McClelland and Stewart, 1977.

Rotella, Elyce J. *From Home to Office: U.S. Women at Work, 1870-1930.* Ann Arbor: UMI Research Press, 1981.

Royce, Marion Y. "Arguments over the Education of Girls—Their Admission to Grammar Schools in this Province." *Ontario History* 67 (1975): 1-13.

Rury, John L. "Vocationalism for Home and Work: Women's Education in the United States, 1880-1930." *History of Education Quarterly* 24, no. 1 (1984): 21-44.

_____. "Women, Cities and Schools: Education and the Development of an Urban Female Labour Force, 1890-1930." (Ph.D. diss., University of Wisconsin, Madison) 1982.

Shaw Correspondence School. *A Business Anchor: A Handbook Explanatory of the Commercial Courses.* Toronto: Central Business College, 1912.

Shaw, W.H. *The Story of a Business School.* Toronto: The Central Business College of Toronto, 1903.

Seath, John. *Education for Industrial Purposes.* Toronto: L.K. Cameron, 1911.

Spark, Keith B. "An Examination of the Development of Technical Education in Ontario between 1800 and 1915, Especially as it Concerns the Founding of Central Technical High School." Toronto: Toronto Board of Education Archives: Photocopy, 1977.

Stamp, Robert M. "The Campaign for Technical Education in Ontario 1876-1914." (Ph.D. thesis, University of Western Ontario) 1970.

_____. "Technical Education, the National Policy, and Federal-Provincial Relations in Canadian Education, 1899-1919." *Canadian Historical Review* 52, no. 4 (1971): 404-423.

_____. "Vocational Objectives in Canadian Education: An Historical Overview." In Ostry, S. (Ed.). *Canadian Higher Education in the Seventies.* Ottawa: Economic Council of Canada, 1972, 241-263.

_____. "Canadian High Schools in the 1920s and 1930s: The Social Challenge to the Academic Tradition." Canadian Historical Association, *Historical Papers* (1978): 76-93.

Tyack, David. *The One Best System.* Cambridge: Harvard University Press, 1975.

Valli, Linda. *Becoming Clerical Workers.* Boston: Routledge and Kegan Paul, 1986.

Weiss, Janice. "Educating for Clerical Work: A History of Commercial Education in the United States since 1850." (Ph.D. diss., Harvard University) 1978.

_____. "Educating for Clerical Work: The Nineteenth Century Private Commercial School." *Journal of Social History* 14, no. 3 (1981): 407-423.

_____. "The Advent of Education for Clerical Work in the High School: A Reconsideration of the Historiography of Vocationalism." *Teachers College Record* 83, no. 4 (1982): 613-636.

"Schooling Women for Home or for Work?" Vocational Education for Women in Ontario in the Early Twentieth Century: The Case of the Toronto Technical High School: 1892-1920[*]

Ruby Heap

Introduction

In his lengthy report on *Education for Industrial Purposes*, published in December 1910, Ontario's Superintendent of Education, John Seath, concluded that "owing to the decadence of the apprenticeship system, no organized means of training the workman now exists in connection with the trades and other industries." The problem was serious since, in the long run, industry "which combines with general intelligence the broadest technical knowledge and the highest skill will command the markets of the world."[1] In order to meet adequately industry's pressing demand for skilled labour, Seath recommended that Ontario be provided with a thorough system of technical education, financed by all levels of government, which would build "a closer connection between our schools and the activities of life."[2]

By using the word "workman," John Seath creates a serious difficulty for the historian interested in the development of vocational education for women at the turn of the century.[3] Is Seath discussing only about male workers? Or he is also including girls and women? In fact, Seath's report does contain various proposals pertaining to the "industrial and technical training" of girls and women. Indeed, the Superintendent believed that girls as well as boys should be provided with such training, wether they were attending public schools or were already in the workforce. For girls who left school at or before the age of 14, Seath proposed "manual training," which should consist of "Household Science and Art Work and Drawing," the last named "dealing chiefly with suitable freehand and elementary designing, and the rest of the course, as in the case of the boy, being intimately related to the life of the pupil."[4] For the much smaller number of girls who remained in school beyond the age of 14 and intended to enter some kind of industrial occupation, Seath recommended the establishment of "specialized industrial schools" offering an "industrial

[*] An earlier version was presented in 1988 to the Canadian History of Education Association in London, Ontario. I am grateful to Alison Prentice for her helpful comments and suggestions.

195

course" along with further instruction in the essential academic subjects. One or two "secondary industrial schools," similar to the Boston High School of Practical Arts and other American technical high schools, could also be established in large urban centres.[5] Finally, John Seath urged that evening classes be provided "for both sexes," contending that the "devotion of five or six hours a week to directed and assisted study, which will increase their wage-earning power, is not so serious a tax upon the ambitious and healthy workman and workwoman."[6]

Accompanying John Seath's recommendations was a plea from Mrs. Huestis, President of the Local Council of Women of Toronto, for the establishment of trade schools for girls. These were necessary, she explained, because "it is becoming quite evident that each year finds girls occupying a more and more important place in the industrial world. It is furthermore admitted by most employers that they enter into this new sphere almost totally unprepared by previous training."[7] Mrs. Huestis' plea as well as John Seath's report indicate that women were indeed part of the increasing public discussions devoted to the sate of technical education in Ontario at the end of the nineteenth century. Neither, as we shall see, were they excluded from the Toronto Technical School, which was the first provincial institution to provide secondary level technical education. Significantly, women's vocational education in English-Canada has a largely unacknowledged history. Indeed, mainstream scholarship on the history of vocational education has largely overlooked gender issues. So far, the vocational area which has received the most attention in this regard is domestic science, whose main purpose was, from the outset, to prepare women for their "natural vocation," that is for unpaid domestic labour in the home.[8] Similarly, while the literature on women and work is expanding rapidly, little is still known of the institutional structures within which girls and women have been trained for the paid labour market. English-Canadian historians have only recently begun to systematically investigate the development of links between educational systems and the labour force participation of women in Canada. Those few scholars who have written on the subject have mainly focussed on the training of girls for clerical work in business colleges and in high school commercial courses.[9] The historical role played by vocational education in the dynamics of gender segregation in the labour market has not been thoroughly examined. What links can we establish between women's position in paid employment for a particular period of time and the educational opportunities that were then offered to them? What role did the state and educational authorities play in the institutionalizing of vocational education for women? How did prevailing attitudes concerning "women's work" determine the provision of vocational education for women?

Schooling Women for Home or for Work?

In turn, what impact did vocationalism have on the definition and provision of women's education? Finally, to what extent did girls and women avail themselves of this new educational avenue? These are only a few of the questions associated to the study of vocational education for women in an historical perspective.

The following paper proposes to shed light on some of these themes by focussing on the activities of the Toronto Technical High School, from its opening in 1892 until 1920. During this period, it was the only institution in the city providing "technical and industrial education" for both day and evening students. Alongside programs designed for male students, it gradually developed gender specific courses and programs which both expanded and diversified during this period. The content and aims of these courses, as well as their evolution in time, will first be examined, in the light of the structure of female paid labour in Ontario and Toronto. Secondly, these courses will be put in relation with the prevailing attitudes concerning "women's work" and "female skills." Finally, the main features of women's participation in vocational education at the Toronto Technical High School will be assessed in the light of the available data on the School.

I—Women's Paid Labour in Ontario and Toronto at the Turn of the Century

As mentioned above, the origins and development of vocational education for women at the Toronto Technical High School must be seen within the context of the evolution of women's paid employment between 1892 and 1920. This evolution, in turn, is related to the development of Ontario's economy during this period.

During last decades of the 19th century up to the First World War, population growth, improved transportation and new technology promoted the expansion of manufacturing and the increasing concentration of industrial activity. Indeed, Ontario witnessed during this period what can be labelled as an "industrial revolution." The province's industrial economy grew impressively, both in terms of output and employment. Capital goods industries and consumer durable industries, including iron and steel products, machinery and electrical equipment, expanded vigorously: output tripled and employment doubled between 1900 and 1910.[10] During the same decade, output doubled and employment increased by over 20% in the consumer goods industries. Some of these industries, such as factory clothing, boots and shoes and patent medicine, tripled their output, while others, like drugs, canning, glove-making, hats, jewellery, soap-making and printing and publishing doubled their outputs.[11] By 1914, the major transformations in Ontario's industrial sector had already occurred. It was now widely diversified, based on large-scale production and oriented both to consumers and producers. Furthermore, the War would give a considerable boost to the province's heavy and capital goods industries, in addition to the clothing and leather industries.[12]

Another significant change in Ontario's economy between 1890 and 1920, which reflects the expansion of capitalist production and the creation of large manufacturing units, was the impressive growth of services. The financial and insurance sector, retail and wholesale trade, public utilities and transportation, personal and professional services, all expanded rapidly during this period. One illustration of this development is the expansion of the clerical labour force. The number of clerical workers increased from 12,000 to over 77,000 between 1891 and 1921. By this time, clerical workers represented close to 7% of the paid labour force.[13]

During this period, Toronto stood as Ontario's leading industrial centre. The city registered an impressive performance throughout. Between 1900 and 1920, the number of workers in industrial employment passed from 42,500 and 66,708, while the value of manufacturing output jumped from 58.4 million to 371.1 million.[14] Furthermore, Toronto greatly benefited from Ontario's increasing urbanization.[15] Its population had already increased dramatically from 59,000 to close to 181,200 inhabitants between 1871 and 1891. Thirty years later, the city's population had almost tripled, reaching some 521,000 inhabitants.[16]

Since the mid-nineteenth century, this population was predominantly female.[17] The closing of agricultural frontiers in Ontario and the resulting out-migration of men of marriageable age were conducive to the delay in the marriage age of women, a factor which, in turn, encouraged the migration of young girls and women to the province's cities. At the beginning of the twentieth century, young immigrant women would follow the same route in large numbers.[18] The young women who moved to cities such as Toronto were above all in search of paid employment. So did all those daughters whose labour within the home had become less necessary with the development of a market economy and the resulting reduction of the family's productive role, but whose wages were now needed in order to purchase the new marketed products geared towards family consumption. In addition, the subsistence of many working-class and immigrant families depended on their children's -girls and boys- waged labour. Existing evidence indicates that these single girls and young women formed the majority of female workers in Toronto at the turn of the century. After a few years in the paid labour force, the majority would

Schooling Women for Home or for Work?

retire and perform unpaid labour in the family as wives and mothers. However, a significant number of older women were also earning wages.[19] These included widows, divorced, separated and deserted women, but, increasingly also, wives of working-class men who were either unemployed or working at insufficient wages.[20]

In Ontario, the participation of women in the paid labour force increased significantly between 1891 and 1921. As Table 1 indicates, the number of female workers more than doubled, their representation in paid employment passing from 13.1% to 17.1%.

Table 1—FEMALE PAID LABOUR FORCE, ONTARIO, 1891-1921

	1891	1901	1911	1921
Number of female workers (10 years and over)	95,612	108,625	154,878	195,106
% of Total Labour Force (male and female)	13.1	14.4	15.6	17.4

Source: *Canada Year Book*, 1939, 777-778.

In 1921, a third of Ontario's female labour force worked in Toronto.[21] Indeed, the number of women in the city's work force increased by 25.6% between 1911 and 1921, while the number of men increased by only 4.7%. By 1921, women's representation in the paid labour force reached close to 27% (Table 2).

Table 2—FEMALE PAID LABOUR FORCE, TORONTO, 1911-1921[1]

	1911	1921
Number of female workers (10 years and over)	42,866	59,834
% of Total Labour Force (male and female) in Toronto	25.3	26.7

[1] The *Census* of 1891 and of 1901 do not provide data on the sexual division of labour in Toronto.

Source: Calculated from the *Census of Canada*, 1911, vol. 6, table 6; 1921, vol. 4, table 5.

What kind of jobs were available to women seeking employment in Toronto between 1890 and 1920? Unfortunately, the *Census of Canada* contains no data on the occupational profile of Toronto working women for 1891 and 1901. However, if we examine the situation of female workers in Ontario during this period, we find that they were then heavily concentrated in three occupational sectors: the most important was personal service, followed by manufacturing, and finally, by professional service.[22] In the first category, women were employed above all in domestic service, which still constituted the single most important occupation for females. In the professional service category, teaching represented by far the leading occupation for women who, in 1891, formed the majority of Ontario's teaching force. Meanwhile, Ontario's industrial revolution was attracting an increasing amount of women in the manufacturing sector. Already in 1891, it employed a third of the female labour force. Women worked above all in the clothing industry as dressmakers, tailoresses, milliners and seamstresses. Many of these women worked in their own homes under the piece and sub-contracting system.[23] However, the transition from skill-craft to industrial production was increasing female paid employment in large and integrated factories. Technological innovation—such as the introduction of the sewing machine—and the development of mechanization led to the fragmentation of the labour process, the simplification of the work performed and the subsequent reduction of the training required to perform this work. In turn, the breakdown of production into simple mechanized operations resulted in what is referred to as a process of "deskilling" [24]and in an increased demand for female workers. In Ontario, these changes promoted the entry of female factory operatives in the knit-goods, boot and shoe and garment industries during the second half of the nineteenth-century.[25]

At the turn of the century, observers noted that female workers could find an increasing number of jobs in manufacturing and that this trend was largely due to technological change and mechanization. In her study on *The Conditions of Female Labour in Ontario*, Jean Thomson Scott observed in 1892 that in recent years, "so many employments have opened up for women that the supply is rather short of the demand."[26] Six years later, factory inspector Margaret Carlyle wrote in her report: "Work of woman is divided among a large and ever-increasing number of occupations." She then explained how during the "past generation...inventions have made machinery almost human, needing directions only, and little manual strength. This has opened up new and wide fields of labour for women. In many cases, it has made it preferable to male labour in the production of many articles." [27]Indeed, during the next two decades, Ontario's industrial development and the maturation of its economy led to a widening of job opportunities for women and also to significant changes in the structure of female paid employment. Fortunately, available census data allow us to observe these changes in Toronto between 1911 and 1921.

Schooling Women for Home or for Work?

The most significant change in the structure of female paid labour in Toronto during the opening decades of the twentieth century: was women's increasing employment in the service sector. In the personal service category, domestic service continued to employ the largest proportion of women.[28] Moreover, in 1911, more than a third of women were involved in the work of cleaning, cooking, catering and caring.[29] The 1921 census records the growing importance of food services as an employer of women. The number of cooks had almost doubled during the last ten years, while waitressing now figured in the data as a distinct occupation, which employed more women than men.[30]

In 1921, there was also a larger proportion of women employed in the professions, as well as in trade and finance, transportation and clerical work. In the first category, teaching predominated. But nursing was rapidly becoming another leading occupation for women, one, indeed, that was exclusively female.[31] Interestingly, a small but significant number of women were employed as art and music teachers.[32] In trade, women were concentrated above all in sales. The expansion of the service sector as well as the development of the large urban department store stimulated the demand for a large pool of female labour. In 1921, there were more saleswomen than salesmen employed in general and departmental stores.[33] In the transportation sector, women worked mainly as telephone operators, an occupation which became feminized with the extension of the telephone system.[34] But it was clerical employment which proved the most attractive, as the rationalization and the mechanization of the office led to the intensive recruitment of women into the specialized and simplified clerical jobs that multiplied at the bottom of office hierarchies.[35]

Increasing female employment in the service sector led to a decline in both the proportion of women working in manufacturing as well as in the female representation of the manufacturing labour force.[36] The absolute numbers of female workers in the latter sector nevertheless increased between 1911 and 1921. During this period, the clothing industry remained the single largest employer of female labour within the manufacturing sector as well as an industry where women continued to predominate.[37] However, mechanization of production and the growth of the factory system led to a sharp decline in the number of dressmakers, milliners and tailoresses engaged in the custom-made trade and, inversely, to an increase in the numbers of female factory operatives working in ready-made clothing.[38]

Within the more general category of textile production, women could, as in the past, find work in the cotton, textile and woollen industries, although in much smaller numbers.[39] On the other hand, as noted previously by factory inspector Margaret Carlyle, women were finding jobs in a wider array of industries within the secondary sector. In Toronto, urbanization and population growth stimulated the food processing industries which, in turn, increasingly employed women. They worked above all as biscuits and confectionery makers.[40] Other industries were also hiring a much larger number of women in 1921 than ten years earlier. Such was the case of printing, publishing and bookbinding, and of "new industries" such as the electrical apparatus and chemical industries.[41]

In the opening decades of the present century, then, Toronto was an industrially mature city with a diversified economy. This led both to an increasing female labour force participation and to new employment options for women. Female workers could be found in factories, restaurants, hospitals, stores and offices. Clerical employment, in particular, was becoming a very attractive choice for young working and middle class girls armed with a high school education. In the manufacturing sector, the clothing industry remained the single leading employer of female labour; however, urbanization and the rapid growth of both the capital and consumer goods industries expanded opportunities for working women.

Nevertheless, in Toronto as elsewhere, the majority of women were employed in a gender-segmented labour market which dictated the main patterns of female labour participation in the city. Firstly, most women were heavily concentrated in a far narrower range of occupations than their male counterparts. At the same time, men and women were located in different types of jobs, with the result that they seldom competed for the same kind of work. Women were said to perform "women's work," while men accomplished "men's work." Finally, most female workers were relegated to the lowest levels of the occupational hierarchy and received wages that were consistently inferior than those paid to male workers.[42] In sum, sex-typing and gender segregation both conduced to make women second-class citizens in the workforce.[43]

II—Women's Vocational Education at the
Toronto Technical High School

A) Evolution of Course Provisions for Women

What links can be drawn between the main patterns in female employment in Toronto during the period examined and the development of vocational education for girls and women in the city's first technical high school? To provide some answers to this question, we must first examine the evolution of

202

Schooling Women for Home or for Work?

the course provisions for girls and women between 1892 and 1920 at the
Toronto Technical High School.

1. Under the Toronto Technical School Board, 1892-1904
On January 25, 1892, the Toronto Technical School opened its doors for the
first time at the old Wycliffe Hall on the north side of College Street, opposite
McCaul Street. This new institution, which was to provide secondary level
technical education, was established by the Toronto City Council, at the urge
of a small group of municipal, industrial and educational leaders in the city,
who felt that industrial expansion necessitated the training of skilled and
intelligent workers in technical schools. The City Council placed the School's
direct supervision in the hands of an appointed body, the Toronto Technical
School Board.[44]

At first, the Board offered only evening classes, all of which were free. The
mandate of the Technical School was the "training and education of artisans,
mechanics and workingmen in such subjects as may promote a knowledge of
mechanical and manufacturing arts."[45] The subjects to be taught were
mathematics, chemistry, descriptive geometry, mechanics, physics and drawing.
No course was specifically designed for women. 305 students registered during
the School's 1892-93 session, a number which clearly surpassed its anticipated
attendance of 150 pupils. During the 1893-94 session, more than 631 students
attended the Technical School.[46] Confronted by such a rapid increase, the
Board of the Toronto Technical School immediately asked the City Council for
a suitable and permanent accommodation that would allow it to "meet the
demands being made upon it in the matter of technical education."[47]

The School's initial mandate suggests that it did not include the
development of a distinct curriculum for women. In 1893, the Technical School
Board set up a Special Committee in order to examine the advisability of
establishing an afternoon class for women. No details are given as to what
subject would be taught in the proposed class. The Special Committee quickly
submitted a report which dismissed the idea on the grounds that it was not the
function of the Toronto Technical School to undertake day classes. The report
was adopted and the matter was not pursued any further.[48] However, sources
available for this early period suggest that women were not, at the time,
excluded from evening classes. Data on female enrolment do not exist, but the
recorded list of occupations held by the students attending the School between
1892 and 1894 includes, amongst others, stenographers, hatmakers, paper box
makers, confectioners, an embroiderer, a governess, public schoolteachers and
telephone operators.[49] Women, then, appeared to be present at the Toronto

Technical School; however, the process of creating a gender-specific curriculum had not yet begun.

The first step was taken in 1896 when the Technical School Board decided to open a "special" class for girls, which would be devoted to domestic economy. This decision was taken upon a petition submitted by a group of Toronto women.[50] The new chairman of the Technical School Board, Albert M. Wickens, then declared that there was no reason why girls and young women should not receive a practical education as much as boys and young men. However, he made it clear that the training dispensed would differ from that offered to male students: "I consider we will not be doing our whole duty as a Technical School Board if we do not do all in our power to attain further opportunities for the practical teaching of subjects suitable for women."[51]

In order to assist the Board in the establishment and operation of the new course, a Ladies' Advisory Committee was set up. Soon after the beginning of the evening class, the Committee reported an "unexpectedly large number of applications," a situation which indicated that the instruction being given met "a much felt public need." The Technical School Board responded by opening a new class and by hiring an assistant teacher.[52] But this also proved to be insufficient and afternoon classes in "Domestic Science" were quickly organized, even though such an arrangement went against official regulations.[53] In 1897, following the recommendation of its School Management Committee, the Technical School Board decided that the assistance of the Ladies' Advisory Committee in the conducting of the domestic science classes was no longer necessary.[54] Since Board members were exclusively male at the time, the abolition of the Ladies' Advisory Committee thus excluded women from the decision-making process at the Toronto Technical School.

According to the 1898-99 Prospectus, domestic science was still classified as a "Special Course."[55] Indeed, it was not attached to any of the existing Departments and it consisted in elementary instruction in theoretical and practical cookery.[56] Two classes were separately held from the beginning of October until the end of April. Applicants, who had to be at least fifteen years of age, were still admitted free of charge. Unlike students enrolled in the various Departments, those successfully completing the domestic science course did not receive a diploma. A silver medal was simply awarded to the student taking the highest stand at the final examination.[57] Obviously, the Technical School Board did not intend at the time to put domestic science on a more solid footing.

The problem was not empty classes since accommodation was provided for about ninety students. General overcrowding, rather, was the Toronto Technical School's main concern at the time. At the end of 1899, better quarters were

Schooling Women for Home or for Work?

provided in the Stewart Building, on the south side of College Street. Finally, in 1901, the decision was taken to offer day as well as evening classes, due to the fact that the "demand for technical education has become more pronounced."[58] Day classes were open to students holding high school entrance and public school leaving certificates. Diplomas would be awarded to those who had attended regularly and passed satisfactorily the required examinations. The day school sessions were composed of three terms extending from September until mid-June, while evening classes went on from October 1st until the end of March. While these remained free, fees were imposed on students admitted to the day classes.[59]

The introduction of day classes led to a major reorganization of domestic science teaching at the Toronto Technical School. No longer confined to a "special course," the subject was awarded a distinct department, responsible for the supervision of four different types of courses: a two-year "normal course" intended for the training of teachers of domestic science; a one year "general course" designed to meet "the needs of young women who desire to learn the fundamental principles of intelligent housekeeping and homemaking;" the "housekeepers' course," which occupied one or more terms, and was intended to train housekeepers and matrons; finally, one term "short courses," which offered instruction in subjects such as plain and invalid cookery, house hygiene and household economics. Diplomas would be awarded to students who had satisfactorily passed the examinations.

The expansion of domestic science at the Toronto Technical School can be viewed as another victory for the urban upper and middle-class women who vigorously promoted domestic science in Ontario at the time. By 1904, they had succeeded in establishing the subject at practically every level of the provincial educational system, including normal schools and university. In addition, the aims and content of the new courses offered by the Toronto Technical School faithfully corresponded to the main objectives which the domestic science movement assigned to such training: prepare young women for their most important roles, that of wife and mother, build a large supply of qualified teachers in domestic science, mainly for public schools, and upgrade the skills and status of domestics servants, whose rapidly declining numbers since the end of the nineteenth century had created what women reformers referred to as the "Servant Problem."[60]

Thus, at the turn of the century, a distinctly female curriculum was emerging at the Toronto Technical School. Significantly, female students were being trained for the main occupations held by girls and women at the time: unpaid labour in the home and, in the job-market, teaching and domestic service.

However, there was one important omission in the course provisions for women at the Toronto Technical School at the turn of the century: there was no possibility to receive training in sewing, dressmaking and millinery, although the clothing and wearing apparel industries were then the most important employers of women in the city. Significantly, in 1901, a group of women had petitioned the School for the establishment of classes in plain sewing and in the cutting and drafting of garments, a request which had not been considered by the Technical School Board at the time.[61] The reasons behind the Board's refusal to provide such classes remain unknown. One may assume that the lack of adequate facilities was a sufficient motive. Indeed, in 1905, the provincial inspector of technical education, Albert Leake, condemned outright the deplorable conditions prevailing at the Technical School. The present building, he wrote in his report, was incapable of providing sufficient space to conduct all the courses. Interestingly, Leake also deplored the absence of separate means of entrance or exit and of separate stairways "for the sexes." According to Leake, the opening of a day school had thus rendered the present site totally unsuitable for technical education.[62]

2. Under the Toronto Board of Education: 1904-1920
a) The expansion of technical education in Toronto in the early twentieth century.
In 1904, the Toronto Technical School was placed under the control of the newly-created Toronto Board of Education. Its status as a secondary level institution was then recognized when it was re-named the "Technical High School."[63] During the next fifteen years, technical education in Toronto and at the Technical High School, more specifically, underwent considerable transformations. At the beginning of the new century, the rapid growth of Canadian manufacturing as well as the growing concentration of industry into large corporations resulted in a campaign for increased technical education. The leadership of the campaign was assumed by the Canadian Manufacturers's Association, which pressed both the federal and provincial governments to provide funds for the creation of technical schools. Such schools, claimed the CMA, would train a sufficient pool of skilled labour to meet the demands of today's industries. In Toronto, the CMA campaign was supported by the Toronto Board of Trade as well as by the Toronto and District Trade and Labour Council.[64]

In 1910, the federal government responded both to capital and labour's lobbying by establishing the Royal Commission on Industrial Training and Technical Education. Three years later, the Commission submitted its findings and recommendations. The report proposed above all that the federal government set aside, for the next ten years, an annual grant of three million dollars for the development of technical education. Most of the money would be distributed to the provinces, which would, in addition, maintain control and regulation over technical education, as over education in general.[65]

In Ontario, the new conservative government of James Whitney had responded earlier than its federal counterpart to the campaign for increased technical education. In 1909, the Superintendent of Education, John Seath, was mandated to examine technical education in the United States and Europe and to recommend policy for Ontario's school system. As we have seen, Seath's report, *Education for Industrial Purposes*, published the following year, strongly defended the principle of provincial financial support for the creation of a comprehensive system of technical education.[66] Interestingly, Seath placed technical high schools — such as the existing Toronto Technical High School- at the top of his proposed system. Indeed, such schools would cater to an "educational elite," being reserved to "those who are designed for the higher directive positions in connection with the industries," positions which required "special technical knowledge" and are of "greater importance and responsibility than those held by skilled mechanics."[67] The Ontario government acted rapidly to implement the report's main recommendations. In 1911, it adopted the Industrial Education Act, which outlined the first comprehensive provincial policy on technical education.[68] The adoption of the Act had immediate effects on the administration of the Toronto Technical High School. In compliance with the legislation, it was placed in 1911 under the management of a local Advisory Industrial Committee, appointed by the Toronto Board of Education and comprising representatives from education, business and labour.[69] Under the Committee's management, technical education in Toronto expanded considerably. Immediately upon its appointment, the Committee decided to develop technical education in a central technical high school — the existing Toronto Technical High School- as well as in branch evening technical schools. During the next two years, three branch evening schools were opened in various collegiate institutes; however, only in 1923 did Toronto's first full-fledged branch technical school, the Riverdale Branch Technical School, open its doors for day as well as for evening classes. At the same time, the Advisory Committee narrowed down the scope of technical education. Since the inception of day classes, the Toronto Technical High School had offered commercial subjects,[70] eventually regrouping these under a Department of Commerce and Finance. In 1911, the Committee decided to move the Department into new quarters, thus operating a definitive split between technical education and commercial education.[71] Meanwhile, in 1915, the newly-named Central Technical School moved to a more spacious building.[72] The provincial director of industrial and technical education, F.W. Merchant, marvelled at the new accommodations which made the School "one of the largest and best equipped in the world for instruction in the type of work to which it is devoted."[73] Merchant was particularly impressed by the provisions made for women's work at the Central Technical School:

> There are four kitchens, a demonstration dining-room, a laundry, sewing and dress-making rooms, millinery rooms, a demonstration house-keeping apartment for teaching practical house-keeping, made up of a suite of rooms, including kitchen, pantry, dining-room, toilet and bathrooms, linen and clothes closet, and entrance hall.[74]

In fact, an entire floor of the new building had been reserved for classes in Domestic Science and Domestic Art.[75] The new Technical School thus served as an impressive symbol of the continuing growth of vocational education in Toronto.

b) Towards a "wage-earning" curriculum: Course provisions for women, 1904-1920.

The wider allocation of resources devoted to the training of female students in the Central Technical School resulted from the expansion of course provisions for women during the previous ten years. At first, the Toronto Board of Education had quickly reorganized them in a three-year Diploma "Home Economics" course, which was placed under the supervision of the new Department of Domestic Science and Art. The course taught a wide variety of subjects. To the traditional cooking classes were now added classes in sewing and millinery. "Household economics" now meant training to care for house furnishings and various appliances, while "Domestic Art" was defined as handsewing and machine sewing. The "scientific" component of the course was represented by subjects such as anatomy and physiology, bacteriology, hygiene and dietetics. Finally, during the third year, a preliminary training course for nurses was introduced.[76] Despite this initiative, the School's calendar did not attribute any real vocational objectives to the Home Economics Course. On the contrary, it was simply designed for those women "desiring to become proficient in the care of the home."[77] The duration of the course, equivalent to that of the other courses offered by the School's various Departments[78], certainly did not allow for the speedy training of girls for a specific trade. In addition, the Toronto Board of Education now aimed to provide all regular day students with some degree of general academic training, a goal reflected in the establishment of the Department of Language and History at the Technical

Schooling Women for Home or for Work?

School. Girls registered in the Home Economics Course were thus required to take subjects such as literature, composition, history, French or German. However, mathematics and science courses did not figure in the curriculum, with the single exception of arithmetic.[79]

Free evening classes also grew in importance under the Toronto Board of Education's management. Their official mandate did not specifically include the training of girls and women for employment. In fact, women were not referred to at all in the Technical High School's calendars, which declared that the purpose of evening classes were to provide "scientific and artistic training for apprentices, journeymen, foremen and others, who are engaged in industrial or commercial pursuits during the daytime, and who desire supplementary instruction in the application of science and art to the trades and manufactures."[80] Nevertheless, night classes for women developed in importance under the Department of Domestic Science and Domestic Art. Indeed, students were now encouraged to take a diploma course in sewing, cooking or in both subjects combined, each one covering two evenings a week for more than three years.[81]

A full-fledged domestic science program was thus on its way to being established at the Technical High School. This is not surprising considering the rapid incursion of domestic science at all levels of Ontario's educational system. Domestic science courses were spreading at the time in other secondary level institutions, especially the collegiate institutes. Already in 1910, close to 18% of the girls attending the latter were enrolled in domestic science. Furthermore, since 1906, graduates from both high schools and collegiate institutes could attend the Faculty of Household Science at the University of Toronto, which offered a four-year program leading to the Bachelor of Household Science.[82] Significantly, female graduates of the Technical High School were not admitted to this program. The School did not offer a matriculation course allowing for their admission, although male students wishing to enter the University's School of Applied Science could follow such a course at the Technical School.

The situation changed under the management of the Advisory Industrial Committee. In effect, this new administrative body soon proceeded to a major reorganization of day classes at the Technical High School. The major changes were inspired by John Seath's 1911 report, including his discussion and recommendations concerning the training of girls and women.[83] The result was a significant shift towards a "wage-earning" female curriculum at the Toronto Technical High School.

Firstly, a tuition-free three-year "industrial course" was established to train girls and young women wishing "to prepare for such occupations as dressmaking, machine operating, millinery, costume designing, industrial designing, catering, cookery for private homes, for public dining-rooms and for hospital patients." For the first time, an explicit statement concerning the vocational training of women for the paid labour force had been made. Although the work of the first year was general in character and included courses such as physics, chemistry, english, history geography and literature, the last two allowed for specialization in order "to meet the needs of the individual students." One of the distinctive features of the new industrial course was the importance granted to drawing and design. Freehand drawing was offered throughout and third-year students wishing to specialize in some form of industrial art work could take classes from the regular Art Course now being offered by the Technical School.[84]

In *Education for Industrial Purposes*, John Seath had stressed the urgent necessity of developing drawing and art education in Ontario as in the United States and many European countries. In 1904, art had been included in the revised curriculum implemented by the Department of Education. Since then, it had progressed in the province's public and high schools, and normal school students were also receiving instruction in the subject. Furthermore, American institutions offering "industrial education" to girls and women at the time generally included regular art courses as well as courses teaching the practical applications of art to the needs of industry.[85] Finally, since 1886, the Toronto School of Art had been imparting to both sexes instruction in various subjects related to art with the financial help of the City of Toronto and of the provincial government. Most of its students were employed in some branch of industry for which training in art was required, but since the late nineteenth-century, a large proportion of those enrolled also studied to become teachers.[86] We can assume that many of these future teachers were women, a trend reflected, indeed, in the census data.[87] Despite this work being done in the area of art education, Seath believed that there was a serious lack of competent teachers. Significantly, the Superintendent of Education considered art instruction to be an integral part of any system of industrial and technical training. He expressed the wish that the Toronto Technical School set up a complete department of Industrial Art and Design, stating that while "such a department cannot be efficient if it does not give due prominence to the artistic side, it will, in function, be auxiliary to the industries."[88]

The Advisory Industrial Committee thus responded to Seath's wishes by establishing a tuition-free three-year course in fine and applied art intended to give "a thorough preparation along art lines for those who desire to follow the work from the pure art standpoint, and especially for those who wish to use it for industrial purposes." More specifically, the course had two main objectives: to prepare art teachers and to train future workers wishing to secure positions in the art departments of various industries, including engraving, lithographing, publishing, illustrating, advertising, decorating and designing of jewelry.[89] The special provisions made for girls enrolled in the industrial course for further training in industrial art thus suggest that the art field was deemed an area suitable for the employment of women, not only as teachers but also as workers in such industries.

In addition to the new industrial course for girls, the Advisory Industrial Committee also introduced, on a part-time day basis, "special short courses of theoretical and practical technology," some of which were specifically designed for girls and women. These included sewing, dressmaking, millinery, lace making, embroidery, cookery and breadmaking. Courses in fine and applied arts, with special adaptation to the industries, were also offered. In addition, short and intensive courses, each lasting four months, were established. The growing presence of women in the health field is reflected in two of these courses. One provided preliminary training for those wishing to enter a hospital to train as a nurse or to supplement their education in this field. The work was carried on in co-operation with Toronto hospitals. In fact, preference would be given to those applicants who had taken the course. Secondly, a course for dietitians was planned for young women whose services were required in the diet kitchens of "modern hospitals." On the other hand, the continuing presence of girls and women in domestic service is illustrated in the creation of a "housekeepers' course" which was designed to "enable the student to meet intelligently the demands of the modern home."[90]

By 1920, the number of part-time and short courses had increased. New part-time courses included textiles and a power operating course which taught the "principles of garment construction," the "use and care of power machines" as well as "shop methods." Short intensive courses in advanced dressmaking and millinery were introduced, both of which put emphasis on trade methods.[91] To these was added a "houseworkers' course," which could be attended by individuals who had obtained the permission of their employer.[92] Both categories of courses were modelled on the "trade-extension courses" introduced in the early twentieth century by American trade and technical high schools. Their main purpose was to enable girls and women already employed to become more proficient in their work or to enable them to progress to a better job.[93]

Evening courses were also restructured on the same lines. Shorter unit courses were introduced, whereby students could select any of the subjects included in the regular diploma courses instead of being required to complete the whole course, which could take up to three years. Designed to give rapid instruction in some narrow, well-defined field, these courses were expected to improve attendance by encouraging students to keep up with their work and, according to the Central Technical School, help them to make progress in their "particular trade or profession."[94]

What about domestic science? It, too, underwent significant changes under the early management of the Advisory Industrial Committee. While the three-years Home Economics Course introduced previously by the Toronto Board of Education was maintained, a much more extensive matriculation course of four years was designed for girls having high school entrance standing and seeking admission to the Faculty of Household Science at the University of Toronto.[95] This course was eventually referred to as a "technical high school course for girls and young women." In 1920, it prepared girls for University Junior Matriculation as well as for entrance to the Household Science General Course established in 1915-16 by the University of Toronto. Furthermore, a second course could be arranged for those who wished to return for a fifth year to take Honour Matriculation and do advanced work in Household Science, in order to enter the Special Course in Household Science or in Physiology and Household Science, also being offered by the University of Toronto.[96] The possibility for female graduates from the Technical High School to obtain university-level training in household science, which John Seath had himself envisaged in 1911,[97] thus modified considerably the aims and content of the domestic science courses. While previous programs aimed mainly to prepare women for unpaid employment in the home, domestic science had now been elevated to include a "technical" course that could lead to university training and to gainful employment, particularly in the area of nutrition and dietetics. In sum, domestic science had definitely entered the vocational stream.

B) Training Women for "Women's Work"
1. Vocational Education and Occupational Segregation
The evolution of course provisions for women at the Toronto Technical High School from 1892 to 1920 provides evidence of the development of linkages between the educational system, female paid labour and prevailing attitudes respecting "women's work." As the first area to offer courses designed for girls and women at the Toronto Technical School, domestic science established from the outset a link between vocational education and women's unpaid labour in the home. The belief, widely spread at the time by the leaders of the domestic science movement, that women were above all responsible for the care of the household and of the family, was thus reinforced by the male promoters of technical education in Toronto. Therefore, one of its main objectives would be

to impart "domestic skills" to women, in order to enable them to ably fulfil their duties more ably.

However, with the broadening of course provisions for girls and women, more particularly under the supervision of the Advisory Industrial Committee, a link was also being drawn between vocational education and women's gainful occupations. Two factors can help explain this development. Firstly, a growing concern for the training of girls and women for paid employment was expressed during the opening decades of the present century at both the provincial and national levels. In 1908, for example, the Whitney Government, which had committed itself to the expansion of technical education in the province, took a direct interest in the issue. It asked Adelaide Hoodless, one of the most fervent promoters of domestic science in Ontario,[98] to visit and report on American trade schools for girls. In the fall of 1908, Hoodless visited some of the most famous, including the Carnegie Technical Schools in Pittsburgh, the Manhattan Trade School for Girls and the Pratt Institute in Brooklyn, New York. Her report, submitted in February 1909, expresses the views of a woman who, although still firmly committed to the belief that housekeeping was the most rewarding occupation for a woman, was nevertheless beginning to recognize the reality of female paid labour. She began by reminding the minister of Education that "about half of the pupils attending the public and high schools are girls, and a large majority of these girls must eventually become wage-earners." Unfortunately, circumstances had compelled women to "follow the various industries into shop and factory, without either mental or technical training," a lack which accounted, in a large measure, "for the lower standard of efficiency, lower wages, and consequent social deterioration of women wage-earners." For Hoodless, this was, beyond a doubt, "a serious social and economic matter."[99] Unfortunately, unlike the United States, Ontario had so far done little to provide vocational education for girls. In fact, Hoodless rightly observed, female workers were largely invisible from the discussions concerning technical education in the province:

> The writer has followed very closely...the various discussions which have taken place among manufacturers, Boards of Trade, special committees, and other organizations concerning technical education, as reported from time to time in the daily newspapers. Not once has there appeared even a reference to the woman wage-earner. The extremely limited provison made in a few schools for instruction in domestic science and sewing is all the consideration allowed for the vast army of women workers.[100]

213

Hoodless thus hoped that her report could secure "greater consideration for girls in any scheme of trade and technical education that may be established in Ontario."[101] The issue of job training for women workers was also put forward to the provincial government in the 1916 Report of the Ontario Commission on Unemployment. The Commission pointed out that, despite the significant number of working women and of those who faced unemployment, the reality of women's work had "been imperfectly appreciated" and that it was still not understood that women workers "form equally with men a part of the world's working force."[102] It then identified a direct link between steady female employment and specialized training: "When little training of any kind is required in an employment, the power of the individual in holding a position seems correspondingly small." The Report therefore recommended that such training be provided whenever possible.[103] Meanwhile, at the national level, the establishment of the Royal Commission on Industrial Training and Technical Education had also generated discussion about the training of women for paid labour. More particularly, national women's groups, including the National Council of Women of Canada, promoted the vocational training of girls and women, especially the training of qualified servants. The Commission's final report, submitted in 1913, endorsed their recommendations.[104]

Finally, World War I and the immediate post-war period generated further interest in women's vocational education. By drawing a large pool of women into paid employment, more particularly in industrial and clerical occupations[105], the war created new expectations regarding their future opportunities in the work force. These were clearly formulated by the various national women's organizations which assembled in February 1918 in a "Woman's War Conference," held in Ottawa at the invitation of the federal government.[106] Significantly, the delegates not only recognized the right of women to engage in paid labour; they also expressed the belief that they could contribute to the war effort by successfully replacing men in non-traditional fields. Measures should also be taken to fight female unemployment, already a problem due to the decrease of munition contracts. Finally, the Conference stressed the necessity of training women for employment in various trades in order to increase their efficiency, as well as the importance of providing such training in technical schools and in vocational night schools. It even requested the federal government to standardize the school system throughout the Dominion so "that the majority of the students may be trained primarily for vocational work."[107]

The post-war period witnessed, on its part, substantial optimism respecting women's future in the workplace. In 1919, Marjorie MacMurchy, whose husband had chaired the Ontario Commission on Unemployment, published,

Schooling Women for Home or for Work?

under the auspices of the Women's Department of the Canadian Reconstruction Association, a brochure proclaiming that "this is the age of the woman at work" and that "to find the best employment is part of our [women's] war readjustment." Again, the necessity of training was underlined, MacMurchy pointing out that "one of the greatest safeguards against poverty and unemployment at any time in her future life which women can possess is experience and skill in some form of useful work."[108] The same year, Marjorie MacMurchy formulated the same kind of advice in one of Canada's first vocational guidance books, *The Canadian Girl at Work*, published by the Ontario Ministry of Education.[109]

Meanwhile, the Ontario government was taking two steps which put the issue of vocational education for women at the forefront. Firstly, the Trades and Labour Branch of the Department of Public Works launched a "Vocational Guidance Investigation" in order to provide schoolteachers and parents reliable information respecting vocational opportunities for girls and boys in various Ontario industries. Such an initiative came largely in response to a series of requests submitted since 1917 by the Dominion Council of Girl Guides, the National Council of Women and the Toronto Home and School Council, for the establishment of a provincial bureau of vocational guidance for girls destined to enter the workplace.[110] But the adoption in 1919 of the Adolescent School Attendance Act, which decreed that, starting in 1921, the age limit for full-time and part-time compulsory school attendance would be raised from 14 to 16 years, also had great significance for women's vocational education. In effect, this law, which was designed to enforce secondary school attendance, was directly related to the Department of Education's policy of expanding vocationalism in the high schools. The training of skilled workers for Ontario's post-war economy was one of the Department's main concerns. F.W. Merchant, who still acted as Director of Industrial and Technical Education, had been a fierce promoter of compulsory legislation designed to further extend general education.[111] Furthermore, as the report of the Ontario Commission on Unemployment suggests, raising the compulsory school leaving age was seen at the time as an essential step in the reduction of the mass of young male and female workers who, having left school at fourteen with no proper training, had drifted in the ranks of unskilled labour and were left with no prospect of permanent employment.[112]

The evidence indicates, then, that the growing emphasis put on the vocational training of girls and women for gainful occupations can be related to an increasing recognition and acceptance of their place and role in the paid labour market. A relationship was being drawn between vocational education and women's work, in which the former was perceived as a means of enhancing women's job prospects, and, more fundamentally, of fighting female unemployment, a problem which was attracting more attention. The development of a "wage-earning" curriculum for girls and women at the Toronto Technical High School undoubtedly reflected these changing attitudes towards women's paid labour.

At the same time, the courses designed for girls and women were clearly perceived as beneficial to local economic interests. The importance of adapting the curriculum of the Toronto Technical High School to the needs of local industries was raised frequently by its promoters, even before the establishment of the Advisory Industrial Committee, where now sat together representatives of the manufacturing interests and of the Toronto Board of Education. In 1906, a Special Committee on Technical Education reminded the Toronto Board of Education that the technical school was meant above all to prepare its students for the workplace and that it should therefore provide instruction "in the science and arts underlying the chief trades of Toronto, i.e. the building trades, the metal trades, the art trades, the power plant trades, the chemical trades, the household trades, and as the school develops, the textile trades and printing trades."[113] The same point had been strongly made before the Special Committee by the Toronto Board of Trade as well as by the Canadian Manufacturers' Association.[114] In 1910, the chairman of the Toronto Board of Education, James Simpson, also expressed his firm intention of developing technical education in order "to serve the industries in the City of Toronto." Simpson noted that "few cities on the North American Continent have had in view the local demands when arranging their technical courses"; therefore, with "a proper appreciation of Toronto's industrial needs and a course to meet these conditions a lesson of great value to other industrial centres can be given."[115]

Did such a concern for the needs of the local labour market imply the training of girls and women in order to supply the former with a steady pool of female labour? Again, the historian is confronted by a gender-neutral discourse which inevitably promotes the invisibility of women workers. Nevertheless, the evolution of course provisions for girls and women at the Toronto Technical High School remains indicative of the kind of relationship which was being established at the beginning of the century between vocational education for girls and women and the local labour market. Thus, with the introduction of wage-earning domestic science courses such as cooking, housekeeping, trade dressmaking, trade millinery, as well as the provision of courses in health and industrial art and design, the Toronto Technical High School was training girls and women for those sectors where they either already formed a high proportion of the workforce (personal service and the wearing apparel industry) or were being increasingly employed (such as food services and the publishing and printing industries), as well as for rapidly growing "female" occupations(dietetics and nursing).[116] Moreover, in establishing courses in "gainful" domestic science, more particularly those for the training of housekeepers and houseworkers, the Toronto Technical High School was responding directly to the persistent and highly vocal call for skilled domestic servants which was being sent by upper and middle-class women and their representatives within various women's organizations.[117] The problem of the "servant shortage" was becoming more acute at the turn of the century due to the expansion of occupational opportunities for girls and women.[118] The development of certified training courses, it was believed, would not only provide employers with a competent body of workers; these courses would also help raise the status of domestic servants, which was much lower than that of other female workers. This point of view was endorsed by the Royal Commission on Industrial Training and Technical Education and the Ontario Commission on Unemployment, which both specifically recommended the creation of various courses in housekeeping and housework for future as well as for present employees.[119]

In sum, vocational education at the Toronto Technical High School prepared girls and women for those few female-dominated occupations that were already open to them in the work place. Itself partitioned by gender, vocational education thus reinforced the two processes of sex-typing and gender segregation. At the same time, it constituted a source of occupational segregation, since the distinctly female curriculum was training girls and women for jobs different from those in which men worked. In sum, while its advocates claimed that vocational education would improve women's job opportunities, help promote stability in female employment and lead to higher wages, the training which was being offered to girls and women could, in fact, change neither the occupational structure of the paid labour market nor the low wages attached to the jobs performed by the majority of female workers.

Indeed, for the promoters of vocational education, there was no doubt that women should be trained, with few exceptions, for female-dominated occupations. According to Marjorie MacMurchy, some women could seek an "exceptional occupation" if they were qualified for it and "not be discouraged by initial failure;" she believed, nonetheless, that "necessary occupations" such as food, health, clothing, household management, teaching, child care and nursing offered women the best prospects of employment as well as a "fair certainty of earning an honourable and comfortable livelihood."[120] In 1919, when the federal government finally decided to act upon the main recommendations of the Royal Commission on Industrial Training and

Technical Education by adopting the Vocational and Technical Education Act,[121] an agreement was subsequently negotiated with the government of Ontario in order to promote the expansion of technical education in the province. Defining the aim of "technical education" as the fitting of "young persons for useful employment or to improve the efficiency of those already employed," the agreement would provide for training in several occupational areas which included, amongst others, typing and stenography, household science, decorating, needlework, millinery, dressmaking, child welfare and the elements of nursing.[122] Such a selection clearly reveals what kind of training was deemed appropriate for future female workers in Ontario.

By 1920, these vocational areas were covered by the female curriculum developed by the Toronto Technical High School, with the exception of typing and stenography courses which had been dropped by this time. At the same time, the range of courses available in the female-dominated areas of employment was limited compared to those offered in areas of male-dominated occupations. For example, they accounted for only thirteen of the forty-six part-time day "industrial courses" offered in 1921.[123] Moreover, the industrial course for girls was one year shorter than the four year industrial course for boys. Girls typically began to specialize and engage in practical work immediately in the second year, while boys did so in the third. In sum, the overall curriculum was less extensively developed in female fields of study than in the male. Ironically, the only four year course was the matriculation course which allowed graduates to enter the Faculty of Household Science at the University of Toronto.

The Toronto Technical High School curriculum reflected prevailing attitudes concerning the nature of "women's work,"for promoters of vocational education for women consistently stressed the dual nature of women's work in industrial society. The unpaid activities women performed in the home were seen as essential components of women's work experience. In fact, the Royal Commission on Industrial Training and Technical Education expressed the fairly common opinion that the work women performed in the labour market, particularly in the clothing and food industries, was virtually the same as the work they did at home before the industrial revolution. The main difference lay simply in the conditions under which this work was performed.[124] In the end, this emphasis on the duality of women's work undermined women's role as paid labourers in two ways. First, women's traditional employment as wives and mothers and as keepers of the home continued to be perceived as their most vital work. Marjorie MacMurchy summed up this point of view by stating that the mother was "the first worker of the nation."[125] Second, since the unpaid labour performed by women in the home was their primary "vocation," it was

Schooling Women for Home or for Work?

expected that girls and young women entering the work force would quit after a brief stay in order to get married. The Ontario Commission on Unemployment stated without hesitation that "home occupations are the ultimate employment of all but a comparatively small percentage of women."[126]

In turn, such perceptions of women's work had important implications for the development of vocational education for women. Its promoters continually stressed the need to prepare girls for their future careers as sustainers of the family as well as for gainful occupations. Thus,while they recognized the increasing role women played in the paid labour market,they were equally fervent advocates of domestic science, along with those who argued, even more conservatively,that the place of women was exclusively in the home. Again, Marjorie MacMurchy summed up this point of view in *The Canadian Girls at Work*:

> The life of the average woman is divided generally into periods of work, that of paid employment and that of homemaking. No adequate scheme of training for girls can fail to take account of this fact. They should be equipped with knowledge and skill for homemaking and assisted in making the best use of their years in paid work.[127]

Furthermore, many believed that since most girls were anxious to earn wages as soon as possible and since they would remain only a few years in the paid labour force before they retired permanently after marriage, they did not require long and intensive job training. Such a view was clearly expressed in 1911 by none other than John Seath:

> Girls...who enter any kind of industrial employment do so earlier than the boys who are to become skilled mechanics, and the courses that result in wage-earning capacity are by them more easily completed than are the corresponding courses for boys. They desire to earn money as soon as possible, and for obvious reasons, they do not look forward to a trade or any other industrial occupation as their life work." [128]

2. Vocational Education and the Construction of Skill

Seath's testimony also raised the important issue of skill in relation to women's paid labour. In effect, his view was that only men had access to skilled jobs and that their training therefore had to be more extensive. Feminist scholarship has effectively challenged prevailing assumptions about what constitutes "skill," however, as well as the labelling of women's jobs as "unskilled." There is now general agreement that, far from being an objective and independent variable, skill is an historical and political construction, reflecting not only the technology of production, but also the complex interaction of gender relations at work and at home, women's lack of representation by strong collective organizations and the mechanisms of capitalist production. The result has been not only that women have been excluded from many skilled occupations but also that men have captured the definition of "skilled" for their own jobs. Women have lacked the workplace power to do the same.[129] According to Anne Philipps and Barbara Taylor, "Skill definitions are saturated with sexual bias." [130]Furthermore, they contend that the "classification of women's jobs as unskilled and men's jobs as skilled or semi-skilled frequently bears little relation to the actual amount of training or ability required for them."[131] However, as Jane Gaskell has pointed out, "the length and form that training will take is [also] decided through political and economic struggle."[132] She thus reminds us that any discussion about the development of skill should include an examination of the role played by the educational system in this process.

More historical studies on gender and skill in various Canadian industries are needed before a systematic analysis of the relationship between vocational education and women's paid labour can be attempted.[133] We have especially to examine more closely the process by which skills have been defined in these industries and the influence exerted by different social groups -employers, unions, educators, legislators and women's associations- on the construction of "female skills." Nevertheless, in view of the evidence compiled for the present case study, the following points can tentatively be made respecting to vocational education and women' skills.

First, with the exception of the three-year industrial course which, by adding academic work, physical education, drawing and design to training for a particular trade, allowed for the development of general intelligence and of broader range of skills, the short, intensive and "special" courses which, by 1920, constituted a significant portion of the "wage-earning" curriculum developed by the Toronto Technical High School, offered a small range of skills with specific and narrow applications. The emphasis was generally put on speed, accuracy, precision and dexterity[134], which were recognised at the time as the main skills involved in most female industrial jobs.[135] At the same time, these courses both reflected and reinforced the belief that "women's jobs" did not require a wide breadth of skills, that these could therefore be learned quickly and, that in any case, longer courses were not warranted for workers who would leave their jobs after just a few years in the labour market.

Schooling Women for Home or for Work?

However, the intervention of the school in the training of girls and women for paid labour constituted in itself a significant development as far as the imparting of skill is concerned. Indeed, the school was taking over a responsibility which the traditional apprenticeship system was still assuming in some female occupations in Toronto, notably dressmaking and millinery.[136] One can postulate that the decline of the small workshops and the ensuing shift toward factory production in the wearing apparel industry during the period examined led educators to provide instruction in the fundamental principles of the trade as well as those job-related skills which the large body of girls and women working in large shops or factories could no longer acquire. In addition, the school might possibly reach what the Ontario Commission on Unemployment had described as the "floating population" of female factory operatives "who have not acquired skill or who have not had the opportunity to acquire it." Mainly girls who had left school at fourteen, these operatives were the first to be laid off in slack seasons and in times of depression and this forced them to drift from one factory to another.[137]

Hence, school-based instruction was becoming a distinguishing feature of women's training for industrial employment. The presence of representatives from the manufacturing sector on the Advisory Industrial Committee suggests that employers did not contest such a development. In fact, there seemed to be a demand for experienced workers in the wearing apparel industry and the possibility of some advancement for female workers in this sector did exist. However, the nature and amount of training required of factory operatives in general was much more problematic. Factors such as the highly seasonal nature of women's industrial jobs and the relatively short period of time supposedly needed to learn most of the processes involved in female industrial work were thus invoked to question the validity, if not the necessity, of school-based training for women. [138]Indeed, John Seath had submitted to the Ontario Commission on Unemployment a rather gloomy testimony on the attitude of Ontario manufacturers concerning the education of their workers:

> So far as...industrial education is concerned, the key to the situation is really the manufacturer. Naturally, his object is to make money and normally he cares little about the education of his employees so long as they can do the work for which he pays them. In most manufacturing industries, labour is subdivided, and the employer is satisfied to have his employee repeat one operation day after day, and year after year. It is none of his business to provide an opportunity for the employee's fitting himself for a higher and more lucrative occupation. Co-operation

221

between the school and the factory might, under suitable
conditions, be to the interest of the manufacturer, but, as yet in
this Province, there is almost no such co-operation.[139]

Such a statement seems to warrant caution against the notion that educational
policy constitutes a direct and faithful reflection of employers' views and needs.
It has already been suggested that the educational system does have a degree
of autonomy in shaping policy while other social groups besides employers can
influence this process.[140] On the other hand, the development of various
programs and courses in domestic science at the Toronto Technical High
School reveals the existence of a wide consensus regarding the necessity for the
institution of the school to provide skill, indeed, to construct skill for purely
female work both in the household and in the paid labour market. As indicated
earlier, the so-called "servant problem" invoked by employers at the turn of the
century implied not only a shortage of domestics but also their lack of proper
training. To raise the skill level of servants was therefore one of their main
concerns. It was shared by the Ontario Commission on Unemployment which
argued that the "greatest advance possible in the future of this occupation
(domestic service) is to make it a skilled trade, with trained workers holding
certificates."[141] One solution was to import a large pool of highly trained
domestics from abroad.[142] Another and more wide-ranging answer was to
turn to the school; hence, the development of "wage-earning" domestic science
courses.

Although they offered certified training, the short and intensive courses
eventually established in housekeeping and houseworking at the Toronto
Technical High School did not do much to raise the level of those traditional
"female" skills involved in both these occupations. In contrast stood the four-
year "technical high school course," which offered students the possibility to
enter the University of Toronto Faculty of Household Science and to eventually
become highly qualified teachers, dieticians and nutritionists. In the meantime,
it allowed girls to acquire valuable skills associated with a general academic
education.[143] One can thus argue that the domestic science movement
increased the further education opportunities of girls by promoting the creation
of such a course at the Toronto Technical High School. Although its campaign
to promote "scientific homemaking" was based on the ideology of the separate
spheres and although it led to the creation of "female" professions, the
domestic science movement nonetheless allowed girls to increase the amount
of education which they possessed and, probably also, their occupational
options.

Schooling Women for Home or for Work?

C) Female Students at the Toronto Technical High School

How did girls and women respond to the development of vocational education at the Toronto Technical High School? Who were the students and what did they study in this institution between 1892 and 1920? Unfortunately, complete and uniform data concerning the enrolment of girls and women in the various courses and programs offered during this period are not available. The fragmented statistics contained in the prospectus and calendars of the Toronto Technical School prior to the take over by the Board of Education are not broken down by gender. Nevertheless, we can see that the establishment of a special evening course in domestic science in 1896 definitely attracted a large number of students. Indeed, during the 1897-98 session, an average of 133 students attended, by far the highest registered at the School for that year. At the same time, over two hundred women were refused admittance to the School owing to lack of accommodation. The list of occupations of pupils provided for this year clearly reveals their growing presence: 3 domestics, 19 dressmakers, 1 milliner, 1 seamstress, 29 housekeepers, 13 nurses, 7 salesladies and 14 schoolgirls figure amongst those female students attending evening classes. A list of the name of students having successfully passed the examinations is also available for the 1897-98 session. It provides a breakdown by course for those students. As expected, the course in domestic science produced the largest number of female graduates, but a significant number could be found in other fields. Indeed, girls and women formed the majority of the successful candidates in industrial design and almost half of those having successfully completed freehand drawing, two courses aimed at providing the artisan with "a better position and increased earnings." Other courses offered by the Department of Freehand Drawing, Design and Decoration, such as clay-modelling, graphic mathematics and mechanical drawing, also counted female graduates, although in much smaller numbers. Finally, a few women were graduating in different branches of physics, chemistry and mathematics.[144]

After the 1904 takeover of the School by the Toronto Board of Education, regular statistics published in the report of the Minister of Education indicate that the number of female students at the Toronto Technical High School multiplied by four from 1905 to 1920, an increase which reflected the School's overall expansion. Except for 1920, women never represented less than 40% of the student population (Table 3).

Table 3—STUDENTS ENROLLED AT THE TORONTO TECHNICAL HIGH
SCHOOL 1905-1920

Year	Male	Female	Total	% of Women
1905	310	290	600	48.3
1910	693	470	1163	40.4
1915	615	689	1304	52.8
1920	1922	1172	3094	37.8

Source: *Report of the Minister of Education of Ontario*, 1905-1920.

Table 4—NUMBER OF STUDENTS IN DOMESTIC SCIENCE AS % OF
TOTAL FEMALE ENROLMENT 1905-1915

Year	No. of Students	% of Total
1905	120	41.3
1910	360	76.5
1915	520	75.4

Source: *Report of the Minister of Education of Ontario*, 1905-1920.

While the number of students enrolled in the various branches of study is not broken down by gender, the report of the Minister of Education between 1905 and 1915 records the total number of pupils enrolled in domestic science. These figures demonstrate an increasing concentration of girls and women in this field following the move to the Toronto Board of Education in 1904 and the ensuing expansion of domestic science as an area of study (Table 4). On the other hand, some women were manifestly taking other courses. The large enrolments recorded in the Toronto Technical High School's commercial course as well as in stenography and typewriting as long as the School was responsible for these classes, suggest that these were very attractive options for girls.[145]

At the end of the period examined, the report of the Minister of Education started to record the number of students enrolled in each subject offered during the day by the Central Technical School. The data indicate that various subjects related to domestic science had a strong attraction. In 1920, cooking classes were widely attended, closely followed by sewing and dressmaking and by millinery. Courses such as housekeeping, laundry, power machine operating and embroidery, on the other hand, attracted less students (Table 5).

Table 5—NUMBER OF STUDENTS ENROLLED IN BRANCHES OF INSTRUCTION RELATED TO DOMESTIC SCIENCE DAY SCHOOL, 1920

Cooking	602	Power machine operating	15
Housekeeping	65	Laundry	73
Home Economics	325	Millinery	540
Home Nursing	136	Embroidery and lace making	48
Sewing and Dressmaking	585	Hygiene and Dietetics	186

Total enrolled: 2576

Source: *Report of the Minister of Education*, 1920, 261.

As for evening classes, regular statistics begin to appear in the report of the Minister of Education following the adoption of the Industrial Education Act in 1911. While no breakdown by gender is included, the total number of students enrolled in each course is available. In the evening as during the day, cooking, sewing and dressmaking, as well as millinery, were clearly the most popular of those branches of instruction related to domestic science.[146] Moreover, the first three subjects consistently enrolled the largest number of students in the School's evening classes, competing only with mathematics.[147] F.W. Merchant, the director of Industrial and Technical Education, noted the "marked difference in the character of the subjects taken by men and women" in evening classes, in his 1918 report: "Men in the industries apparently need most the elements of a general education and the theoretical subjects related to their occupations. The women, on the other hand, chiefly attend classes for practical subjects."[148]

Merchant's observations suggest another reason for the lower skill requirements attributed to female occupations as well as the limited range of courses and levels of study available to girls. Women, indeed, may not have been attracted by theoretical subjects. At the same time, the patterns of enrolments described above show how the development of a gender-segregated curriculum at the Toronto Technical High School probably influenced the choices and occupational preferences of those girls and women attending. By

225

1920, they were heavily concentrated in those branches that constituted the female curriculum. The annual list of diplomas, scholarships and prizes awarded to students of both day and evening classes clearly confirms this trend.[149] Indeed, in contrast to the earlier years, girls and women were almost totally absent from classes in mathematics, physics and chemistry. The general knowledge courses where they could be found were mainly English and Modern Languages. On the other hand, a continuing trend was the attraction of female students to art and design courses. Indeed, they often represented an overwhelming majority of graduates in the day art course and they frequently collected the scholarships and prizes awarded to the best students enrolled in the day and evening art and design classes.[150]

The Toronto Technical High School, then, was attracting an increasing number of girls and women into the vocational stream in the early twentieth century. It was at the same time funnelling this clientele in a highly segregated curriculum. Art and design constituted a more "neutral" terrain. Nonetheless, by 1920, this area of study was itself strongly feminized.

Who were the girls and women attending the Toronto Technical High School and why did they enrol in its classes? These two questions are the most difficult to answer in the view of the available data. We know that students originated overwhelmingly from Toronto.[151] Secondly, students came mainly from the working-class, although those heads of families who were engaged in commerce formed an important group throughout, except for a sharp drop in 1915.[152] Significant, also, was the number of those without occupations as well as the increasing proportion of those heads of families whose occupations were not specified (Table 6).

The motives and concerns which induced women to attend the Toronto Technical School during the period examined are, obviously, very difficult to discern. For those who enrolled in the full-time day courses, we can agree with Geraldine Joncich Clifford that the supplementary amount of schooling which they received was in itself important. By staying in school, they would probably widen their options in the paid labour force, all the more as the day vocational courses offered by the School contained the essentials of an academic education.[153] Secondly, one can assume that most who attended the various part-time and short courses, as well as the evening classes, were concerned either with increasing their chances of getting a job or with improving their position in the workplace by improving their job-related skills or by acquiring new skills which would allow them to switch jobs.[154] F.W. Merchant thus observed in 1914 that outside of Toronto, evening classes did not really prepare women for paid employment since, contrary to the situation which prevailed in this city, "there has not as yet been an urgent demand for a training for women

Schooling Women for Home or for Work?

in industrial work for the purpose of earning wages."[155] Furthermore, the increasing number of girls graduating from the special short course for dietitians despite its relatively high costs, seems to indicate a particular interest in training for new occupational avenues in the health field.[156] The reasons behind the educational choices made by women attending the Toronto Technical High School, however diverse, were surely linked largely to the necessity of earning wages, mostly as daughters, but possibly also as married women from the working-class or as working women living outside the family.[157]

Table 6—OCCUPATIONS OF HEADS OF FAMILIES OF STUDENTS
ENROLLED AT THE TORONTO TECHNICAL HIGH SCHOOL 1905-1920

Categories*	1905	1910	1915	1920	Total
Commerce	300	384	26	263	973
Agriculture	6	35	17	28	86
Professions**	60	46	23	57	186
Mechanical Occupations	216	547	n.a.	n.a.	763
Trades	n.a.	n.a.	470	397	867
Labouring Occupations	n.a.	93	200	79	372
Without Occupations	n.a.	n.a	300	164	464
Other	24	58	263	330	675

 * Categories used in the report of the Minister of Education
 ** Includes teachers for 1915 and 1920.
Source: *Report of the Minister of Education of Ontario*, 1905-1920.

On the other hand, the desire to improve their skills as unpaid homemakers may have induced girls and women to enrol in the various evening domestic science classes offered by the Toronto Technical High School. It remains to see why they felt the need to do so. Certainly, the upper and middle-class promoters of domestic science education presumed that these female students shared their conviction that women's true place was in the home and that homemaking constituted their true "vocation." However, working-class women

227

might themselves have hoped to better contribute to the family economy and help improve their family's standard of living by learning how to cook and sew or by acquiring the more modern techniques in these areas. The vital role played by working-class wives, mothers and daughters in family economics was likely a major factor accounting for the participation of women in late 19th- and early 20th-century vocational education.

Conclusion

I have attempted to provide some answers to the many questions related to the development of vocational education for women and to the links which exist between the education of girls and women and their position in the paid labour market for the period in question. It seems clear, first of all, that the development and institutionalizing of women's vocational education at the Toronto Technical High School was related to three basic factors: the growing intervention of the provincial and federal governments in the field of technical and industrial education; the domestic science movement, the upper and middle-class promoters of which stressed the importance of schooling in the training of both servants and future housewives; and the increasing recognition of the reality of women's participation in the paid labour force. The needs of the local industrial economy must also be considered and these certainly preoccupied the promoters of technical education in Toronto, even though manufacturers themselves seem to have been divided as to the necessity of such training for female workers. For those who did believe in its value, school-based training was undoubtedly beneficial in that it relieved employers of the cost of educating workers.

By 1920, vocational education at the Toronto Technical High School was more closely linked to women's paid labour than had previoulsy been the case. The development of a "wage-earning" curriculum went along, however, with the establishment of a distinct female curriculum within the walls of a co-educational institution. This evolution illustrates the complex reciprocal relations between vocational education and the dual nature of women's work. On one hand, the promoters of this type of education never overlooked the indispensable unpaid labour performed by women in the home; hence, their commitment to domestic science. On the other hand, women's vocational education at the Toronto Technical High School developed close links with the gender-segregated paid labour force. Not only did it reflect the existing occupational structure of the labour market; it also became itself a source of

Schooling Women for Home or for Work?

occupational sex segregation by preparing most of the students for a limited range of female-dominated occupations.

Finally, prevailing attitudes concerning the nature "women's work" and of "female skills" were important in the shaping of a distinct female curriculum at the Toronto Technical High School. The range of courses offered girls and women was narrower, the training tended to be shorter and it focussed more on practical applications than on theory. In conclusion, I would suggest that the significance of the development of women's vocational education at the Toronto Technical High School at the turn of the century resided not so much in its ability to redefine and raise women's low level of recognised vocational skills, but more fundamentally, in the role which the school, as an institution, was assuming as a provider of skills. Indeed, the absence of a formal apprenticeship system for women workers, the lack of opportunities for promotion within most female industrial occupations and the weakness of women's industrial organization in unions all conduced to bring job-training in the classroom. One can believe that many of the girls and women attending classes at the Toronto Technical High School had come to the same conclusion.

Notes

1. John Seath, *Education for Industrial Purposes. A Report*, Toronto, 1911, 281-282.
2. Ibid., 345.
3. By "vocational education," I refer to the training for jobs classified generally as skilled, semi-skilled or technical, as opposed to managerial and professional occupations.
4. Ibid., p. 283.
5. Ibid., p. 290
6. Ibid., 295.
7. Ibid., 291.
8. See, for example, Terry Crowley, "Madonnas before Magdalenes: Adelaide Hoodless and the Making of the Canadian Gibson Girl," *Canadian Historical Review*, LXVII(1986): 520-547; Marta Danylewycz, Nadia Fahmy-Eid and Nicole Thivierge, "L'enseignement ménager et les 'Home Economics' au Québec et en Ontario au début du 20e siècle. Une analyse compareé," in J. Donald Wilson, ed., *An Imperfect Past: Education and Society in Canadian History*, Vancouver, 1984, 65-119; Diana Pedersen, " ' The Scientific Training of Mothers' " : The Campaign for Domestic Science in Ontario Schools, 1890-1913," in Richard Jarrell and Arnold Roos, eds., *Critical Issues in the History of Canadian Science, Technology and Medecine*, Tornhill: HSTC Publications, 1983, 178-194; Robert M. Stamp, "Teaching Girls their 'God-Given Place in Life': The Introduction of Home Economics in the Schools," *Atlantis*, 2(1977): 18-34.
9. See, for example, Jane Gaskell, "Sex Inequalities in Education for Work: The Case of Business Education," *Canadian Journal of Education*, 6 (April 1981):54-72; Nancy S. Jackson and Jane S. Gaskell, "White Collar Vocationalism: The Rise of Commercial Education in Ontario and British Columbia, 1870-1929," *Curriculum Inquiry*, 17, no 2 (Summer 1982): 177-201 (reproduced in this volume); Graham S. Lowe, "Women, Work and the Office: The Feminization of Clerical Occupations in Canada, 1901-1931," *Canadian Journal of Sociology,* 5 (1980):361-379. Ruth Pierson and Marjorie Cohen have also written a very enlightening article on "Government Job-Training Programs for Women, 1937-1947," in Ruth Pierson, *"They're Still Women After All: The Second World War and Canadian Womanhood,"* Toronto, 1986, 62-94.

10. Ian M. Drummond, *Progress without Planning. The Economic History of Ontario from Confederation to the Second World War*, Toronto, 1987, 104-110.
11. Ibid., 109-110.
12. Ibid., 150.
13. Ibid., 363, table 2.2.
14. Ibid., 413, table 10.2.
15. In 1891, 38.74% of Ontarians lived in cities, while thirty years later, the percentage reached 58.17% *Canada Year Book*, 1932, 102.
16. Ibid., 103.
17. *Census of Canada*, Vol. 2, 1931, table 19.
18. Marjorie Cohen, *Women's Work, Markets, and Economic Development in Nineteenth Century Ontario,* Toronto, 1988, 120-123; Alison Prentice and *al., Canadian Women. A History*, Toronto, 1988, 115-116.
19. In 1900, the National Council of Women of Canada noted that in Canada, "the ages of the women engaged in active employment range from sixteen to forty years." See *Women in Canada. Their Life and Work*, 1900, 102.
20. Revealing of this trend is the analytical table of applications for positions prepared in 1916 by the Toronto Women's Patriotic League. Of the 1963 applicants, 46.7% were single, 33.7%, married, 16.1%, widows and 3.3%, deserted. See Ontario, *Report of the Ontario Commission on Unemployment*, Toronto, 1916, 196. Earlier, in 1892, Jean Thomson Scott had concluded that the "employment of married women in factories and stores in Ontario is not general." Jean Thomson Scott, *The Conditions of Female Labour in Ontario*, Toronto, 1892, 25. Finally, as noted by Michael J. Piva, a significant number of married women were applying at the Women's Department of the Toronto Public Employment Bureau after the latter opened its doors in 1916.See his study on *The Condition of the Working Class In Toronto—1900-1921*, Ottawa, 1979, 40, 43.
21. Toronto's working women represented 27.6% and 30.6% of Ontario's paid female labour force(women 10 years of age and older) in 1911 and 1921 respectively. Calculated from the *Census of Canada*, 1911, vol.6, table 6, and the *Census of Canada*, 1921, vol.4, table 5, and from the *Canada Year Book*, 1939, 778. In 1891 and 1901, the Census does not provide data on the sexual division of labour in Toronto.
22. In 1891, 43.6% of Ontario's female labour force(10 years and over) was in personal service, 33.7% in manufacturing and 9.4%, in professional service. *Canada Year Book*, 1939, 778.
23. Marjorie Cohen, *Women's Work*, 134.

24. This process has been described by Harry Braverman in his seminal study, *Labour and Monopoly Capital: The Degradation of Work in the Twentieth Century*, New York, 1974.

25. Marjorie Cohen, *Woman's Work*, 141-143; Joy Parr, *The Gender of Breadwinners. Women, Men and Change in Two Industrial Towns, 1880-1950*, Toronto,1990, 70-72; Mercedes Steedman, "Skill and Gender in the Canadian Clothing Industry, 1890-1940," in Craig Heron and Robert Storey, eds., *On the Job: Confronting the Labour Process in Canada*, Kingston, 1986, 152-155. In 1892, Jean Thomson Scott observed in her study on *The Conditions of Female Labour in Ontario*, that the "very fact of there being a number of employments requiring unskilled labour has led, no doubt, to the increased employment of young girls and women." Scott, *The Conditions...*, 19.

26. Jean Scott, *The Conditions of Female Labour in Ontario*, Toronto, 1892, 19.

27. Ontario, Department of Agriculture, *Report of the Inspectors of Factories*, 1898, 30.

28. In 1911, there were 5,962 female servants in Toronto. Their number went down slightly to 5,598 in 1921. Nevertheless, servants represented more than 50% of the total number of women employed in domestic and personal service in 1921, as compared to 56% in 1911. All data on women's employment for 1911 and 1921 used in this section, unless otherwise cited, are from the *Census of Canada*, 1911, vol. 6, table 6, and from the *Census of Canada*, 1921, vol. 4, table 5. All calculations are my own.

29. 37.6% of women in the personal and service category thus worked as housekeepers, charworkers, cooks, laundresses, nursemaids, restaurant, hotel and boarding housekeepers and employees, charitable institution workers and in "other domestic and personal service."

30. The number of women employed as cooks passed from 360 to 668 between 1911 and 1921. In 1921, the census records 776 waitresses and 672 waiters working in Toronto.

31. In 1921, women represented more than 76% of the teaching force in Toronto. The number of nurses increased from 844 to more than 2870 between 1911 and 1921. The data for 1921 also includes nurses-in-training.

32. In 1911, there were 434 women employed as musicians and music teachers in Toronto while in 1921, their number totalled 568. The art field attracted less women but their numbers also increased between 1911 and 1921. In 1911, the census records 86 women artists and painters in Toronto, but does not specify how many worked as teachers.

Ten years later, one finds 116 women in the category "artists and teachers of art," which suggests that teaching constituted a growing area of employment for women in the art field.

33. In 1921, the Census recorded 2,893 women and 2,589 men employed in general and departmental stores. Ten years later, the number had passed to 6,037 and 5,248 respectively. *Census of Canada*, 1921, vol. 4, table 5; 1931, vol. 7, table 57.

34. See Michèle Martin, "Feminization of the Labour Process in the Communication Industry. The Case of the Telephone Operators, 1876-1904," *Labour/Le Travail*, 22 (Fall 1988): 139-162. In 1921, there were more than 2,377 female telephone operators in Toronto, compared to only 99 men.

35. See Graham S. Lowe, *Women in the Administrative Revolution. The Feminization of Clerical Work*, Toronto, 1987. The *Census of Canada* does not record in a separate category the total number of female clerical workers in Toronto in 1911 and in 1921. However, in 1911, 82,5% of stenographers and typists were women, while ten years later, women outnumbered men as office clerks and employees in the trade, finance and service categories combined, as well as in unspecified industries.

36. Female representation in Toronto's manufacturing sector dropped from 33,7% to 26,5% between 1911 and 1921.

37. In 1911, for example, the clothing and allied products industries regrouped 54.7% of all women employed in manufacturing; at the same time, 60.1% of their labour force was composed of women.

38. The number of dressmakers, milliners and tailoresses dropped from 6,590 to 2,234 between 1911 and 1921, while the number of clothing factory workers increased from 1,074 to 3,582 during the same period.

39. In 1921, 1,155 women were working in the primary production of textiles in Toronto. The majority were working as factory employees in the cotton, knitting, woollen and textile industries.

40. Between 1911 and 1921, the number of women working in the food industries passed from 905 to 1,485, which represented an increase of 24%. The large majority worked as biscuit and confectionery makers, whose number increased from 690 to 1,099 during the same period. At the same time, the number of fruits and vegetable canners more than doubled, passing from 14 to 36 between 1911 and 1921.

41. In 1911, the census recorded 714 female printers and engravers in Toronto. Ten years later, 1,405 women worked in the printing and bookbinding industries. If we discount the 577 office employees, the majority of other workers were bookbinders(426). In the paper products

industry, the number of women making boxes, bags and stationary passed from between 1911 and 1921. In the leather and rubber products industry, the number of female workers increased from 378 to 1,130 during the same period. Only 36 women were electrical supplies makers in 1911, while ten years later, their number had increased five times, reaching 184. Interestingly, women outnumbered men as lamp and lantern makers during this period. Their numbers passed from 47 to 59 between 1911 and 1921. Finally, in the chemical industry, the number of female workers more than doubled, increasing from 206 to 457 between 1911 and 1921. Women by then outnumbered men as chemical products makers and as drugs and medicine makers.

42.   On women's paid labour in Ontario and Toronto in the early twentieth century, see Janice Acton and *al.*, eds., *Women at Work. Ontario,1850-1930*, Toronto, 1974; Michael Piva, *The Condition of the Working Class in Toronto, 100-1921*; Marjorie Griffin Cohen, *Women's Work, Markets and Economic Development in Nineteenth-Century Ontario.*

43.   Sex-typing refers to the process by which jobs are ascribed to one sex or the other; gender segregation refers to the way in which women and men are located in different types of jobs. For recent discussion on both processes, see Harriet Bradley, *Men's Work, Women's Work. A Sociological History of the Sexual Division of Labour in Employment*, Cambridge, Great Britain, 1989; Rosemary Crompton and Kay Sanderson, *Gendered Jobs and Social Change*, London, 1990; Pat Armstrong and High Armstrong, *Theorizing Women's Work*, Toronto, 1990.

44.   The Technical School Board was made up of representatives from the City Council, the Board of Trade, the Canadian Manufacturers' Association and the School of Practical Science. For a brief history of the Toronto Technical High School at the turn of the century, see Keith B. Spark, "An Examination of the Development of Technical Education in Ontario between 1800 and 1915, especially as it concerns the founding of Central Technical High School, Toronto," unpublished paper, Ontario Institute for Studies in Education, January 1977. For a history of technical education in Ontario in the late nineteenth and early twentieth century, see Robert M. Stamp, "The Campaign for Technical Education in Ontario, 1876-1914," unpublished PHD, University of Western Ontario, 1970.

45.   Ontario Archives(thereafter OA), Gov. Doc. A/B1/SL, Ontario Bureau of Industries, *Reports on Labour, Wages and Cost of Living, 1884-1889*, Toronto, 1893, 35.

46.   Ibid., 37; 41; 47.

47. Ibid., 49.
48. Toronto Board of Education Archives(thereafter TBE), Minutes of the Technical School Board of the City of Toronto, 1891-1899, Meeting of September 26, 1893.
49. In 1892-93, of the 305 registered students, we find 57 clerks, 3 stenographers, 2 confectioners, 1 governess and 1 telephone operator. There is also 1 paper box maker, an occupation which was opened to women in Toronto. In 1893-94, of the 631 registered pupils, there were 92 clerks, 5 stenographers, 4 public schoolteachers, 2 hatters, 2 telephone operators, 1 embroiderer and 1 hatmaker. Ontario Archives, Ontario Bureau of Industries, *Reports on Labour, Wages and Cost of Living, 1884-1889*, Toronto, 1893, 41, 46-47.
50. Whose names remain unfortunately unknown.
51. Ibid., Meetings of February 26 and of April 28, 1896.
52. Ibid., Meeting of October 15, 1896.
53. Ibid., Meeting of November 24, 1896.
54. Ibid., Meeting of February 23, 1897.
55. Along with "Mineralogy, Geology and Metallurgy" and "Electricity, Steam and Gas Engines." TBE Archives, Toronto Technical School, *Prospectus*, Session 1898-99, 7.
56. Ibid. The five Departments included Physical Science, Machine Construction, Architecture and Building Construction, Chemistry and finally, Freehand Drawing, Design and Decoration.
57. Ibid., 5-6; 32.
58. Spark, 12.
59. TBE Archives, Toronto Technical School, *Prospectus*, Session 1903-04, 5.
60. See Marta Danylewycz, Nadia Fahmy-Eid et Nicole Thivierge, "L'enseignement ménager et les 'Home Economics' au Québec et en Ontario au début du 20e siècle: une analyse compareé," 94-109. See also, Diana Pederson, "The 'Scientific Training of Mothers': The Campaign for Domestic Science in Ontario Schools, 1890-1913," 178-194.
61. TBE Archives, *Minutes of the Toronto School Board of the City of Toronto*, March 21st, 1901.
62. TBE Archives, Toronto Board of Education, *Minutes*, 1905, 159-161.
63. Spark, 14-15. The creation of the Toronto Board of Education resulted from the amalgamation of the Technical School Board, the High School Board and the Public School Board.
64. For the campaign for increased technical education in Canada, see Robert M. Stamp, "The Campaign for Technical Education in Ontario, 1876-1914;" see also Stamp, "Technical Education, the National Policy

and Federal-Provincial Relations in Education, 1899-1919," *Canadian Historical Review*, 52(1976): 404-423.

65. See Canada, *Report of the Royal Commission on Industrial Training and Technical Education*, Ottawa, 4 vol., 1913-14.

66. See page 195.

67. Seath, *Education for Industrial Purposes*, 3, 289.

68. "An Act Respecting Education for Industrial Purposes," *Statutes of the Province of Ontario*, Toronto, 1911, 525-30.

69. The Advisory Industrial Council was composed of twelve members. Six were selected from the Toronto Board of Education; six were chosen from manufacturing, three being employers and the other three, employees.

70. These included bookkeeping, shorthand, typing, commercial arithmetic, business correspondence and business forms and practice. During the first decade of the century, the Department of Commerce and Finance offered a three-year business course intended for those who wanted to "enter upon a business career as office assistant, or later in some managerial capacity." TBE Archives, *Calendar of the Technical High School, Toronto,* 1907-1908, 7.

71. In 1916, the Central High School of Commerce opened its doors on Shaw Street. It was the first commercial high school in the province of Ontario. See Honora M. Cochrane, ed., *Centennial History. The Board of Education for the City of Toronto, 1850-1950*, Toronto, 1950, 120-21.

72. The new building, which was four storeys in height, was located on Lippincott Street. In 1930, there were four branch technical schools in Toronto.

73. *Report of the Minister of Education of Ontario*, 1915, Appendix E, 56.

74. Ibid.

75. TBE Archives, *Calendar of the Technical Schools, Toronto*, 1925-1926, 11.

76. TBE Archives, *Calendar of the Technical High School*, Toronto, 1907-1908, 22-23.

77. Ibid. 7.

78. These included the Departments of Commerce and Finance, Drafting and Design, Physics, Chemistry, Mathematics, and Language and History. Ibid., 8.

79. Ibid., 11.

80. Ibid., 25.

81. Ibid., 31.

82. See Marta Danylewycz, Nadia Fahmy-Eid and Nicole Thivierge, "L'enseignement ménager et les 'Home Economics' au Québec et en

Ontario au début du 20e siècle. Une Analyse comparée," 101, Table 2; 104.

83. See above, 195.

84. TBE Archives, *Calendar of the Technical Schools*, Toronto, 1913-14, 52-59.

85. Such was the case of the School of Industrial Art and Technical Design for Women, founded in 1881 in New York City, and of the Drexel Institute of Art, Science and Industry, a co-educational institution which opened in Philadelphia in 1892. In the first institution, for example, women were taught designing for calico, muslin, woods, jewelry and stained glass. They could also learn the "workings of machinery and the technicalities of design as applied to various industries, as carpet designing, wall paper, oil-cloth, linoleum, lace, chintz, silk, leather, book covers, etc." See Ontario Bureau of Industries, *Reports on Labour, wages and cost of living, 1884-1889*, 89, 91. See also Bernard McEvoy, *Report on Technical Education*, Toronto, Ontario Department of Education, 1900, 21-23.

86. G. Campbell, *Community Colleges in Canada*, Toronto, 1971, 41.

87. See note 32.

88. Seath, *Education for Industrial Purposes*, 308-11.

89. TBE Archives, *Calendar of the Toronto Technical Schools*, Toronto, 1913-1914, 39.

90. Ibid., 60-67.

91. Classes were held five days a week for three months.

92. Classes for the houseworkers' course were held two afternoons a week for three months. TBE Archives, *Calendar of the Technical Schools of Toronto*, 1919-20, 87-90.

93. See David Spence Hill, *Introduction to Vocational Education*, New York, 1920, 374-75; Theodore Struck, *Foundations of Industrial Education*, New York, 1930, 275.

94. TBE, *Calendar of the Technical Schools of Toronto, 1919-20*, 91. See also the *Report of the Minister of Ontario*, 1919, 12. Thus, instead of completing the whole diploma course in domestic art, a student could simply follow a class in sewing, dressmaking or millinery. Again, these unit courses constituted one of the major reforms introduced in American vocational schools in the early twentieth century, including those attended by girls, after it had been recognized that a two or three-year full course of study in evening schools had been an almost complete failure due to poor attendance. See Albert H. Leake, *The Vocational Education of Girls and Women*, New York, 1918, 321-23.

95. Ibid., 8.

96. *Calendar of the Technical Schools of Toronto*, 1919-20, 59. By 1920, the entire course cost $45.00, the first year being offered for free.
97. Seath, *Education for Industrial Purposes*, 290-1.
98. See Cheryl MacDonald's biography, *Adelaide Hoodless. Domestic Crusader*, Toronto and Reading, 1986.
99. Adelaide Hoodless, *Report to the Minister Of Education, Ontario, on Trade Schools in Relation to Elementary Education*, Toronto, 1909, 3.
100. Ibid., 4.
101. Ibid., 15.
102. Ontario, *Report of the Ontario Commission on Unemployment*, Toronto, 1916, 59.
103. Ibid., 69.
104. *Report of the Royal Commission on Industrial Training and Technical Education*, Ottawa, 1913, Part II, 336; Part I, 50-51.
105. See Ceta Ramkhalawansingh, "Women during the Great War," in Janice Acton *and al.*, eds., *Women at Work. Ontario, 1850-1930*, 261-307.
106. The Conference included representatives of organizations such as the National Council of Women in Canada, the Imperial Order of the Daughters of the Empire, the Young Women's Christian Association, the Women's Christian temperance Union and the Canadian Suffrage Association. See the *Report of the Women's War Conference*, Ottawa, 1918, 3.
107. Ibid., 19-21;30.
108. Marjorie MacMurchy, *What Shall I do? How to Work for Canada in Peace*, Winnipeg, Toronto and Montreal, 9, 3.
109. Marjory MacMurchy, *The Canadian Girls at Work*, Toronto, 1919.
110. Ontario Provincial Archives, RG7-12-0-42: *Vocational Guidance(Girls) 1917-1919*. See the correspondence exchanged between these associations and the Trades and Labour Branch of the Department of Public Works.
111. RMEO, 1918,26-27; 1919,15-18.
112. *Report of the Ontario Commission on Unemployment*, 73. The Commission had suggested raising the compulsory school leaving age from fourteen to fifteen years old.
113. TBE Archives, *Minutes* of the Toronto Board of Education, 1906, 176-77. The Board adopted the Committee's report.
114. Ibid.
115. TBE Archives, *Minutes*, 1910, appendix no. 2, 7.
116. As will be shown below, the Toronto Technical High School had also been training girls and women as clerical workers for the rapidly expanding tertiary sector in its Department of Commerce and Finance,

238

prior to the separation of technical education from its commercial counterpart in 1911

117. Marta Danylewycz, Nadia Fahmy-Eid et Nicole Thivierge, "L'enseignement ménager et les 'Home Economics'," 107-08.
118. Scott, *The Conditions of Female Labour in Ontario*, 19.
119. *Report of the Royal Commission in Industrial Training and Technical Education*, vol.1, part II, 52-53; *Report of the Ontario Commission on Unemployment*, 168. The former recommended short and intensive courses, while the latter proposed the establishment of training schools in connection with Welcome Hostels for immigrant women, of training classes in connection with technical schools and of part-time training classes for those already employed as houseworkers.
120. MacMurchy, *What Shall I Do?*, 9.
121. The Act allowed the federal government to share up to fifty percent of the provincial expenditures for technical education. For this purpose, ten million dollars would be spent over a ten-year period. See R. M. Stamp, "Technical Education, the National Policy, and Federal-Provincial Relations in Canadian Education, 1899-1919," 419-23.
122. AO, Education, RG 2, series P-3, 73\1, ? 1919.
123. These courses included sewing, dressmaking, millinery, embroidery, power operating, textiles, cookery, bread making and canning and pickling.
124. *Report of the Royal Commission on Industrial Training and Technical Education*, Part I, 49-52.
125. MacMurchy, *What Shall I Do?*, 6.
126. *Report of the Ontario Commission on Unemployment*, 63.
127. MacMurchy, *The Canadian Girl At Work*, Introduction.
128. John Seath, *Education for Industrial Purposes*, 290.
129. See Barbara Pocock, *Demanding Skill. Women and Technical Education in Australia*, Sydney, 1988, chapter 2.
130. Anne Philipps and Barbara Taylor, "Sex and Skill: Notes towards a Feminist Economics," *Feminist Review*, 6, 1980: 79.
131. Ibid.
132. Considering the training of clerical workers, Gaskell contends that women's unskilled status "is produced at least in part by training that is widely accessible and formally short." See "Conceptions of Skill and the Work of Women: Some Historical and Political Issues," *Atlantis*, vol. 8, no.2, Spring 1983: 14, 23.
133. Recent studies include: Mercedes Steedman, "Skill and Gender in the Canadian Clothing Industry,1890-1940," in Craig Heron and Robert Storey, eds., On the Job: Confronting the Labour Process in Canada,

Montreal, 1986, 151-176; Joy Parr, *Disaggregating the Sexual Division of Labour: A Transatlantic Case Study*, Queen's Papers in Industrial Relations, no. 5, Kingston, 1987; Michèle Martin, "Feminisation of the Labour Process in the Communication Industry: The Case of the Telephone Operators, 1876-1904," *Labour/Le Travail*, 22 (Fall 1988): 139-62; Margaret McCallum, "Separate Spheres: The Organization of Work in a Confectionary Factory: Ganong Bros., St. Stephen, New Brunswick, *Labour/Le Travail*, 24 (Fall 1989): 69-90 and Shirley Tillotson, "The Operators Along the Coast: A Case Study of the Link Between Gender, Skilled Labour and Social Power, 1900-1930," *Acadiensis*, 20, 1 (Autumn 1990): 72-88.

134. According to Arthur D. Dean, chief of the Division of Trade-Schools in the New York State Department of Education, "A Worker with skill of hand, reinforced with a general education, has the opportunity to rise in her vocation. An occupation that calls for a little knowledge as well as for dexterity becomes immediately a stimulus to the intelligence." Dean, *The Worker and the State. A Study of Education for Industrial Workers*, New York, 1910, 82.

135. Albert Leake observed in 1918 that "skill is not easily defined, as it varies according to the industry. In many cases it simply means speed in processes such as sewing on buttons, folding pamphlets, or operating an envelope machine. In strawsewing, machine embroidery, and the making of lace skill means accuracy and delicacy of touch. In the work of a designer or the work of a forewoman, in addition to deftness of hand the term 'skill' includes imagination, organizing ability, and general intelligence." Leake, *The Vocational Education of Girls and Women*, 256.

136. The 1921 Census reported the following apprentices: 94 dressmakers and seamstresses; 106 milliners and 92 tailoresses. They could also be found in the food industry(12 bakers) and in the printing and bookbinding industry(183 printers and bookbinders). *Census of Canada*, vol. 4, 1921, table 5.

137. *Report of the Ontario Commission on Unemployment*, 170;174-75. As indicated earlier, the Commission proposed raising the age of compulsory schooling as one of the main solutions to the problem of this large pool of unskilled workers.

138. According to the Ontario Commission on Unemployment, the clothing industry preferred the experienced worker. In addition, a female worker could become a designer if she had the artistic ability while factory operatives could become head of a section and have charge and control of work. On the other hand, the Commission noted that in other industries, manufacturers preferred to train their own workers and that

in response to an enquiry "as to what school training would be of help to the woman operative in factory employment, the only answer received was that a knowledge of power machinery in clothing trades would be valuable." The Commission thus recommended a study of factory employment "with a view to learning how far the training obtained from work in factories gives skill that ensures employment" as well as an enquiry "as to what special training for factory workers can be provided in schools." *Report of the Ontario Commission on Unemployment*, 172;175.

139. Ibid., 204.

140. Gaskell,"Conceptions of Skill and the Work of Women," 16. See also Michael Apple, *Education and Power*, Boston, 1982.

141. *Report of the Ontario Commission on Unemployment*, 167.

142. Such a policy was actively pursued by governments, churches, benevolent associations and nation-wide women's organizations such as the National Council of Women of Canada and the Young Woman's Christian Association. For a thorough study of domestic service at the turn of the century, see Genevieve Leslie, "Domestic Service in Canada, 1880-1920," in Janice Acton and *al.*, *Women at Work*, 71-125.

143. The course, which prepared girls for University Junior Matriculation, included the study of Physics, Mathematics, Biology, Chemistry, Latin, French and English. Domestic science subjects were far from predominant. In fact, they were absent from the fourth year curriculum. TBE Archives, *Calendar of the Technical Schools of Toronto, 1919-20*, 59-67.

144. TBE Archives, Toronto Technical School, *Prospectus, 1898-99*, 36-39. The School's Prospectus for 1903-04 confirms the definite attraction of girls and women to the domestic science course, which continued to record the highest attendance. Housekeepers, housemaids, dressmakers and domestics constituted the largest groups of female workers attending the evening classes. Other female occupations recorded included that of milliner, maid, householder, governess and housewife. TBE Archives, Toronto Technical School, *Prospectus 1903-1904*, 29.

145. Such an attraction is revealed by the fact that in 1920, girls made up 70% of the Central High School of Commerce sudent body. See the article by Susan Gelman in this volume.

146. This was a province-wide trend at the time. *Report of the Minister of Education of Ontario*, 1918, 20

147. In 1916, more than 1123 students were enrolled in cooking classes and 516, in sewing and dressmaking. Mathematics came in between, with 648 students. *Report of the Minister of Education*, 1916, 64-65.

148. *Report of the Minister of Education of Ontario*, 1918, 20. Merchant continued as follows: "The academic subject in greatest demand by men is arithmetic; then follow in order, English composition, reading and literature, shop mathematics, mechanical drawing, electricity, algebra and geometry, etc."

149. These lists are included in the Commencement Programs which started to be published regularly following the establishment of the Advisory Industrial Committee. A Scholarship Fund was then created. Scholarships of $25.00 each were awarded each year to both boys and girls attending the School's day classes. Girls were awarded at first 12 scholarships while the boys received 8. The difference is due to the fact that four scholarships were granted to the home economics course. Significantly, in 1920, girls now only received 19 scholarships whereas more than 27 were awarded to male students. For example, 20 scholarships were granted to the industrial course for boys and only 10 to the industrial course for girls. See TBE Archives, Commencement Programs, Central Technical School.

150. Significantly, one could still find girls and women enrolled in industrial design classes, although their number was quite small. The presence of women in this branch of instruction, which had a direct link with the paid labour market, would certainly merit further study.

151. In 1905, 97% of the students were from municipalities composing the High School District. Ten years later, 93% of the students were in this category. The remainder came from municipalities within the County of Toronto and from other Counties. *Report of the Minister of Education of Ontario*, 1905, 57; 1915,189.

152. This sharp drop can possibly be attributed to the establishment of an autonomous Department of Commerce and Finance in 1911.

153. See Geraldine Joncich Clifford, "'Marry, Stitch, Die, or Do Worse': Educating Women for Work," in Harvey Kantor and David B. Tyack, eds., *Work, Youth and Schooling*, Stanford, California, 1982, 242; 267-68.

154. In her study on public evening schools for girls in New York City, Mary Van Kleeck noted that most of the girls and women enrolled in courses such as dressmaking, millinery and machine power operating worked in factories during the day and wished to acquire additional knowledge skills in order to get better positions and better wages. She concluded: "Their decision to attend evening school to acquire more training was therefore the more significant of the need which they felt, and of the failure of the industries themselves to provide adequate training." See her *Working Girls in Evening School*, New York, 1914, 132.

155. *Report of the Minister of Education of Ontario*, 1914, 694.

Schooling Women for Home or for Work?

156. While the dietitians'course counted only four graduates in 1914, by 1920, it counted twenty-two. It also extended over six months and cost $14.00.
157. Thus, the special short course for housekeepers usually counted married women amongst its graduates.

Part Four:

Special Privilege:
The Quest for Higher Education

"Manners and Morals"? Or "Men in Petticoats"? Education at Alma College, 1871-1898[1]

Johanna Selles-Roney

An advertisement for Alma College in St. Thomas, Ontario, claimed that "Students need bring nothing with them for their comfort other than would be required going to a first-class hotel."[2] Furthermore, the circular stated that "A student in residence in the Institution has complete control of her time for the purpose for which she is sent to school. In residence at Alma she will be constantly under the eye of competent teachers and governesses, ever watchful of her health, habit and morals...." The comparison of a ladies' college to a first-class hotel confirms the general impression left by these schools, namely, that they were finishing schools for daughters of the affluent.[3] Until recently, the absence of ladies' colleges from Ontario's educational history has done little to correct this misconception.[4] As R.D. Gidney and W.P.J. Millar argue in *Inventing Secondary Education*, the history of private schools is a necessary ingredient for a complete understanding of Ontario education. Developments in the private sector were played against an increasing state control which served to undermine the autonomy of private schools. Despite this eventual loss of autonomy, the primacy of denominational innovation in schooling in the 1800s must be kept in perspective.[5]

The preoccupation of ladies' colleges themselves with form and appearance has also contributed to their association with accomplishments rather than academic rigour.[6] Yet their curriculum often marked the beginnings of a serious attempt at higher education and the acquisition of mental discipline. The fact that this type of curriculum constituted, in many cases, a radical departure from contemporary stereotyped expectations about a woman's ability meant that the colleges had to cultivate an image which did not appear to challenge accepted notions of female behaviour.

In Canada, academies and seminaries offering "superior" education for women emerged in the 1820s and 1830s.[7] By 1847 there were a number of seminaries for women in Ontario; three in Cobourg, five in Toronto, and one each in Niagara, Kingston, Hamilton, and Cornwall.[8] The Rev. A. Burns, principal of the Hamilton Ladies' College, reported the existence in 1888 of seven ladies' colleges established by denominational patronage without state assistance.[9] Although many of the schools were sponsored by specific denominations, they shared a common belief that women could and should be educated. The belief in the importance of higher education was a distinguishing characteristic of the academy or seminary movement which, throughout North America, attempted to imbue female education with the same degree of seriousness that had been associated with male education and particularly seminary training for the ministry.[10] Ladies' seminary education was a training for a female "ministry" which led, not to ordination, but to vocations in family, teaching and church work or social reform. Alma College was part of this seminary movement for women.

Origins of the College

Bishop Carman of the Methodist Episcopal Church of Southwestern Ontario was convinced, by the 1860s, that Western Ontario needed a college for young ladies. Carman had long been involved in educational matters; he had served, for example, as principal of Albert College, Belleville, from 1858 to 1875.[11] Carman was thus familiar with the question of education for girls and he considered St. Thomas an excellent location for such a school. The existence of several railroad lines, the healthy climate of the area and the availability of fresh fruit and vegetables were cited as reasons for the choice of St. Thomas. An added advantage, particularly for the establishment of a girls' school, was the fact that St. Thomas was "comparatively free from the vices and snares incident to overgrown cities."[12] A college circular, dated Spring 1881, claimed that: "The best bred lady in the land cannot find there anything to wound her delicacy, or to repress her taste; while to nearly all, the arrangements tend to elevate, to inspire a higher and purer ambition for the personal habits and modes of thought of the perfect woman."[13]

The attention to architectural style was no accident. Helen Horowitz describes the seminary model as a single building wherein students could be kept "physically in place and thus secure in a limited sense."[14] The seclusion of students in a single building made an intense disciplinary regime possible, with a routine similar to life in an asylum. At the Ipswich Female Seminary in Massachusetts, for example, almost every moment of the day was accounted for and bells marked the tasks required. Yet this closely supervised schedule gave students time for either domestic work, prayer or study and provided them with a sense of mental mastery. Mt. Holyoke Seminary also used an enlarged version of a nineteenth-century private house, with a clear division between parents and children in the seminary family.[15] This model closely resembled the structure of Alma College. Furthermore, rural and small town locations were important to both the family ideal and to the goal of protection, and the location of Alma College in St. Thomas was no exception.[16]

The congruence between design and purpose was noted at the cornerstone ceremony by the Minister of Education, Hon. Adam Crooks: "I have not seen in this country—I have not seen anywhere else—a design in better harmony with the objects of the institution."[17] The college, built in a Victorian style, was designed by the architect James Balfour of Hamilton, and consisted essentially of one grand building with 50 rooms able to accommodate 100 students. A great stairway led to the upstairs floors, which were arranged with two parallel rows of rooms divided by a hall. Two towers at each corner and a central tower lent an air of stately elegance to the building. The plan was to provide "every degree of comfort possible" including steam heating, ventilation, and gas light.[18] The building housed the principal, the lady principal and governess, in addition to providing apartments for the teachers.

The college board consisted of twenty-one members: seven St. Thomas citizens and thirteen members of the Methodist Church, along with Bishop Carman. A charter was granted in 1877 and by 1881 the college was declared open "to afford young ladies a liberal course of instruction in all that tends to make their lives useful and happy, and their tastes elevated and refined."[19]

The Principalship of B.F. Austin

The life of the college was guided by the leadership of the principal. B.F. Austin successfully headed the school through its trial years. By 1897, however, the relationship between the board and the principal had become tense. The board felt that Austin was not devoting enough of his time to the school. On his part, Austin wrote to the board revealing mixed feelings about his commitment to the college:

> Finding a reprieve of at least a year necessary for straightening my financial affairs, I am undecided whether it is better in the school interests and my own to ask for a year's furlough or to tender my resignation. While the above reasons seem to me of weight, I must confess that family affliction and much anxiety of mind over various matters have rendered me somewhat distrustful of my own judgment.[20]

Austin's personal confusion may have been due to the death of his young daughter in 1896.[21] In 1897, Austin did resign his position;[22] the following year he was to be tried for heresy and expelled from the Methodist ministry. Austin left the College with an unpaid debt and a commitment to follow his interests and belief in spiritualism.[23]

The official histories of Alma College deal only briefly with the principalship of Austin. Edwards claimed that his adventures outside his immediate duties as principal were for the most part "unfortunate." Austin's publishing ventures were costly and, according to Edwards, financial problems precipitated his resignation or dismissal.[24] Riddell only briefly mentions Austin's resignation, claiming that he moved to California to edit a magazine on spiritualism, "a subject in which he had been deeply interested for some time."[25] Austin was succeeded by Professor Warner, who had previously served as a professor of modern languages and literature. The college minutes do not discuss Austin further, and it is thus impossible to conclude whether he had a following among students or staff.

Yet, a quite interesting figure emerges from sources other than those of the college. Indeed, Austin held distinct views on the education of women. These are summarized in a volume of essays which he edited and published in 1890, entitled *Woman: Her Character, Culture, and Calling*.[26] In a chapter called "What Christ Has Done for Woman, and What Woman Has Done for Christ," Austin argued that Christianity conferred a special honour on woman, and the birth of Christ rendered motherhood forever glorious.[27] Woman was exalted to a position wherein she partook in the "blessings, responsibilities, and duties of Christian life," but, in addition, woman had the "signal glory of womanhood."[28] The "queen of the home" had been lifted up by Christ's birth, not only to equality, but to a distinctive calling. Austin wrote that any Biblical passages which appeared to endorse the submission of women could be explained—and ignored—by placing them in the context of the culture for which they were written.

Women were exalted not only for their role as mothers, but also for special qualities which they possessed including such passive virtues as gentleness, meekness, patience, self-denial, and obedience.[29] These virtues were not indigenous to a man's heart, but they bloomed naturally in a woman's. Austin explained that women used their talents to serve others, evangelize, support missions, and fight the battle for social and moral reform.[30]

Austin's exaltation of women as mothers was not inconsistent with his educational mission at Alma. Indeed, Austin proclaimed the necessity of educating women. He argued that a woman should be educated in a way that would give her a specialty or a useful art by which she could earn a living, rather than being forced to marry to escape poverty. The "ornamental" education dispersed by many ladies' seminaries needed to be replaced by the teaching of practical arts.[31] Austin urged the employment of women in outdoor labour, horticulture, telegraphy, civil service, art work, art teaching, house decoration, design, and medicine. By outdoor labour, Austin meant any light farm work which would have a more wholesome effect on women's health "than the miserable slave life many women lead in factories, shops and stores where long hours, promiscuous associations and poor pay are the general rule."[32] Austin envisioned that even traditionally female occupations such as domestic service would help them escape from their current slavery. Domestic service would require women who had greater intelligence and culture, thus entitling them to greater recognition in the home as trained, scientific housekeepers or governesses. The higher remuneration and respect which Austin deemed necessary for domestics was also recommended for another female profession, namely, teaching. The inequality in the salaries of female, as opposed to male, teachers was unjust and discriminatory. In addition to these occupations, Austin claimed Christian service as a calling for women. The home, school and church were spheres in which woman was all-powerful. Her influence on society was crucial since "if society is ever to become thoroughly permeated with the Christian doctrine and spirit...it must be by the agency of Christian women."[33] Professions, then, which traditionally employed women needed to be revalued in terms of status and remuneration, while those which had previously excluded women workers needed to be reconsidered.

Austin rejected the two main arguments commonly used against the higher education of women, which were that women were unable to absorb higher education and that evil results derived from educating women. He believed that women were physically and mentally capable of higher learning. The claim that education produced evil results such as "strong-minded women" and "men in petticoats" was inaccurate because higher Christian education could only foster humility, not conceit. Proper education should provide physical development, intellectual training, and religious culture.[34] In sum, the major goal of education was the development of character, as opposed to "mere skill or accomplishment."[35]

Austin's message was shaped by conservative rhetoric, tainted with radical connotations.[36] His recognition that not all women were destined to marry, and that marriage should never be an alternative to economic necessity or boredom was clearly progressive. He also rejected traditional reasons why women should not be educated and advocated their ability to learn and perform a variety of occupations. His views were particularly innovative on the subject of "practical" education and on vocational goals for women. The suggestion that women could work in non-traditional jobs opened the door for women's further participation in the public sphere. He sanctioned the public involvement of women by suggesting that society would benefit from their special qualities.

However, arguments for equality, higher education, and vocational innovation were couched in a conservative rhetoric which ultimately left her reigning as queen of the home. Woman's distinctive qualities prepared her to influence society; "in the Church, in the school, in all moral and social reforms, woman's powerful influence is felt."[37] The conservative aspect of the rhetoric emerged even more clearly in an article published in Austin's book by the Rev. Morgan Dix. This article strongly supported the use of single-sex education to underline God-given differences between the sexes. The harmony between the sexes had to be maintained by education in which "the woman shall be enabled to be to the man all that he needs, while he shall hold her in the honour and devotion which are her due."[38]

The complexity of Austin's position derived from the fact that his views were neither strictly radical nor conservative; nor did he advocate a completely private or totally public sphere of influence for women. Rather, his views combined all these elements in a way that mirrored the education given at Alma College. Indeed, Austin's views must be seen in the context of nineteenth-century expectations for women. By the latter part of the century, the presence of women in social reform movements, church life and professions such as teaching was undeniable. Moreover, advanced education continued to challenge the boundaries of women's role by offering them options. The support of the ladies' college, however, was still derived from parents, individuals and churches, who believed in the primacy of the domestic sphere. Early reformers and proponents of girls' education worked from inside this model, borrowed from its language, and thus achieved their goals.

Recent American studies show that this strategy was quite successful. According to Anne Scott, the Troy Female Seminary in Troy, N.Y., combined "an allegiance to certain well-defined ideas about what was proper for women with subversive attention to women's intellectual development."[39] Emma Willard, the head of Troy Seminary, combined traditional views of woman's role with a commitment to her progress; Willard's success lay in the fact that, at Troy, "feminist values co-existed with traditional ones but also spread more easily when attached to 'correct' views of women."[40] A similar phenomenon is illustrated by the life of Francis Willard, who both spoke at Alma and wrote an introduction to Austin's book. A local newspaper enthusiastically described Willard's speech at the school's annual closing lecture in 1891, held at the First Methodist Church in St. Thomas: "She speaks simply, as a lady always does, and she speaks with charity towards all, as a woman always should."[41] Willard called for "mother-hearted women to be the saviours of the race."[42] Using the rhetoric derived from the "cult of true womanhood" and the "cult of domesticity," Willard spoke in a language that was immediately accessible to her audience.[43] Yet the fact that she spoke in public was a continuing contravention of the norms of womanly behaviour.

The concept of woman's special nature which was basic to the ladies' college tradition was also manifest in social reform movements throughout Canada.

"Manners or Morals"? Or "Men in Petticoats"?

Members of the Women's Christian Temperance Union of Canada believed that "woman was and should be the moral guardian of society."[44] Maternal feminism also provided the rationale for the National Council of Women; its members believed that mothering was not to be restricted to the household but that it should extend throughout society. The connection between ladies' colleges and reform or club movements has not been adequately explored. Veronica Strong-Boag suggests that ladies' college graduates were both ideal women of the Victorian middle class and promising candidates for the club movement.[45] We need to know more about these connections. The life of one graduate, Annie Gardner, can serve to illustrate these links. Gardner graduated from the Brantford Collegiate Institute and the Brantford Young Ladies' College with highest honours. In 1893 she graduated from Alma College with a diploma in painting. She married George Brown, who became the Lieutenant-Governor of Saskatchewan, and had two children. She worked with the W.C.T.U., the Y.W.C.A., the Women's Musical Club and the Ladies' Aid of the Metropolitan Methodist Church. In addition, she was involved with the Local Council of Women, the Hospital Aid Society, the Daughters of the Empire, and the Aberdeen Association.[46]

Curriculum

Students travelled from Southern Ontario and the northern United States to attend Alma College. A subscription list from 1879 shows that they came from Strathroy, Woodstock, Delaware, and Glencoe in Ontario, and from Buffalo and Bergen in New York, among other places.[47] The young women chose courses within a preparatory, academic, or collegiate department. Preparatory courses consisted of reading, primary elocution, spelling, grammar and arithmetic. The academic course included the more advanced work in all preceding studies, as well as geometry, algebra, natural philosophy, French and Latin. The collegiate department covered a three-year course of study, which embraced the Junior and Senior Matriculation of the University of Toronto and which consisted of ancient classics, modern languages and literature, advanced science, metaphysics, Christian evidences, and ethics.[48] Students could also study at the conservatory of music, art academy or the school of fancy work, as well as the commercial department, all contained within the institution.[49] Diplomas offered by the school included the Mistress of English Literature (M.E.L.) and the Mistress of Liberal Arts (M.L.A.).

Physical activity involved at least one daily walk and calisthenic exercises. The school's concern with the students' welfare also extended to dietary restrictions: "Good health depends largely on habits of diet. All boxes of rich pastry etc. will be returned to the sender."[50] In 1885-86, Alma College added a department of domestic economy to the curriculum, since "the vast majority of young ladies go from school and college, not to enter professional life, but to control the HOME—the fountain of health and strength, and of moral and religious reforms to the people."[51] The establishment of a commercial department, as well as the school of elocution, also reflected a practical orientation. The latter offered graduates the potential to teach elocution privately or in conjunction with an established school.[52] Similarly, the earning potential of a music graduate was recognized from the beginning:

> The income of the girl who can teach the piano and, perhaps, the violin, or singing, will always be greater than that of her less fortunate sister in the factory or counting-room.[53]

Although the academic program was regarded with great seriousness, students were encouraged to participate in extracurricular clubs organized on the basis of activities considered appropriate for young girls. By 1899, the college calendar listed the following clubs: The Alumnae Association; the Almafilian Literary Society; the Alma College Missionary Society; the Tennis Club and reading circles such as Sorosis.

Religious and moral development was a central goal of the school's program. The college advertised that it was non-sectarian, but still distinctively and positively Christian in its character and teachings.[54] Students attended the church of their parents' or guardians' choice, accompanied by a chaperon. All students had to follow a Bible course during their stay. The school intended to provide a complete environment for students and this environment was shaped by good manners and morals: "Good manners are founded on good morals, and our wish and effort is to utilize every occasion and means for inculcating a knowledge of polite forms...Our true ideal is the perfect culture—that of brain, soul and social being."[55]

The moral instruction was enforced by a system of discipline and a clearly defined code of behaviour. Girls were given demerit points for infractions such as misconduct in church, unexplained absence from class, receiving a caller without permission and pranks, such as concealing the college bell. Room doors had to be left open during study hours. On Saturdays between four and six, students could receive visitors but were forbidden to walk or ride in public without attendance by some adult and responsible member of the family."[56] Restrictions on behaviour extended to all the details of daily life. Students were allowed, for example, to write only one letter per week to anyone outside their immediate families, and were permitted to cut their hair only with their parents' permission. Two students lost all their social privileges for the term because they threw snowballs at a visitor to the college.[57] Although the college claimed to be non-sectarian, there were also limits to tolerance. In 1891, Professor Warner moved at a council meeting that the presence of Negro students might prove prejudicial to the financial interests of the school and might "imperil the usefulness of the school for the purposes contemplated in its foundations."[58] The motion passed.

Pressures were also mounting from outside the college to redefine its curriculum. In 1898, the Deputy Minister of Education wrote to the principal of Alma College, suggesting that the secondary level be abandoned:

> Why, might I ask, should the work required in the institution of such subjects such as English, Literature, French, Chemistry, Latin, Algebra, etc., be duplicated by having separate classes in a city like St. Thomas? My suggestion is that Alma College or, in fact, any ladies' college should abandon the work of instruction in those subjects for which ample provision is made in the High Schools and Collegiate Institutes.[59]

The Deputy Minister argued that the proper role of the ladies' college was teaching the accomplishments, such as music and art, for which school boards were unwilling to pay. He suggested that young ladies from the college be allowed to attend classes in geometry, botany, or history at the collegiate institute.[60] The Department of Education was therefore increasing pressure on Alma College to refrain from duplicating secondary school functions and to become strictly a ladies' "accomplishments school."[61]

The option of seeking university affiliation was settled in 1891, when the college affiliated with the University of Toronto and Victoria University, thus giving Alma a status similar to a junior college.[62] This affiliation meant that Alma students were examined according to standards set by the university. Although the exact amount of credit given for Alma College courses was determined through negotiations with the university, by 1898, Alma College clearly was engaged in university preparation as opposed to university level teaching. This type of relationship meant that the curriculum at Alma was consciously shaped to adapt to external standards, which in this case were set by the university.[63] The adaptation to external standards increased in 1909 when the government's "approved school" scheme meant that all schools, including private schools such as Alma, had to pass certain inspection standards and adjust their curriculum to address priorities set by the Department of Education.

Financial Difficulties

Financial problems plagued the college from its very beginnings in 1871, dependent as it was on fees and donations collected by agents throughout the circuits. Bishop Carman remained optimistic in the face of continuous financial crises and he believed that the college was "bound to rise above all the clouds of financial difficulties to where perpetual sunshine shall settle upon it."[64] The building plans for the college, in addition to the costs of furnishing it and hiring competent staff, outstripped the funds which had been collected. Edwards estimated that the total cost of the college was $60,000.[65] The success of the fundraising tactics varied; some agents were skilful and raised a great deal of money, but in rural districts located far from Alma, people did not feel called to support the college.

The union of Methodism in 1883 created additional problems for Alma. The Act brought together the Ontario Ladies' College and the Wesleyan Ladies' College with Albert, Alexandra, and Alma College.[66] The affiliation increased competition for available resources. Although the college encouraged its supporters to consider making large endowments, with the exception of the Massey endowment of $35,000, there were no significant offers of patronage. The recruitment of agents to canvass the circuits was in itself an added cost, since the agents were generally paid $1,000 per year. Alma College acquired a debt during its first decade which also taxed the financial status of the college. Although the generation of income from tuition helped to meet some of the college's costs, it was evident that this income would not help reduce the amount of indebtedness. After union, the Board of Alma decided to reduce the debt, but increased enrolment at the college strained the facilities until a new residence hall was built in 1886 at the cost of $50,000. The expanded facilities contained a music hall with seating for five hundred, fifty dormitory rooms, a fine art studio, several class rooms and a museum.[67] Grandeur could not be compromised even in the face of relentless financial problems.

The Board attempted to hire financial agents with proven expertise to tackle the debt. Not only was the debt a problem, but school attendance declined due to a general economic depression.[68] The minutes of the Board record an awareness of the gravity of the situation: "A crisis is upon us...and [that] if the Alma College is to live and grow we have reached the time of extraordinary vigorous measures in the way of economy."[69] The extraordinary measures included reducing staff, asking staff to return part of their salary to the school and decreasing the use of food and fuel.[70] Alma eventually received assistance from the Massey estate in 1896 and by 1898 the financial situation was improving.[71]

Public perception of the college's image was important because Alma depended on contributions and on the resources generated by student tuition. Parents needed reassurance that their daughters were adequately supervised and were taught the essential social graces and academic subjects. Any discrepancy between parental expectations and the students' experience at the school provoked emotional responses. One parent, who was informed by his daughter that girls at the school regularly danced in the halls, wrote to the principal:

> Have we as Methodists come to this—that we cannot send our daughters to a Methodist school without contamination with this curse and spirit of worldliness...when in our own Methodist Ladies' College our daughters are encouraged to disrespect and violate the very rules of our church, and are allowed to give themselves over to this soul-destroying pleasure, to sap the vital spark of spirituality should they happen to possess any.[72]

The student's father believed that if students were organized into praying circles, this would soon destroy the "insatiable" desire for dance. The father paid the college for the "sacred safeguard" of his daughter and was outraged at its failure to fulfil this mandate.

Safeguarding its patrons was such a major part of the college's task that this type of incident was potentially harmful to the image of the school and more importantly to its financial basis. Increased competition for students and funds resulted from the perceived "proliferation" of ladies' colleges and the board, well aware of the competition from other institutions, recognized that the school could not afford to tarnish its image. A special report was commissioned in the late 1880s to investigate the reasons why Alma was not attracting more students or support.[73] The rumour that Alma College attracted "a lower class of students" was reported to be one detrimental factor. Yet at the same time, the rate charged by Alma meant that the college could not compete with convent schools, which charged only one hundred and six dollars per year. The author of the special report thus quoted the Sisters of Loretto, who claimed that fifty percent of their students were Protestant, a fact that could be explained by the cheaper cost of Catholic education.[74]

Financial problems lent some urgency to the discussion of Alma's status as a school. Board meetings grappled with the problem of how the college would fit into the larger school structure of the province. In June 1889 the Board recommended that the Senate reconstruct the curriculum to bring it into harmony with the high schools and collegiate institutes "so far as practicable."[75] In 1882, the Board had suggested that the Executive Committee take the necessary steps to secure university affiliation for Alma College. The importance of maintaining the central place of the Bible in the curriculum was underscored in 1895.[76] These three proposals were of vital importance for determining the college's relationship to the university and to the secondary school, while at the same time expressing a desire to retain the Christian and Biblical basis of its curriculum.

To withstand pressures from the provincial educational authorities, the Alma College Board needed a clear vision of why Alma was distinct and necessary. A major part of this mandate was Alma's claim to offer Christian education for women. Rev. R.I. Warner, Professor of Modern Languages, who succeeded B.F. Austin in 1898 to the principalship of Alma College, described his vision for the future of the college to the London Conference in 1891:

> Is not our Provincial system of education ample to meet all the necessary demands? I unhesitatingly answer, No! And when I do so please do not misunderstand me. There is no one here who feels a deeper sense of patriotic pride, when viewing our splendid school system, than I feel, yet I most unmistakably declare that this splendid national school system fails to supply all that the country demands in respect to the education of women.[77]

Warner believed that only the church could fill the "lack" in public education. According to Warner, Roman Catholics, those "enterprising propagandists," had seen the need for special girls' education and had successfully started schools in Southwestern Ontario, which had captured more than half of the available Protestant girls. Warner conceded that the convent model successfully met a need in the education of girls, but he warned the audience of the dangers of letting education be controlled by Catholics:

> It is claimed by many that the Roman Church has its hand on the Governments at Ottawa and Toronto, and exerts a controlling influence on our politics: that it has its hand on the school system and is destroying the basis of our national education—the public school—through the system of separate schools; and that the convent system is a shrewd effort to get the hand of that church upon the homes of the land by securing the education of the homemakers of the future.[78]

"Manners or Morals"? Or "Men in Petticoats"?

Warner believed schools should be based on Christian benevolence in the same way as convents, that is, the church provided the land and the nuns did the work as a labour of love—a system which was as effective as a heavy endowment. The Protestant colleges had survived by means of joint stock companies which often undertook the work at a financial loss. Warner thus suggested that the church, rather than individuals, carry this burden. Warner referred to the Presbyterian church's sponsorship of Ottawa Ladies' College and Senator McMaster's endowment of Moulton Ladies' College as an illustration of the potential role for the church in education.

For those who were unconvinced about the need to educate girls or the necessity for church-sponsored education for girls, the question was framed in the rhetoric of an eventual takeover by Catholics of both culture and society. Yet, the question remains, why did Warner and the Board believe that Alma College was needed as a "power for culture, for church, and for Christ in this empire province of Ontario?"[79]

In an appeal to "men of wealth" to donate money to the college, Warner underlined the virtue of giving to the cause of girls' education: "whoever thus gives a thorough Christian education to a young woman is exalting and ennobling a queen of the home and a leader in society, and is thus scattering broadcast the blessings of his benevolence upon the world."[80] The author referred to examples of endowments to ladies' colleges in the United States in order to encourage the Canadian man of wealth to do the same. This investment would "preserve his name in perpetual fragrance in the Christian church, and prove more endurable than any monument of brass or marble."[81]

Despite this appeal, the endowments, which in the United States played a major role in establishing women's colleges, were not forthcoming. Alma College was rescued, at least in part, by the Massey estate, and by other smaller endowments, as well as by campaigns organized by the alumnae. The management of Alma was aware that the key to their development and stability was tied to the attainment of these endowments. In 1902, it reported to the Board of the College:

Alma College as the only chartered residential Protestant school in Ontario West of Toronto should with the start it has and with proper encouragement make St. Thomas the educational centre West of Toronto for the higher education of young women. With a Mathew Vassar or a Dr. Goucher behind it Alma could easily have an enrolment of 500 Students and be a measureless blessing in the life of our Canadian people.[82]

Gender And Education In Ontario: An Historical Reader

Conclusion

Why did leaders in the women's education movement believe that this education was both necessary and distinct from public education? General agreement among Methodists that higher education was important and necessary for future mothers fuelled the impetus for schools such as Alma College. In a healthy, chaperoned environment with a balance of exercise and mental exertion, and a biblically based Christian instruction, young Protestant women could be carefully cultivated to full blossoming of both culture and belief. The vision had religious reasons as well as patriotic impulses. For both God and country, men must be persuaded to part with their wealth to support the total environment of the ladies' college.[83] Although the family was an important influence on a girl's life, the substitute family found in the college was better equipped to guide girls and prepare them for their future roles. The residential school was described as a splendid transition between the home and the outside world. In this microcosm the student would learn self-dependence as well as become aware of her role in the larger "sphere of citizenship in the commonwealth, to which commonwealth the college is the largest portal."[84] Alma College was a Protestant improvement on the convent theme: the college offered dormitory life supervised by substitute "mothers," yet provided male teachers representing learning and prestige. The substitute mothers had the advantage that they could help girls "over that crisis so trying to many mothers and to many girls, namely, the transition between childhood and womanhood."[85]

The school offered refinement and culture and this aspect of the girl's education was a marketable commodity. The development was not left to chance or mere exposure—female students were carefully guided. Morals and manners were seen to be inseparable and it was this vision which attracted parents of girls from towns in Southern Ontario and the United States and led them to pay for their daughters' education. The secondary schools and collegiate institutes could offer neither the prestige nor the protection offered by Alma College. The college saw its mission, not as in competition with the provincial school system, but rather as its complement.[86]

Thus, ladies' colleges represented denominational initiatives in the nineteenth century for the education of young ladies. Once girls' education was recognized as an important step in the formation of Christian mothers, various denominations competed with each other to provide the "grandest" facilities in the land. The growth of facilities for girl's education increased the competition during the 1880s and 1890s for funds and students. Since the financial burden of these schools rested with the boards, and income was derived from fees, the ladies' colleges were generally not profit-making enterprises. The lack of state support or direct denominational funding left these schools in a vulnerable position, particularly as cheaper alternatives in the form of secondary schools and collegiate institutes became a prevalent and acceptable option for parents. The continued existence of Alma, Ontario Ladies' College and Bishop Strachan School, however, indicates that there was a demand for the type of education which nineteenth-century ladies' colleges offered.

In Ontario, schools such as Alma College developed in the midst of denominational imperatives and provincial politics which affected the structure of the curriculum and ultimately the survival of the school. Although Alma had one of the first domestic science departments in Ontario, the presence of schools such as the Lillian Massey School of Practical Science in Toronto and the Macdonald Institute in Guelph moved the study of domestic science away from the ladies' college into the university.[87] The rise of commercial schools throughout Ontario also undermined Alma's claim to this territory. Similarly, art schools and conservatories of music duplicated the curriculum available at the ladies' college. The necessity to attain status as a school "approved" by the province meant that ultimate authority over the curriculum and teacher's qualifications, as well as facilities, was gradually surrendered to the state.[88]

Although the number of graduates does not represent the total number of students who attended the college, the graduate certificates of Alma until 1900 included 12 Mistress of Liberal Arts; 35 Mistress of English Literature; 46 Music diplomas; 43 in Elocution; 49 in Commercial; 8 in Domestic Science.[89] The figures indicate a strong preference for diplomas which were perceived to offer employment opportunities such as music, elocution and commerce. The calendar for 1889/90 claimed that Alma students had won over 400 certificates from the Ontario School of Art, including 22 Grade B and 13 Grade A and advanced teachers' certificates, as well as several public schoolteachers' certificates within the previous four years. Some alumnae continued studies in Europe or the United States, and others took up positions in schools throughout North America and Japan. Thus, the students' preference for programs perceived as having earning potential contrasts rather sharply with the college's stated intention to emphasize motherhood and homemaking. At the same time, were not these graduates answering Principal Austin's call for women's further involvement in the public sphere?

Gender And Education In Ontario: An Historical Reader

Notes

1. I am grateful to Professors John Moir and Alison Prentice for comments and suggestions on earlier drafts of this paper. The staff of the United Church Archives in Toronto provided invaluable assistance during the research for this paper. I would also like to thank Heather Meier of Alma College.

2. *Minutes*, Executive Council, 1881, Collection on Educational Institutions in Canada, Alma College papers, United Church Archives, Toronto. Subsequent references to this collection will be indicated by UCA.

3. When C.B. Sissons was questioned about the lack of information on the Wesleyan Ladies' College of Hamilton in his history of Victoria University, Sissons replied: "I suppose Hamilton [Ladies' College] had nearly run its course when women were first enrolled in Victoria in 1880." Sisson's mother had been a student at the WLC in the 1860s but according to him it was merely a finishing course. See C.B. Sissons to Freda Walson, 14 May 1954, Wesleyan Ladies' College, Special Collections, Hamilton Public Library, Hamilton, Ontario.

4. Recent work includes Marion V. Royce, "Landmarks in the Victorian Education of Young Ladies Under Methodist Church Auspices," *Atlantis* 31 (Fall 1977); Kate Rousmaniere, "To Prepare the Ideal Woman: Private Denominational Girl's Schooling in Late Nineteenth Century Ontario," (M.A. thesis, University of Toronto, 1984); Kathleen Moorcroft, "Character Builders: Women and Education in Whitby, Ontario, 1900-1920," (Ed.D. thesis, University of Toronto, 1979); Elizabeth Smyth, "The Lessons of Religion and Science: The Congregation of the Sisters of St. Joseph and St. Joseph's Academy, Toronto, 1854-1911," (Ed.D. thesis, University of Toronto, 1989). See also, John Reid, "The Education of Women at Mount Allison, 1854-1914," *Acadiensis* 12, 2 (Spring 1983), 3-33.

5. R.D. Gidney and W.P.J. Millar, *Inventing Secondary Education: The Rise of the High School in Nineteenth-Century Ontario*, (Montreal: McGill-Queen's University Press, 1990) Chapter 2.

6. See Marjorie Theobald, "'Mere Accomplishments?' Melbourne's Early Girls Schools Reconsidered," *History of Education Review* 13, 2 (1984), 15-28.

7. Susan E. Houston and Alison Prentice, *Schooling and Scholars in Nineteenth-Century Ontario*, (Toronto: University of Toronto Press, 1988) 34-45.

8. Ibid., 43.

9. These seven colleges included three Methodist ones: Wesleyan Ladies' College, Hamilton; Ontario Ladies' College, Whitby; Alma College, St. Thomas. There were also two Church of England schools: Bishop Strachan School, Toronto, and Hellmuth Ladies' College, and the Brantford Ladies' College. See Rev. Alexander Burns, "Female Education in Ontario," in J.G. Hodgins ed., *The Establishment of Schools and Colleges in Ontario 1792-1910* (Toronto: Cameron, 1910) 232-34.

10. Helen Horowitz, *Alma Mater. Design and Experience in the Womens' Colleges from their Nineteenth Century Beginnings to the 1930s* (New York: Knopf, 1984) 4.

11. Albert College had been established in 1857 as Belleville Seminary. The school contained a separate female department called Alexandra College. Carman's two sisters had studied at the ladies' college.

12. Quoted in Rev. Wesley Edwards, *The History of Alma College* (St. Thomas, Ont.: Alma College, 1927) 4.

13. Edwards, *Alma College*, 8-9.

14. Horowitz, *Alma Mater*, 5.

15. Ibid., 12.

16. On the ideal of the family as a model for schools, see Alison Prentice, "Education and the Metaphor of the Family: The Upper Canadian Example," in Michael B. Katz and Paul H. Mattingly eds., *Education and Social Change* (New York: New York University Press, 1975) 110-32.

17. Hon. Adam Crooks, speaker at the ceremony. Quoted in Edwards, *Alma College*, 5.

18. Katharine Riddell ed., *Alma College Centennial Book 1877-1977* (St. Thomas: Phibbs, 1977) 7.

19. Ibid., 5.

20. B.F. Austin to the Board, 21 May 1897, Box 10, UCA.

21. Ramsay Cook, *The Regenerators* (Toronto: University of Toronto Press, 1985) 69-78. See also B.F. Austin Personal Papers, Family Scrapbook, UCA, for an obituary of his daughter, Kathleen, who died of pneumonia in 1896 at the age of 2.

22. Secretary of the Board to B.F. Austin, 1897, Box 10, UCA.

23. The family scrapbook contains a clipping which states that Austin left Alma to be on the editorial board of Linscott Publishing.

24. Edwards, *Alma College*, 32. According to Henry Morgan ed., *Canadian Men and Women of the Time* (Toronto: Wm. Briggs, 1912). Austin became president of the William Smith College for Women, Geneva, N.Y., in 1903 and in 1906 served as pastor of Plymouth Spiritual Church of Rochester, N.Y. He was a trustee of the N.Y. State Spiritual

Association and editor of a journal called *Reason*. Austin lived in Los Angeles from 1913 until his death in 1936 and was involved with the Central Spiritual Church during his time there.

25. Riddell, *Alma College*, 20.
26. B.F. Austin ed., *Woman: Her Character, Culture, and Calling* (Brantford: Book and Bible House, 1890) 199-209.
27. Ibid., 200.
28. Ibid., 200.
29. Ibid., 206.
30. Ibid., 206.
31. Ibid., 34.
32. Ibid., 36.
33. Ibid., 38.
34. Ibid., 376.
35. Ibid., 382.
36. For a critical study of women's rhetoric, see Karlyn Kohrs Campbell, *Men Cannot Speak For Her* (New York: Praeger, 1989). Campbell points out an important principle of rhetoric, which could be applied to some male speakers, such as Austin, namely that "rhetorical invention is rarely originality of argument, but rather the selection and adaptation of materials to the occasion, the purpose, and the audience." See Campbell, *Man Cannot Speak*, 9.
37. Ibid., 380.
38. Rev. Morgan Dix, "The Education of Woman for Her Work," in *Woman*, 451.
39. Anne Firor Scott, "The Troy Female Seminary," *Making the Invisible Woman Visible* (Urbana and Chicago: University of Illinois Press, 1984) 83.
40. Ibid., 83.
41. Quoted in the *Almafilian*, July 1891, Box 24, UCA.
42. Quoted in Carolyn DeSwarte Gifford, "For God and Home and Native Land," in Hillah Thomas and Rosemary Skinner Keller eds., *Women in New Worlds* (Nashville: Abingdon, 1981) 315.
43. Nancy Hardesty, *Women Called to Witness: Evangelical Feminism in the 19th Century* (Nashville: Abingdon, 1984) 152. For the cult of true womanhood, see Barbara Welter, "The Cult of True Womanhood: 1820-1960," *American Quarterly* 18 (Summer 1966), 151-74; and Nancy Cott, *The Bonds of Womanhood: Woman's Sphere in New England, 1780-1835* (New Haven: Yale University Press, 1975). See also Mary P. Ryan, *Cradle of the Middle Class: The Family in Oneida County, New York,*

1790-1865 (Cambridge: Cambridge University Press, 1981); and Lynn D. Gordon, *Gender and Higher Education in the Progressive Era* (New Haven: Yale University Press, 1990).

44. Wendy Mitchinson, "The W.C.T.U.: 'For God and Home and Native Land': A Study in Nineteenth-Century Feminism," in Linda Kealey ed., *A Not Unreasonable Claim: Women and Reform in Canada 1880s-1920s* (Toronto: Women's Press, 1979) 151-67. For a study of women's activism in the American context, see Nancy A. Hewitt, *Women's Activism and Social Change. Rochester, New York, 1822-1872* (Ithaca and London: Cornell University Press, 1984).

45. Veronica Strong-Boag, *The Parliament of Women: The National Council of Women of Canada 1893-1923* Canada, National Museum of Man, Mercury series/History paper, no. 18 (Ottawa: National Museums of Canada, 1976) 11. See also, Theodora Penny Martin, *The Sound of Our Own Voices. Women's Study Clubs 1860-1910* (Boston: Beacon Press, 1987) for a study of the American club movement.

46. *Almafilian* 7, 1 (Thanksgiving 1910), 2, UCA.

47. Subscription List, 1879, Box 7, 3, UCA.

48. See the discussion in Gidney and Millar, *Inventing Secondary Education*, 11-17, concerning the distinctions between beginners and more advanced students and how these levels were integrated within the schools.

49. Announcement, Alma College 1884, Albert Carman Papers, Box 4, vol. 1, file 10b, UCA.

50. *Calendar*, 1885-86, UCA.

51. Ibid.

52. The profession of elocution offered employment possibilities as described by M.L. Rayne, *What Can A Woman Do; or, Her Position in the Business and Literary World* (Petersburgh, N.Y.: Eagle, 1893) 159-68. Rayne claimed that a professional elocutionist could earn 15-25 dollars by entertaining wealthy society ladies for an evening. Schools of elocution also offered graduates opportunities for teaching. Finally, elocution claimed to benefit its students by strengthening lungs, improving health, acquiring a graceful manner as well as general culture. Rayne, 160.

53. "Music as a Bread Winner for Girls," *Almafilian* 5, 1 (July 1891).

54. *Calendar*, 1884-85, UCA.

55. *Minutes*, Executive Council, Sept. 1883, Box 15, 1, UCA.

56. Ibid.

57. *Minutes* of the Council, Jan. 1891, Box 15, 1, UCA.

58.   Ibid. Foreign students were, however, already at the college in the mid-1880s. The *Christian Guardian*, 23 Jan. 1884, announced that rooms at Alma were engaged for two young ladies, Eugenie and Mamie Dupuch, from the Bahamas, who would commence studies in May 1885. The minutes of the Executive committee noted that in Jan. 1886, Miss Eugenie Dupuch was appointed Assistant Teacher of Music. The *Almafilian* in 1912 recorded that Mrs. Mamie Dupuch-Bone died in 1912 after having served for many years as a principal of the Girl's Model School at Nassau. See *Almafilian* (April 1219) 8, 4, UCA. Much later, in 1929, the admission of Jewish girls was debated and no motion was passed but the recommendation was made that the Principal should register no more than four to five girls at any one time. See *Minutes*, Board of Management, 17 Sept. 1929, Box 5, 4, UCA.

59.   John Millar to Prof. Warner, 22 June 1898, Alma College, Box 10, 3, UCA.

60.   John Millar to Prof. Warner, 22 June 1898, Alma College, Box 10, 3, UCA.

61.   See also Gidney and Millar, *Inventing Secondary Education*, 294-5.

62.   Alma had affiliated in 1884 "for examination purposes" with the Ontario School of Art. This meant that students who passed the exam were given licence to teach drawing and painting in the public schools and collegiate institutes of the province. See Report by B.F. Austin to the Board of Management, 17 April 1884, Box 12, 19.

63.   Gidney and Millar indicate that there was some overlap between the university and the high school in the form of the senior matriculation, which was also the work of the first year of university. In 1880, "the vast majority of students entered university through the junior matriculation examination." *Inventing Secondary Education*, 272. Adaptation to external standards increased in 1909 when the government's "approved school" scheme meant that all schools, including private schools such as Alma, had to pass certain inspection standards and adjust their curriculum to address priorities set by the Department of Education.

64.   Ibid., 10.

65.   Edwards, *Alma College*, 7.

66.   Nathaniel Burwash, *A History of Victoria College* (Toronto: Victoria College Press, 1927). The union created an additional complication, which was that ministers of the Methodist Episcopal Church, in order to enter union on an equal ground with Wesleyan ministers, were required to contribute to their superannuation fund. Many were unable to do so and consequently retired or moved to the United States. The notes

which these ministers had signed were lost income for the college. See Edwards, *Alma College*, 13.

67. Edwards, *Alma College*, 10.

68. Ibid., 18.

69. *Minutes* of the Board, 6 Oct. 1893, Box 1, 1, UCA.

70. The minutes record that coal tar was recommended instead of coal for heating; that special fees for German, Italian, and French be increased, and that Miss Brooks be hired in lieu of the full services of Prof. Bell-Smith. Furthermore, less expensive arrangements for calisthenics were recommended. See *Minutes* of the Board, June 1887, UCA.

71. *Minutes* of the Board, Alma College, Oct. 1896, Box 1, 2, UCA.

72. Parent to Dr. Warner, Feb. 1910, Box 13, UCA.

73. The report concluded, "So far as I can understand the failure of patronage has arisen mainly from competition and the stringency of the times and possibly to some extent from external causes. When Alma opened in 1881 there were fewer schools in competition. The two conservatories of music, Moulton College, Havergal College, and the Presbyterian Ladies' College, Toronto, have all come into competition since 1881. See Report to the President and Board of Management [undated, possibly late 1880s], by the Alma College Committee on Agency, Box 12, 17. Gidney and Millar observe that the multiplication of girl's boarding and day schools in the seventies and eighties demonstrated that some parents continued to prefer segregated schooling. *Inventing Secondary Education*, 244.

74. Special report to the Board of Management, *Minutes*, n.d., Box 13, 22.

75. *Minutes* of the Board, Alma College, 25 June 1887. The entrance into the collegiate course was made dependent on passing exams in the same subjects as were required for high school entrance; the academic course contained the same subjects and options as the departmental regulations for third class public schoolteacher's certificates; the collegiate course contained the same subjects and options as the second class certificate. By October 1889 the *Christian Guardian* reported that the college work had been brought into line with the public school requirements for second and third class certificates, and that provision had been made for a full course for first class certificate and university matriculation work.

76. *Minutes* of the Board, 25 June 1889.

77. Quoted in the *Almafilian*, 5, 1 (July 1891), 1.

78. Ibid., 1.

79. *Almafilian*, 5, 1 (July 1891), 2.

80. Ibid., 2.

81. Ibid., 2.

82. Report to the Board of Alma College, 20 Nov. 1902, Box 12, 20, UCA.

83. Paul Bennett, "Little Worlds: The Forging of Identities in Ontario Protestant Schools and Special Institutions, 1850-1930," (Ed.D. thesis: University of Toronto, 1991).

84. Quoted in Rev. Warner's Inaugural Address, 1897, and reprinted in an article entitled "Principal Warner's Decennial," *Alma* 2, 2 (June 1907), 1-4.

85. "The Boarding School for Girls and Its Advantages," *Alma* 1, 1 (July 1903), 3. In a report on education this role was connected explicitly to women, as it stated: "Again the teachers of women should be largely women. We do not say exclusively so. The influence of a manly man calls out womanly development in some directions, mental as well as social. But no greater mistake can be made than for a man to attempt to correct the defects of a young women. Only motherly insight and sympathy can do that. The education of women, especially during the formative period from 14 to 20 should be chiefly in the hands of women and those the best that the country can find." See Report to the Board of the Educational Society of the Methodist Church, 1916/17, Alma College, Box 13, 23, UCA.

86. "Ladies' Colleges in the Educational System of Ontario," *Almafilian* 1, 1 (July 1903), 5.

87. See Principal Warner's Report to the Board, 24 November 1908, Box 12, 20, UCA.

88. Conflict between Alma and the Department of Education emerges in the correspondence on the subject of teacher qualifications. See RG2, P-3, Box 32-5/74, CodeI-270/1917: Private Schools, Public Archives of Ontario.

89. Graduates of Alma College, Box 21, 2, UCA.

"A Noble Proof of Excellence": The Culture and Curriculum of a Nineteenth-Century Ontario Convent Academy

Elizabeth Smyth

[Some people] would take it to be some great college devoted to instruction of the sterner sex. But these are the days of feminine progress and nowhere is that progression more marked and rapid than in the matter of education; parents demand the best alike for their daughters and sons and unfortunately too many Catholics think to secure great temporal advantage to their daughters by sending them to the Protestant High Schools and Colleges, under the impression that Catholic institutions for women are behind the times. Never was there a greater nor more fatal mistake. St. Joseph's [Academy] is one of the noblest proofs of the excellence to which female education has attained within the Catholic Church.[1]

Although written in 1897, this journalist's description of the school administered by the Sisters of St. Joseph at their Toronto motherhouse is a fitting place to begin a contemporary analysis of gender and education in one nineteenth-century Ontario convent academy.[2]

From the mid-nineteenth century on, most Ontario cities and major towns had at least one, and sometimes two, convent academies. In spite of this fact, their presence and their influence have been neglected in the current standard reference works on nineteenth-century education in Ontario. Like their sister Protestant denominational private girls' schools, colleges and female academies, convent academies have, for too long, been dismissed as places focussing solely on moral education or on social graces. Unlike American scholars, who have traced the impact of nineteenth-century female academies in the development and formalization of women's secondary and tertiary education,[3] and Australian researchers, whose analysis of Australian girls' denominational and private boarding schools of the nineteenth and early twentieth centuries has called into question the labelling of this form of education as an exercise in "mere accomplishments,"[4] Ontario historians have largely overlooked the study of nineteenth-century Ontario Catholic institutions for girls and young women.[5]

This article explores the culture and curriculum of one nineteenth-century Ontario convent academy, St. Joseph's Academy, Toronto, from its foundation in 1854 to the turn of the century. It focusses on the evolving definition of appropriate education for Catholic girls and young women evident in the curriculum—those subjects taught—and the culture—the practices and physical surroundings—of the convent academy. It will show that within this fifty year period, the meaning of the phrase "a noble proof of excellence" changed considerably. As the author of the opening excerpt suggests, by the turn of the century, St. Joseph's Academy could not be labelled as being "behind the times." Rather, it was one of the leading academic institutions for Ontario's young women. The academy offered its pupils the opportunity to gain provincially recognized certification in a variety of programs. Finally, within the first decade of the twentieth century, the academy actively and successfully pursued affiliation as a Catholic women's college within the federated University of Toronto.

I: Origins of the Order and of the Academy

Convent education is, by definition, associated with an order of religious women. To explore a convent academy necessitates an examination of the order under whose ever-present and watchful eye it grew. St. Joseph's Academy was the second convent academy established in Toronto. It was founded in 1854 by members of the Congregation of the Sisters of St. Joseph, an uncloistered order of religious women which had its origins in seventeenth-century France. The order had as its mission "Christian perfection and . . . service of their neighbour,"[6] which, when translated into practice, meant that it was an order whose members were engaged in both teaching and social service.

The Congregation as a whole was regulated by a constitution, but it operated as a series of decentralized administrative units organized along diocesan lines. Each diocesan unit, or community, had its own local superior and novitiate. Although the communities were linked to each other by their common constitution, each motherhouse operated independently of the others. While the diocesan bishop issued the invitation to the order to establish a local foundation and oversaw both the Sisters' spiritual and temporal activities, the local superior ultimately decided how her community was to carry out the order's mandate of "Christian perfection and . . . service of their neighbours."[7] It was she who was called upon to balance the needs of her bishop and diocese with the strengths of her community and decide where the Sisters would give service: in parish schools, academies, hospitals, orphanages or other charitable institutions.

In 1836, the Congregation set up its initial North American foundation in Missouri. Fifteen years later, at the invitation of Bishop Armand François

A Noble Proof of Excellence

Marie de Charbonnel, four members of the order came to Toronto to staff an orphanage. The following year, the Sisters were asked by de Charbonnel to teach in the city's parochial schools. By 1854, the Sisters were operating a boarding school for young women. One can speculate why the community made this decision. The four women who established the Toronto foundation all had experience teaching in and administering boarding schools in France and in the United States. They thus would have had first-hand knowledge that a boarding school was fiscally and practically rewarding. A tuition-charging boarding school could be a revenue-generating enterprise and a place of employment for the members of the expanding community. Capitalizing on the Sisters' artistic, musical and linguistic talents, the community could also earn additional monies by offering pupils instruction in these skills.

It has been suggested that religious communities viewed the operation of a boarding school as a means of replenishing the order with new members.[8] The evidence collected on the Toronto community of the Sisters of St. Joseph indicates either that this was not a primary goal of the boarding school, or that the Sisters were not very successful in achieving this objective. Less than 5% of the girls attending the school as boarders entered the community as novices.[9]

There seems to have been a more pressing reason for the establishment of a convent-academy in Toronto. Both the Sisters and their bishop realized that a boarding school would meet the educational needs of an underserved sector of society: adolescent girls of all religious denominations. Because of the lack of state-sponsored schools for young women, private education was the only option available in the early to mid-nineteenth century for families who wished their daughters to engage in further study. It was this need that stimulated the establishment of the original Toronto convent academy—Loretto Academy.

In 1847, Bishop Michael Power invited members of the Institute of the Blessed Virgin Mary (the Loretto Sisters), to journey from Ireland to Toronto in order to establish a school for the education of young women. The Loretto Sisters' educational enterprise had a most inauspicious beginning. The deaths of several Sisters caused the boarding school to close in March 1851. When it reopened the following September, only five of the boarders returned. It appears that Bishop de Charbonnel saw the state of girls' education was suffering because of the illness and death which had plagued the Loretto community. It may be reasonable to suggest that de Charbonnel and Mother Delphine, the St. Joseph's superior in Toronto, decided that the needs of the diocese and St. Joseph's mandate of "service to neighbour"[10] overruled the order's traditional veto on competition with others in educational endeavours.

It is clear that, from the outset, the Sisters of St. Joseph had the managing of a large and growing school as a long term goal. The attendance books and other record-keeping volumes which date from the late 1850s had been specifically printed for the school. When plans were drawn for a new motherhouse building at Clover Hill, careful consideration was given to the design to ensure that it accommodated both a sisters' and boarders' quarters. Ample room was left for expansion within both the structure of the building and the surrounding space.

By the beginning of the twentieth century, it was obvious that the Sisters had achieved this long-term goal. The order had duly incorporated regulations concerning the administration of the convent academy into its constitution. Over two thousand pupils of all religious denominations had attended the academy as boarders.[11] The large and flourishing school within the motherhouse complex was visible proof of the commitment which the Congregation of the Sisters of St. Joseph had made to the education of young women.

II: A Curriculum for the Education of Young Women

Sound intellectual and moral training while meeting the pupils' physical and social needs were the major goals pursued by St. Joseph's Academy, as evidenced by its nineteenth-century prospectuses. Yet, in the course of the nineteenth century, the purposes of the "sound intellectual training" changed from one almost exclusively focussed on excellence of achievement within the home and charitable work within the neighbourhood to one which offered many options, including preparation for a career outside of the home as well as university education.

From its establishment, the academy advertised itself as providing "every branch suitable to the complete Education of Young Ladies, with strictest attention to their moral and polite deportment."[12] The initial *Prospectus* issued in 1866 for the school's relocation to Clover Hill, offered a rather comprehensive, and rather typical, array of studies:

English, French and Italian Languages, Reading, Writing, Grammar, Geography, History, Intellectual and Practical Arithmetic, Algebra, Geometry, Book-keeping, Elementary Chemistry and Botany, Natural Philosophy, Logical Analysis, Astronomy and Use of Globes, Rhetoric, Vocal and Instrumental Music, Drawing, Painting, Plain and Ornamental Needle-work, Wax Fruit and Flowers, & c.[sic].[13]

A Noble Proof of Excellence

The curriculum closely parallelled that of secular private schools for young women in Ontario and Australia.[14] However, while the fine arts and musical studies so commonly associated with a nineteenth-century young ladies' education were offered, they were not considered as part of the core curriculum covered by the standard tuition fee. Instead, they were available to the pupils at considerable cost, well exceeding the annual fee charged for a day pupil to attend the school.[15] Also noteworthy is the fact that from its beginning the academy held public examinations of its graduating students, with local clergy taking the role of examiners. The patrons of the academy offered in all classes a number of prizes and medals for achievement in both intellectual and artistic pursuits.

Attendance and participation in the academy's program were well regulated. The Sisters required a commitment from the pupils to stay for at least a quarter term. Until the turn of the century, a young lady wishing to be "crowned" as a graduate of the academy had to be a boarding pupil for at least one term, in order to fully experience the rights and rituals of a convent academy. The academy was to be a place of serious work, not merely a place of refuge for young women experiencing a "slow season" in their social calendars.

From the beginning, the academy accepted pupils of all religious denominations (See Table 1). Its *Prospectus* announced that "no distinction of religion will be made in the admission of Pupils; but all will be required to conform to the general rules of the House."[16]

There was some variation in the "general rules" for Catholic and non-Catholic pupils. Non-Catholic pupils were not required to attend all religious ceremonies; in fact, when a retreat or other celebration preceded a holiday, the non-Catholic pupils found themselves with a few more days of vacation. Although they were free and indeed encouraged to practice their own faith, it would have been virtually impossible to escape the fact that Catholic faith and practices were integrated into virtually every aspect of the pupils' life. The pupils' dress reflected the simplicity of the order's habits. The pupils' dormitory games imitated key experiences in the religious formation of a Sister.[17] From in-class to extracurricular to co-curricular activities, the Catholic influence was most pervasive.[18]

Although students lived in the same building as a community of religious women, the pupils and the Sisters led separate and separated lives. The separation of the secular from the religious was implicit in the plan of the first architect-designed motherhouse and school building. Unlike the two previous temporary residences of the community, the Clover Hill buildings were especially constructed to accommodate the needs of both the community and

273

its boarding and day schools. The design of the building incorporated the architectural features of a large Victorian home and a generously endowed educational institution. With its dormered roofs and a veranda surrounding the building, the motherhouse sat amidst extensive grounds which were planted with orchards and ornamental trees[19] and landscaped to become "beautiful gardens, rare collections of shrubs, spacious playgrounds."[20]

Table 1—RELIGION OF PUPILS REGISTERED AS BOARDERS IN
ST. JOSEPH ACADEMY, TORONTO 1854-1920

Date	# Boarders	# Catholic	% Catholic	# Non-Catholics	% Non-Catholics	# Unknown	% Unknown
pre 1860	24	24	100%	0	0	0	0
1861-1870	161	146	90.7%	15	9.3%	0	0
1871-1880	279	215	77.1%	64	22.9%	0	0
1881-1890	370	272	73.6%	86	23.2%	12	3.2%
1891-1900	271	217	80.1%	54	19.9%	0	0
1901-1911	495	423	85.5%	72	14.5%	0	0
1911-1920	738	624	84.6%	105	14.2%	9	1.2%
Total	2338	1921	82.2%	396	16.9%	21	0.9%

Source : "Register [1856-1920]," Box 5, ASSJ.

For both the original building and subsequent additions, the constitutions of the community provided the architects with some of the details of the interior layout. As the building was to serve as a motherhouse, novitiate and boarding school, the needs of these three distinct groups had to be accommodated. The 1881 *Constitution of The Sisters of St. Joseph* instructed that "great care must be taken that the apartments of the Sisters be entirely separate from those of the seculars."[21] Thus, the building was constructed and expanded to be divided into two houses which were, to a certain extent, mirror images of each other. In this way, the Sisters and the boarders were accommodated quite independently, thus allowing them to lead quite separate lives while living under the same roof. Sharing only the main entrance areas and the chapels, the Sisters and the boarders had their separate parlours for receiving visitors, their separate recreation areas, libraries, study spaces, dining facilities, sleeping areas and infirmaries. This separation extended beyond the walls of the house proper. Even out of doors, the Sisters had their own enclosed garden area, which was separated from the boarders' gardens.

A Noble Proof of Excellence

The gardens and orchards were to serve a variety of functions in the academy's religious ceremonies and academic programs. The gardens were to be the sites of processions and pilgrimages to celebrate the feasts of Corpus Christi and the Blessed Virgin Mary. As well, they were to serve as an outdoor laboratory for the study of botany. Finally, these pleasant surroundings presented "many inducements to healthful and invigorating exercise,"[22] thus providing a space for those outdoor activities considered proper and beneficial for young ladies in the nineteenth and early twentieth centuries. There were croquet pitches and tennis courts. There were stables for the horses and space to accommodate the riding lessons given by Major Darnely, who also served as the calisthenics instructor at the academy.[23] The major may have held some of his classes in the gardens, and he definitely led his brisk walks through the flower and vegetable gardens, the vineyards and pear, peach and apple orchards. Even when weather proved inclement, "the large verandas afforded a pleasant promenade for the young ladies in wet weather."[24] However, it was not until well into the twentieth century that a gymnasium was added to the edifice.

In 1873, within a decade of its construction, the main building was expanded. A new wing, with a new chapel and a "distribution hall" was added to the motherhouse complex.[25] A newspaper report described this addition as "render[ing] St. Joseph's, one of the largest, as it is already acknowledged, as one of the best institutions for young ladies in Canada."[26] The chapel was the site of many of the religious festivals and ceremonies of both the school and the community. The distribution hall or concert hall hosted many more secular ceremonies and events. Its construction further reinforced the desire of the order to provide a public space for the demonstration of the knowledge and skills acquired by their pupils within the academy's walls.

Chronicling the evolution and use of the distribution hall yields a significant perspective on the order's definition of appropriate education for their young lady pupils. Public performance of their talents was a priority. Visitors included clergy of many denominations and orders, government officials, royalty and ecclesiastical and political dignitaries. In addition to housing the prestigious annual closing exercises and distribution of prizes, graduation recitals, allegorical plays and public lectures, it was the site of countless benefit concerts and "entertainments."

These "entertainments" took many forms: calisthenics displays, recitations in English and foreign languages, musical and vocal performances, dramas written by members of the order to celebrate the visit of special guests. From the "minims," the most junior of the school's pupils, to graduates who returned to visit their alma mater, the young ladies of St. Joseph were expected to and were called upon to share their talents before the community, the clergy and the public at large.

Table 2—DAILY EXERCISES, 1871

A.M.	
5:20	Rising and Morning Prayers
6:00	Mass
6:30	Breakfast
7:00	Study Recreation and Study
9:00	Class
10:00	Recreation
10:10	Class
11:45	Dinner
P.M.	
12:15	Visit to Blessed Sacrament
12:30	Recreation
1:00	Class
2:45	Recreation
3:00	Class
4:00	Recreation
4:20	Study
6:00	Tea
6:15	[Rosary] Beads
6:30	Recreation
7:30	French Conversation
8:20	Night Prayers

Source: "Yearly Regulations for the Boarding and Day School of the Convent of St. Joseph, Together with names of Sisters employed in teaching in the different schools," Box 8, ASSJ.

The pupils were well prepared for their public appearances. The formal presentations were well rehearsed and subsequently analysed. Throughout the latter decades of the nineteenth century, the mother superior held weekly "Conversations,"—opportunities for the pupils to perform for each other and for their teachers. By the end of the century, "Deportment" was a regularly scheduled session led by Sister Emerentia Lonergan. A pupil remembered that while listening to Sister Emerentia's instructions concerning the exact width of a ladylike smile, the exact rhythm of a curtsey, the exact position of the head, feet and arms and hands, while sitting, standing and walking, the exact intonation of polite speech,[27] her classmates snickered and chatted among themselves. Yet, she reflected, these lessons provided in later years not only grace and poise but "good posture and good nerves."[28]

The distribution hall was also the site of the public demonstration of the pupils' academic achievements. The final examination of graduating pupils were public events. The examiners were drawn from the ranks of the Toronto ecclesia and the staff of St. Michael's College. The proceedings were covered in both the Catholic and secular press. Invariably, favourable comments were made concerning the role of the Sisters in providing appropriate educational opportunities for young women. These public proceedings were thus meant to give prominence to the community and its school.

III: Restructuring the Curriculum

Significant changes occurred in the academy's curriculum during the decades of the 1870s and 1880s. These were the result of the interaction of a number of factors: strong community leadership and a refining of community roles, episcopal support for a more academically oriented program and, undoubtedly, the discussion of the appropriate curriculum for young women which was stimulated by the restructing of the Ontario secondary school curriculum during the 1870s and 1880s.[29] The order's new constitution, which had been drafted under Mother Superior Philomena Sheridan and submitted to Rome for pontifical approval in 1877, set out, in considerable detail, regulations and directions for the operations of the academy and for the education of its staff. The emphasis given to teacher selection and education in the constitution indicates that the order was rapidly progressing toward the formalization of instruction in its schools and academies. The implementation of the changes set out in the constitution, coupled with the factors mentioned above, resulted in the academy becoming an institution which offered "secondary education," as it was defined by the provincial collegiates of Ontario.

While analysing the curriculum delivered at St. Joseph's Academy, it is useful to examine the evolution of the mandate of the Congregation of the Sisters of St. Joseph for educating young women. The constitution which initially governed the Toronto community, the 1847 *Constitution of Congregation of the Sisters of St. Joseph*,[30] "scarcely mentioned the instruction of young women.... Hence, no rules were written for teachers."[31] Yet by 1881, when the Toronto community published its own constitution, education of children in general, and of young women in particular, had become one of the order's major activities. The *Constitution and Rules of the Congregation of the Sisters of St. Joseph in the Archdiocese of Toronto* (1881) consequently attached great importance to the selection of teachers:

> One of the most important works for the service of neighbour and the progress of religion is the education and instruction of young girls. This duty requires peculiar qualifications of those who are employed therein; therefore the choice and education of the Sisters who are destined to be teachers should be to the Congregation a special object of solicitude.[32]

The new Constitution systematically outlined the duties and responsibilities of the women engaged in teaching, with special attention given to the directress of the academy. This office was described as "one of the most important [charges] of the Congregation." It was filled by appointment by the mother superior on the advice of her counsellors. The directress was given the responsibility "to see that, while making continual progress in science," the young lady pupils of the academy "also advance in piety and virtue."[33] She had a broad array of powers over the pupils and the staff. She interviewed the pupils applying to the academy and assessed them for placement in classes. She could, but only after receiving permission from the mother superior, reject a pupil "whose admission might be injurious to the school." She was responsible for ensuring that "the teachers use the books and follow the methods of teaching that have been pointed out to them." In order to "ascertain what progress they make in their studies, [and] whether they apply to them with diligence," the directress was empowered to "interrogate [the pupils] in regard to what they have learned" and was to reward excellence in study with "premiums and notes of approbation." She was to "assemble the teachers once a week to confer with them concerning the general good of the academy."[34]

The teachers were also given specific direction on their behaviour and "deportment." By their presence in the classroom, they were to model "religion and science." "Once given their teaching assignment by the directress, they shall previously prepare the lessons they are to give their classes so that while understanding perfectly what they teach, they may be able to communicate it to their pupils with clearness and precision. They shall devote to their own improvement all the time that is necessary, but they shall not study any other branches than those prescribed by the superior or directress in order that their progress in science may be accompanied by their progress in humility and obedience."[35]

A Noble Proof of Excellence

This somewhat contradictory mixture of encouraging intellectual curiosity while maintaining a pious humility is perhaps one of the most salient features of the Constitution of 1881. The Sisters were to celebrate and reward achievement in their pupils but also teach them humility. For themselves, they were to "refer to God all glory resulting from any talent with which he may have gifted them" and "seek humility, not pride from it."[36]

Three final points concerning the regulations for teachers should be made. The teachers were instructed to "take proper care of their health" as their job required "much exertion of the voice and great application of the mind."[37] At the first sign of any fatigue or illness, they were to notify the superior. These noteworthy items indicated that the community was concerned about not overworking its members and thus rendering them useless to the order. Secondly, the teachers were to respect the directress. Instructing women who are bound by obedience to show respect may in fact be a reference to discontent among the academy staff. As in any educational institution, the implementation of change is, for some, a painful and grief-ridden process. The purpose of this directive, therefore, may have been destined to quell any further objections. Finally, and perhaps most significantly, the new Constitution directed the teachers to attend conferences, organized by the mother superior, on "the methods of teaching."[38] These annual conferences strikingly parallelled a contemporary professional development program for late twentieth-century teachers.

The year 1882 is a critical one in the history of the academy. Indeed, the staff was well on its way to fully implementing the directives set out in the order's new constitution. While it still rewarded "lady-like deportment" and achievement in the fine arts, the pupils' academic achievements were more emphatically celebrated and highlighted in the Annual Prize Distribution. More significantly, the achievement of one pupil in the Department of Education matriculation examinations suggests that the subjects offered to the pupils of the academy closely parallelled those offered by the public high schools of the province. Gertrude Lawler, the academy's Gold Medal graduate of 1882, sat the provincial matriculation examinations at Jarvis Collegiate, achieved first class honours and embarked upon a brilliant academic career at the University of Toronto. The fact that Lawler, fresh from her academy graduation, was able to successfully sit the provincial examinations may indicate that in addition to her own abilities, her academy experience had given her mastery of the content and the skills necessary to pass the exams.

Lawler's success, coupled with the emphasis on academic achievement and teacher education found in the Constitution of 1881, the *Annals* and other sources, seems to indicate that change in the curriculum offered to the pupils of the academy was taking place. However, the academy's movement toward applying to the Ontario Department of Education for permission to nominate its own candidates for the provincial matriculation examinations was not initiated, but rather accelerated, by Lawler's success.

During the first decade of its existence, St. Joseph's Academy appears to have offered its pupils a curriculum generated and regulated by the order. As a private institution, the academy presented its own certificate of achievement to those graduating students who met its internally generated standards. It seems that the academy neither sought nor subscribed to the curricular requirements set out by the Ontario Department of Education. Yet, by the end of the 1880s, the academy's curricular orientation had changed. The academy's experience was like that of many private schools which in the 1880s "tied [themselves] to the curricular prescriptions and standards set by the department [of Education]."[39] According to R.D. Gidney and W.P.J. Millar, the growth of a system of matriculation, examinations and certificates sponsored by the Department of Education and endorsed by all universities and professional associations "eliminated...[the option] for private schools to negotiate with the universities about their own academic programs and thus reserve a degree of curricular independence."[40]

At the same time, one can speculate that the Sisters also understood that a provincially recognized certificate of matriculation was a valuable educational currency. Deprived of the ability to grant this certification, the academy risked the loss of pupils to other public and private institutions. Equally as important, with the matriculation examination came the licence to teach. Teaching was viewed as an intermediary step between school and a career in the home. Thus, it was to the academy's advantage to offer this option to its pupils. By the end of the 1880s, the academy was presenting its own candidates for provincial matriculation.[41] The order's successful bid for this designation indicates that the academy's curriculum met with the standards established for matriculation in the provincial high schools and collegiate institutes.

At the end of the nineteenth century, the Sisters of St. Joseph offered their pupils the choice of three courses: a Collegiate Course, an Academic Course and a Commercial Course. Each of these courses was affiliated with an external institution which examined the pupils and awarded certification to successful candidates. The pupils in the collegiate program were examined by members of the Department of Education. Success in this program qualified the pupils for admission to university as well as teaching and nursing programs. The academic courses included those subjects previously defined as the "accomplishments": foreign languages, music and fine arts. Like the collegiate courses, these programs led to external certification and yielded credentials for employment. Successful completion of the music program would result in the acquisition of a University of Toronto Music Degree. The art program was affiliated with the Toronto School of Art. A graduate could use these credentials to advertise her services as an instructor. The third program, the Commercial Course, was affiliated with a number of Toronto business schools including the Nimms and Harrison Business College.[42] The fact that this program was offered indicates that the academy realized the necessity to provide some of its pupils with training enabling them to compete for the opportunities available to women in the growing commercial sector.

The pupils and their parents certainly had many options from which to choose. By the first decade of the century, they had even more. In 1911, the academy successfully affiliated itself with St. Michael's College and the University of Toronto. Yet, it is noteworthy that even as the school was increasing its focus on academic achievement, the arts remained an integral part of the pupils' educational experience. The graduates who went on to have outstanding careers in the public and academic sector, fondly and frequently commented on the musical and artistic skills which they had acquired during their academy days.

IV: *The Young Lady Pupils*

An analysis of the development of St. Joseph's Academy in the nineteenth century reveals that the Sisters of St. Joseph, like their colleagues in lay female educational institutions, the provincial school inspectors and their ecclesiastical superiors, held similar and equally contradictory views on the subject of appropriate education for nineteenth century young women. In analysing the variety of comments available from contemporary sources, it is apparent that the questions surrounding the purpose of further education for the young women of St. Joseph's Academy illustrate the variety of opinions held during the nineteenth century on both the purpose and nature of education for young women.

At the end of the century, St. Joseph's Academy offered its pupils a sound academic footing which, for the majority, served as preparation for marriage and motherhood. At the same time, through the religious women who made up its staff and a small but significant number of exemplary graduates who became career women, the academy provided its pupils with examples of women who had achieved an independent lifestyle separate from marriage and motherhood.

Proponents of changes in the academy's curriculum such as Archbishop Lynch believed that marriage and motherhood were the goals of girls' education. The Archbishop delivered the following remarks to the 1871 Annual Examination and Prize Distribution:

> the superior advantages of conventual education and the great and marked influence it has in giving the proper shape to society...the influence of mother in forming the family which is the ground work—the nucleus of society and showed how vast her authority may be used for good and evil. The usefulness of conventual education is beginning to be recognized throughout the length and breadth of this land—and hence it is that our convents are always full.[43]

Lynch thus supported the realignment of the academy's curriculum as a means of assisting the pupils in becoming better wives and mothers. Yet, these changes allowed some of the graduates to gain the certification and skills which enabled them to lead lives as economically independent women, independent of motherhood and family and outside of a religious community.

A minority of the pupils of St. Joseph's Academy became independent career women while some joined the order. However, the majority followed the traditional path of marriage and motherhood. But regardless of the choices that were made, the academy remained an important part of the lives of a substantial number of graduates. In the early decades of the academy's existence, informal links characterized the pupils' association with their former teachers and classmates. In 1891, the Alumnae Association was formed.[44] It offered its members opportunities for further intellectual growth within a social setting. Through its meetings and publications, it enabled St. Joseph's graduates to further develop and speak on their interests and activities, share their talents, and discuss in a formal manner critical issues of the day. The association funded scholarships, administered a literary journal and actively participated in national and international organizations supporting women's issues—particularly the higher education of women. Through a brief scan of its activities, one observes the opportunities for life-long association which the academy provided to some of its graduates.[45]

The achievements of two graduates of the decade of the 1880s who were both actively involved in the formation and development of the Alumnae Association, illustrate how broadly a "noble proof of excellence" could be defined by the turn of the century. Gertrude Lawler was representative of those students who pursued public lives as independent women. For her part, Mary Austin belonged to the minority of students who joined the Congregation of the Sisters of St. Joseph and assumed a leading role in the order. They graduated from the academy during perhaps the most critical decade in its development

A Noble Proof of Excellence

and publicly demonstrated the high calibre of education available at the academy.

Gertrude Lawler is perhaps the most outstanding graduate of the decade. She became a teacher in the Toronto Board of Education and was a pioneer advocate of pay equity for females in the teaching profession. Her efforts on behalf of higher education for women are most evident in her work as the first female senator of the University of Toronto. As part of its centenary celebrations in 1927, the University awarded her an honourary Doctor of Law. An active practising Catholic, the niece of a high ranking priest, Lawler did not follow what may have been perceived to be the path open to educated Catholic women. She did not choose to teach in either the separate school system or the convent-academy. She spent all her teaching career in the public secondary schools of Stratford and Toronto. Though she remained single, she did not enter religious life. She was a member of the laity, practising her faith but outside the confines of traditional Catholic social and educational institutions.

But she remained closely tied to the academy and was a founding member of both the Alumnae Association and the "Lilies," the alumnae literary and news magazine. Lawler was highly regarded by the academy and her memory is still honoured through an annual scholarship for achievement in English Literature.

Mary Maud McKay Warnock, a contemporary of Lawler, represented the less than 5% of pupils who joined the Sisters of St. Joseph. In 1894, Mary Warnock was received into the order as Sister Mary Austin and began her career as a teacher in St. Joseph's Academy. Almost immediately, she began preparation for the University of Toronto examinations. She was a brilliant student and the recipient of many scholarships and awards. After the affiliation of St. Joseph's with the University, Sister Austin became part of the St. Joseph's College faculty. She died, unexpectedly, in 1916, as a result of complications following surgery for appendicitis.

Sister Austin's obituaries reveal much about the public perception of the work accomplished by the St. Joseph's community. While many mourned the loss of an outstanding scholar, one used the occasion of Sister Austin's death to reflect upon her achievement and the demands placed on her. The writer commented that "thirty-six hours a week, about three times the number of hours calculated for the ordinary professional instructor, was the regular labour for years of this frail nun." The writer continued:

> The life of the modern nun that we thoughtlessly indicate by the
> familiar phrases of the silence and tranquillity of the cloister,
> retirement from the bustling scenes of solicitous material life and

its struggles, unbroken communion with the world beyond, neglect of cares of this fleshy existence seems very misleading and very inaccurate.[46]

Gertrude Lawler and Mary Maud McKay Warnock represent a small but significant minority of academy students. Their achievements were celebrated by the academy's staff and by their former classmates, who themselves were pursuing lives as wives and mothers. Through the network of the Alumnae Association, which Lawler and Warnock took an active role in shaping, the former pupils of the academy were also able to maintain and renew their ties to the school and one another. Thus, the academy and the order clearly expressed the desire to continue shaping the lives of their graduates.

V: Conclusion

This study of St. Joseph's Academy provides some evidence of the changing role of the convent-academy in the promotion of higher education and increased economic opportunities for nineteenth-century Ontario women.

In the course of the nineteenth century, the Sisters of St. Joseph and the actions of their young lady pupils gave new definition to the phrase "appropriate education for convent-educated young women." From a program of "accomplishments" with academic training, the curriculum of the academy evolved to include provincially regulated and recognized certification in teaching, business studies, music and art. These credentials gave the pupils the means to seek a lifestyle economically independent of family or religious community. A few of the pupils chose this lifestyle as a permanent one; many more pupils pursued these options before marriage and motherhood became their full time career.

At the academy, the girls and young women could develop leadership skills which were later exercised in both secular and religious spheres. Upon graduation, the academy became an intellectual and spiritual home for many of the alumnae: a network of supportive women, a place to seek comfort in times of personal crisis; a place to celebrate public achievement.

Was this convent-academy typical of other such institutions in nineteenth-century Ontario? Only more research on the history of the education of girls in schools administered by both Catholic and Anglican orders of religious women in Ontario will yield the answer to this question. Only then can we also attempt a comparative analysis of the convent experience in Ontario, Quebec and in the rest of Canada. First and foremost, one needs to explore thoroughly the relationship between the convent-academies and the dominant cultural and religious orientation of the population in order to properly assess the similarities and differences observed.

Gender And Education In Ontario: An Historical Reader

Notes

1. "St. Joseph's Convent" "Written for the *Register*" *Scrapbooks of the Sisters of St. Joseph*, vii (1897), 25 (hereafter *Scrapbooks*). Archives of the Sisters of St. Joseph, Morrow Park (hereafter ASSJ).

2. The definition of gender employed here is based on the writings of Joan Wallach Scott, who in her study *Gender and the Politics of History* (New York: Columbia University Press, 1988), defines gender as "the knowledge which establishes meaning for bodily differences" (p.2). Scott suggests "these meanings vary across culture, social groups and time since nothing about the body, including women's reproductive organs, determines unequivocally how social divisions will be shaped" (p.2).

3. David F. Allmendinger, Jr., "Mount Holyoke Students Encounter the Need for Life-Planning, 1837-1850," *History of Education Quarterly* 19 (Spring, 1979): 27-46; Ann D. Gordon, "The Young Ladies Academy of Philadelphia," in *Women of America: A History*, ed., Carol R. Berkin and Mary Beth Norton (Boston: Houghton Mifflin Co., 1979), 68-87. This work is somewhat different from the others insofar as it analyses a Philadelphia school between 1787 and 1830. See also Helen Lefkowitz Horowitz, *Alma Mater* (Boston: Beacon Press, 1984); Rosalind Rosenberg, *Beyond Separate Spheres: Intellectual Roots of Modern Feminism* (New Haven: Yale University Press, 1982); Anne Firor Scott, "The Ever-Widening Circle: The Diffusion of Feminist Values from the Troy Female Seminary 1822-72," in *Making the Invisible Woman Visible* (Urbana: University of Illinois Press, 1984), 64-89 and Barbara Miller Solomon, *In the Company of Educated Women* (New Haven: Yale University Press, 1985).

4. In her article, "'Mere Accomplishments?' Melbourne's Early Ladies' Schools Reconsidered," *History of Education Review* 13 (1984): 15-28, Marjorie Theobald defines an education in the accomplishments as one which advocated "excellence in music, modern languages and painting with an understanding that female achievement must not be used in the public sphere." Also see the following works: Alison Mackinnon, *The New Women: Adelaide's Early Women Graduates* (Adelaide: Wakefield Press, 1986); A. Mackinnon, *One Foot on The Ladder: Origins and Outcomes of Girls' Secondary Schooling in South Australia* (St. Lucia, Queensland: University of Queensland Press, 1984).

5. Robert Stamp's *The Schools of Ontario 1876-1976* (Toronto: University of Toronto Press, 1982) contains no references to convent education in the later nineteenth and early twentieth centuries. Susan Houston and

A Noble Proof of Excellence

Alison Prentice's *Schooling and Scholars in Nineteenth Century Ontario* (Toronto: University of Toronto Press, 1988) has more to say about schools for girls and young women but scarcely deals with nineteenth-century-convent education. R.D.Gidney and W.P.J.Millar's *Inventing Secondary Education: The Rise of the High School in Ontario* (Montreal: McGill-Queen's Press, 1990) a fine study of secondary education, with many references to private girls' education, discusses the convent schools in passing but does not assess their contribution nor that of the female religious orders to the development of secondary education. Even more startling observations come from an examination of the standard work on Ontario's Catholic education. Franklin Walker's two volume history of Catholic education in Ontario *Catholic Education and Politics in Upper Canada*, vol. 1 and *Catholic Education and Politics in Ontario*, vol. 2 (Toronto: Federation of Catholic Education Associations of Ontario, 1976) gives only the briefest of mention to convent schools and the religious communities who administered them.

Unlike their Ontario colleagues, historians in Quebec and in other parts of Canada have certainly found convent education a fruitful area for study. Especially significant is the work of Marta Danylewycz, *Taking the Veil: An Alternative to Marriage, Motherhood and Spinsterhood in Quebec, 1840-1920* (Toronto: McClelland and Stewart, 1986); Micheline Dumont and Nadia Fahmy-Eid eds., *Les Couventines: L'éducation des filles au Québec dans les congrégations religieuses enseignantes 1840-1960* (Montréal: Boréal, 1986); Marie-Paule Malouin, "L'Académie Marie-Rose, 1876-1911," (M.A. thesis, Université de Montréal, 1980).

6. *Constitution and Rules of the Congregation of the Sisters of St. Joseph of the Archdiocese of Toronto* (Toronto, 1881), 11 (hereafter *Constitution of 1881*).

7. *Constitution of 1881*, 11.

8. Marta Danylewycz, *Taking the Veil*. Barbara Cooper, "'That We May Attain to the End We Propose to Ourselves...' The North American Institute of the Blessed Virgin Mary, 1932-1962," (Ph.D. diss., York University, 1989).

9. Significantly, though, this small proportion of women assumed positions of leadership within the order and the enterprises it administered. This confirms Marta Danylewycz's thesis concerning religious life as an attractive "alternative" career for women.

10. *Constitution of 1881*, 11.

11. An analysis of the Academy Register reveals that 16.9% of its pupils were non-Catholic. "Register [of St. Joseph's Academy] 1856-1920," ASSJ.

12. *Prospectus*, [1870?]. Box 8. ASSJ.

13. *Prospectus*, [1866]. Box 8. ASSJ.

14. For other examples of curriculum in Ontario, see Gidney and Millar, *Inventing Secondary Education*, 15-19; for Australia see Theobald, "Mere Accomplishments," 15-28.

15. The annual fee of $16.00 was charged for a day pupil to attend the school. Harp lessons were $50.00 a year. Piano lessons cost $28.00. Annual tuition for Vocal Music, Guitar, Drawing (Pencil and Crayon Drawing, Painting in Water Colours) was $20.00 per subject. *Prospectus*, [1866] ASSJ.

16. *Prospectus*, [1866] ASSJ.

17. The alcove bedrooms and dormitories were the site of many of the games. In her memoirs of her convent education, Mary Ryan Smith wrote of the Saturday night game of reception "when Sisters were at prayer. We dressed in the bed clothes and solemnly went through a 'Convent Reception'...[we] divided into two groups—those entering and those 'making vows.' All wanted to enter because that gave them a chance to wear a train—a bedquilt—whereas the 'vowers' only carried a candle. The bishop, of course, went all out in the matter of costumes. He had his pick of the quilts." Mary Ryan Smith, "Reminiscences," *St. Joseph Lilies Centennial Issue 1851-1951*, v.xl, #2, 200.

18. See Table 2.

19. *Community Annals of the Sisters of St. Joseph of Toronto*, 26 May 1868, 13 (hereafter *Annals*).

20. *Scrapbooks*, v.3, 26 June 1873, xcx.

21. *Constitution of 1881*, 13-4.

22. *Scrapbooks*, vii (circa 1882-1903) 3.

23. *Annals*, 19 December 1878, 81.

24. *Scrapbooks*, v.vii, (1881-1903) 3.

25. It is noteworthy that the contractor was not a Catholic at the time of the building of the addition. The *Annals* record his death commenting that he died "fortified with the sacraments of the church, having been baptized a Catholic a few days previously." *Annals*, 31 May 1876, 53.

26. *Scrapbooks*, v.3, 19 March 1873, n.p.

27. Ruth Agnew, "Bonitatem et Disciplinam et Scientiam Doce Me," *St. Joseph Lilies Centennial Issue 1851-1951*, vol. xl, no. 2, 217.

28. Agnew, "Bonitatem," 217.

29. Gidney and Millar, *Inventing Secondary Education*, 293.
30. Sisters of St. Joseph of Carondelet, *Constitution of Congregation of the Sisters of St. Joseph* (St. Louis: Mullin, 1847).
31. "Introduction," *Constitution of 1881*, 9.
32. *Constitution of 1881*, 32.
33. *Constitution of 1881*, 54.
34. *Constitution of 1881*, 87-8.
35. *Constitution of 1881*, 90-1.
36. *Constitution of 1881*, 91.
37. *Constitution of 1881*, 90.
38. *Constitution of 1881*, 91.
39. Gidney and Millar, *Inventing Secondary Education*, 318.
40. Gidney and Millar, *Inventing Secondary Education*, 317.
41. *Annals*, 9 July 1889, 162.
42. "St. Joseph's Convent," *Catholic Register*, 21 June 1900, "Scrapbooks" vol. vii, 23-25. Neither this article nor others written on the academy at the turn of the century specify who examined the pupils in foreign languages. Perhaps those sisters who had studied languages, or perhaps the staff of St. Michael's College (who, the *Annals* document, were used to examine a variety of "collegiate subjects") examined the pupils.
43. *Scrapbooks*, v.3, 27 June 1871, lxii.
44. Also called the "Literary and Musical Association." *Annals*, 11 November 1891, 171-2.
45. Much more work needs to be done on the Alumnae Association to analyse its development and influence and to compare it to its sister associations in Ontario and Quebec. For certain, the Alumnae Association attracted a considerable number of women. Over 300 alumnae attended the 1912 banquet ("Alumnae Banquet" 26 October 1912. *Scrapbooks*, x.xvii, 25). Its literary journal, "The Lilies" was published until January 1954. This last edition contained no reference to the fact that this would be the final and to date no reason has been found to explain the abrupt termination of this publication. In another vein, the executive of the Alumnae Association played a leading role in the establishment of the International Federation of Catholic Convent Alumnae Associations, founded in 1919. Through the presence of executive members at Alumnae Activities, there is evidence of close links between the Alumnae Association and the Catholic Women's League, the Rosary Hall Society, the St. Elizabeth Nursing Society and The Catholic Women's Club of Toronto University.

46.   Unsigned obituary, "Modern Nun: Sister Austin," *Scrapbooks*, v. xviii, xiv.

Kale Meydelach Or Shulamith Girls: Cultural Change and Continuity Among Jewish Parents and Daughters—a Case Study of Toronto's Harbord Collegiate Institute in the 1920s[1]

Lynne Marks

For young Jewish women attending high school in Toronto in the 1920s Harbord Collegiate was the place to be. Former students who transferred from Jarvis or Parkdale later recalled how much happier they had been at Harbord. As Toronto's Jewish community moved west of University Avenue in the 1920s, Harbord became "the Jewish high school," with Jewish students making up over half of Harbord's student body.[2] These Jewish students were the children of Eastern European immigrants who came to Canada in the late nineteenth and early twentieth centuries.[3]

Why were Canadian-born Jewish students so much happier attending school with other Jews? Did this simply reflect the attitudes of their immigrant parents and the anti-Semitism of Canadian society, or was it something more complex? An exploration of patterns of interaction between Jewish and non-Jewish young women provides some answers. An equally intriguing set of questions relates to the very presence of Jewish young women at high school. For European Jews, education—while valued—had been largely a male prerogative. Had Old World attitudes towards education and proper gender roles been replaced by Canadian values among immigrant parents?

A close look at Harbord Collegiate in the 1920s shows how the history of schooling can address more than traditional questions of school attendance and upward mobility. It also demonstrates the insights to be gained within ethnic history by focussing on gender. Using Harbord's records and the recollections of former students this paper explores patterns of cultural continuity and adaptation among Jewish immigrant parents and their daughters.[4] Clearly, many immigrant parents modified traditional perceptions of proper female roles by allowing their daughters to attend an academic high school such as Harbord. Although modified, traditional attitudes were not transformed. Males remained privileged in terms of access to education.

The self-perception of the first Canadian-born generation is critically important: I study it here through an examination of student interaction and extra-curricular activities among Harbord students. One finds that these young women defined for themselves a new sense of Jewishness which allowed them to adapt to Canadian society, while continuing to identify themselves as Jews. An exploration of Jewish reactions to the subtle and not so subtle efforts at assimilation which occurred at Harbord helps to identify the limits of Canadianization for both parents and daughters.

Before looking at female Jewish students at Harbord Collegiate it is essential to understand what the lives of these young women would have been like had their parents remained in Europe. Among Eastern European Jews, men and women were expected to fulfil different roles. Women's primary role was in the home, while the ideal sphere for men was the *shul* or synagogue, where they prayed and studied Talmud. The value placed on male scholarship made it acceptable and often imperative that wives earn money to support scholarly husbands. This emphasis on religious male scholarship resulted in very different patterns of education for male and female children. Boys entered all-male religious schools at four or five, and attended them until at least age thirteen. The longer they could study, the more status they and their families acquired. In sharp contrast to this pattern, girls usually attended more informal female schools for a few years, where they learned to read Yiddish and perhaps a bit of Hebrew. They spent most of their girlhood at home, helping their mothers and learning domestic skills, until they became *kale meydelach*, girls of marriageable age. In the *shtetls*, the Jewish towns of Eastern Europe, it was assumed that "for girls study is marginal to their primary activities, while for the boys it is the major occupation and goal."[5]

For Canadian-born Jews who attended Canadian public schools, the Jewish education which had been dominant in Eastern Europe was relegated to after-school hours. However, in other respects this education remained unchanged. Most young women received a few years of Yiddish or Hebrew lessons, but their education continued to be much less extensive than that provided for their brothers. For example, Mrs. Goodman mentioned that she went to a Hebrew evening school for a few years, but that her brothers studied for much longer. She commented that "on Friday night my father would question my brothers on what they learned in Hebrew school and they would review the *sedra* (reading from the Pentateuch) of the week...I would sit in and listen, because I was interested."[6]

Jewish parents were less likely to discriminate against daughters with regard to public school education. However, an examination of Jewish attendance at Harbord suggests some continuity with Old World patterns of male privilege. Among Jewish students entering Harbord in 1923, 71 percent were male and only 29 percent were female. In comparison, slightly over half of the non-Jewish students were female. Two years later the pattern among entering students was

Kale Meydelach Or Shulamith Girls

similar, although among Jewish students the gender differential, at 59 percent male to 41 percent female, was not quite as extreme:

Table 1—PERCENTAGE OF STUDENTS ENTERING FIRST FORM AT HARBORD COLLEGIATE: BY SEX, FATHER'S SOCIO-ECONOMIC RANK, AND RELIGION, 1923 AND 1925

Socio-Economic Rank*	Jewish				Non-Jewish			
	Male	Female	Total		Male	Female	Total	
	%	%	%	N	%	%	%	N
1923								
1	48	52	100	21	70	30	100	24
2	71	29	100	42	41	59	100	64
3	73	27	100	55	50	50	100	36
4	90	10	100	20	50	50	100	20
Other	66	34	100	3	0	100	100	4
Total	71	29	100	141	48	52	100	147
1925								
1	44	56	100	41	40	60	100	30
2	57	43	100	35	51	49	100	43
3	66	34	100	82	57	43	100	42
4	75	25	100	12	57	43	100	21
Other	40	60	100	5	33	66	100	3
Total	59	41	100	175	51	49	100	139

* 1 = professional/managerial
2 = small business/clerical
3 = skilled workers
4 = semi-skilled and unskilled workers

Source: Toronto Board of Education Archives, Harbord Collegiate Records, Student Cards and Class Lists, 1923-1926.

While the minority position of Jewish female students at Harbord clearly reflects continuity with European patterns among immigrant parents, the presence of these young women also reveals certain changes in immigrant attitudes. How far had attitudes shifted? Did Jewish parents send daughters to high school with the same dreams of professional careers that they had for their sons?

It seems that, for Toronto Jewish women, vocational ambitions were to be limited. After leaving school women worked until marriage, which remained their ultimate destiny. Clerical work, which was clean and respectable but inherently temporary and dead end, was the common experience of all women interviewed for this study. Moreover, they suggested that it was the experience of almost all female Jewish students at Harbord. The 1931 census reinforces their claim. In this year almost half of Canadian-born Jewish women in the labour force did clerical work—two and a half times the proportion of all Canadian-born women in the clerical field. Conversely, the proportion of all Canadian-born Jewish women working as teachers, the most "professional" occupation attainable by most Canadian women, was only a quarter that of all Canadian-born women. A reluctance to hire Jewish teachers in the public school system no doubt played a role here, but traditional expectations of women's proper role may also have narrowed Jewish women's occupational options even more than was the case for most Canadian women of the 1920s.[7]

Since female students were destined for clerical work, why did parents send daughters to an academic high school such as Harbord? Miriam Cohen has argued that by the 1930s New York Italian young women stayed in school for longer periods because parents came to see the economic value of schooling in providing the necessary training for clerical jobs.[8] However, for young Jewish women in Toronto the Central High School of Commerce, situated only a few blocks from Harbord, most readily provided such training. Harbord did not teach clerical skills. In fact, after leaving Harbord most female students took a short course at Central Commerce or a private business school to equip them for a clerical job. What then can explain parental decisions to send daughters to Harbord?

Parents seem to have transferred the traditional Jewish respect for scholarship to the new secular Canadian education. This education was clearly not exclusively masculine. Immigrant parents could see that Canadian young women attended Harbord as readily as young men. Also, the secular education offered at this school had never been denied Jewish girls, as had the all-male religious learning of the *shtetl.* As a result, the attendance of daughters could be justified and even encouraged.

According to Mrs. Singer, "it was considered by the community to be really fine if parents could send their daughters to an academic high school."[9] High school educated daughters gave both parents and the daughter at least some of the status which in Eastern Europe was reserved for male scholars.

Kale Meydelach Or Shulamith Girls

Interviewees made it clear that a commercial high school education was considered second best. Immigrant parents who were unfamiliar with the school system sometimes sent elder daughters to Central Commerce, but when they realized that this school did not provide an academic education, they sent younger daughters to Harbord. All interviewees said that their parents were strongly committed to their attending Harbord and expected that they do well at school. As Mrs. Levy commented, "in my home you simply couldn't bring home bad reports."[10]

Interviewees did not suggest, however, that parents viewed attendance at Harbord as leading to a career. For most Canadian women the major vocational justification for attending an academic high school was a teaching career, which few Jewish women enjoyed. Rather, immigrant parents sent their daughters to Harbord because such academic education was valued in itself. Attendance at Harbord could actually limit employment opportunities. Mrs. Kuperman lamented the fact that her parents had insisted that she and her sister attend an academic high school, since this meant that they lacked the skills needed to get a well-paying clerical job.[11]

Although female education was accepted and even valued within the Jewish community, it remained less important than male education. It is clear that, when family resources were limited, sons came first. In both 1923 and 1925 Jewish students at Harbord with professional or managerial parents were marginally more likely to be female than to be male, while among students with parents in clerical, small business or blue collar occupations, the proportion of young women was much lower than that of young men (see Table 1). Among non-Jewish students, gender ratios in school attendance do not appear to be correlated to father's occupation.

Among Jewish families the economic strain of university attendance was rarely justified for a daughter. Mrs. Goodman, the only interviewee to attend university, stated that if one of her brothers had wished to attend she would not have been able to do so.

Mrs. Kay's brothers attended university, but she did not. Mrs. Kuperman commented matter-of-factly that "if there were boys in the family, naturally the boys went."[12] In some cases daughters appear to have internalized traditional beliefs in their subordinate role. Mrs. Levy's parents wanted her to attend university, but she refused to go. She would not accept her parents' financial sacrifice and recognized her younger brother's desire to attend university.[13]

It is not surprising that male needs were placed first, given the near monopoly men had over education in traditional Jewish culture. Also, in Canada high school and university were valued for the economic rewards they offered to young men. Traditional Jewish attitudes may have shifted to accept the education of daughters, but vocational goals for women remained limited. Women were not expected to have real careers: as their ultimate destiny was marriage and motherhood, their education could more readily be sacrificed. It remains clear, however, that some value was placed on female education, at least at the high school level, since attendance was usually encouraged if family resources allowed.

Faced with the opportunities offered by Harbord Collegiate, Jewish parents modified but did not transform traditional values. What about their daughters, who were actually attending Harbord? By examining the interaction of Jewish and non-Jewish young women and the extra-curricular activities of female Jewish students, one sees how the first Canadian-born generation created their own sense of themselves and of their place in Canadian society. As one former student commented with regard to extra-curricular activities, "you had to make your own way, parents did not know about these things..."[14]

A preference for Harbord among young Jewish women reflected the fact that most socializing took place within one's own ethnic group. All former students interviewed for this study recalled that all or most of their friends were Jewish. They may have been friendly with non-Jewish female students in class, but even while walking to school or eating lunch they associated primarily with Jewish young women. This sense of division may explain the very limited involvement of female Jewish students in organized extra-curricular activities at Harbord. Among young women involved in extra-curricular activities, non-Jewish women outnumbered Jewish women by more than two to one.[15] Few interviewees attended Harbord dances and those who did associated primarily with Jewish students at these affairs.

This sense of division can be explained in various ways. Certainly anti-Semitism played an important role. Interviewees suggested that, in the early 1920s, the division between Jewish and non-Jewish students was based largely on such sentiment. Mrs. Palmer, who entered Harbord in 1922, stated that when some non-Jewish girls with whom she had been friendly learned she was Jewish, their friendship cooled considerably. Students entering later in the decade argued that anti-Semitism was less of a problem. They suggest that they remained separate from non-Jewish students partly because their parents preferred this, but also because they too felt more comfortable among Jews.[16] Reasons for Jewish reluctance to become involved in general extra-curricular activities become clearer once these activities are examined. The Girls Club, the main club for female students at Harbord, was affiliated with the YWCA; its meetings ended with vesper services and the club undertook to provide Christmas dinners for poor families. It is not surprising that only one Jewish student can be found on the large executive of this club. Jewish students, particularly those from observant homes, could not have been comfortable in such an atmosphere.

Although their Jewishness meant that Jewish female students remained distinct at Harbord, it did not mean that they retained their parents' lifestyle. They had housework to do, but they did not spend all of their non-school time as apprentice housewives, or working to help support the family, as their mothers had. Since they did not wish to be involved in the Christian extra-curricular activities at Harbord, they created their own unofficial Jewish Girls Club. This club had a Hebrew name, the *Shulamith* Girls, and was largely composed of Harbord students, with a few Jewish students from other schools.[17]

The existence of this group suggests a sense of difference among young Jewish women. However, the activities of the club and other activities of Harbord students reflected Canadian patterns and interests, although with Jewish overtones, more than they did the Jewish traditions of Eastern Europe. The *Shulamith* Girls were involved in activities similar to those of the official Harbord Girls Club, which in turn reflected activities common to most Canadian women's clubs of the period. At the Jewish club there was some attempt to keep minutes; there were bridge games, teas, and outings. Fundraising events were also organized, the only difference from the Girls Club being the object of the charity: the *Shulamith* Girls raised money for a Jewish orphanage.[18] They held parties, inviting male Jewish students from Harbord. Some of the women interviewed were also involved in other Jewish groups which seem to have been modelled on Christian organizations. These groups included an all-Jewish Girl Guides, the National Council of Jewish Juniors and a social service group affiliated to Mount Sinai Hospital.[19] All of these organizations had a Jewish membership and were concerned with Jewish issues. However, they were very different from immigrant organizations such as the *landsmanshaften*, mutual benefit societies which were organized by European place of origin, and held firmly to European traditions. These organizations and most Jewish groups in Europe were exclusively male. The very existence of female organizations reflected an adaptation to Canadian society.[20]

The experience of young Jewish women at Harbord demonstrates patterns of both acculturation and continuity among the first Canadian-born generation. Young women adopted Canadian ways, while retaining a strong sense of themselves as Jews. This ethnic identification led Jewish students to prefer each other's company and to join groups with some Jewish content. As Deborah Dash Moore states in the American context: "Through the process of becoming...American, second generation Jews redefined the meaning of

Jewishness...they established the limits of their assimilation into American society."[21]

The extent to which the Jewish female students of Harbord Collegiate identified with a new sense of "ethnic Jewishness," incorporating both Jewish and Canadian elements, is illustrated in a story told by Mrs. Lerner. In the 1920s a young Jewish woman recently arrived from Germany entered Harbord. Having a pronounced accent, she was perceived by the other female Jewish students as being foreign, with the result that she was largely ignored and not included in their activities.[22] Obviously the Jewish-Canadian synthesis which bound the *Shulamith* Girls together was very different from the European Jewishness of their parents and of this young woman.

Although this new sense of ethnic Jewishness was forged by the Canadian-born, it required some acceptance by immigrant parents. As long as daughters "stayed with their own," most activities were acceptable to Socialist and Orthodox parents alike.[23] Little objection was made to club membership or attendance at movies or parties, even though such activities differed from those of young Jewish women in Eastern Europe. This reflects a further weakening of traditional gender expectations among immigrant parents. Certain women interviewed suggested that this willingness to allow daughters to accept new ways was linked to parental eagerness that they, and more particularly their children, become more Canadianized, and thus better able to succeed in Canadian society.[24]

To what extent were Jewish parents willing to accept the Canadianization of their children? Immigrant parents sent their children to Canadian schools which saw the Anglicization of the immigrant as one of their primary roles. Both parents and children seem to have accepted the process of Canadianization offered by the schools—but only as long as it did not threaten their Jewishness. Jewish students willingly accepted the guidance of Harbord's Anglo-Saxon teachers. Interviewees spoke of teachers with respect and admiration and clearly viewed them as role models. However, overt attacks on the students' Jewish identity were not passively accepted. A speech given by the principal, attacking Jewish students who did not wish to write an examination on a Jewish holiday, drew parental protest. More than half a century has not entirely dispelled the bitter resentment at the principal's tendency to change the names of Jewish students, and at his comment to those who protested that "I can't help it if your parents are too ignorant to know what to name their children."[25]

Parents and children welcomed much of what Harbord offered, both its academic opportunities and its lessons in Canadian culture. Parents saw such lessons as helping their children to advance and to integrate into the new

Kale Meydelach Or Shulamith Girls

society. However, Canadianization had its limits for both generations, limits which were far narrower than those of Canadians who saw the schools as a means of solving the "immigrant problem" through assimilation. Toronto's Jews were not easily moulded into ideal British Canadian citizens: Jewish parents and their daughters were active agents. Parents modified but did not transform traditional gender roles in response to Canadian society and the educational opportunities it offered. Daughters took up new activities and redefined their Jewishness to incorporate much of Canadian culture. Despite substantial adaptation, it is clear that neither generation was prepared to compromise with Canadian culture when it threatened their self-defined sense of Jewishness.

Notes

1. I would like to express my thanks to the women who agreed to be interviewed for this study. I would also like to thank Robert Harney for whom this paper was originally written and Jackie Buncel, Ruth Frager, Chad Gaffield, Susan Houston, Franca Iacovetta, Susan Laskin and Ian Radforth for their comments on drafts of the paper.

2. By 1914 66% of Toronto Jews lived between Spadina and Bathurst, and they continued to move west in the 1920s. See Stephen Speisman, *The Jews of Toronto* (Toronto: McClelland and Stewart, 1979).

3. In the 1920s many of these immigrants had attained a modest prosperity, which allowed them to forego their children's earnings and send them to high school. However, in this period not all Jews could afford a high school education for their children. This paper therefore does not represent the experience of all Canadian-born Jewish adolescents of the 1920s.

4. Nine former Jewish female students of Harbord were interviewed for this study. Their names have been fictionalized to retain their privacy.

5. Mark Zborowski and Elizabeth Herzog, *Life is With People: The Culture of the Shtetl* (New York: Schocken Books, 1952) 125.

6. Interview with Mrs. Goodman, July 25, 1983.

7. Canada, *Census of Canada*, 1931, volume 7, Tables 46 and 49. For a discussion of the options open to Canadian working women in the 1920s, see Veronica Strong-Boag, "The Girl of the New Day, Canadian Working Women in the 1920s," *Labour/Le Travailleur*, 1979.

8. Mirian Cohen, "Italian-American Women in New York City, 1900-1950: Work and School," in Milton Cantor and Bruce Laurie, eds., *Class, Sex and the Woman Worker* (Westport, Conn.: Greenwood Press, 1977).

9. Interview with Mrs. Singer, July 25, 1983.

10. Interview with Mrs. Levy, August 9, 1983.

11. Interview with Mrs. Kuperman, August 10, 1983.

12. Mrs. Goodman, Mrs. Kuperman and interview with Mrs. Kay, July 19, 1983.

13. Mrs. Levy.

14. Mrs. Singer.

15. Mrs. Levy, Mrs. Kay and interview with Mrs. Palmer, August 8, 1983.

17. Mrs. Kuperman and Mrs. Levy. *Shulamith* is a Hebrew woman's name. It has no particular significance in this context that I have been able to discover.

18. Mrs. Kuperman and Mrs. Palmer.

19. Mrs. Landau, Mrs. Goodman, Mrs. Singer and Mrs. Tobias.

20. See Paula J. Draper and Janice B. Karlinsky, "Abraham's Daughters: Women, Charity and Power in the Canadian Jewish Community," in Jean Burnet, ed., *Looking into my Sister's Eyes: An Exploration in Women's History* (Toronto: Multicultural History Society of Toronto, 1986) for a discussion of Jewish women's organizational involvement.

21. Deborah Dash Moore, *At Home in America: Second Generation New York Jews* (New York: Columbia University Press, 1981) 4.

22. Mrs. Lerner.

23. Orthodox young women were not permitted to be involved in such activities on the Sabbath. Mrs. Goodman.

24. Mrs. Kuperman and Mrs. Kay.

25. Mrs. Kuperman.

The Academic Life of Canadian Coeds, 1880-1900*

Jo LaPierre

On October 15, 1889, just two weeks after she registered as a first-year student in Arts at University College, Toronto, Bessie Scott recorded in her diary: "Decide to give up Math and take Moderns."[1] Mathematics had been Bessie's best subject when she wrote her junior matriculation exams in Ottawa the previous spring and she had only received third-class standing in French, German, and English.[2] She also enjoyed mathematics; the following May she again confided to her diary: "Our *last* exam in Mathematics. How strange it seems *never* to write on my beloved Math again."[3]

Why did Bessie decide so quickly to switch to modern languages? Unfortunately we shall probably never know. What we do know is that a great many of the first generation of women who attended Canadian universities made very similar decisions. At a time when Canadian universities were expanding their Arts faculties and offering new options in different fields, particularly in science, female students increasingly clustered in modern languages and music. Very few women, except for female medical students, took science or mathematics beyond the required minimum, and practically no women took Greek.

In this paper, part of a larger study on the first generation of female students at Queen's, McGill, and the affiliated colleges of the University of Toronto,[4] I want to examine the academic aspects of women's university experience: what courses were available to them and which they chose to take, how the professors and male students reacted to their presence in the classrooms, how they felt about the faculty, how hard they worked and how well they did academically. I also want to examine how, and if possible why, their experience differed from that of male students.

This is not an easy task. Women slipped so silently into the classrooms of Canadian universities that they left remarkably little record of their presence.

---

* I presented an earlier version of this paper at the CHEA Conference in London, Ontario, in October 1988. I would like to thank Paul Axelrod, Chad Gaffield, Ruth Pierson, Alison Prentice, Donna Ronish and Kit Szanto for their comments and suggestions on how to improve it. I would also like to thank OISE and the SSHRCC for their financial support, which permitted me to carry out the research involved.

Gender And Education In Ontario: An Historical Reader

Tolerated rather than welcomed within these very patriarchal institutions, they were careful not to draw any undue attention to themselves. Any complaints or criticism which they dared to express were very muted. Conscious that they were embarking on a potentially dangerous and controversial undertaking, they knew that their behaviour would be carefully scrutinized, particularly by those who had opposed their admission in the first place. As a result they seem to have made themselves almost invisible.

We can piece together the outlines of their academic life from calendars and students records but it is much harder to assess how they were perceived by other groups within the universities or how they themselves felt about the whole adventure. Official bodies within Canadian universities rarely debated "the woman question" at any length. Once the decision to admit women was reached, any other decisions about how to integrate female students were usually deferred to a later meeting or delegated to another body which rarely got around to reporting back on the question.[5] Consequently most decisions affecting women students were reached on a very temporary and *ad hoc* basis, after minimal debate. Occasional comments by or about the women students appeared in student journals or local newspapers and these provide some insights, as do alumnae memoirs, although these, usually written much later, often appear quite romanticized and must be used with considerable caution. It is only from the very rare contemporary sources, like Bessie Scott's diary, that we can begin to reconstruct the day-to-day experience of these early students.[6]

It has become a cliche to say that students have been left out of most of the history of higher education in Canada, but it is still true, and it is particularly true of women students. Almost none of the histories of Canadian universities have paid much attention to their students.[7] However, this situation is finally beginning to change and several recent articles and the collection of essays entitled *Youth, University, and Canadian Society* give evidence of a growing interest in the largely undiscovered field of student life, including that of women students.[8]

Another problem has been the institutional nature of nearly all the work on Canadian higher education. With the exception of Robin Harris's *History of Higher Education in Canada,* there are no general works which look at more than one institution.[9] There are a few unpublished Ph.D. theses on the development of English-speaking universities in Canada in the nineteenth century;[10] however, none of these works raises the question of gender differences at Canadian universities.[11]

Until very recently the focus of most of the literature on women and higher education has been on the debate over the admission of women to universities, not on their experience once they got there.[12] This lack is more serious in Canada than in several other countries. In England, in addition to some excellent works on the struggles of Emily Davies and others to gain entry for women to the universities of London, Oxford, and Cambridge, there are several fascinating new studies on the experience of female university students.[13] The literature on women university students in the United States is less rich than for England, but here too research has progressed well beyond the traditional institutional history.[14] Thomas Woody's sixty-year-old study of women's education is still useful and there are several newer works which focus on the experience of female university students.[15] There has also been some interesting work on early university women in Australia.[16]

The best works on gender differentiation, both generally and, in several cases, in specific educational institutions, have originated in England, although there are also several recent works which look at girls' secondary school experience in Australia.[17] In Canada, there is still remarkably little published material on secondary education for girls.[18] Nor has there been much attention given to gender differentiation at the university level, at least for this first generation of women.[19]

The original debate in England over the admission of women to university focussed on whether they were intellectually equal to men and capable of following the same curriculum.[20] Emily Davies was adamant that female students had to take exactly the same courses as male students, including both mathematics and Greek, even when it brought her into conflict with those demanding a reform of the traditional classical curriculum at Cambridge and Oxford.[21] M. Carey Thomas was equally insistent about the curriculum at Bryn Mawr College.[22] In Canada, although the idea that girls and boys had different educational needs had emerged very clearly in the debate over girls' position within the grammar schools of Ontario,[23] there was almost no discussion of what courses women would take once they were admitted to university.[24] The grammar school debate did serve to focus public attention on the needs of Canadian girls for access to more (or higher) education, and Egerton Ryerson's efforts to keep girls out of the grammar schools ultimately failed. By 1880, when women first entered the Canadian universities discussed here, the debate over women's comparable intellectual abilities was pretty well over, although whenever female students actually surpassed males for academic awards it continued to generate comment for years to come.[25]

The curriculum available to the newly admitted women students at Canadian universities, the courses they chose to take, and how well they did in them are the most easily documented aspects of their academic life. University calendars show the slow evolution of Canada's small denominational colleges, primarily dedicated to training candidates for the clergy, into multi-faculty institutions serving a far more varied population. Class and prize lists show which courses women chose to take and where they tended to excel. At the beginning of the 1880s, all the universities considered here still offered a traditional, highly structured, classical Arts program, but they were becoming aware that as their student body became more diverse, there was a growing demand for a more varied and practical curriculum.[26] There was remarkably little theoretical debate about the shift away from classics in Canada, which is surprising since nearly all the professors involved, who had themselves been trained in either England or Scotland, must have been aware that the traditional, classical curriculum was coming under attack in Britain.[27] Nor was there ever any discussion about making any changes in the Arts curriculum in order to accommodate women students.

Since women had absolutely no power in any of the decision-making bodies of Canada's universities, they played no role in the discussions of which new courses should be offered, but as curricular changes were introduced, particularly an increasing number of modern language courses, and more courses in English literature,[28] women students were quick to take advantage of them. They were much less inclined to pursue the increasing range of science and social science courses which were also being added to the Arts curriculum. In addition to this expansion in the number of courses offered, the other major change in the Canadian Arts curriculum in the closing decades of the nineteenth century was the development of the Honours B.A. First introduced at the University of Toronto,[29] it was quickly copied by Queen's, always very sensitive to a possible loss of students to the provincial university. Once an Honours B.A. became the required prerequisite for a specialist teacher's certificate,[30] women students, for whom high school teaching was often the most attractive career option available, quickly switched to Honours programs.

Frederick Rudolph has referred to the late nineteenth century as a period of "disarray" in the American university curriculum. This was equally true in Canada, although here there were no fiery debates like those which followed Charles William Eliot's introduction of a free choice of options at Harvard in 1869.[31] In Canada, for purely economic reasons, no dramatic overhaul of the curriculum was possible. Canadian universities could not afford enough faculty to offer the degree of specialization available in the older, larger, and wealthier American institutions; yet they shared with Eliot a recognition that they had to offer their increasingly diverse student bodies a less structured and limited curriculum.

All these changes were just beginning when Annie Fowler became the first woman to register as a full-time student in the Faculty of Arts at Queen's

The Academic Life of Canadian Coeds

University on October 24, 1880. Annie was soon joined by Laura Allen, the daughter of a Kingston shoemaker, and Jennie Greaves, whose father was dead. Both Laura and Jennie had attended the Kingston Collegiate Institute. Laura was twenty-one, Jennie and Annie were seventeen. Annie had graduated from high school in Fredericton, New Brunswick, and moved to Kingston when her father accepted the position of Lecturer in Natural Science at Queen's.[32]

The arrival of women was just one of a number of changes at Queen's that year. In the spring of 1880 the Faculty of Arts at Queen's consisted of five professors, with another three positions listed as vacant. James Fowler filled the vacancy in natural science, and Professor George Ferguson, who already taught history and English, undertook to teach French and German as well until a lecturer in modern languages was appointed.[33] A new Arts Building was officially opened on October 16, and there were high hopes that this would help attract new students to the University, which had conferred only six B.A. degrees the previous spring. However, no official body within the university ever wrote one word about including women among these new students and no changes were made in the Arts curriculum to accommodate them.[34]

The Queen's Arts program presented the student with minimal curricular decisions. It offered a four-year B.A., which required the student to complete thirteen of the nineteen courses offered within the faculty. All students had to take junior and senior Latin and junior mathematics. Greek could be avoided by taking both French and German in its place; junior philosophy, English literature, and one of either physics or chemistry were also required.[35] Students took three or four courses per year, writing monthly exams in each subject and final exams in April. Supplemental exams could be written in September. Students who had not written the University's own matriculation exams for entrance were judged to have matriculated successfully in a subject once they had passed their monthly exams during the fall term.[36] In order to proceed to the final exam a student had to have achieved at least 25% on the monthly exams and scholarships and prizes were awarded only to students who had obtained at least 50%.[37] Students had to attend four-fifths of all classes in order to be permitted to write the final examinations. Classes were offered on a standard grid; nearly all classes met five times a week for a one-hour period, between nine and four o'clock, with a two-hour break for lunch from twelve to two. The University recommended a set order in which the students should take their courses, although exceptions were made and gradually this practice was abandoned, creating a lot of problems with the timetable. The average student's workload was therefore either fifteen or twenty hours of lectures a week, plus a fairly demanding schedule of tests and examinations.

Gender And Education In Ontario: An Historical Reader

In addition to this very structured course load, students were surrounded with regulations. In order to be admitted they had to produce a character certificate from their minister "or some respectable person" and sign a declaration promising "due respect and obedience" to the University authorities, diligent attention to their studies, and "courteous and peaceable" behaviour towards their fellow students. There was a hierarchy of punishments for insubordination, immoral conduct, gross neglect of study, and other offences.[38] The library regulations were also severe. A one-dollar deposit had to be made for each book borrowed, to a maximum of three books, which had to be returned within seven days or a fine of three cents a day would be charged up to the price of the book. No student had access to the shelves and the library was open only three hours a day during the week and one hour on Saturdays.[39] Women students had the same access as the men but always studied in their own reading room.

Annie Fowler and Jennie Greaves proceeded quite smoothly through their courses; Laura Allen apparently dropped out almost immediately. Annie won a prize for junior French in the spring of 1881 and another for senior French in 1882.[40] French was also Jennie's best subject,[41] but having completed ten of the thirteen courses required for a degree she left the University after three years, quite possibly for economic reasons since her mother was a widow.[42]

In 1881 three more women registered in Arts; one of them was Eliza Fitzgerald, a grocer's daughter who had attended the St. Catharines Collegiate Institute. Eliza was twenty-two by the time she reached Queen's. She had already passed the matriculation exams of University College, Toronto, in 1879, but the Principal, Daniel Wilson, was so adamant that University College would not become co-educational that he refused to admit women to lectures, so Eliza came to Queen's. Unlike most of the early women students, she pursued her study of both Greek and Latin, and graduated, along with Annie Fowler, in April 1884, winning the Gold Medal for classics.[43] The Chancellor of Queen's, Sir Sanford Fleming, was so delighted at the prospect of "capping" a woman that he ordered a special pin from Tiffany's in New York "consisting of a silver mortar-board with tassel and a spray of silver bay leaves...with the words 'Laureated, 1884' enamelled on the mortar board." Principal Grant, who was to present the award, realized that there would actually be two women receiving their B.A. degrees and ordered a second pin from Tiffany's.[44]

After 1884, Queen's women students were treated less effusively. They continued to graduate in small numbers, often excelling in modern language courses, but also often dropping out without completing their degrees. They lived a life apart from the male students, sitting separately at the front of the classrooms, studying in their own reading room. Publicly they voiced few

The Academic Life of Canadian Coeds

complaints or comments about their professors or courses, although John Watson[45] and Principal Grant, who had both supported their admission to Queen's, were their favourites. While the male students often expressed their views on all aspects of the University in the *Queen's College Journal,* the women students only initiated a regular column called "The Ladies' Corner" in the *Journal* in 1889 when they first used it to plead for a larger reading room.[46]

In contrast to Queen's, women entered the Arts faculties in the fall of 1884 at both McGill and University College, Toronto, in a blaze of controversy and publicity. However, the outcome for the women students involved was not very different, except that at McGill they took some of their lectures in separate classes. The big issue for both Sir William Dawson at McGill, and his close friend, Sir Daniel Wilson at University College, was not what women should learn but whether they should do it in a co-educational setting as was being done at Queen's, or in what they called a "ladies' college." Dawson won his fight for separate education, at least in part; Wilson lost his. At Queen's the question really never came up, at least not in the Faculty of Arts.[47]

The story of women's entrance to McGill, the unexpected gift of Donald Smith (later Lord Strathcona), and the public debate over the creation of what finally became Royal Victoria College has already been told in detail.[48] Much less has been written about the academic life of the women who pursued their Arts degrees at McGill between 1884 and 1899, when RVC finally opened. Like Queen's, in 1884 McGill offered a four-year B.A. with a heavy emphasis on the classics and mathematics and a limited number of options.[49] The female students at McGill, called somewhat coyly the Donaldas in honour of their benefactor, Donald Smith, had to matriculate in Latin, Greek (or German), mathematics, and English. As at Queen's, students who had not completed the matriculation requirements could enter as partial students. If they took at least three subjects "of the ordinary course of study," they could then "make good their standing as Undergraduates at the Christmas or Sessional Examinations." There were also occasional students, described as "Ladies desirous of taking one or two Courses of Lectures," who did not intend to write the examinations.[50] All the female students were taught separately, usually between twelve and five o'clock, since the professors were busy teaching duplicate courses to the male students in the mornings.

For their first two years the female students at McGill followed a set curriculum of Latin, mathematics, chemistry, and English, and, preferably, Greek, plus one modern language (either French or German). However, students could substitute German for Greek, and take French as their modern language. In their second year they took Latin, mathematics, Greek (or German), logic, French, botany, history, and English. Each of these years involved fourteen to sixteen hours of lectures. In their third and fourth years the female students had greater flexibility: mathematics and either Greek or Latin were still required as part of the "ordinary" course, plus three of a long list of "additional" courses including physics, zoology, English, logic, astronomy, philosophy, French, and German. These women's courses were also concentrated late in the day, while the men were taught between nine and one o'clock. Women could also take Honour courses, which were "mixed" (with male students), in classics, mathematical physics, mental and moral philosophy, English language and literature, history, geology, and "other Natural Sciences."[51]

The disciplinary regulations for students at McGill were also similar to those at Queen's. The women students lived very separate lives, closely chaperoned and protected from all possible dangers by the "aid and oversight of a competent Lady Superintendent."[52] Originally women were instructed not to wear "academic dress"; then, when they protested this decision, the regulation was changed to require them to do so.[53] Otherwise the regulations were "the same as for men," which meant strict rules concerning attendance at class (professors often locked the classroom door after calling the roll), and orderly conduct. Although the McGill library was open from nine to four every day, its regulations were also severe: a deposit of five dollars permitted a student to take out up to three books for two weeks with fines of five cents a day for lateness. An additional deposit of four dollars permitted a student to take out another two books but any student accumulating a fine of over one dollar could be "debarred from the library." No students had access to the library shelves or "alcoves" and no conversation was permitted in the library.[54]

Whereas at Queen's the women students were charged a fee for use of the gymnasium, but denied access to it,[55] at McGill the female students' need for physical education was recognized fairly quickly. Although there were complaints that the women were assigned the less desirable hours in the gym, a physical education "instructress" was appointed in December 1888 to teach optional courses in gymnastics.[56] However, the lack of equal athletic facilities for women continued well into the twentieth century until the RVC gym and pool were finally built.[57] There were other discriminatory pinpricks along the way: one was the lengthy debate over the names of the degrees that women would be granted. The Senate considered calling the women's degrees *baccalaurea, magistra,* and *doctrix* instead of *baccalaureus, magister,* and *doctor,* but this idea was ultimately dropped.[58] There was also a lot of concern about the strain of competition for women, which led to a discussion of whether or not the women's marks should be ranked with the men's. Although the decision was made to rank the women separately it was never carried out and the

The Academic Life of Canadian Coeds

practice of integrated ranking became institutionalized. The women students wrote the same exams as the male students, but wrote them in different rooms.[59]

In spite of their marginalized role within the university, McGill's early women graduates remembered their student days very fondly. Georgina Hunter, one of the first eight women to graduate in 1888, wrote about the "liberality" of the University towards women, but then went on to recall the leaking roof in the women's classroom and the "occasional invasion of rats."[60] Elizabeth Hammond, who graduated in 1890, also wrote of how "the snow silted in overhead through the skylight."[61] Octavia Grace Ritchie, another member of the class of 1888, who went on to study medicine in the face of much opposition, was more critical of McGill and its belief that "there were still subtle distinctions to be maintained between the men and women students." She also expressed her gratitude to John Clark Murray, the Professor of Philosophy, who was a steady defender of co-education and the rights of the women students.[62] Carrie Derick, another graduate in 1890, who was to become McGill's first woman faculty member, was also critical of the University and recalled the double standard imposed on the female students and "the weight of formulated womanhood" which they had to bear.[63]

Grace Ritchie and several other members of the first class of women to graduate from McGill in 1888 were excellent students. Most of them had gone through the High School for Girls together. In fact Georgina Hunter had taught many of them there before she joined her former students in McGill's first class of women. Though the High School for Girls supposedly duplicated the Boys' High School, the girls' curriculum did not include Greek, and German was offered only as an option, so that to prepare themselves for the McGill entrance exams many of the women had to arrange for private tutoring in order to be able to present the required number of subjects. Rosalie McLea, a particularly brilliant student, managed to cover the three-year course in Greek in a single year with the help of a private tutor. In the examinations for Associate in Arts in the spring of 1884, Rosalie was at the top of the list for the province while Grace Ritchie stood second.[64] Rosalie went on to win prizes in Greek, Latin, French, and chemistry at McGill and Ritchie did equally well in mathematics, English, and German.[65] Although Rosalie dropped out of McGill after two years, most of the original eight graduated successfully and several went on to do graduate work after leaving McGill; Donalda McFee went to Cornell and later to Leipzig where she earned a Ph.D. in 1895, and Grace Ritchie became a doctor.[66]

The McGill Arts curriculum developed slowly over the next fifteen years, but as the staff expanded from its 1884 level of eight professors the women's separate classes could be spread more evenly through the day. By 1896, botany, logic, physics, and modern history were being offered to the women students along with the core subjects of Latin, Greek, French, German, and mathematics.[67] Principal William Peterson, who succeeded Dawson, was determined to improve and expand McGill's Arts program, hoping to create new chairs in zoology, philosophy, economics, political science, education, geography, art, music, and additional modern languages. These ambitions often brought him into conflict with Donald Smith (by then Lord Strathcona), since the latter was determined to maintain separate classes for women and his original aim had been to offer "identical education for both sexes." Peterson felt the duplication of work this involved for his staff was becoming an increasing burden.[68] When Royal Victoria College finally opened in the fall of 1899, a Music Department for the women students was added, and Resident Tutors and Lecturers took over some of the teaching of the women students, as did the Lady Principal, later retitled the Warden. Yet the College staff were rarely recognized as full members of the McGill faculty, and more and more of the courses, particularly those in science, were only offered on a "mixed" basis.[69]

Daniel Wilson, the Principal of University College, Toronto, thought that McGill's solution to the problem of admitting women to the university was ideal. Wilson disliked the idea of co-education even more strongly than Dawson and refused even to consider allowing women students to attend classes until he was ordered to do so by the provincial government.[70] While trying to avert this growing threat, Wilson approved the setting up of a scheme of Local Examinations for Women, to permit women throughout the province to write the junior and senior matriculation examinations in their own communities. The scheme involved the formation of local committees prepared to guarantee at least six candidates, to pay the University for all costs involved, to provide overnight lodgings for any candidates coming a considerable distance, and to arrange for at least two lady members of the local committee to assist in supervising the exams. There were two levels of examinations, equivalent to the University's junior and senior matriculation examinations. The passing grade was to be not less than 25% on each paper, and 50% on the total number of marks.[71]

The scheme was an instant success: twenty-four candidates passed in 1878, twelve of them with first- or second-class honours. One of these was Eliza Fitzgerald, who would turn up at Queen's three years later. The following year another twenty-four candidates passed, eight with first- or second-class honours, and two of the previous year's candidates went on to pass the second examination.[72] However, several other members of the first group proceeded

The Academic Life of Canadian Coeds

to write the regular matriculation examinations, including Eliza Fitzgerald and Henrietta Charles from the St. Catharines Collegiate Institute, and Alice Cummings from the Hamilton Collegiate Institute, who won one of the Junior Matriculation Scholarships that year.[73]

Actually a small number of women had begun writing the matriculation exams as far back as the spring of 1877, just when the scheme of Local Examinations was being discussed in the University Senate. In the spring of 1880 Henrietta Charles won a double first in modern languages and general proficiency in the first year Arts examinations.[74] Obviously Wilson's scheme had not solved the problem of women attempting to get in to the University, and the numbers went on increasing: in 1877, two women passed the regular matric exams; in 1878, three; in 1879, eighteen; in 1880, nine; in 1881, twenty-one; in 1882, eighteen; in 1883, thirteen; in 1884, fifteen.[75] Meanwhile a growing number of other women were still writing the Local Examinations for Women, and the University Senate had been forced to allow women winning scholarships to be granted their awards, even though they were still being refused the right to attend lectures.[76] Henrietta Charles was one of several women who wrote Principal Wilson requesting admission to classes, to no avail; as a result she did not receive her B.A. until 1888.[77] In all, of the ninety-nine women who had passed their matriculation examinations before they were granted admission to classes at University College in the fall of 1884, only nineteen ever completed their degrees.[78]

The B.A. curriculum to which women finally gained access at Toronto was not unlike that offered by Queen's and McGill. It was a four-year program after junior matriculation, involving four years of Latin, English, and one modern language, plus at least one course in mathematics, physics, chemistry, history, or philosophy in the first two years. In the third year students had the choice of two of history, political science, philosophy, and physics, and in the fourth year, two of political science, philosophy, mathematics, and physics.[79] This added up to between fifteen and twenty hours of lectures each week, with the year being divided into three terms stretching from early October until late May.[80] Students taking the Honours B.A. also had certain core requirements in Latin, English, mathematics, and a modern language, but could concentrate more heavily in their Honour subject, particularly in the third and fourth years. There were no special accommodations made for women students. Many of them entered the expanding field of modern languages, which soon included Italian and Spanish as well as French and German, or the growing Honours program in English language and literature.[81] As Robin Harris has pointed out, the most prestigious Arts subject in the 1890s was philosophy, which included economics, political science, and psychology. It was usually taught in fourth year

313

and its teachers were often the stars among the faculty: Watson at Queen's, Murray at McGill, and George Paxton Young at Toronto.[82]

The period at which women entered Canada's major universities was one of dramatic expansion and change, particularly at Toronto. Classics were in decline in spite of the efforts of the energetic new classics professor, Maurice Hutton. This gave modern languages a new appeal and prestige. At the same time, English history was splitting away from general courses called English, and English literature was replacing rhetoric as a field of specialization.[83] Although many were concerned about the reduced emphasis on the classics, Toronto proceeded with the development of two distinct Arts courses, Pass and Honours, and other Canadian universities followed this lead. The introduction of a dual level of entrance, either by pass (junior) matriculation, or by remaining an additional year in high school and writing the honour (senior) matriculation, reinforced this division; it also saved the students money. Since this development coincided with the introduction of the specialist certificate for teachers, it had an important impact on women students, who often saw high school teaching as an appealing career option.[84]

Bessie Scott, whose diary I quoted at the beginning of this paper, was typical of the early women students in many respects. She was never a particularly strong student; in fact at the end of her first year at University College, where she was taking the Honours course in modern languages, she was classed as "below the line" in French, although she escaped having to write a supplementary exam in the fall.[85] By the end of her second year she was doing quite a bit better, and got a first class in English, Spanish, and Italian. For reasons that are never explained, she did not return for her third and fourth years, and never graduated. This decision seems to have been reached over the Christmas break in 1890, and during that spring her mother apparently helped her to look for a teaching job for the following fall, successfully as it turned out. She was hired by Ottawa Collegiate Institute (later Lisgar Collegiate) to teach English, at a salary of $650, and although sad about not rejoining her friends at Varsity, she was delighted about getting the job and left Toronto hoping to return in 1892. Many of her friends also dropped out, which makes her typical in another respect; all the early female classes had very high dropout rates.

The delightful aspect of Bessie diary is her outspoken frankness about all aspects of her university experience, recorded each day in the diary she kept for her two years at U.C. After her arrival in October 1889, we see her making new friends, searching for somewhere to live, reacting, both favourably and unfavourably, to her professors, and throughout the two years working incredibly hard. She liked Professor Squair, the French professor, but described Professor Hutton as "perfectly abominable." Professor Chapman, who taught geology, was seen as "very funny, a dear old man—denies that he objects to ladies," and later "poor Prof. Chapman overcome at sight of 8 girls." Her botany lectures are "fearfully dry," and history, with Principal Wilson, is "not much better, dry lists of colonies." Early in February of her first year she was in the library, consulting "last year's exam papers." A few days later she reported on the terrible fire at University College, and the readjustment of classrooms it necessitated. In mid-April, lectures stopped, and for the next two weeks Bessie put in thirteen- to fourteen-hour days studying for the nineteen two-and-a-half hour exams she had to write between May 2 and May 19.

The following October, Bessie returned. That year she took French, German, Italian, Spanish, English, Latin, history, logic, and psychology. She seemed more confident about her work, and skipped a lot of lectures, particularly in German. She still found Professor Hutton "horrid," reporting to her diary: "Livy! I don't believe I will go any more." In spite of her heavy workload she agreed to replace a friend teaching at the high school in Smithville for two weeks. After her first day of teaching she reported:

Fine clear morning—oh! what mingled feelings I had on setting out to teach in a High School—nice school and fine order but as I had no time to prepare work found it rather hard to put in time, prepared for tomorrow until 9 and then begin Varsity work until 11.

By Christmas she was discussing the possibility of teaching in a Model school in Ottawa, but returned to put in another busy term of studying, often working until 1:30 in the morning and getting up at 5:00 a.m. That year she wrote twenty-two final exams. On May 23, 1891, Bessie wrote:

Last day of exams! I am glad and yet oh! *so* sorry—last day with the girls of '93! how many have dropped already who started with us...still more next year—Bertha and I...Bid goodbye to all the girls...dear, dear, old '93...if only, but no I *must* not think of coming back.[86]

Bessie never did "come back." Her diary stops that spring and as with so many of her fellow students we know only the outlines of her later life.[87]

Bessie left the University of Toronto just before it began to change dramatically in both size and structure. The University Federation Act of 1887 set up the structure it was to function under for almost a century and serious negotiations for federation with both Victoria University at Cobourg and Queen's at Kingston quickly followed. Queen's formally rejected the possibility of federation soon after but negotiations with Victoria continued until finally, in 1892, Victoria moved to Toronto, maintaining its own Arts and Theology faculties. Victoria, which had a much longer tradition of women's education than University College, continued to offer its women Arts students a curriculum integrated with that of the University, which took over responsibility for the technicalities of registration and recording grades.[88]

Another university offering higher education to women in Toronto at this time was Trinity, which also considered federation with the University of Toronto in the 1880s, but rejected the idea then, only to reverse that decision later and become another federated College, offering Arts and Theology, in 1902. Like University College, Trinity first permitted women to write the Arts examinations and receive certificates, but not to attend lectures or be awarded degrees. The first "Course of Study for Women" appeared in the 1884 calendar, following a decision reached in June 1883.[89] This action was apparently in response to a request from the Principal of the Bishop Strachan School.[90] Trinity quickly made some adjustments to its matriculation requirements, permitting women to take one of Greek, German, or Italian, and to substitute elementary harmony for algebra. These same exceptions were carried forward into the Arts curriculum: harmony could be taken instead of mathematics, and any two of Greek, French, German, and Italian were required. In the final year geology and mineralogy could be substituted for Greek.[91] Women were also admitted to take the examinations in the Music faculty, as many quickly did. Emma Mellish had already registered in Music in 1883, to be joined the following year by Helen Gregory and Lillian Howland.[92]

In the face of further pressure, the Trinity authorities, who shared many of Daniel Wilson's fears about the dangers of co-education, agreed to set up St. Hilda's College. As at McGill, the women had separate classes, with the Trinity faculty repeating their lectures, except at the Honours level where the female students joined the men. This system lasted from 1888 until 1894, when, largely because of a financial crisis at Trinity due to the bursar having defrauded the University of a considerable portion of its endowment, stringent financial measures were instituted, including the abolition of separate classes for women. From 1894 on, St. Hilda's College functioned primarily as a women's residence.[93]

St. Hilda's students thus enjoyed residential facilities, something the women at Queen's, University College, McGill, and Victoria lacked.[94] The tiny College continued to operate very much in the shadow of Trinity, and its small band of women students remained as modestly silent as those elsewhere, if not more so.[95] While St. Hilda's still offered some of its own courses, two of its early graduates joined the staff: Emma Mellish, who graduated in Music, taught harmony, and Clara Martin, later Canada's first woman lawyer, taught mathematics.[96] The majority of Trinity's women students registered in the Faculty of Music, nearly 150 in the period covered in this paper, of whom only twenty-seven actually graduated, although several others went on to be employed as music teachers.[97]

By the turn of the century each of the institutions discussed here had integrated a small minority of women into their Arts faculties. This had not been an entirely painless process for any of the participants. Male faculty members nearly all displayed great uneasiness when confronted with female students. Some professors responded with courtly formality, others with obvious hostility. Male students were equally equivocal in their reactions. The female students recognized the inherent dangers in their position and did nothing to challenge their very marginalized role within the universities. Instead, they developed strategies to permit them to follow what they, and society, perceived as an appropriately "feminine" route to the B.A. degree. In doing so they were extremely careful not to challenge any of the accepted norms of feminine behaviour, although by focussing their efforts on subjects like music and modern languages, already acknowledged to be appropriate female "accomplishments," they also curtailed their future career options. Bessie Scott, who so enjoyed her brief time as a student and went on to put her training to profitable use as a teacher, expressed some of the pressures she and her fellow students felt in an unpublished essay entitled "College Women," written some time before the turn of the century:

> All honour to those brave women who were willing to bear that sobriquet and to have a slur cast upon their very womanhood. We who humbly follow in their footsteps are able to do so with a very slight share of adverse criticism though we are not entirely free from this yet.[98]

Gender And Education In Ontario: An Historical Reader

Notes

1. Bessie Mabel Scott Lewis, Diary, 1889-90, University of Toronto Archives [hereafter Scott Diary and UTA] 15 Oct. 1889.
2. *University of Toronto, Class and Prize List, 1890*, UTA, "Junior Matriculation, July 1889," 10.
3. Scott Diary, 10 May 1890.
4. For the purpose of this study these include University College, Victoria College (which federated with the University of Toronto in 1892) and Trinity College, although it did not formally join the federation until 1902. It does not include St. Michael's College since the college did not accept women during the time covered in this study.
5. This practice occurs too often to cite specific examples here; it will be documented for important incidents elsewhere in this study.
6. To date I have found only five diaries among approximately 1,000 women who attended the universities I am looking at; Bessie Scott's is one of the most detailed. Personal diaries must, of course, be used with caution and weighed against other more concrete forms of evidence before any generalizations can be made.
7. This is not true of John Reid's *Mount Allison University: A History to 1963. Volume I: 1843-1914* (Toronto: University of Toronto Press, 1984) and his article, "The Education of Women at Mount Allison, 1854-1914," *Acadiensis* 12 (Spring 1983).
8. One of the first of these to appear was Lynne Marks and Chad Gaffield, "Women at Queen's University, 1895-1905: A 'Little Sphere' All Their Own?" *Ontario History* 78 (Dec. 1986), which raised many of the questions I am interested in exploring, although unfortunately the other universities I am looking at do not have as complete records as Queen's does. See also Keith Walden, "Respectable Hooligans: Male Toronto College Students Celebrate Hallowe'en," *Canadian Historical Review* 67 (Mar. 1987); Nicole Neatby, "Preparing for the Working World: Women at Queen's During the 1920s," *Historical Studies in Education* 1 (Spring 1989); and Paul Axelrod and John G. Reid, eds., *Youth, University and Canadian Society: Essays on the Social History of Higher Education* (Montreal: McGill-Queen's University Press, 1989).
9. Robin S. Harris, *A History of Higher Education in Canada, 1663-1960* (Toronto: University of Toronto Press, 1976). Harris does provide a useful comparison of the curricular developments at Canada's major universities, stressing particularly the development of the Honours

318

course in Arts, but he pays little attention to women students and makes no reference to any gender differences within the Arts curriculum.

10. David Ross Keane, "Rediscovering Ontario University Students of the Mid-Nineteenth Century," (Ph.D. diss., University of Toronto, 1981); Janet C. Scarfe, "Letters and Affection: The Recruitment and Responsibilities of Academics in English-Speaking Universities in British North America in the Mid-Nineteenth Century," (Ph.D. diss., University of Toronto, 1982); Marni de Pencier, "Ideas of English-Speaking Universities in Canada to 1920," (Ph.D. diss., University of Toronto, 1977); Patricia Jane Jasen, "The English Canadian Liberal Arts Curriculum: An Intellectual History," (Ph.D. diss., University of Manitoba, 1987).

11. In a review essay of Margaret Gillett's *We Walked Very Warily: A History of Women at McGill* (Montreal: Eden Press, 1981) Nancy Sheehan discusses the problem of trying to write women into the history of higher education in Canada while we are still lacking any general analysis of the role of Canadian universities: see, "Collegiate Women in Canada," *History of Education Quarterly* 24 (Spring 1984).

12. The most complete survey on the admission of women to Canadian universities is Donna Yavorsky Ronish, "Sweet Girl Graduates: The Admission of Women to English-Speaking Universities in Canada in the Nineteenth Century," (Ph.D. diss., Université de Montréal, 1985); see also Nancy Ramsay Thompson, "The Controversy Over the Admission of Women to University College, University of Toronto," (M.A., University of Toronto, 1974); and Paula J.S. LaPierre, "Separate or Mixed: The Debate Over Co-education at McGill University," (M.A., McGill University, 1983).

13. There is a wealth of materials on this subject. Some of the latest and best are chap. 4 of Martha Vicinus, *Independent Women: Work and Community for Single Women, 1850-1920* (Chicago: University of Chicago Press, 1985); and "One Life to Stand Beside Me: Emotional Conflicts in First-Generation College Women in England," *Feminist Studies* 8 (Fall 1982); Perry Williams, "Pioneer Women Students at Cambridge, 1869-81," in Felicity Hunt, ed., *Lessons for Life: The Schooling of Girls and Women, 1850-1950* (Oxford: Basil Blackwell, 1987); and chaps. 1 and 2 of Susan J. Leonardi, *Dangerous by Degrees: Women at Oxford and the Somerville College Novelists* (New Brunswick, N.J.: Rutgers University Press, 1989). All of these works make extensive use of published and unpublished diaries and autobiographies by early women students. Unfortunately Canadian sources of this nature are much rarer.

14. David Allmendinger, *Paupers and Scholars: The Transformation of Student Life in Nineteenth Century New England* (New York: St. Martin's Press, 1975); and Helen Lefkowitz Horowitz, *Campus Life: Undergraduate Cultures from the End of the Eighteenth Century to the Present* (New York: Knopf, 1987) are two good examples.

15. Thomas Woody, *A History of Women's Education in the United States,* 2 Vols. (New York: Science Press, 1929); and Maxine Schwartz Seller, "A History of Women's Education in the United States: Thomas Woody's Classic—Sixty Years Later," *History of Education Quarterly* 29 (Spring 1989). The best modern overview is Barbara Miller Solomon, *In the Company of Educated Women: A History of Women and Higher Education in America* (New Haven: Yale University Press, 1985); see also Helen Lefkowitz Horowitz, *Alma Mater: Design and Experience in the Women's Colleges from Their Nineteenth-Century Beginnings to the 1930s* (New York: Knopf, 1984).

16. Ailsa Zainu'ddin, "The Admission of Women to the University of Melbourne, 1869-1903," *Melbourne Studies in Education* (1973); Alison Mackinnon, *The New Women: Adelaide's Early Women Graduates* (Netley, S.A.: Wakefield Press, 1986).

17. Felicity Hunt, "Divided Aims: The Educational Implications of Opposing Ideologies in Girls' Secondary Schooling, 1850-1940," in *Lessons for Life*, and her Introduction to the same volume; Carol Dyhouse, *Girls Growing Up in Late Victorian and Edwardian England* (London: Routledge, 1981) and Paul Kegan, "Towards A 'Feminine' Curriculum for English Schoolgirls: The Demands of Ideology, 1870-1963," *Women's Studies International Quarterly* 1 (1978); "Good Wives and Little Mothers: Social Anxieties and the Schoolgirls' Curriculum, 1890-1920," *Oxford Review of Education* 3 (1977); and "Social Darwinistic Ideas and the Development of Women's Education in England, 1880-1920," *History of Education* 5 (Spring 1976); Joan Burstyn, *Victorian Education and the Ideal of Womanhood* (London: Croom Helm, 1980); Anna Davin, "Mind That You Do As You Are Told: Reading Books for Board Schoolgirls, 1870-1902," *Feminist Review* 3 (1979); "Imperialism and Motherhood," *History Workshop Journal* 5 (Spring 1978); Sara Delamont, "The Contradictions in Ladies' Education," in Sara Delamont and Lorna Duffin, eds., *The Nineteenth Century Woman: Her Cultural and Physical World* (London: Croom Helm, 1978); Deborah Gorham, *The Victorian Girl and the Feminine Ideal* (Bloomington: Indiana University Press, 1982); Alison Mackinnon, *One Foot on the Ladder: Origins and Outcomes of Girls' Secondary Schooling in South Australia* (Queensland: University of

Queensland Press, 1984); Marjorie Theobald, " 'Mere Accomplishments'? Melbourne's Early Ladies' Schools Reconsidered," *History of Education Review* 23 (1984); and Ailsa Zainu'ddin, *They Dreamt of a School: A Centenary History of the Methodist Ladies' College, Kew, 1882-1982* (Melbourne: Hyland House, 1983).

18. Even the vocabulary raises problems. The modern division of schooling into elementary, secondary, and post-secondary levels did not exist in the nineteenth century. The most commonly used term, particularly in reference to female students, was "higher education," but it is very unclear exactly what level preceded "higher education." In the case of girls' schools the terms "academy," "college," and "seminary" appear interchangeable. Marion Royce's work on denominational education for girls is still useful: "Education for Girls in Quaker Schools in Ontario," *Atlantis* 3 (Fall 1977), and "Methodism and the Education of Women in Nineteenth Century Ontario," *Atlantis* 3 (Spring 1978). There are also several interesting M.A. theses: Ann Margaret Gray, "Continuity in Change: The Effects on Girls of Co-educational Secondary Schooling in Ontario, 1890-1910," (M.A. University of Toronto, 1979); and Kate Rousmaniere, "To Prepare the Ideal Woman: Private Denominational Girls' Schooling in Late Nineteenth Century Ontario," (M.A. University of Toronto, 1984). The best works on women's education in Quebec are Micheline Dumont and Nadia Fahmy-Eid, eds., *Maîtresses de maison, maîtresses d'école: femmes, famille et éducation dans l'histoire du Québec* (Montréal: Boréal, 1983); and *Les couventines. L'éducation des filles au Québec dans les congrégations religieuses enseignantes, 1840-1960* (Montréal: Boréal, 1986).

19. In addition to Gillett, *We Walked Very Warily*, there are a few books sparked by anniversary celebrations: Margaret Gillett and Kay E. Sibbald, eds., *A Fair Shake: Autobiographical Essays of Women at McGill* (Montreal: Eden Press, 1984); Anne Rochon Ford, *A Path Not Strewn with Roses: One hundred Years of Women at the University of Toronto, 1884-1984* (Toronto: University of Toronto Press, 1985); Joy Parr, ed., *Still Running...Personal Stories by Queen's Women Celebrating the Fiftieth Anniversary of the Marty Scholarship* (Kingston: Queen's University Alumnae Association, 1987); and Barbara Sutton, ed., *Sanctum Hildam Canimus: A Collection of Reminiscences* (Toronto: St. Hilda's College, 1988).

20. See Burstyn, *Victorian Education*, chaps. 4 and 5.

21. Vicinus, *Independent Women*, 125-26.

22. Solomon, *In the Company of Educated Women*, 49.

23. The lengthy debate over Ontario's secondary schools and the creation of the collegiate institutes which educated so many of the women who went on to university is discussed in R.D. Gidney and D.A. Lawr, "Egerton Ryerson and the Origins of the Ontario Secondary School," *Canadian Historical Review* 60 (Dec. 1979); R.D. Gidney and W.P.J. Millar, *Inventing Secondary Education: The Rise of the High School in Nineteenth-Century Ontario* (Montreal and Kingston: McGill-Queen's University Press, 1990); and George S. Tomkins, *A Common Countenance: Stability and Change in the Canadian Curriculum* (Toronto: Prentice Hall, 1986). The position of girls in the grammar schools is also discussed in Marion Royce, "Arguments Over the Education of Girls—Their Admission to Grammar Schools in This Province," *Ontario History* 67 (March 1975), and Susan E. Houston and Alison Prentice, *Schooling and Scholars in Nineteenth-Century Ontario* (Toronto: University of Toronto Press, 1988) 321-28.

24. There was more discussion of women's role in the university at the turn of the century when new, female-dominated faculties such as nursing, social work, and library science were being established. The most interesting debate, still largely ignored in Canada, was over the addition of domestic science to the university curriculum early in the twentieth century.

25. Women who excelled in classics aroused particular comment, as did women in traditionally "masculine" faculties like medicine or law.

26. Jasen, "The English Canadian Curriculum," 37-49, 157-66. Since the vast majority of Canadian women entered Arts, I have focussed attention on the Arts curriculum, although in this same period smaller numbers of women were also entering Medicine at Queen's, Trinity, Victoria, and Toronto, and Music at Trinity and Toronto.

27. Many Canadian faculty members maintained close ties to Great Britain, often returning for visits over the summer, and new faculty members were routinely recruited in Great Britain. British politics and debates were followed closely through British publications as well as in the Canadian press. In addition Canadian periodicals such as the *Canadian Monthly and National Review* and the *Canadian Educational Monthly* frequently published articles on educational questions. *The Week*, a Toronto periodical founded in 1883, published lengthy articles on the question of co-education at both University College and McGill University during the 1880s.

28. Jasen, "The English Canadian Curriculum," 47, 49, 166-69, 173-78.

29. Harris, *Higher Education*, 42-43, 129-30; Jasen, "The English Canadian Curriculum," chap. 2; Alan Franklin Bowker, "Truly Useful Men: Maurice Hutton, George Wrong, James Mavor and the University of Toronto, 1880-1927," (Ph. D. diss., University of Toronto, 1975) 9-14.

30. At Queen's the first formal reference to the need for an Honours degree to teach high school appeared in 1889: *The Calendar of Queen's University and College, Kingston, Canada for the Year 1889-90* (Kingston 1889) 36.

31. Frederick Rudolph, *Curriculum: A History of the American Course of Study Since 1636* (San Francisco: Jossey Bass, 1977) 135-38, 191-96.

32. Queen's University, Register of Students, Queen's University Archives [hereafter QUA] #1129 (Fowler), #1139 (Allen), #1157 (Greaves).

33. *The Calendar of Queen's University and College, Kingston, Canada for the Year 1880-81* (Toronto, 1880) 4; The Board of Trustees at Queen's was already irked that Ferguson had been teaching German at the Royal Military College, and recommended his salary be reduced if he continued to do so. Queen's University, Board of Trustees Minutes, QUA, 29 Apr. 1880, 6-7.

34. Queen's is usually credited with having formally agreed to the admission of women to Arts in the fall of 1878 (Ronish, "Sweet Girl Graduates," 125, 139; Ford, *A Path Not Strewn with Roses*, 6; Ramsay Cook and Wendy Mitchinson, eds., *The Proper Sphere: Women's Place in Canadian Society* (Toronto: Oxford University Press, 1976) 120; Marks and Gaffield, "Women at Queen's," 333, but there is no record of such a decision in any of the Queen's records. I have concluded that the error originated in a rather fanciful history of Queen's entitled the "Domesday Book" which was compiled to commemorate the success of a money-raising campaign begun in 1888. Written by James Williamson, the Professor of Natural Philosophy and Mathematics, and Miss Lois Saunders, the Librarian, it stated that "early in the session of 1878-1879" the authorities of Queen's announced that "the University course would henceforth be thrown open to women" (Domesday Book, QUA, 1: 842-43). Quoted but not acknowledged in D.D. Calvin, *Queen's University at Kingston: The First Century of a Scottish Canadian Foundation, 1841-1941* (Kingston: Trustees of the University, 1941) 237, this error has since crept into most of the secondary Canadian literature.

35. *Queen's Calendar, 1880-1881*, 24-25.

36. Keane, "Rediscovering Ontario Students," 29-31, discusses the problem of the admission of unmatriculated students at different universities.

37. These figures seem very low by modern standards but they are reasonably typical for this period: Queen's College, Senate Minutes, QUA, 26 Apr. 1880, 3: 113. They were raised slightly at Queen's but were then the source of much discussion when a common entrance examination for all Ontario universities was being agreed upon. The whole question of how "hard" university was compared to today is very difficult to answer.

38. Apparently the female students never received any of these penalties, although the Senate minutes record numerous cases involving male students, the most common problems being drinking and cheating on examinations. See Queen's College, Senate Minutes, 7 Oct. 1880, 3: 114-16; 4 Mar. 1885, 3: 277; 6 May 1896, 4: 378; 12 Mar. 1897, 4: 392; 22 Apr. 1899, 5:26.

39. Each calendar contains some of these regulations, which were also discussed regularly by the Senate; a fairly complete compilation appeared in *The Calendar of Queen's University and College, Kingston, Ontario, 1889-90* (Kingston, 1889) 1-4. See also Queen's College, Senate Minutes, QUA, 1 Oct. 1888, 4: 42 concerning the library regulations.

40. *The Calendar of Queen's University and College, 1881-82* (Kingston, 1881) 47; *The Calendar of Queen's University and College, Kingston, Ontario, 1882-83* (Kingston, 1882) 48; Queen's University, Register of Students, QUA, Fowler (#1129).

41. Queen's College, Senate Minutes, QUA, 23 Apr. 1881, 3:139.

42. Queen's University, Register of Students, QUA, Greaves (#1157).

43. See *University of Toronto, Class and Prize List, 1880,* "Matriculation Examinations, 1879," 7-8. Eliza got first-class honours in English, French, and history and third-class in classics and mathematics; she had also written the Local Examinations for Women in 1878 (ibid., 1879, 9) and passed mathematics, English, and German, without receiving honours, but got second-class honours in history and geography and French. At Queen's, Eliza also won a prize for junior chemistry in 1883. *The Calendar of Queen's University and College, Kingston, Ontario, 1883-84* (Kingston 1883) 54; *The Calendar of Queen's University and College, Kingston, Ontario, 1884-85* (Kingston 1884) 62-63; Queen's University, Register of Students, QUA, Fitzgerald (#1231).

44. "Closing Ceremonies," *Queen's College Journal* 12 (Midsummer 1884) 141; *Daily British Whig,* 30 Apr. and 1 May 1884.

45. John Watson took over the Chair in philosophy at Queen's when John Clark Murray, another strong advocate of women's education, moved to

McGill. See John Watson, "Female Education," *Queen's College Journal* 4 (27 Jan. 1877) 3.

46.   *Queen's College Journal* 16 (19 Jan. 1889) 54. It was suggested that the women's gym fee of $1.00 be used to buy furnishings for their reading room.

47.   The conflict over co-education in the Faculty of Medicine at Queen's has been discussed in Veronica Strong-Boag, ed., *'A Woman with a Purpose': The Diaries of Elizabeth Smith, 1872-1884* (Toronto: University of Toronto Press, 1980); A.A. Travill, "Early Medical Co-education and Women's Medical College, Kingston, Ontario, 1880-1894," *Historic Kingston* 30 (Jan. 1982); Hilda Neatby, *Queen's University, Volume I: 1841-1917* (Montreal: McGill-Queen's University Press, 1978); and Ronish, "Sweet Girl Graduates," 138-52. There were a few discussions about Queen's affiliating with different ladies' colleges, but nothing came of them. See Queen's University, Board of Trustees, Minutes, QUA, 27 Apr. 1882, 78.

48.   LaPierre, "The Debate Over Co-education at McGill"; Ronish, "Sweet Girl Graduates"; Stanley B. Frost, *McGill University: For the Advancement of Learning, Volume 1: 1801-1895* (Montreal: McGill-Queen's University Press, 1980); Gillett, *We Walked Very Warily.*

49.   *Annual Calendar of McGill College and University, Session 1884-85.* (Montreal 1884) 19-53.

50.   *Annual Calendar of McGill College and University, Session 1885-86.* "Special Course for Women" (Montreal 1885) 63-69.

51.   *Annual Calendar of McGill College and University, Session 1886-87.* "Special Course for Women" (Montreal 1886) 65-69.

52.   Ibid., 68. The Lady Superintendent was Miss Helen Gairdner, one of the original members of the Montreal Ladies' Educational Association.

53.   McGill University, Faculty of Arts, Minute Book, McGill University Archives [hereafter MUA] 20 Oct. 1887, 3, 148 and Corporate Minute Book, 26 Oct. 1887, 386. See also *Annual Calendar, 1885-86,* 63, vs. *Annual Calendar, 1889-89,* 72 for the change in regulations, and *McGill Fortnightly* 2 (8 Dec. 1893) 117 for a letter complaining about the rigidity with which the regulation was enforced.

54.   *Annual Calendar, 1884-85,* 39-41.

55.   The gym fee had been a cause of controversy for years; in 1886 the Senate exempted "ladies" from paying it but it apparently was reimposed later. See Queen's College, Senate Minutes, QUA, 30 Sept. 1886, 3, 343.

56. McGill University, Faculty of Arts, Minute Book, MUA, 30 Nov. 1888, 205; 14 Dec. 1888, 207; 22 June 1892, 360-63.

57. See Zerada Slack, "The Development of Physical Education for Women at McGill University," (M.A. McGill University, 1934).

58. McGill University, Faculty of Arts, Minute Book, MUA, 19 Dec. 1885, 72; 23 Jan. 1886, 75-77; 6 Feb. 1886, 77; 20 Feb. 1886, 80; 6 Mar. 1886, 83-84; 25 Mar. 1887, 131; 7 Jan. 1888, 160-61.

59. Ibid., 29 Oct. 1884, 14; 28 Nov. 1884, 20; 10 Dec. 1884, 22-23.

60. Georgina Hunter, "In the Beginning," *McGill News* 10 (Mar. 1929) 14-15.

61. Elizabeth A. Irwin, [Hammond] "Women at McGill," *McGill News* 1 (Dec. 1919) 40-42.

62. Grace Ritchie England, "The Entrance of Women to McGill," *McGill News* 16 (Dec. 1934) 13-17.

63. Carrie M. Derick, "In the 80s," *Old McGill,* 1927, 29, 200.

64. Ibid., 15; Gillett, *We Walked Very Warily,* 50.

65. *Annual Calendar, 1885-86.* Special course for women, 145.

66. England, "Entrance of Women to McGill," 16-17; Gillett, *We Walked Very Warily,* 107.

67. *Annual Calendar of McGill College and University for Session 1896-97.* Special course for women (Montreal 1896), 64-68.

68. For Peterson's plans for the Faculty of Arts, see Peterson Papers, MUA, RG 2, Peterson to Smith, 12 Oct. 1896; memo, Peterson's hand, 17 Apr. 1897; Peterson to Strathcona, 17 Feb. 1898; Faculty of Arts, Minute Book, MUA, 1 Mar. 1897, 124-27.

69. Hilda D. Oakeley, *My Adventures in Education* (London: Williams and Norgate, 1939) 73-74. (Miss Oakeley was the first Warden of RVC.)

70. Thompson, "Admission of Women to University College"; Ford, *A Path Not Strewn with Roses*, 6-16.

71. University of Toronto, Senate Minutes, UTA, 28 May 1877, 163-66; University of Toronto, Applications for Examinations in Arts, A-70-0051/001-003, 1881-82, and A-73-0051-270-21, 1882-88, UTA. It appears that the local exams were exactly the same as the regular matriculation exams and were held simultaneously, the only difference being that it cost only $1.00 to write them as opposed to the $5.00 fee charged for the regular matriculation exams.

72. *University of Toronto, Class and Prize List, 1879,* "Local Examinations for Women: First Examination," 9; *University of Toronto, Class and Prize List, 1880,* "Local Examinations for Women: 1879," 9.

The Academic Life of Canadian Coeds

73. *University of Toronto, Class and Prize List, 1880,* "Arts: Matriculation Examinations, 1879," 7-8 and "Scholarships: Matriculation, 1879," 22.

74. *University of Toronto, Class and Prize List, 1880,* "Faculty of Arts: First Year," 23.

75. John Squair, *The Admission of Women to the University of Toronto* (Toronto, 1924) 1-3. (John Squair, who was a contemporary of many of these women and went on to university with some of them, had a long career at University College as the Professor of French.)

76. University of Toronto, Senate Minutes, UTA, 4 Mar. 1881, 406; *Calendar of University College, Toronto for 1885-86,* Appendix (Toronto 1885) 62-63; Squair, *Admission of Women,* 6.

77. Her letter to Wilson dated 31 Dec. 1881 is quoted in Squair, *Admission of Women,* 6. It was also published in the *Mail,* 1 Oct. 1883.

78. Squair, *Admission of Women,* 2-3.

79. Harris, *Higher Education,* 124.

80. *Calendar of University College, Toronto 1884-85* (Toronto 1884) 6, 13-15, 39.

81. *Calendar of University College, Toronto 1890-91* (Toronto 1890) 29-33.

82. Harris, *Higher Education,* 135; Jasen, "The Liberal Arts Curriculum," 42.

83. Ibid., 46-48.

84. Ibid., 65-81.

85. *University of Toronto, Class and Prize List, 1890 and 1891*; and Student Record, A73-0006/052,UTA.

86. Scott Diary, 1889-90, n.p.

87. Bessie was the first woman teacher employed at the Ottawa Collegiate Institute and taught English and calisthenics there until her marriage in 1906. In 1924 she returned as librarian and remained at the school until her retirement in 1939. She attended the school's centenary celebrations in Nov. 1943 and died in 1951. I hope to publish her diary. See *A History of the Ottawa Collegiate Institute, 1843-1903* (Ottawa 1904) 63, 66; *Lisgar Collegiate Institute, 1843-1943* (N.p., n.d.) 16, 102, 119; Charlotte Whitton, "Times Have Changed—Or Have They?" *Chronicle* 48 (1975-76) 8.

88. Ronish, "Sweet Girl Graduates," chap. 2, covers the admission of women to Victoria College when it was still located at Cobourg, Ontario.

89. Trinity University Committee of the Curriculum, Minutes, 29 June 1883, Trinity University Archives [hereafter TUA]; *University of Trinity College, Calendar for 1884.* Course of study for women (Toronto 1885) 62-66.

90. Trinity University, Committee of the Curriculum, Minutes, 29 June 1883; Corporation Minutes, 14 Mar. 1883, TUA. The Bishop Strachan School

apparently had a particularly bright graduating class in 1885; six students wrote the Trinity matriculation exams and one the University of Toronto exams.

91. *University of Trinity College, Calendar for 1885,* "Course of Study for Women" (Toronto 1885) 62-66. Trinity was the only university discussed here which made specific adjustments to its Arts curriculum, such as offering courses in Italian, which were available only to "ladies."

92. *Trinity Calendar, 1884,* 85.

93. Trinity University, Corporation Minutes, 19 Feb. 1894, 10 Oct. 1894; St. Hilda's College, Council Minutes, 16 Jan. 188 to 20 Nov. 1894, TUA.

94. Royal Victoria College did not open until the fall of 1899. Victoria's first women's residence, Annesley Hall, opened in 1903. Queen's and University College did not provide residences for their women students until well into the twentieth century.

95. St. Hilda's students only began to contribute a regular column to the *Trinity University Review* in March 1895; the *St. Hilda's Chronicle* was started in 1901.

96. St. Hilda's College, *Educational Report of the Lady Principal for the Year 1888-1889,* TUA; Constance Backhouse, "'To Open the Way for Others of My Sex': Clara Brett Martin's Career as Canada's First Woman Lawyer,". *Canadian Journal of Women and the Law* 1 (1985).

97. See *University of Trinity College Calendar, 1883-1900,* for lists of students in Music; the Appendix to Earl Davey, "The Development of Undergraduate Music Curricula at the University of Toronto, 1918-68," (M.A. University of Toronto, 1977) lists the members of the Associated Musicians of Ontario, 1899-1900, several of whom were Trinity women; Harris, *Higher Education,* Appendix, lists the numbers of men and women in different faculties but omits (625 n.9) the Trinity students registered in Music.

98. Bessie Scott, "College Women," 1, UTA.

Preparing for the Working World:
Women at Queen's During the 1920s[1]

Nicole Neatby

World War I brought changes that many hoped would radically improve women's status and role in society. Women had extended their fields of action in the working world and they were encroaching on professional male preserves. By 1918, most women had finally obtained the right to vote at most levels of government. And yet the following decade did not live up to feminist expectations. As Veronica Strong-Boag has pointed out, "Predictions of major, even revolutionary change for feminists and anti-feminists turned out far wide of the mark."[2]

Instead of building on or even consolidating these advances, the post-war period was one in which women seemed to have lost ground. Historians have noted that after the Great War, women generally ended up following the dictates of domesticity, essentially orienting their goals towards marriage and raising children. As the authors of the most recent textbook on Canadian women's history have written, "Given the loss of 60,000 Canadian lives during the war, motherhood acquired an enhanced practical and symbolical importance." Furthermore, "the tremendous social and economic dislocation the nation experienced at war's end reinforced the belief that women should not compete for men's jobs."[3] Even their newly acquired voting power was neutralized by the fact that most wives voted as their husbands did.

But can we assume that women's fight for equality was at a standstill in the 1920s or even that the clock had been turned back? Recent studies reveal that although the women's movement of the early twentieth century appeared to have "lost its way,"[4] significant changes in women's lives were nonetheless taking place, changes which helped to enhance female autonomy. A closer look at the 1920s thus seems in order. This post-war decade may not have brought about the dramatic progress hoped for by the suffragettes and other feminists of the earlier generation, yet this must not preclude the study of other types of important transformations.

Certainly changes in higher education support the claim that the 1920s saw improvements in the status of women. Very little has been written on the experience of Canadian female university students of that decade, but some significant changes were taking place.[5] It was a time when more women were going to university than ever before. Total registration rose over the decade and more significantly, in relative terms, the proportion of female students rose from 16.3% of total enrolment in 1919/20 to 23.5% in 1929/30.[6] These statistics suggest that something was happening.

Gender and Education in Ontario: An Historical Reader

Could this increased enrolment be linked to the adoption of feminist principles? Were female students turning to higher education for better-paying jobs? Was this an attempt to extend their sphere of activity into male territory? More specifically, one needs to ask why women went to university in the 1920s. What did they, or their parents, expect to gain from these additional years of higher education?

The experience of female students who attended Queen's University in the 1920s suggests some answers to these questions. The Queen's records provide information on most of the students' place of origin, religious denomination, father's occupation, intended profession, and course selection. Of these files, 847 document the women who registered at Queen's during the decade. The small number in any one year makes it difficult to create valid annual samples for the whole decade. This study therefore concentrates on the records of the first-year students of 1925. The data covers 62 of the 76 female students starting university that year as well as 61 of their male colleagues, one-third of the total male enrolment.[7] The men were included to see whether the social and economic backgrounds of students varied according to gender. The *Queen's Journal,* the student newspaper, was the major source of information on student interests, attitudes, and activities. The archival record was supplemented by interviews with 23 women and eight men living in the Kingston and Ottawa areas who were graduates in the 1920s.[8]

By the 1920s the presence of female students in the universities was no longer a novelty. Earlier generations had convinced an increasing segment of the population that university education for women was an acceptable expense. Some even upheld it as a necessary prelude to a financially productive female life. By the 1920s, paid work even for women of the middle class was no longer seen as an aberration. At least in the brief interlude between the end of education and marriage, "maturity was increasingly associated with paid work. Like their brothers, women came to expect to spend at least some of their adult life in the labour force."[9] Fathers and brothers were progressively being relieved of the financial responsibility of supporting single female family members who were old enough to work. Mary Vipond makes the point that the popular magazines of the period even publicized the notion that paid employment would make women better homemakers.[10] It was clearly understood that this prescribed working period in a woman's life was meant to be temporary, an interregnum before she began her true vocation, that of wife and mother.[11] In the case of women who might "unfortunately" never marry, there may have been the reluctant awareness that this temporary working period might become permanent. The spinster would then be in a position to avoid her traditionally dependent status and become financially self-sufficient.

Women at Queen's During the 1920s

When a period of paid employment is taken for granted, higher education might well be seen as a passport to the more suitable occupations. This, of course, would be mostly true for women of the middle class. If women were expected to work even for a brief period in their lives and if education was to be, at least in part, a preparation for this experience, then higher education for women would increasingly be recognized as a preparation for the working world. In other words, the purpose of university education for women would resemble more and more that of the men's. This would not necessarily eliminate the fact that career expectations for men and women were still very different. Women would still not be welcome in the more prestigious liberal professions. But they would gain admission to potentially more rewarding occupations. This could still be consistent with and might even be seen as training for an eventual career as mother and housekeeper.[12] There would not be a revolution. A university education which would prepare women for the work world would still "not fundamentally threaten the primacy of the family headed by the male breadwinner."[13] But, if there was no revolution, attitudes were changing.

Does the experience of female students who went to Queen's in the 1920s bear witness to such an evolution? The women graduates of Queen's who were interviewed clearly did not consider themselves as pioneers. When asked whether they had expected to go to university when they were in high school, 18 of the 23 women graduates answered in the affirmative. Without any hesitation, the majority claimed that they took university education for granted: "It came as a natural progression."[14] Only two respondents remembered any opposition from relatives or friends to the pursuit of higher education. Attending university did not make these women feel different or unusual; it seemed a normal thing to do. University had become an acceptable environment for women. What had once been an act of defiance was now an appropriate option.

In some ways, however, they were still exceptional. They were still part of a definite minority. In 1920, only 1% of all women in Canada between the ages of 20 and 24 were attending university.[15] At Queen's University there was an average of 300 female students per year in an average student population of 1816 during the 1920s.[16] These statistics seem to contradict the belief among the women interviewed that higher education was a "natural progression." However, the statistics for the Faculty of Arts paint a different picture. Female students were about 40% of the Arts students.[17] In this area, therefore, women were comparatively well represented. Understandably in these circumstances, they may not have felt out of place.

Gender and Education in Ontario: An Historical Reader

Yet these figures do not tell us which women came to university. In the 1920s, according to Frederick Gibson, Queen's had the reputation of being a poor man's college, "performing a vital service in eastern Ontario, as well as for the province," in "helping the backward and unfortunate" to get a university education.[18] Students "were on the whole people of modest means and uncertain prospects."[19] Nonetheless, at Queen's as elsewhere, the middle class was overrepresented.[20] For an earlier period, from 1895 to 1905, Lynne Marks and Chad Gaffield have pointed out that "Queen's students tended to have fathers in higher status occupations but...they were not from a homogeneous wealthy elite."[21] In the 1920s, according to Gibson, "the sons and daughters of professional parents [were] the largest single group of Queen's students"[22] and the proportion increased during the decade, from 30% of the total freshman class in 1920/21 to 39% in 1928/29.[23]

Within this student body, however, the social origins of the women differed from those of the men. The most direct way of establishing the social origins of Queen's students is to look at their fathers' occupations.[24] The student records show that one-quarter of the women came from professional backgrounds and more than half were born into business families.[25] Thus the great majority of these women (three-quarters) had fathers in these two occupational categories. Male students, on the other hand, only had half as many fathers in professional and business categories, representing slightly more than one-third of the total occupations listed. Apparently male students were more likely to come from families with less "prestigious" occupations.

The interview samples reflected the same pattern. Of the 23 women questioned, half came from professional backgrounds and one-third from business families, while six of the eight men interviewed belonged to skilled artisan or primary producer families. Unfortunately, as Lynne Marks and Chad Gaffield pointed out for an earlier period, "the records contain no information about the father's actual income or wealth, a consideration especially important in the case of farmers."[26] Nonetheless the findings make clear that the Queen's women had fathers with higher status jobs and probably with higher incomes than the fathers of Queen's men.[27]

This conclusion is strengthened by the evidence that the women's education was largely financed by their parents. Among the female graduates interviewed, only two financed their own education; another five contributed, whereas three-quarters of those interviewed (16) said that their fathers paid for everything. On the other hand, the evidence suggests that sons were, more often than not, expected to finance their university education themselves. Six out of the eight male graduates said that they paid their own way through college and claimed that this was usual for male students.

332

Women at Queen's During the 1920s

The summer activities of these students underline the difference between the two groups. The interviews suggest that for female students the summer months were almost holidays. The great majority (17) did not work to earn money. They either "just had fun"[28] or helped around the house, some of them taking care of younger siblings. In fact, a few claimed that applying for a summer job "wasn't the thing to do."[29] In some cases, it was the parents of the graduates who objected to the idea. They wanted to keep their daughters at home, perhaps to look after younger brothers or sisters, or work around the house.[30] Earning money in the summer apparently was not considered an appropriate female activity. By contrast, each of the male graduates questioned worked for wages in the summer. Again, for them it was the "normal thing to do."[31] One of them explained that they "all worked: it was a poor man's university";[32] another said that "everyone was struggling to get through."[33] Even during the school year most of them held part-time jobs. None of them remembered any female students who had worked in the summer time. The men and women may have gone to classes together but when summer came their paths diverged.

There is some evidence to suggest that at Queen's the pattern was changing. Attempts were made to find summer jobs for women. Ideally this would make female students less dependent on financial assistance from parents and would facilitate access to university for the less fortunate. Charlotte Whitton played an active role in such endeavours, along with other Queen's alumnae, by forming a Committee on Employment of Women after World War I. They also proposed that "an employment bureau be established for men and women of the University."[34] A few years later, an article in the *Queen's Journal* commended the work done by the Employment Service of the University "in bringing placement to many graduates and undergraduates who are anxious to secure the necessary funds to keep the home fires burning."[35] And there certainly are sources to suggest that some female students were working in the summer out of economic necessity. Thus, when in 1920, Dean O.K. Skelton addressed the Alma Mater Society, he commented that

> Queen's students as a rule come from homes where boys and girls are accustomed to look after themselves and many even pay part of their college expenses by working in the summer...[36]

Among the six former graduates who held a summer job, one recalled how she and her friends all worked out of need despite the fact that "of course, there were always wealthy ones who went to their summer cottages in the summer."[37] Finally, it is noteworthy that these six women did not think of their experience in retrospect as being out of the ordinary.

These signs of evolution, however, cannot conceal the fact that above all, Queen's continued to cater to female students who came from financially secure backgrounds. The Employment Service had only a limited impact. The bitter complaints voiced by Charlotte Whitton in 1928 leave no doubt that women attending Queen's were not driven by the same pressures as men to find additional sources of income.

> Women students desiring summer employment have evinced their interest and given their names in reference to various lines of work, but when openings have been obtained after considerable effort, it has been found that many of those applying therefor [sic] have changed their minds and those who have reserved positions for them have consequently been disappointed.[38]

It is also important to keep in mind that even if female students did obtain a summer job, women's wages were such that female students could not earn as much as male students to finance their university attendance. Thus the financial context of the 1920s still made it difficult for the less fortunate women to enter Queen's.

But why did the women who could afford to go to Queen's want a higher education? Parental hopes seem to have had some influence in pushing the women graduates towards a higher education. This is not surprising when we take into account the dependence of many women on their fathers' financial support to enter university. In this situation, a daughter's decision to pursue a higher education could not have been a completely autonomous one. The great majority of female graduates questioned (21 out of 23) clearly remember that their parents wanted them to have a university education. This strong desire to see their daughters college-educated is particularly striking considering the fact that most of the parents had never attended university. Seven of the fathers had a public school education, six of them had finished high school, and nine attended university. The mothers had even less education. Three of them had had public school education, sixteen had a high school education, one attended Normal School, and three went on to university for two years or less. In spite of this, mothers were often singled out as the dominant force in pushing for the higher education of their daughters. Indeed, six women graduates pointed to their mother as the parent with the most desire to see them go on to university. Only three mentioned their fathers. Clearly this distinction cannot be attributed to a more advanced education on the part of the mothers. Is it possible that they had been influenced by the notions of women's rights and status promoted during the pre-war era? These women could have been looking back on their own limited education as a disadvantage and possibly did not want to see their daughters frustrated or deprived in the same way as they had been. The evidence is not conclusive but one thing is certain: both fathers and mothers felt that higher education was a benefit which they wanted their daughters to acquire.

The nature of this anticipated benefit is not clear. The interviews leave no doubt that parents eventually hoped to see their daughters marry. One can wonder if they felt the university offered young women opportunities to meet eligible and "suitable" male companions? It seems highly likely that parents would be well aware of the favourable social context provided by the campus. Indeed registering at Queen's certainly could enhance their daughter's chances of making an "interesting" match. Yet nothing in the responses of the former female graduates suggests that parents openly expressed such hopes.

One thing seems certain from the interviews: for some parents the advantages of a university education were undoubtedly economic. One female graduate recalled how her father used to say, "Go on to school and get an education so that you don't have to work as hard as I did all my life."[39] Implicit in the attitude of many of the parents was the expectation that their daughters would at one point enter the working world and earn a living. When one considers that the mothers of 20 of the 23 female graduates had not worked for wages before their marriage, it is obvious that parental attitudes towards single women's employment had changed. In fact, some women graduates remembered that their parents had been quite outspoken on this issue. One mentioned that her mother was

> determined that we would be able to earn our living. If we married, O.K., but you might need it anyway. She was determined that there would be a vocation other than just a degree.[40]

These parents clearly wanted to guarantee their daughters' economic independence. It no longer seemed acceptable for single women to be without income. More than this, investing in university education could be seen as a way of ensuring their child's lifelong financial security—every woman after all was a potential spinster. As one graduate explained, her parents felt that

> a woman should have some means of self-support—not just be left to sit. You mightn't marry and you should be able to support yourself and not be dependent on relatives.[41]

However, there was also the assumption that a university degree meant not just a job and financial autonomy but a higher status job. Indeed, since parents wanted their daughters both to attend university and to find a job, it seems probable that they were not ready to see their daughters accept just any form of employment. It must be noted that three-quarters of the women could not recall their mothers or fathers expressing any specific hopes as to what they would become. The choice of their course program was left up to them. But one female graduate who was thinking of becoming a teacher remembered that her father strongly encouraged her to aim for a "specialist degree" in teaching, which implied some form of university training,[42] so she could hope for more prestigious employment:

> My father instilled that [idea in me]. He said, "if you become a specialist you have a much better career in teaching than if you aren't. You can become a Department Head. You'll have more advancement."[43]

Nonetheless, whatever the perceived advantages of higher education for women, parents gave a higher priority to their sons' university attendance. When a parent died or if younger siblings needed care, older sisters who were at university were more likely to be called back home to help than their male counterparts.[44] This was clearly demonstrated during the Depression years, a time when parents' financial resources were reduced. As Hilda Laird, the Dean of Women, noted in 1932-33, "a young man unable to find employment is sent to the university: a young woman is kept at home to help with domestic work."[45] Indeed, female enrolment at Queen's dropped from 404 in 1928/29 to 347 by 1932/33, whereas male enrolment in applied science and medicine rose during that period.[46] This suggests that parents still did not consider higher education as important for their daughters as for their sons. Yet it remains clear that when circumstances allowed, affluent parents in the post-war decade encouraged their daughters to enter university.

But what of the aspirations of the female students themselves? What were their goals upon entering university? Why did they think a university education was a worthwhile endeavour? For one thing, did they enter university in the hope of meeting a "suitable" husband? Although inconclusive, the available evidence certainly does not allow us to suppose that female students were registering at Queen's to find "Mr. Right." The notion of a "marriage market" at Queen's did inspire some comment in the student newspaper. More precisely, one finds female students responding vehemently to their male colleagues' accusations that the women on campus were attending university to catch a husband. This touched a sensitive chord among some female students,

Women at Queen's During the 1920s

provoking denials from the offended. Although one female journalist was ready to admit that "the desire for finding a husband is always more or less present in a girl's mind, whether consciously or unconsciously expressed," she was not at all prepared to accept the idea that higher education had anything to do with this "latent" desire: "it is absurd and unreasonable to think that the average girl enters an institution of higher learning for four years—where the % of marriages among students is very low—for the primary purpose of husband hunting." She explained that "most of us at Queen's are serious about this business of education and intend on going on into careers. They don't give B.A.'s to dumbbells, nor do they take them in responsible positions."[47] Some denials were much more categorical. Thus one incensed Queen's woman protested in a letter to the editor that

> we are at Queen's because we aim at a career. We would not be here spending our parents' hard-earned pennies if it were a husband and a good time we sought—we would go some place where such things are to be had. As a class the Queen's students are far from the ideal husband.[48]

Another female student analysed the situation in a more detailed fashion. After asking, "Is Queen's a matrimonial agency, or to put the question in another form, does the average girl come to Queen's to grab a husband," she answered,

> Levana, to a woman, howls an emphatic "no." But some man may murmur as he disconnects his telephone, "Methinks the lady protests too much." The fact remains, however, that a college education is not an asset, but rather a handicap in the matrimonial race. By raising a girl's standards, it narrows her choice of a husband, by increasing her earning power it lessens her need for one.[49]

Judging from the interviews, marriage does not appear to have been a major motivating factor pushing female students to seek a higher education. In fact, out of the 23 female graduates interviewed, seven remained single and only two of those who did get married (16) met their future husbands at Queen's. When asked whether they had hoped to be married or engaged by graduation, most of the married female graduates (12) answered "no." Some of them could not remember thinking about marriage at that time while others were more definite. For instance, one graduate exclaimed: "Oh! no, no, it

337

wouldn't even occur to me to think of such a thing, because I wanted to earn my living.... Marriage wasn't on my mind at all."[50]

One could argue that wanting to earn a living was a far more widespread and pressing goal at this stage in these young women's lives. Indeed the great majority of the female graduates interviewed (20) had expected to work after university. Was higher education seen as a preparation for employment? Female students writing for the *Queen's Journal* certainly lend support to such a supposition. According to one female journalist "somewhere behind the arrival of almost every woman at Queen's is lurking the hope of ultimate independence." More specifically, the Queen's woman was aspiring to

> greater knowledge, broader culture, and a more refined sense of the pleasure in things, and that most material advantage increased earning power.[51]

However, further evidence suggests a more complex reality. Students who registered at Queen's were asked to identify their "intended profession." About half of the female students left this blank. Indeed, from the student records, Hilda Laird established the intended profession of the total female population for the years 1925/26, 1926/27, 1927/28 and published her findings in the Principal's Reports. In her first survey of 1925/26, she discovered that out of a total female registration of 293, more than half (162) had no "intended profession" upon entering Queen's.[52] The following years provided much the same results.[53] The interviews also lend support to these findings. Once again, half of the former graduates questioned remembered registering at Queen's without established plans, unsure of their future professional occupations. At first glance, this type of evidence appears to undermine the suggestion that female students were at Queen's to prepare for the working world. How could they be, when so many of them did not have a precise occupation in mind upon arriving at university?

There is no doubt that the Dean of Women's statistics point to widespread professional indecision among the female population at Queen's. Yet indecision does not necessarily mean purposelessness. One can argue that simply by deciding to go to university, female students were actually revealing some kind of vocational ambition. This is all the more likely when one takes into account the prospects the working world held out for women in the 1920s. Employment options were clearly limited. What is more, most of the jobs available to women did not require a higher education and most professions that did require a university degree were closed to them.[54] All the former women graduates questioned had shared the experience of having to choose a vocation from only

Women at Queen's During the 1920s

a few possibilities. One of them recalled how "in those days there were only 3 choices for girls—you taught, or you became a nurse or you were a secretary."[55]

To register at Queen's was in fact rejecting the possibility of working in some of these fields—namely employment in the lower status occupations of nursing and secretarial work for which a different kind of preparation was required.[56] One female graduate's recollections certainly lend support to this suggestion:

> You see, there weren't an awful lot of interesting things for women in those days and the girls who didn't go to college had gone in and done secretarial work, taken a course at a business college.[57]

Presumably for the women deciding to enter Queen's, these less prestigious occupations had no appeal. Presented in this light, the undeniable pattern of indecision among female students concerning their "intended profession" cannot simply be dismissed as a lack of vocational ambition. These "undecided" women had in fact chosen to reject less prestigious forms of employment open to them. This is a decisive first step in the process of committing oneself to a profession. In all probability, these female students had not yet gone beyond this stage in their search for an appealing vocation. But they were searching. That there should be a delay is not surprising when one considers the limited career options open to university-trained women. It is also interesting that a sampling of the first-year male students of 1925 shows that one-third (28) of the men had no specified "intended profession." Clearly, widespread vocational indecision was not an exclusively female phenomenon. At this stage, even men, on whom society exercised a strong pressure to find a lifelong career, could be undecided about their professional future.

What about those women who registered at Queen's with a specific professional goal in mind? An overwhelming majority opted for teaching. The Dean of Women's study points out that out of the female population in 1925 almost all of those who stated a career option intended to teach (118 out of 131).[58] She found the same pattern in 1926/27 and again in 1927/28.[59] In addition, seven out of the eleven "decided" former graduates interviewed also remember opting for teaching at the outset of their university education.

What engendered this constant and overwhelming interest in teaching? For one thing, teaching was one of the rare female occupations for which a university degree was a significant advantage. In Ontario, those who obtained their B.A. and spent a subsequent year at the Ontario College of Education could qualify to teach at the high school level. Teachers at this level were assured of better salaries and more prestige than their non-university trained colleagues in the primary schools. In theory, they could also become eligible for advancement into various high-ranking positions in school administrations. Some female students appreciated these advantages and saw the extra years of training at university as worthwhile. One former graduate remembered thinking that

> if I were going to teach it was better to have a specialist standing.... It means a better salary and you're more apt to be head of your department.[60]

Deciding to become a teacher, in effect, meant that not only would one enjoy relatively good working conditions compared to those found in other occupations open to women but one would benefit from enviable social prestige. As one female commentator put it,

> The rewards of the profession are not money or leisure merely. Teachers have the respect and affection of the community to a degree enjoyed by few other workers.[61]

Thus, the large proportion of aspiring teachers at Queen's lends support to the notion that women were seeking a university education in order to prepare themselves for higher status employment.

But these statistics also tell another story. They provide yet another clear illustration of the restricted job opportunities for women in the 1920s. There is some evidence to suggest that the choice of becoming a teacher was often made without much enthusiasm for the profession as such. In some cases the choice seems to have been made out of resignation rather than positive inclination. It was one, as one graduate remembered, "guided by what you *could* get."[62] In her case, she explained that

> I wasn't at all sure that I would [like to teach], but I did. It seemed to be the only thing left and I knew I didn't want to be a nurse and I knew I didn't want to be a secretary.[63]

Through her surveys, Hilda Laird noticed much the same kind of reluctant choice. For the year 1925, she reported that "many of the 118 future teachers have repeatedly stated that they plan to be teachers only because they do not know what else to do."[64] One graduate probably expressed a widespread feeling when she admitted that she was "afraid teaching may have been [her] choice by elimination."[65] Therefore if teaching proved to be the most frequently mentioned "intended profession" of Queen's female students, it was probably because for many it seemed the only interesting career option available, the only profession for university-trained women which guaranteed a certain status and good working conditions.

A striking contrast emerges when we look at the options declared by the "decided" male students. The men of the 1925 sample mentioned ten different career options.[66] Although the majority (16) of these men did choose teaching, they did so in considerably smaller numbers than the "decided" women. What is more, there is no evidence to suggest that they made their choice as a last resort. Why should they? Unlike their female counterparts, they had a whole range of possible careers to choose from.

Whatever the motivations behind the "undecided" and "decided" female students at Queen's, one thing seems obvious: these women had decided that they were going to have to earn their living—at least for a few years. In order to do so, some were even ready to prepare for a profession that left them far from enthusiastic. Thus by the 1920s attitudes towards women's paid work had evolved. Queen's women, unlike their mothers, had come to expect to gain some kind of financial independence—at least for a few years during their adult lives. In this respect, their life after graduation was becoming increasingly comparable to the experience of their male colleagues.

However, if expectations had changed by the 1920s concerning women's paid employment, the Queen's material leaves no doubt that many traditional assumptions about female roles and capacities remained. Female students were still excluded from several male professional preserves. Furthermore, there is no evidence to suggest that Queen's women showed a desire to challenge their exclusion. Some remember being first attracted to male professions but they were soon discouraged from pursuing their initial interest. The segregated working world at the time made little effort to accommodate female recruits who wanted to operate outside traditionally prescribed fields of employment. For instance, one of the former graduates recalled that she had wanted to be a lawyer but before making any decision she talked to the only female lawyer in Ottawa at the time:

She was in the process of moving to Toronto because she said: "There's nothing in law for women at the moment. All you are allowed to do is make wills and sign leases, because the interesting work was not given to women at all." Also she said: "You need a private income because you make nothing."[67]

Discouraged to find that law was not a vocation for women who worked to support themselves, she was forced to reconsider: "So I thought: Oh! dear, I'll take a teacher's course. Not that I particularly wanted to be a teacher."[68]

The large percentage of "undecided" female students and the high concentration in teaching aroused some concern at the university. At a Levana dinner given in 1924, Charlotte Whitton, at that time President of the Alumnae Association, was invited to speak. She "emphasized the seriousness of a college course and advised the girls to plan their careers from the beginning."[69] What seemed particularly worrisome, however, was the fact that teachers were graduating in large numbers during the 1920s, leading to a serious overcrowding in the profession.[70] As a response, the Dean of Women persistently pushed for "some kind of vocational guidance."[71] She wanted to make Queen's women aware of various career possibilities other than teaching. Through her initiative, counselling was made available and conferences were set up on alternative women's professions. In 1925, she presented her first series of lectures on "Professions for Women," explaining that

> there is no doubt about the fact that almost all of the students do wish
> to prepare themselves to enter some profession. The difficulty is that
> they lack information regarding the nature of the work, the scale of
> salaries and the living conditions in different professions and regarding
> the qualifications which are necessary to enter them.[72]

Although Hilda Laird was somewhat disappointed to report that "the attendance at the lectures was not large: it varied from 50 to 100," she remarked nonetheless that "the students were greatly interested."[73] The Dean of Women remained fully convinced of the necessity "to interest a large number of students in professions other than teaching."[74] Thus a program of conferences on women's occupations was established for the following years as well. In 1927/28, however, "on account of the lack of funds," the lectures were not given.[75] It seems that interest in the project did not prove strong enough among the supporting societies that year, including Levana and the Alumnae Association. Miss Laird regretted that both these groups "turned deaf ears to my appeals."[76] But as it turned out, this apparent apathy proved temporary: for the next two years, the vocational talks reappeared on the agenda. To what can we attribute this lull in interest? Although it seems clear that the Dean's initiative never engendered overwhelming enthusiasm among her protegees, the sources make it difficult to conclude much more. One thing is certain: women at Queen's were being encouraged to seek employment once they graduated and they were also being pushed to broaden their professional horizons.

Women at Queen's During the 1920s

Through her endeavours, Hilda Laird was lending support to the newly emerging pattern of single women's work.

Yet a brief overview of the lectures on alternative women's professions reveals that the Dean of Women was also abiding by the constraints imposed on women in the predominantly male working world. Women at Queen's were not being encouraged to challenge the pre-established sexual divisions of labour. For one thing, some lecturers advocated preparation for purely traditional female occupations. Out of a total of 20 conferences given between 1925 and 1930, half discussed the advantages and requirements for employment clearly associated with women. Thus, four lectures were given on social work; one on public health and nursing; two on household science; one on teaching; one on interior decorating; and one on library work. Furthermore, the lecturers appear to have endorsed the current assumption that women's work was to be but an interim activity before embarking on the lifelong career of homemaking. They often underlined the benefits of various employment training courses in terms of their usefulness for the future homemaker. In their view, professional training for women at university could also be seen as a preparation for marriage and motherhood. How else are we to interpret what was said at the conference on Household Science?

> Miss Laird pointed out that this course [offered at Varsity] was an ideal one for women for, whether or not they ever intended to use it professionally, it fits them for the greatest career of all, that of marriage.[77]

A couple of years later, the advantages of training as an interior decorator were presented in similar terms:

> There have been more requests for a lecture on interior decorating than for any other subject. Indeed it is something in which every women may very well be interested even if not from a professional point of view. There are homes everywhere which can be and should be made more attractive; more comfortable and more home-like.[78]

It remains true, nonetheless, that female students were advised to seek professional training for new types of vocations, to diversify their interests. Indeed, the ten other conferences offered vocational counselling of a much less traditional nature. Thus, women at Queen's were encouraged to look into journalism, business, physical education, law, medicine, and music as well as opportunities in large department stores, in biology and chemistry, and to consider scientific work in the civil service or employment in the field of insurance. It must be noted that while the lecturers encouraged female students to extend their vocational horizons they also took care to present the obstacles and the constraints imposed by male discrimination. They do not appear to have encouraged their audience to challenge these limitations. The idea was to bring out the types of positions women were allowed to hold in these traditional male domains. Thus, at a session on women and business, female students were told by Miss M. MacMahon (manager of the Employment Bureau of the Underwood Typewriter Company and President of the Women's Business Club of Toronto) that

> a position in a larger corporation is splendid for experience but promotion is difficult. In smaller concerns [however] there are dozens of women occupying positions of office manager or secretary-treasurer.

She also entreated them to try journalism while warning that "in Toronto at least, there seems to be a concerted effort on the part of the newspaper men to see that [women] remain only reporters." In spite of this, Miss MacMahon felt that a female journalist "does not become segregated or isolated as, for instance, a schoolteacher almost invariably does."[80]

Although the idea was not to push them to rebel against existing discrimination, female students at Queen's were at least made aware of its prevalence and its implications for their employment prospects. In the case of some Queen's women, this awareness may have helped them look at the working world differently. An awareness of the sexual division of labour was a necessary first step in recognizing the role of male chauvinism.

Not all Queen's officials were as enthusiastic as Hilda Laird when it came to encouraging female students to discover new kinds of employment. Principal Taylor, for instance, seems to have shown signs of resistance. Although he appeared somewhat concerned over the vocational future of the female population on campus, agreeing that "professions for women are still few in number," he also went on to warn the female students that finding alternative vocations "requires the spirit of adventure while success seldom means the safe monthly cheque."[81]

This kind of conservative advice appears to have had a sympathetic audience. Indeed, we know from other sources that throughout the 1920s, teaching remained the preferred vocational option among single women. As Veronica Strong-Boag points out,

344

Women at Queen's During the 1920s

What counsellors failed to note was that, so long as women were particularly socialized to see their futures as involving children and were restricted to a few sex-labelled employments, the problem of overcrowding was bound to remain.[82]

Certainly, the experience of the graduates interviewed confirms this dominant trend. Of the 21 who ended up working after leaving Queen's, close to half of them (nine) taught.

More significantly, however, the professional future of these Queen's women confirms the changes that had taken place by the 1920s and which have been underlined in this study. As we have seen, these women entered university expecting to be employed after graduation. All but two of them fulfilled this expectation. Indeed, in addition to those who opted for teaching, five others worked as librarians, three worked in journalism, two became dieticians, one worked as a secretary, and one became a bank administrator. Getting a job for a few years thus appears to have been a definite goal among Queen's female students. Like their male colleagues they looked forward to employment after graduation—if only for a short period.

The temporary nature of this work period, however, needs to be underlined. The experience of the former graduates can serve as an illustration of this dominant pattern during the 1920s. Indeed, 14 of the 23 women interviewed who eventually became wives and mothers conformed to the traditional dictates of domesticity by stopping work. Two others who chose to ignore this well-established convention of "early retirement" after marriage were definitely made to feel uncomfortable. One recalled that while she worked as a supply teacher "they used to look down their noses at me for doing it after I was married."[83] In fact, this convention more often than not became a condition of employment. When applying for her first job teaching in a high school a female graduate of Queen's remembered being asked by the principal of the school if she was engaged. She replied, "Oh! no" and he said:

"You have to promise that you won't get married for 6 years (or something like that) because you're no good to a school until you've been teaching at least that long." I would have promised never to get married at this point! So I got the job.[84]

Nevertheless, by the 1920s women would gain some experience in the working world.

But the evidence from Queen's points to another significant development. Indeed, it appears that the expectation of employment had an influence on women's attitudes towards higher education. More specifically, university training was increasingly seen by women students, and their parents, as a preparation for their interim career between graduation and marriage. The sources make clear that female students at Queen's did not just want a job—they wanted a higher status job. And by the 1920s these women felt that a university training would prepare them to attain this goal. The large number of aspiring teachers on campus confirms this attitude. These women were not only aiming to teach—they were preparing themselves to teach at the high school level and become eligible for promotion to various administrative posts in the educational system. In other words, they were seeking to qualify themselves for the rare positions open to women at that time which offered prestige and better working conditions.

The Dean of Women's sustained efforts at vocational guidance provides yet another indication of the evolving role of women's higher education. That such a close supervisor of the female population on campus was encouraging female students to diversify their professional interests in both traditional and non-traditional fields of work could only serve to reinforce the notion that women should be thinking about their future occupations while at university. In this way those who arrived at Queen's without an "intended profession" would inevitably be exposed to some kind of professional counselling.

The notion that single women should become economically independent, even temporarily, had radical implications. At least for a brief interlude in their lives, women would be employed and have the possibility of managing their own finances. For those who did not marry, this economic independence could be prolonged for a lifetime. Not only would single women no longer be dependent on relatives for financial support, but, with an income, they were also in a position to postpone marriage. What is more, those who married might very well decide to continue working until they became mothers. Certainly the experience of Queen's suggests that traditional attitudes towards paid employment and higher education for women were being eroded in the 1920s.

Women at Queen's During the 1920s

Notes

1. This article is a revised version of my 1986 Queen's University M.A. research paper, "Women at Queen's in the 1920s: A Separate Sphere." I would like to thank Joy Parr, Chad Gaffield, Rebecca Coulter, Dominique Jean, and Jacqueline Neatby for their very useful comments on earlier drafts.

2. Veronica Strong-Boag, *The New Day Recalled: Lives of Girls and Women in English Canada, 1919-1939* (Toronto: Copp Clark Pitman Ltd., 1988) 2.

3. Alison Prentice et al. *Canadian Women: A History* (Toronto: Harcourt, Brace, Jovanovich, 1988) 218.

4. Veronica Strong-Boag, "Canadian Feminism in the 1920s: The Case of Nellie McClung," *Journal of Canadian Studies* 13 (1977) 67.

5. There are no specialized studies on Canadian women in higher education in the 1920s. There are only a few articles discussing women at university for the preceding or following decades. See John Reid, "The Education of Women at Mount Alison University, 1854-1914," *Acadiensis* (Spring 1983); Lee Stewart, "Women on Campus in B.C.: Strategies for Survival, Years of War and Peace, 1906-1920," in K. Latham and R. Pazdro, eds., *Not Just Pin Money* (Victoria: Camosum College, 1984); Lynne Marks and Chad Gaffield, "Women at Queen's University, 1895-1905: A Little Sphere All Their Own?" *Ontario History* LXXXVIII, 4 (Dec. 1986); Paul Axelrod, "Moulding the Middle Class: Student Life at Dalhousie University in the 1930s," *Acadiensis* XV, 1 (Autumn 1985) 84-122.

6. Mary Vipond, "The Image of Women in Mass Circulation Magazines in the 20s," in Susan Mann Trofimenkoff and Alison Prentice, eds., *The Neglected Majority* (Toronto: McClelland and Stewart, 1977) 118.

7. The records of the 14 other female students were missing from the files. The total number of first-year male students for 1925-26 was 199. The sample of 61 male students was created by choosing every third man from the student records. Male students in engineering were not included in the sample.

8. In the case of the female graduates, an effort was made to interview an equal number of graduates for each year. All years except 1920 and 1922 were represented. Some male students were also interviewed to see whether their backgrounds and attitudes were similar. The cities of Kingston and Ottawa were selected for reasons of convenience. The graduates agreed to be interviewed on condition that they would not be

given any personal publicity. Their anonymity was therefore guaranteed. However, each female graduate student has been given a number to identify her in the footnote; the men have been given a letter.

9. Strong-Boag, *New Day Recalled*, 41.
10. See Vipond, "The Image."
11. Mary Vipond points out that about 90% of the gainfully employed women were single, while married women only made up about 3% of the labour force during the 1920s. She notes that during that decade Canadian women "turned to their real careers, marriage and motherhood" at the average age of 25. See Vipond, "The Image," 117, 118, and 120.
12. See the discussion of companionate marriages in the 1920s in Prentice, *Canadian Women*, 254-55, and Axelrod, "Student Life," 44.
13. Strong-Boag, *New Day Recalled*, 25.
14. Int. #22.
15. Based on data from M.C. Urquhart and K.A.H. Buckley, eds., *Historical Statistics of Canada* (Toronto: MacMillan, 1965) 601; and R.S. Harris, *A History of Higher Education in Canada, 1663-1960* (Toronto: University of Toronto Press, 1976) 351-52.
16. Statistics compiled from the *Principal's Reports of Queen's University* (hereafter cited as *PR*) and the *Calendars of the Faculty of Arts* from 1919/20 to 1929/30, Queen's Archives.
17. Statistics taken from the *Report of the Dean of Women* (hereafter cited as *R of DW*) in the *PR* of 1928/29 and 1929/30, Queen's Archives.
18. Frederick W. Gibson, *Queen's University, Vol. II, 1917-1961: To Serve and Yet Be Free* (Kingston: McGill-Queen's University Press, 1983) 32 and 111.
19. Ibid., 110.
20. See Vipond, "The Image," 118, and Axelrod, "Student Life," 4.
21. Marks and Gaffield, Women at Queen's, 338.
22. Gibson, *To Serve,* 103.
23. Ibid., 448.
24. After looking at the occupational groupings from the *Sixth Census of Canada, 1921 Occupations,* vol. 6, xxxiv, and those drawn up by Paul Axelrod in his study on students at Dalhousie University in the 1930s, I compiled a list of six occupational categories in order to determine the social origin of Queen's students: 1. Professions (teachers, ministers, civil servants, doctors, engineers); 2. Business (merchants, real estate agents, insurance agents, contractors); 3. White Collar (railway agents, newspaper employees, customs service officers); 4. Artisan-Skilled

(electricians, carpenters, printers, musicians); 5. Unskilled (labourers); 6. Primary Producers (farmers, millers, market producers, fishermen).

25. In the female student sample, 11 did not specify their father's occupation. In the case of the men's, 7 left out this information.
26. Marks and Gaffield, "Women at Queen's," 337.
27. Ibid., 338.
28. Int. #17.
29. Int. #11.
30. One graduate explained that "my mother had died by then and my father said: 'You don't need to (work)'—but my brother did." Int. #9.
31. Int. D.
32. Int. G.
33. Int. H.
34. Charlotte Whitton, quoted in an article addressing female students in the *Queen's Journal* (hereafter cited as *QJ*), February 25, 1921.
35. *QJ*, January 22, 1924.
36. *QJ*, October 15, 1920.
37. Int. #14. Out of the six, three worked for one summer only.
38. *QJ*, December 7, 1928.
39. Int. #5.
40. Int. #1.
41. Int. #6.
42. "Qualification for teaching in the public high schools was a university degree and a training course at a Normal School or, as in Ontario, at a College of Education...the universities of Canada were not involved in the training of elementary schoolteachers in 1920. This was done in Normal Schools." Harris, *A History of Higher Education,* 296.
43. Int. #9.
44. One former graduate recalled interrupting her studies after the B.A.: "actually I intended to go back for my M.A.: when my mother died you see, I didn't...so I stayed with dad till I got married"; Int. #23. And another graduate remembered being allowed to register at university because "I was the eldest in the family and they didn't need my help in bringing up the family so I could go"; Int. #8.
45. Quoted in Gibson, *To Serve,* 103.
46. Gibson, *To Serve,* 102-3. The national statistics tell much the same story: "The ratio of female to male undergraduates declined throughout the 1930s." Prentice, *Canadian Women,* 241-42. In Strong-Boag, *New Day Recalled,* 24, the author calculates that between 1930 and 1935 the

percentage change in undergraduate enrolment for women was +.89% whereas for the men it was +7.79%.

47. *QJ*, November 18, 1927.
48. *QJ*, November 15, 1927.
49. "Levana" is the name given to the female students' association at Queen's. *QJ*, March 2, 1926.
50. Int. #16.
51. *QJ*, March 2, 1926.
52. Queen's Archives, *R of DW, PRD*, 1925/26, 65.
53. Thus the first-year students of 1926/27 did not change these proportions: the findings for the 326 female students of that year also showed how more than half (190) left the "intended profession" category blank when they registered; Queen's Archives, *R of DW, PR*, 1926/27. The Dean of Women's results for the year 1928/29 reveal the same pattern: out of a total 377 female students more than half (199) were "silent"; Queen's Archives, *R of DW, PR*, 1927/28. My sample study of 1925 only served to confirm the Dean of Women's findings. Half (34) of the "freshettes" (first-year female students) left "intended profession" blank on their student file.
54. Thus, for instance, at Queen's female students were not admitted into medicine or into the engineering program.
55. Int. #14.
56. Usually through short training sessions given in specialized schools or the actual workplace. See Marjorie MacMurchy, *The Canadian Girl at Work* (Toronto: King's Printer, 1919) and Ellen Knox, *The Girl of the New Day* (Toronto: McClelland, 1924). It must be noted that progressively throughout the decade, women were able to train in universities for some of their occupations. Thus, in 1919, "the first university degree program in nursing in the British Empire was established at the University of British Columbia" (Prentice, *Canadian Women*, 225). Universities started to give out certificates, diplomas, and finally degrees in library training. A degree in household science was also created at some universities. Queen's, however, was still not granting these specialized degrees during that period.
57. Int. #6.
58. Queen's Archives, *R of DW, PR*, 1925/26, 65. The sample of the first-year students in 1925 confirms this result: of the 28 who gave an "intended profession," almost all (23) chose teaching.
59. In 1926/27, teaching as before was by far the most popular occupation, attracting 124 out of 136 female students; Queen's Archives, *R of DW,*

PR, 1926/27, 58. In 1927/28, of the 178 who did declare a profession, 143 opted for teaching; Queen's Archives, *R of DW, PR,* 1927/28, 38.

60. Int. #15.
61. MacMurchy, *The Canadian Girl at Work,* 36.
62. Int. #6.
63. Int. #6
64. Queen's Archives, *R of DW, PR,* 1925/26, 65.
65. Int. #4.
66. Teaching, law, commerce, wrecking, business, business administration, foreign trade, ministry. As for the women, apart from those who chose teaching, three opted for secretarial work, one for journalism and another wanted to become a dietician. This pattern was reflected at the national level: "While men were widely dispersed over a broad range of industrial groups, women were heavily concentrated in far fewer, with 70.9% of women in only 6 of the 25 categories covered by the census..."; Strong-Boag, *New Day Recalled,* 51.
67. Int. #6. The impossibility of earning a living as a "lady lawyer" was confirmed by another graduate as well. She recalled that "I wanted to be a lawyer but my father said: 'You couldn't earn your living and you're going to have to earn your living.'" Int. #16.
68. Int. #6.
69. *QJ,* March 4, 1924.
70. See Strong-Boag, *New Day Recalled,* 64-5.
71. Queen's Archives, *R of DW, PR,* 1925/26, 65.
72. Ibid.
73. Queen's Archives, *R of DW, PR,* 1927/28, 66.
74. Queen's Archives, *R of DW, PR,* 1926/27, 58.
75. Queen's Archives, *R of DW, PR,* 1927/28, 66.
76. Ibid.
77. *QJ,* February 22, 1927.
78. *QJ,* February 19, 1929.
79. This is brought out, for example, in some of the conference titles: *Opportunities in Large Department Stores, Opportunities in Biology and Chemistry, Women in Business.* They certainly were not led to believe they could compete for the same jobs as men at all levels.
80. *QJ,* March 19, 1926.
81. Queen's Archives, Principal Taylor, *PR,* 1927/28, 6.
82. Strong-Boag, *New Day Recalled,* 64-5.
83. Int. #16.
84. Int. #12.